Many Voices, ONE NATION

Frontispiece.
Immokalee Statue of Liberty, created by Kat Rodriguez, 2000. This rendition of the Statue of Liberty is holding a tomato in her right hand instead of a torch, and a tomato basket in her left hand instead of a tablet. The papier-mâché and mixed-media sculpture linked the struggles of migrant farm workers with a powerful symbol of immigration to the United States. National Museum of American History, Smithsonian Institution, gift of Coalition of Immokalee Workers.

Many Voices,
ONE NATION

MATERIAL CULTURE REFLECTIONS ON RACE AND MIGRATION IN THE UNITED STATES

Edited by

Margaret Salazar-Porzio and Joan Fragaszy Troyano

with

Lauren Safranek

A Smithsonian Contribution to Knowledge

Smithsonian Institution
Scholarly Press

Washington, D.C.
2017

Published by
SMITHSONIAN INSTITUTION SCHOLARLY PRESS
P.O. Box 37012, MRC 957
Washington, D.C. 20013-7012
www.scholarlypress.si.edu

All photos by Jaclyn Nash unless otherwise credited.
All images courtesy of the National Museum of American History unless otherwise credited.

Front cover image: Detail of eagle with motto *E Pluribus Unum*, nineteenth century, National Museum of American History, Smithsonian Institution, gift of Joel Barlow (see Lilienfeld, Figure 1).
Back cover image: Uncle Sam figure from National Papier Mache Works, Milwaukee, Wisconsin, created in the early 1900s. National Museum of American History, Smithsonian Institution (see Lilienfeld, Figure 3).

Library of Congress Cataloging-in-Publication Data:

Names: Salazar-Porzio, Margaret, editor. | Troyano, Joan Fragaszy, editor. | Safranek, Lauren. | Smithsonian Institution Scholarly Press, publisher.
Title: Many voices, one nation : material culture reflections on race and migration in the United States / edited by Margaret Salazar-Porzio and Joan Fragaszy Troyano, with Lauren Safranek.
Other titles: Smithsonian contribution to knowledge.
Description: Washington, D.C. : Smithsonian Institution Scholarly Press, 2017. | Series: A Smithsonian contribution to knowledge. | Includes bibliographical references and index.
Identifiers: LCCN 2016040060 | ISBN 9781944466091 (cloth) | ISBN 9781944466114 (ebook)
Subjects: LCSH: Minorities—United States—History. | Immigrants—United States—History. | United States—Emigration and immigration—History. | United States—Race relations—History. | United States—Social life and customs. | United States—Civilization.
Classification: LCC E184.A1 A288 2017 | DDC 305.800973—dc23 | SUDOC SI 1.60:M 11
LC record available at https://lccn.loc.gov/2016040060

ISBN: 978-1-944466-09-1 (cloth)
ISBN: 978-1-944466-11-4 (ebook)

Printed in the United States of America

♾ The paper used in this publication meets the minimum requirements of the American National Standard for Permanence of Paper for Printed Library Materials Z39.48–1992.

Contents

1   Welcome
    John L. Gray

3   Foreword
    Gary Gerstle

11 Introduction
    *Margaret Salazar-Porzio and
    Joan Fragaszy Troyano*

SECTION ONE

27 Unsettling the Continent, 1492–1776
    Barbara Clark Smith

45 Exploring the Colonial History
    of New Mexico Through Artifacts
    Ramón A. Gutiérrez

57 Native American Objects of Memory
    and Journey from the National Museum
    of the American Indian
    Christopher Lindsay Turner

69 Now/Then, We/Them? Toward a More
    Global U.S. History
    John Kuo Wei Tchen

SECTION TWO

81 Creating and Expanding the Nation,
    1776–1900
    Bonnie Campbell Lilienfeld

101 Communities of Refuge in Frontier
    Illinois
    Nancy Davis

111 African American Expression
    in Antebellum America:
    The Story of Dave Drake
    Kym Rice

123 Lady in the Harbor: The Statue
    of Liberty as American Icon
    Alan M. Kraut

SECTION THREE

137 Contesting the Nation, 1900–1965
    Fath Davis Ruffins

165 Education and Americanization:
    The Language of Community
    *Joan Fragaszy Troyano and
    Debbie Schaefer-Jacobs*

179 Chicago's "Concentric Zones":
    Thinking Through the Material History
    of an Iconic Map
    Davarian L. Baldwin

193 Pulling at the Threads:
    A Korean American Diptych
    Sojin Kim

SECTION FOUR

205 New Americans, Continuing Debates,
    1965–2014
    Margaret Salazar-Porzio

231 Old South, New Migrations
    L. Stephen Velasquez

245 Beyond Apology and Assertion
    in *Beyond Bollywood*
    Masum Momaya

257 The Desert Colossus: Fragments
    of Twenty-First-Century
    Undocumented Migration
    Jason De León

269 Epilogue: Our Polycultural Past
    and Future Century
    Scott Kurashige

277 Acknowledgments
279 Contributors
285 Index

Welcome

The Great Seal of the United States contains the 13-letter Latin phrase *E Pluribus Unum*, which translates to "Out of Many, One." And when we think of the "One," we think of the one nation that has been forged from the "Many."

Many Voices, One Nation is a historic and dynamic look at the peopling of our country. The National Museum of American History is dedicated to using our unparalleled collection of national treasures to help us understand the past in order to make sense of the present and shape a more humane future. The role of the National Museum is to tell the story of how our people have come together to participate in the growth and development of an ever-evolving national narrative. So how do we share stories that will foster greater understanding, empathy, and connection among the many and the one?

This publication and exhibition highlight the Smithsonian's greatest strengths. We draw upon the collections and expertise of colleagues across the Institution. As a nexus between some of the nation's foremost scholars and the American people, we are very pleased to feature contributors from academic institutions across the country.

We invite you to explore the many stories within our shared history and discover the commonalities that bring us together as a people.

John L. Gray
Director
National Museum of American History

Foreword

Gary Gerstle

The peopling of America is one of the most vivid and consequential stories in the country's history. Across more than five centuries, somewhere between 70 and 80 million individuals journeyed as free people or as unfree laborers to what would become the United States. Millions more became part of the United States as a result of the new republic's expansion and conquest of land that had belonged to other empires and nations. Over time, the major movements of people and redrawing of borders rendered the United States as heterogeneous a society as any on the planet, home to a remarkable diversity of nationalities, races, and ethnicities. How, exactly, does one tell this American story of movement, exchange, and conflict comprehensively? How can one do justice to all the groups who have become part of America, to their experiences here, and to their encounters with each other?

The Smithsonian has told portions of this story, and done so brilliantly, in numerous exhibits focused on specific groups of migrants and minorities, first in the National Museum of American History and the National Museum of Natural History, and later in the National Museum of the American Indian and the National Museum of African American History and Culture. But the last effort by the Smithsonian to grasp the peopling story in its entirety occurred a long time ago—in 1976, the year of the Bicentennial, when *A Nation of Nations* debuted at the National Museum of History and Technology, the forerunner of today's National Museum of American History. I was finishing college and preparing for graduate school when I first visited *A Nation of Nations*. The exhibit enthralled me, and I returned to see it again and again. I did not yet know that I would spend a good part of my career studying immigration history, but, in retrospect, my engagement with that exhibit was an early sign of a subject that would sustain my interest across decades.

A Nation of Nations successfully distilled the knowledge of immigration history as it existed at that time, and conveyed it through the display and inter-rogation of objects: clothing, paintings, ceremonial objects, tools, weapons, in-ventions, a classroom, and a World War II army bunk all appeared in the exhibit. In the wake of the civil rights movement, no credible effort to represent the past could celebrate America as a place of unmitigated freedom, or as a place where everyone had melded into one undifferentiated shape. *A Nation of Nations* docu-mented slavery and its consequences; the history of American Indians hovered at the exhibit's edges, not well integrated into the exhibit but sufficient to register the indigenous presence on the North American continent.

Reckoning with African and indigenous Americans, groups that had ei-ther not been allowed to integrate into American life or had not wanted to, had also prompted the exhibit creators to challenge the metaphors that had been deployed across the first half of the twentieth century to make sense of how America had managed its diversity. Among the most popular of these was the notion of a melting pot into which all immigrants had been tossed, emerging from it as new men and women, fully American and shorn of their Old World customs, habits, and languages. Outside museum walls, Ameri-cans everywhere were, by the 1970s, themselves challenging the concepts long used to describe the American encounter with diversity. Phrases such as "pluralism" and "multiculturalism" had begun to supplant "assimilation" and "Americanization" as the watchwords for understanding the American experience. The roster of contemporary books and films contributing to the rethinking of American belonging and identity includes such classics as Dee Brown's *Bury My Heart at Wounded Knee* (1970), Michael Novak's *The Rise of the Unmeltable Ethnics* (1972), Francis Ford Coppola's *The Godfather* (1972), Irving Howe's *World of Our Fathers* (1976), and Alex Haley's *Roots* (1976). The 1970s was also the decade in which Philip Roth and Woody Allen became breakout artists, writing fiction and making movies for all kinds of audiences and not just Jewish ones. *A Nation of Nations* registered this ferment. Its ar-chitects wanted to show that America was a nation, to be sure, but one in which the older nations or peoples from which bicentennial Americans were descended remained very much alive in folkways, humor, patterns of cultures, and memories of injustice.

One can still experience that 1976 exhibit by studying the book of the same title that was published in conjunction with it. Anyone doing that will be struck, however, not just by what that exhibit accomplished but by how much its interpretation has aged, and how much we need a new reckoning with the peopling saga. That new reckoning is the purpose of this book, *Many Voices, One Nation*, and of the exhibit by the same name associated with it. The contributors to this volume have immersed themselves in and mastered the remarkable scholarship on the peoples of America that has been produced across the last 40 years. And while they write on very different kinds of objects and time periods, reflecting the variety of their expertises, they are united by three principles discernable in every one of the essays. Together these principles have yielded a way of interpreting the history of America's peopling that is different in important respects from the one animating *A Nation of Nations*. The first principle is that any story of the peopling of America must be genuinely continental in scope, a goal to which *A Nation of Nations* aspired but did not accomplish. The second principle is that none of the groups involved in the peopling of America can be represented by a single voice, or single object, no matter how eloquent the voice or revealing the object in question. The third principle is that the story of the peopling of America is not something that can safely be tucked away as history—as something that is past. It is something very much a part of our present. Let me elaborate on each of these principles.

CONTINENTALISM RATHER THAN REGIONALISM

As much as *A Nation of Nations* aspired to be a story of the entire United States, most of the objects appearing in that exhibit and the book resulting from it were drawn from the northeast section of the country, north of the Ohio River and east of the Mississippi. This eastern and northern bias reflected in part the central role of the 13 British colonies, all located on the Atlantic Seaboard, in fashioning the American republic. It reflected, too, the fact that the country's northeast quadrant became the nation's industrial heartland in the nineteenth and early twentieth centuries. This is where the need for labor was greatest and where the largest percentage of immigrants settled. These regional developments are important aspects of America's peopling story and will forever remain so. The scholarship of the past two generations, however, has made clear the importance of other European empires, most notably the Spanish and French, to the peopling of North America. For a long time, the Spanish Empire was the largest and most powerful in the New World, eclipsing even that of the British. Accounting for its influence requires that we pay as much attention to the western half of North America as to its eastern half.

Making the West integral to the story requires a recognition, too, that the peopling mix in the West was different from the East, and that patterns of ethnic mixing and hierarchy therefore took different forms as well. So, too, did the global movements of commodities, armies, and people out of which these western patterns emerged. This book, and the exhibit with which it is associated, achieves its continental aspirations, and compels us to situate them in global processes, in ways in which *A Nation of Nations* was never able to do.

MANY VOICES

The contributors to this volume are committed not just to registering the presence of once-ignored groups—American Indians, Africans, Asians, Mexicans, and others—but to giving them voice. Giving voice means allowing groups to speak in their own words and through objects of their own creation. It also means treating groups not as undifferentiated masses but as complex and internally differentiated societies. Barbara Clark Smith makes this point when she writes that American Indian nations "were diverse and changing." So does Nancy Davis in her examination of New Philadelphia, Illinois, the first town, Davis writes, "founded and platted by an African American." The African Americans who lived and, for a time, prospered in New Philadelphia were hardly typical of their race in antebellum America, but their experiment in building a free, autonomous, and integrated community, and locating it in close proximity to the still-flourishing slave regimes of Kentucky and Tennessee, compels us to ask new questions about the aspirations and achievements of blacks in nineteenth-century America. We want to be able to ask new and fresh questions about every group that has peopled America. This book helps us to do so. Sometimes, asking fresh questions requires us to admit, as John Kuo Wei Tchen poignantly notes, how little we know about a group in question, and how each item collected on that group, no matter how exquisite, may well conceal a world "full of stories yet to be recovered and retold." Humility can be an important antechamber to the temple of knowledge.

CONTINUITY BETWEEN PAST AND PRESENT

The creators of *A Nation of Nations* believed they were telling a story of America's peopling that had substantially ended. There is no recognition in the book they produced to accompany their exhibit that a vast and varied new population of immigrants was just beginning to arrive—Mexicans, Dominicans, Cubans, Haitians, Chinese, Koreans, Vietnamese, Indians, Nigerians, Sudanese, Somalis, and many others. This lack of recognition supports the view of scholars who have argued that the purpose of the Hart-Celler Immigration and Nationality Act of 1965 was less to open America's immigrant gates to the world once again than it was to make amends to those groups already in America—most notably eastern and southern Europeans—who had been stigmatized by past immigration laws as racially inferior and thus unwelcome. It should be humbling to policymakers—and fascinating to historians—that so few experts anticipated that this 1960s reform would trigger such a vast migration, its numbers equaling the total of 35 million who came in all of the nineteenth century. This immigrant wave has reconfigured the American population and intensified both cultural exchange and conflict in profound ways.

This volume is among the first to situate this wave—the focus of Section Four of this book—fully within the centuries-old story of the peopling of America of which it is part. That in itself is an achievement. But the contributors to this volume compel us to do more than simply understand that this latest wave is continuous with one of the great dramas of American history. They also compel us to look in new ways at the connections between past and present. The contributors help us to understand how past exchanges and conflicts among the peoples present on this continent still reverberate through American society. They help us to see that we are the legatees of these past exchanges and conflicts, and that we have been shaped by them. At the same time, this volume makes clear that America is not a finished nation. The cultural exchanges that are at the heart of the peopling of America are ongoing. They have the potential, of course, to trigger new forms of conflict and coercion; but they are also indispensable, as they always have been, for sustaining and replenishing the remarkable dynamism and creativity of American life.

Given the vast diversity of American life, and the very different experiences of those who have become part of America, in what sense can we still talk of America as constituting one nation? To this important question, this volume offers an intriguingly traditional answer: that Americans are bound together by a love of liberty, and by an aspiration to live their lives in circumstances of freedom. The dream of freedom is universal, of course, but has special meaning in the United States because the ideals of life, liberty, and the pursuit of happiness are inscribed in the country's founding documents. This association of nation and liberty was reinforced after the Civil War through the gift by France to the United States of the Statue of Liberty, and its placement in New York Harbor in 1886. The statue was not intended to salute America as a land of liberty for immigrants from other lands, as Alan Kraut reminds us in his essay. Rather it was meant to celebrate the ending of slavery on the North American continent and a new birth of liberty for France's sister republic. It was only in the twentieth century that the Statue of Liberty became a beacon to immigrants, at a time when the vast majority of European immigrants entered the United States by sailing past the Lady on the way to Ellis Island, and when Emma Lazarus's 1883 poem, *The New Colossus* (with its famous line, "Give me your tired, your poor, your huddled masses yearning to breathe free") became affixed to an indoor wall that was part of the statue's pedestal.

In recent decades, invoking the Statue of Liberty as a symbol of the immigrant experience in the United States has been subjected to critique. Many have charged that this symbol has reinforced the Eurocentric bias in immigration studies, privileging the experiences of those who came to America through New York Harbor (most of whom were European), and marginalizing the experience of those who entered the United States through the Southwest and West Coast. That these latter groups were largely perceived as nonwhite, their racial status diminishing their opportunities both to enter the United States and to enjoy the freedom made available here, further underscored the inappropriateness of using a symbol of liberty to frame stories about the peopling of America.

This critique is a cogent one. Still, it may be wrong to dispense with the Statue of Liberty as a symbol around which to organize American notions of nationhood and belonging. It is interesting in this regard that this image is the only one to appear three times in this volume. It has to appear, of course, in the essay on the statue itself that Kraut has written. But it also appears in Margaret Salazar-Porzio's essay on post-1965 immigrants, in the form of a sculpture created by Latina artist and labor activist,

Kat Rodriguez, to support Mexican, Haitian, Mayan, and Guatemalan agricultural workers in their struggle for better working conditions and racial equality. Even more startlingly, it appears in Jason De León's essay, "The Desert Colossus," as an image printed on the back of a shirt recovered from the backpack left behind by an unknown migrant somewhere in the U.S. portion of the Sonoran Desert. The representation of the statue on the back of this shirt is not at all "lady-like." To the contrary, it is rather threatening, predatory, even zombie-like.

What are we to make of such a shirt in the possession of a migrant trying to make it to safety and employment in the United States? On one level, it is interesting to note that the shirt's designers surrounded the statue with images of skyscrapers and airplanes—common representations of twentieth-century New York City. It is not inconceivable that a snarling image of King Kong would appear on the shirt's front. The mixing by the shirt's designers (American? Mexican? Chinese?) of a nineteenth-century French icon of liberty with twentieth-century U.S. pop culture exemplifies what both Ramón Gutiérrez and Salazar-Porzio refer to as the "process of blending and borrowing, of mixing and melding," of "crossing and defying," that they see as intrinsic to cultural development in the United States. On another level, it seems strangely appropriate that this unknown migrant marching through an unforgiving desert would have had a shirt with a rather ghoulish representation of Lady Liberty in his possession. We can imagine this version of the Lady declaring, "America might make you free, if it does not kill you first." A desert colossus indeed! And yet the appearance of Lady Liberty in an abandoned backpack in Sonora underscores the power of this icon to cut through time and space, and to transcend region, nationality, race, and ethnicity.

Why not use this icon, then, as a rallying point for all the peoples who have come to America? Not primarily for reasons of celebration, or for hiding the coercion that has been so much a force in this land of liberty. Indeed, the French makers of the original Statue of Liberty would not want us to do that. The broken chain on which the real Statue of Liberty stands, visible for all to see and meant to symbolize the freeing of the slaves, makes clear that America has never been a pristine nation, free of sin or wrongdoing. Rather, the point of putting the Statue of Liberty forward is to bring together all the groups who are in the United States to discuss the state of their liberty—who has it, who does not—and what needs to be done for the promise of the statue and of the Declaration of Independence to be fulfilled. Out of such discussions a nation that all Americans recognize as their own may yet emerge.

Introduction

Margaret Salazar-Porzio and
Joan Fragaszy Troyano

OUT OF MANY, ONE

For the month of October 2014, anyone flying into or out of Ronald Reagan Washington National Airport or climbing to the top of the Washington Monument could have seen the 840 foot long and 230 foot wide face of a young man peeking through the trees alongside the reflecting pool on the National Mall (Figure 1). Aiming to "create a dialogue about the concept of identity" and "the role models who are chosen to represent us in the public sphere," Cuban American artist Jorge Rodríguez-Gerada took photographs of 50 randomly selected young men from different racial and ethnic backgrounds around Washington, D.C. to compose this portrait. The portrait was then mapped onto the earth by hundreds of workers and volunteers using GPS technology, more than 10,000 wooden pegs, miles of string, 2,300 tons of sand, and 800 tons of soil.[1] Alluding to the translation of our de facto national motto,[2] *E Pluribus Unum*, Rodríguez-Gerada called his landscape portrait, or "facescape," "Out of Many, One."[3]

A collaboration between the National Park Service, the Trust for the National Mall, and the Smithsonian Institution, "Out of Many, One" appeared on the Mall as a statement on both national identity and race in the United States. Though cross-racial identification and morphology has its own problematic legacy in the United States,[4] Rodríguez-Gerada superimposed multiple faces into one face to illustrate that

11

Figure 1.
"Out of Many, One," landscape portrait by artist Jorge Rodríguez-Gerada, 2014. This composite portrait of 50 men was temporarily installed along the south side of the Lincoln Memorial Reflecting Pool. The project was a collaboration between the National Park Service, the Trust for the National Mall, and the Smithsonian Institution. Courtesy of the National Portrait Gallery, Smithsonian Institution, photography by Mark Gulezian.

"Diversity is the backbone of the nation."[5] Although *E Pluribus Unum* became popular in the early Republic to convey the need for unity among newly founded states, each with distinct colonial histories, Rodríguez-Gerada's "Out of Many, One" demonstrates how more contemporary interpretations reveal a growing desire among many Americans to embrace a diversity of peoples and perspectives (Figure 2).

The repurposed phrase *E Pluribus Unum* helps capture the motivation of this edited collection and the related exhibition at the National Museum of American History; we reinterpret the phrase for our title, *Many Voices, One Nation*. The metaphor of "Many Voices, One Nation" provides a meaningful framework to integrate both familiar and unfamiliar stories found in our material heritage into a more textured history that spans five centuries, multiple continents, and many different peoples. Rather than assert that we are or could be "one" made of many, this book pays attention to the *many* and allows readers to contemplate whether and how the *one* may be possible.

Salazar-Porzio and Troyano

Figure 2.
United States Diplomatic Medal imprinted with the Great Seal, 1876, copied from a 1792 medal. *E Pluribus Unum* was first adopted as a component of the Great Seal in 1782, and is still on U.S. currency today. National Museum of American History, Smithsonian Institution, Government Transfer, Library of Congress.

    The *Many Voices, One Nation* exhibition and this companion book draw on decades of historical scholarship that critically examines the complicated relationships among migration, race, nation, and our notions of *E Pluribus Unum*.[6] This exhibition and book come four decades after the Bicentennial exhibition *A Nation of Nations* (1976) opened to the public. *A Nation of Nations* was on display from 1976 to 1991, and it explored the history of the "peopling" of the United States with an emphasis on immigration and cultural pluralism.[7] Since its installation, more recent scholarship, significant historical events, and acquisitions to the national collection have called for a more contemporary interpretation of this topic. *Many Voices, One Nation* updates and confronts these histories and legacies by focusing on the processes of importation, immigration, incorporation, and transnationality. We include a variety of overlapping stories in U.S. history to avoid dismissing or glossing over endeavors that were foundational to the nation but subjugated certain communities, such as slavery and Native American displacement and removal. This provides an important point of departure from *A Nation of Nations,* which provided a relatively inclusive history but did not feature key debates that have confronted our nation over the years: Who is free? Who is equal? Who is welcome? And how do these questions impact what it means to be American?

    This global history of movement, of both people and political borders, necessarily includes stories of voluntary and involuntary immigration and migration. Even as treaties and borders changed, every generation has confronted issues of the many and the one. The importation of enslaved peoples and the subjugation and incorporation of those already on the continent are fundamental parts of this history. Sovereign Native American nations negotiated and struggled with European powers over land, trade, culture, language, and political power. The various European colonies jostled with each other and exploited enslaved Africans and native tribes to advance their financial and political agendas. Mexicans, Californios, Tejanos, and Native Americans in the Southwest contended with Anglo squatting and settlement during American conquest, which culminated in the U.S.–Mexican War. The history of the peopling of the nation is a particularly dynamic entry point for understanding the nuances of our many voices and one nation.

The book and the exhibition are organized chronologically into four sections that span the period from Europeans' arrival in North America (around 1492) to the near present (around 2000). Each chapter covers a particular historical era and includes an overview essay that focuses on national trends supported by material culture, followed by shorter essays about specific objects, places, and peoples. The book and the exhibition are not meant to be comprehensive, nor could they be. Instead, they are an introduction to unexpected objects and stories of everyday people that connect us across time and space.

Essays in this volume provide examples of evolving ideas and ideals within the nation as diverse peoples constantly influence each other and their surroundings. In the *Many Voices, One Nation* exhibition, visitors encounter this history through more than 600 artifacts and images that tell stories about many different people, places, and arenas of interaction. The exhibit spotlights key debates about freedom, equality, and belonging that influenced the context in which people produced and used their artifacts and images. This volume enriches the exhibition experience—and stands on its own—by offering a deeper dive into the meaning of artifacts that reflect histories of migration and race in the United States. Readers of this volume will likewise find the objects and essays offer nuanced and critical inquiry into the ways we interpret and tell stories about our interconnected pasts.

Original artifacts are primary sources that connect us to experiences and values in enduring ways. We use material culture case studies to highlight key arenas of interaction, dynamic demographic changes, and migration experiences. For museum visitors, finding something familiar from long ago, or an early version of something they hold dear, can provide a compelling entry point to the past. Researchers consider objects to help understand the evolution or distribution of ideas and experiences of the past. Material culture can demonstrate processes of

Salazar-Porzio and Troyano

intellectual shifts or technical development. It can offer intimacy and a connection with the creator or user, or evidence of a blatant disregard for feelings of others through caricature or harmful rhetoric. Through material culture, one can hold and trace the links between peoples, memories, and cultures.[8]

In this book and exhibition, material culture reveals shifting understandings of migration, race, and nation that have informed social interactions and cultural narratives locally, nationally, and globally. Reading objects and images through this lens helps to uncover their meanings, distort stereotypes, and even expose power relations. We look at material artifacts that range in size and scope from "Out of Many, One," an ephemeral art piece tilled back into the earth after 30 days, to more permanent fixtures in our national and individual imaginations, such as the Statue of Liberty. For the most part, we focus on everyday objects and stories that have made up our many diverse experiences.

We cast a broad net in pursuit of a complicated history to help us understand how people from different backgrounds have struggled for a place among the many who have made up the United States over time. Objects described in this volume allow us to interpret the experiences of unique individuals through, for example, the creative work of an enslaved African American potter or a transplanted woodworker from Germany. Others speak to a shared experience of community, such as Pueblo tribes forging alliances in the sixteenth century or a bilingual parochial school in the twentieth century. Still others visualize the political nation state through iconography on a diplomatic medal or a symbolic statue in a harbor (Figure 2). We intentionally provide objects of history at multiple levels—from personal stories and local experiences to national trends and global forces—because change occurs on these multiple levels simultaneously. This multilevel analysis of objects provides moments for connecting individual stories to broader social and cultural dynamics and to each other.

Historical objects give us insight into the exchanges of material goods, intellectual ideas, and lived experiences. Porcelain from China and a shirt with an image of the Statue of Liberty journeyed internationally because of their valued function or aesthetics; these items offer insight into trade and consumer taste. Intellectual ideas, also, are manifest in material objects that are produced for others and sometimes for oneself; a religious painting on elk hide and a demographic map of Chicago reveal the thinking of their creators. Representations of experience range from a large formal portrait of a wealthy South Carolinian planter to a small drawing by a Kiowa Indian remembering his tribe's lost freedoms and sovereignty.

As our increasingly diverse American population meets in civic and economic spaces, a book of this nature is essential to provide a foundation for understanding our multiple histories. The *Many Voices, One Nation* exhibition and book aim to prompt deep thinking about the timeworn concept of *E Pluribus Unum* so that as a nation we might go beyond simple acknowledgement of our past, present, and future diversity to focus on building an equitable and inclusive society.

MANY AND ONE: MIGRATION, RACE, AND NATION

The United States has been made of diverse elements from even before its founding, but there is no one conclusive translation of *E Pluribus Unum*.[9] Does "*e pluribus*" refer to many states, many peoples, or many beliefs? Does the noun "*unum*" refer to one nation, one population, or one path forward? And perhaps most tellingly, there is no verb in the phrase; the method to achieve "one out of many" is left to the imagination. These questions—Who are the many? What is the one? And how does this ideal work?—still challenge us.

At first glance, a Latin phrase originally espoused by the founders of the United States in the eighteenth century may not seem provocative for a volume on these themes in the twenty-first century. But the concept of *E Pluribus Unum* has global resonance and longevity that helps us tease out issues of migration, race, and nation. In the 1500s, long before this motto was adopted as a banner uniting thirteen colonies into the American Republic in 1782, Spain intentionally connected the Old World and the New on its money with the phrase *utraque unum* or "both are one."[10] (See Figure 4 in John Kuo Wei Tchen's essay in this volume.) More recently, South Africa, the European Union, and Indonesia have adopted mottos that also express unity out of diversity.[11] A reconsideration of *E Pluribus Unum* can tie together our seemingly disparate histories across time and space.

The motto itself reveals great debates about our history. For some, the phrase remains a Eurocentric relic that elides a national history of conquest and inequality. Some argue that the phrase places too great an emphasis on unity, and leads to the creation of a triumphant national narrative that trivializes oppressive acts of forced assimilation and ignores the experiences of marginalized groups. For others, the phrase prompts a shared appreciation of American concepts of freedom and democracy, without which it could be argued we would have no nation. Still others might place an emphasis on the "many" more than the "one"—or the "one" more than the "many."

Salazar-Porzio and Troyano

Interpretations of the Latin phrase have directly influenced the political rights and civic freedoms of people living in the United States throughout our history. Local communities, states, and the nation itself have determined who among the many could have the privileges of belonging, and who could not; and who among the many could have the freedom to remain distinct, and who would be forced to change.[12] Citizenship was officially and inextricably linked to race in the Declaration of Independence and confirmed again in the 1790 Naturalization Act when it was declared that only "free white men" of "good moral character" could come to the United States, naturalize, and gain citizenship. Indeed, this 1790 naturalization law offered precedent for monitoring and managing immigration and migration based on race until the 1965 Immigration and Nationality Act.[13] Ideas about belonging have been irrevocably linked to ideas of race and national identity over the course of this history. When viewed through this lens, visual and material culture reveals disputes over the very meaning of what it means to be American.

For example, in the nineteenth century, immigrants from Ireland and central Europe faced anti-Catholic prejudice. For them, identification as "white" became a critical link to political inclusion. In 1882 the cartoonist Thomas Nast illustrated just how tenuous this identification might be in the popular *Harper's Weekly* magazine, with a German man and an Irish man, "Fritz" and "Pat" respectively, worrying that they might be labeled "green" and excluded as the Chinese had been[14] (Figure 3).

Figure 3.
"Which color is to be tabooed next?" cartoon by Thomas Nast published in *Harper's Weekly*, 1882. In this political cartoon a German immigrant and an Irish immigrant discuss how the precedent set by the Chinese Exclusion Act may affect them. Courtesy of the Library of Congress, Prints & Photographs Division.

Figure 4.
This magazine cover asks readers to consider how the country's increasing racial diversity will change the nation. From *Time* magazine, 9 April 1990 (Volume 135 Number 15) © 1990 Time Inc. Used under license.

Fast-forward a century to a *Time* magazine cover from 1990, which visualized new demographic shifts through the changing colors of the national flag (Figure 4). This magazine cover can be read in different ways. Some might be shocked or insulted by the change from white stripes to black, brown, and yellow. Others might imagine this new flag as a banner proclaiming the incorporation of diverse peoples into the nation. This cover uses stereotypical colors to represent racialized skin tones to make a statement on the connection between race and nation. Colors do not inherently have racial associations, but over time, racial meanings have been ascribed to the different colors featured on the *Time* cover. Designers depended on a common racialized understanding of these colors to get their point across.[15] At the same time, the cover is laden with multiple meanings, and it provides one example of just how interconnected ideas about race and nation have been in our visual and material culture.[16]

As the political cartoon and *Time* magazine cover illustrate, few issues in American history are as controversial, or as critical, as race and nation. Historically, popular representations have shown race as a divisive concept that threatens to tear apart a unified nation. Yet, as these representations demonstrate, racial and national identities are mutually constitutive. Race and nation are intertwined in such fundamental ways in the United States that we must consider them together; their creation, redefinition, and tension is central to our history.

As essays in this volume suggest, after many years of debate, we still require a fuller understanding of how these terms of self-definition and identity work. We do know, however, that their meanings find powerful expression in material culture.[17] For generations, national narratives of America as a safe haven for immigrants, a frontier for pioneers, or a capitalist Eden for entrepreneurs have been reinforced in our consciousness through cultural products in our everyday lives.[18] The landscape portrait, diplomatic medal, political cartoon, and magazine cover featured above demonstrate how broadly and widely the concepts of race and nation have circulated. Likewise, the objects and images in this book and exhibition show us a society fraught by racial conflict that simultaneously spurred attempts to build relationships across difference and transform the larger social order.

We hope to convince readers that the real opportunity of the phrase *E Pluribus Unum* is its simultaneous flexibility and tension: "one" and "many" are not fixed and neither is dominant. Reconciling the inherent tensions between "one" and "many" is not an easy task, but the phrase can tie together the strands of migration, race, and nation. The "Many Voices, One Nation" metaphor can provide a common place to begin a conversation among those with competing visions of the nation's past.

BECOMING US

How a nation conceives of its past—its origins, its traditions, and historically dominant values—influences how it acts in the present. As a nation, we must question why we tell the stories we do and how they shape our shared values. As institutions committed to both the public good and to the preservation of historical artifacts, museums are poised to demonstrate through material culture how our communities have existed and continue to persist in complex intersection.[19] Deep understanding of the histories of diverse groups plays an important role in our ability to, in the words of education scholar Walter C. Parker, "live together justly, in ways that are mutually satisfying, and which leave our...differences, both individual and group, intact and our multiple identities recognized."[20]

This edited collection of essays by curators and affiliated scholars demonstrates the value of expanding both the types of historical evidence used and the kinds of stories told to help us understand the past. Material culture broadens our understandings of intellectual concepts such as cultural exchange, personal agency, and the construction of race, community, and nation. The objects featured in this volume, along with hundreds of others in the *Many Voices, One Nation* exhibition, indicate the nuances of our diverse American histories. In addition, they provide a model for how historical artifacts, such as those within the national collection, can speak to unique or shared experiences. We hope to create opportunities for visitors and readers to connect with history and to each other in ways that promote discussions about the meanings of America's dynamic past in order to create a more humane future together.

By linking disparate stories, this volume aims to help readers appreciate different facets of U.S. history through empathy and imagination—keys to a healthy democracy. A highly diverse and globally engaged democracy like ours is dependent upon a knowledgeable and civically literate citizenry. According to philosopher Martha Nussbaum, civic literacy comprises three capacities: critical thinking, proficiency in bridging and understanding different cultures, and the ability to imagine and sympathize with the situation of others.[21] Full civic literacies cannot be garnered only by studying books. Our civic knowledge and capabilities are honed through active engagement with differing perspectives about how to address problems that affect the well-being of the nation and the world.[22]

The *Many Voices, One Nation* book and exhibition cultivate for readers a "narrative imagination"—the ability to enter into worldviews and experiences that are different from our own.[23] Since our democratic system involves voting for laws and policies that will ultimately affect both ourselves and others, understanding what others' lives are like and how our decisions impact those around us can only enrich our civic engagement.[24] Indeed, our Republic depends on Americans' understanding of how our political system works and how we might influence it. But beyond political engagement it is also important that we comprehend cultural and global contexts in which democracy is both deeply valued and hotly contested in order to appreciate the differing perspectives and life experiences of our peers.[25] Considering objects, images, and first-person accounts of a variety of people across time can cultivate our narrative imaginations and help us better understand our diverse nation.

Included in this volume is a sampling of American stories. Our history is messy, complex, and multifaceted. Just as there is no simple story, there is no single account of history. This book and exhibition offer readers and visitors entry points for envisioning oneself as part of different communities—a practice that encourages better understanding of our diverse histories and enables us to act in the world in more humane ways. The presentation of our seemingly disparate pasts inspires possibilities for a shared future as we constantly reinterpret our *E Pluribus Unum*—our nation of many voices.

NOTES

1. Artist's Statement, http://npg.si.edu/exhibition/ out-many-one-jorge-rodriquez-gerada. For details on the production of the site, see Wendy Moonan, "How the Artist Behind the Giant Landscape Portrait on the Mall Used a Super-Precise GPS Satellite System as a Paintbrush," *Smithsonian*, 26 September 2014, http://www. smithsonianmag.com/smithsonian-institution/ how-artist-behind-giant-landscape-portrait-mall-used-super-precise-gps-satellite-system-paintbrush-180952856/; and Moonan, "Want to See the New Massive Portrait on the National Mall? Go Up," *Smithsonian*, October 2014, http://www.smithsonianmag.com/smithsonian-institution/want-see-new-massive-portrait-national-mall-go-180952785/.

2. In this phrase, "*e*" is a preposition that can be translated as "out of" or "from" and is used to express a source of place, material, or time. "*Pluribus*" translates simply to "many." Possible translations of the phrase include "one from many," "one out of many," or the more poetic English translations "out of many, one" or "from many, one."

3. In 1956 during the height of the Cold War, the official motto of the United States became "In God We Trust," but *E Pluribus Unum* remains on our currency and is a key phrase in American society. The original interpretation was intended to bring 13 colonies into one nation, but Pierre Eugène du Simitière's design for the Great Seal included an English rose, Scottish thistle, Irish harp, French lily, German eagle, and Belgian lion to invoke a diversity of European peoples who came together in the new United States republic. Not surprisingly, du Simitière made no mention of Africans or Native Americans as part

of the new nation. For a summary and analysis of traditional material culture related to the idea of *E Pluribus Unum*, including du Simitière's design, see David Hackett Fischer's chapter "E Pluribus Unum, Pluralist Solutions" in *Liberty and Freedom: A Visual History of America's Founding Ideas* (Oxford: Oxford University Press, 2005), 130–36. Since the 1960s a more robust and inclusive version of this interpretation has become more resonant.

4. For a compelling look at artists' uses of racial morphology in visual and material culture, see Jennifer Gonzalez, "Morphologies: Race as a Visual Technology" in *Only Skin Deep: Changing Visions of the American Self*, edited by Coco Fusco and Brian Wallis (New York: International Center of Photography, 2003), 379–93.

5. Jorge Rodríguez-Gerada quoted in Moonan, "Want to See the New Massive Portrait on the National Mall? Go Up."

6. This project, initiated by National Museum of American History curators Fath Davis Ruffins and William Yeingst, has taken multiple forms and resulted in years of important conversations about American cultural identity through the lens of immigration and migration. Their hard work has allowed this *Many Voices, One Nation* exhibition and book to build on the tradition of previous exhibit projects such as *A Nation of Nations* (1976).

7. For more on *A Nation of Nations*, see chapter 5, "Finding National Unity through Cultural Diversity: The Smithsonian and the Bicentennial" in William S. Walker, *A Living Exhibition: The Smithsonian and the Transformation of the Universal Museum* (Amherst: University of Massachusetts Press, 2013), 153–195.

8. For more readings on the importance and use of material culture as a historical resource, see, among others, Arjun Appadurai, ed., *The Social Life of Things: Commodities in Cultural Perspective* (Cambridge: Cambridge University Press, 1986); Bill Brown, "Thing Theory" in *Critical Inquiry*, 28(1) (Autumn, 2001):1–22; Sandra H. Dudley, ed., *Museum Objects: Experiencing the Properties of Things* (London and New York: Routledge, 2012); Grant David McCracken, *Culture and Consumption: New Approaches to the Symbolic Character of Consumer Goods and Activities* (Bloomington: Indiana University Press, 1990); Robin Bernstein, "Dances with things: Material culture and the performance of race" in *Social Text*, 27(4) (2009):67–94.

9. While the nation's founders likely were thinking of "*e pluribus*" as many colonies becoming one Republic, technically it could also be translated as many places, materials (such as peoples), or times.

10. Ellen R. Feingold, *The Value of Money* (Washington, D.C.: Smithsonian Institution Scholarly Press, 2016), 50.

11. Upon independence from the Netherlands in 1945, Indonesia adopted the phrase *Bhinneka Tunggal Ika*, translated to "unity in diversity, although different, yet one;" in 2000 the newly formed European Union adopted "United in Diversity," and, also in 2000, the first post-apartheid government of South Africa adopted *!ke e: /xarra //ke*, written in Khoisa and translated as "diverse people unite." See: Filomeno V. Aguilar, "Citizenship, Inheritance, and the Indigenizing of 'Orang Chinese' in Indonesia" in *Positions: East Asia Cultures Critique*, 9(3) (Winter 2001):501–33.

12. For important scholarship that connects race, class, and American laws, see: Ian Haney López, *White By Law: The Legal Construction of Race* (New York: New York University Press, 2006); Mae Ngai, *Impossible Subjects: Illegal Aliens and the Making of Modern America* (Princeton: Princeton University Press, 2004); Robert A. Williams, *The American Indian in Western Legal Thought: The Discourses of Conquest* (Oxford: Oxford University Press, 1993); and Aristide R. Zolberg, *A Nation by Design: Immigration Policy in the Fashioning of America* (Cambridge, Mass.: Harvard University Press, 2006).

13. See, for example, Zolberg, *A Nation by Design* and Ngai, *Impossible Subjects*.

14. Erika Lee, *At America's Gates: Chinese Immigration during the Exclusion Era, 1882–1943* (Chapel Hill: University of North Carolina Press, 2003); David R. Roediger, *The Wages of Whiteness: Race and the Making of the American Working Class*, rev. ed. (London: Verso, 1999); Matthew Frye Jacobson, *Whiteness of a Different Color: European Immigrants and the Alchemy of Race* (Cambridge, Mass.: Harvard University Press, 1998).

15. Racialization is the set of processes through which racial meanings and identities are constructed over time through various practices, representations, and social interactions. Here we refer primarily to Omi and Winant's seminal work, *Racial Formation in the United States*, for a working definition. Omi and Winant start from the understanding that race is an intractable and enduring feature of the United States; racial meanings are pervasive and shape individual identities, collective action, and social structures and interactions; and while race is an "unstable and 'decentered' complex of social meanings constantly being transformed by political struggle" (68), it also remains an organizing principle of social life. Racialization thus refers to specific ideological—and we add historical and representational—processes through which shifting meanings of race are produced by the practices of different social groups over time, in this case, through representation. See Michael Omi and Howard Winant, *Racial Formation in the United States*, 2nd ed. (New York: Routledge, 1994).

16. See, for example, Leo Chavez, *Covering Immigration: Popular Images and the Politics of the Nation* (Berkeley: University of California

Press, 2001); Anna Pegler-Gordon, *In Sight of America: Photography and the Development of U.S. Immigration Policy* (Berkeley: University of California Press, 2009); Elena Tajima Creef, *Imaging Japanese America: The Visual Construction of Citizenship, Nation, and the Body* (New York: New York University Press, 2004).

17. Among others, see Martin A. Berger, *Sight Unseen: Whiteness and American Visual Culture* (Berkeley: University of California Press, 2005); Shawn Michelle Smith, *Photography on the Color Line: W. E. B. Du Bois, Race, and Visual Culture* (Durham, N.C.: Duke University Press, 2004) and *American Archives: Gender, Race, and Class in Visual Culture* (Princeton: Princeton University Press, 1999); Grace Elizabeth Hale, *Making Whiteness: The Culture of Segregation in the South, 1890–1940* (New York: Pantheon, 1998); and Alexander Saxton, *The Rise and Fall of the White Republic: Class Politics and Mass Culture in Nineteenth-Century America* (London: Verso, 1990).

18. See, among others, Robert L. Fleegler, *Ellis Island Nation: Immigration Policy and American Identity in the Twentieth Century* (Philadelphia: University of Pennsylvania Press, 2013); Robert Hariman and John Louis Lucaites, *No Caption Needed: Iconic Photographs, Public Culture, and Liberal Democracy* (Chicago: University of Chicago Press, 2007); Ardis Cameron, ed., *Looking for America: The Visual Production of Nation and People* (Malden, Mass.: Blackwell, 2005); Martha A. Sandweiss, *Print the Legend: Photography and the American West* (New Haven: Yale University Press, 2002); Gregory M. Pfitzer, *Picturing the Past: Illustrated Histories and the American Imagination, 1840–1900* (Washington, D.C.: Smithsonian Institution Press, 2002); Michael G. Kammen, *The Mystic Chords of Memory: The Transformation of Tradition in American Culture*, 1st Vintage Books ed. (New York: Vintage Books, 1993); Angela L. Miller, *The Empire of the Eye: Landscape Representation and American Cultural Politics, 1825–1875*

(Ithaca, N.Y.: Cornell University Press, 1993); and William H. Truettner and Nancy K. Anderson, eds., *The West as America: Reinterpreting Images of the Frontier, 1820–1920* (Washington: Smithsonian Institution Press, 1991).

19. Among others, see David Gelles, "Museums Showcase Attitudes and Beliefs as Well as Objects," *New York Times* (16 March 2015, New York Edition, sec. F); Daniel J. Walkowitz and Lisa Maya Knauer, *Contested Histories in Public Space: Memory, Race, and Nation* (Durham, N.C.: Duke University Press Books, 2008); Ivan Karp, Corrine A. Kratz, Lynn Szwaja, and Tomás Ybarra-Frausto, eds., *Museum Frictions: Public Cultures/Global Transformations* (Durham, N.C.: Duke University Press, 2006); Alison Landsberg, *Prosthetic Memory: The Transformation of American Remembrance in the Age of Mass Culture* (New York: Columbia University Press, 2004); Daniel J. Walkowitz and Lisa Maya Knauer, eds., *Memory and the Impact of Political Transformation in Public Space* (Durham, N.C.: Duke University Press Books, 2004); and Jennifer L. Eichstedt and Stephen Small, *Representations of Slavery: Race and Ideology in Southern Plantation Museums* (Washington, D.C.: Smithsonian Books, 2002).

20. Walter C. Parker, *Teaching Democracy: Unity and Diversity in Public Life* (New York: Teachers College Press, 2003), 20.

21. Martha Nussbaum, *Cultivating Humanity: A Classical Defense of Reform in Liberal Education* (Cambridge, Mass.: Harvard University Press, 1998).

22. For more information on experiential learning and its importance to democratic engagement, see Scott London, *Doing Democracy* (Dayton, Ohio: Kettering Foundation, 2010).

23. Martha Nussbaum, "Cultivating the Imagination," *New York Times* (17 October 2010).

24. Nussbaum, "Cultivating the Imagination."

25. Larry Diamond, "A Report Card on Democracy," *Hoover Digest* 3 (30 July, 2000), http://www.hoover.org/research/report-card-democracy.

BIBLIOGRAPHY

Aguilar, Filomeno V. "Citizenship, Inheritance, and the Indigenizing of 'Orang Chinese' in Indonesia." *Positions: East Asia Cultures Critique*, 9(3) (2001):501–533.

Appadurai, Arjun, ed. *The Social Life of Things: Commodities in Cultural Perspective*. Cambridge: Cambridge University Press, 1986.

Berger, Martin A. *Sight Unseen: Whiteness and American Visual Culture*. Berkeley: University of California Press, 2005.

Bernstein, Robin. "Dances with things: Material Culture and the Performance of Race." *Social Text*, 27(4) (2009):67–94.

Brown, Bill. "Thing Theory." *Critical Inquiry*, 28(1) (2001):1–22.

Cameron, Ardis, ed. *Looking for America: The Visual Production of Nation and People*. Malden, Mass.: Blackwell, 2005.

Chavez, Leo. *Covering Immigration: Popular Images and the Politics of the Nation*. Berkeley: University of California Press, 2001.

Creef, Elena Tajima. *Imaging Japanese America: The Visual Construction of Citizenship, Nation, and the Body*. New York: New York University Press, 2004.

Diamond, Larry. "A Report Card on Democracy." *Hoover Digest*, (3) (30 July 2000). http://www.hoover.org/research/report-card-democracy (accessed 4 November 2016).

Dudley, Sandra H., ed. *Museum Objects: Experiencing the Properties of Things*. London and New York: Routledge, 2012.

Eichstedt, Jennifer L., and Stephen Small. *Representations of Slavery: Race and Ideology in Southern Plantation Museums*. Washington, D.C.: Smithsonian Books, 2002.

Feingold, Ellen R. *The Value of Money*. Washington, D.C.: Smithsonian Institution Scholarly Press, 2016.

Fischer, David Hackett. *Liberty and Freedom: A Visual History of America's Founding Ideas*. Oxford: Oxford University Press, 2005.

Fleegler, Robert L. *Ellis Island Nation: Immigration Policy and American Identity in the Twentieth Century*. Philadelphia: University of Pennsylvania Press, 2013.

Gelles, David. 2015. "Museums Showcase Attitudes and Beliefs as Well as Objects." *New York Times*, 16 March 2015, F.

Gonzalez, Jennifer. "Morphologies: Race as a Visual Technology." In *Only Skin Deep: Changing Visions of the American Self*, eds. Coco Fusco and Brian Wallis, pp. 379–93. New York: International Center of Photography, 2003.

Hale, Grace Elizabeth. *Making Whiteness: The Culture of Segregation in the South, 1890–1940*. New York: Pantheon, 1998.

Haney López, Ian. *White By Law: The Legal Construction of Race*. New York: New York University Press, 2006.

Hariman, Robert, and John Louis Lucaites. *No Caption Needed: Iconic Photographs, Public Culture, and Liberal Democracy*. Chicago: University of Chicago Press, 2007.

Jacobson, Matthew Frye. *Whiteness of a Different Color: European Immigrants and the Alchemy of Race*. Cambridge, Mass.: Harvard University Press, 1998.

Kammen, Michael G. *The Mystic Chords of Memory: The Transformation of Tradition in American Culture*. 1st Vintage Books ed. New York: Vintage Books, 1993.

Karp, Ivan, Corrine A. Kratz, Lynn Szwaja, and Tomás Ybarra-Frausto, eds. *Museum Frictions: Public Cultures/Global Transformations*. Durham, N.C.: Duke University Press, 2006.

Landsberg, Alison. *Prosthetic Memory: The Transformation of American Remembrance in the Age of Mass Culture*. New York: Columbia University Press, 2004.

Lee, Erika. *At America's Gates: Chinese Immigration during the Exclusion Era, 1882–1943*. Chapel Hill: University of North Carolina Press, 2003.

London, Scott. *Doing Democracy*. Dayton, Ohio: Kettering Foundation, 2010.

McCracken, Grant David. *Culture and Consumption: New Approaches to the Symbolic Character of Consumer Goods and Activities*. Bloomington: Indiana University Press, 1990.

Miller, Angela L. *The Empire of the Eye: Landscape Representation and American Cultural Politics, 1825–1875*. Ithaca, N.Y.: Cornell University Press, 1993.

Moonan, Wendy. "How the Artist Behind the Giant Landscape Portrait on the Mall Used a Super-Precise GPS Satellite System as a Paintbrush." *Smithsonian Magazine*, 26 September 2014. http://www.smithsonianmag.com/smithsonian-institution/how-artist-behind-giant-landscape-portrait-mall-used-super-precise-gps-satellite-system-paintbrush-180952856/?no-ist (accessed 4 November 2016).

———. "Want to See the New Massive Portrait on the National Mall? Go Up." *Smithsonian Magazine*, October, 2014. http://www.smithsonianmag.com/smithsonian-institution/want-see-new-massive-portrait-national-mall-go-180952785/?no-ist (accessed 4 November 2016).

Ngai, Mae M. *Impossible Subjects: Illegal Aliens and the Making of Modern America*. Princeton: Princeton University Press, 2004.

Nussbaum, Martha. *Cultivating Humanity: A Classical Defense of Reform in Liberal Education*. Cambridge, Mass.: Harvard University Press, 1998.

———. 2010. "Cultivating the Imagination." *New York Times*, 17 October 2010.

Omi, Michael and Howard Winant. *Racial Formation in the United States*. 2nd ed. New York: Routledge, 1994.

Parker, Walter C. *Teaching Democracy: Unity and Diversity in Public Life*. New York: Teachers College Press, 2003.

Pegler-Gordon, Anna. *In Sight of America: Photography and the Development of U.S. Immigration Policy*. Berkeley: University of California Press, 2009.

Pfitzer, Gregory M. *Picturing the Past: Illustrated Histories and the American Imagination, 1840–1900*. Washington, D.C.: Smithsonian Institution Press, 2002.

Rodríguez-Gerada, Jorge. "Out of Many One." http://npg.si.edu/exhibition/out-many-one-jorge-rodriquez-gerada (accessed 4 November 2016).

Roediger, David R. *The Wages of Whiteness: Race and the Making of the American Working Class*. Rev. ed. London: Verso, 1999.

Sandweiss, Martha A. *Print the Legend: Photography and the American West*. New Haven: Yale University Press, 2002.

Saxton, Alexander. *The Rise and Fall of the White Republic: Class Politics and Mass Culture in Nineteenth-Century America*. London: Verso, 1990.

Smith, Shawn Michelle. *American Archives: Gender, Race, and Class in Visual Culture*. Princeton: Princeton University Press, 1999.

———. *Photography on the Color Line: W. E. B. Du Bois, Race, and Visual Culture*. Durham, N.C.: Duke University Press, 2004.

Truettner, William H. and Nancy K. Anderson, eds., *The West as America: Reinterpreting Images of the Frontier, 1820–1920*. Washington: Smithsonian Institution Press, 1991.

Walker, William S. *A Living Exhibition: The Smithsonian and the Transformation of the Universal Museum*. Amherst: University of Massachusetts Press, 2013.

Walkowitz, Daniel J. and Lisa Maya Knauer. *Contested Histories in Public Space: Memory, Race, and Nation*. Durham, N.C.: Duke University Press Books, 2008.

Walkowitz, Daniel J. and Lisa Maya Knauer, eds. *Memory and the Impact of Political Transformation in Public Space*. Durham, N.C.: Duke University Press Books, 2004.

Williams, Robert A. *The American Indian in Western Legal Thought: The Discourses of Conquest*. Oxford: Oxford University Press, 1993.

Zolberg, Aristide R. *A Nation by Design: Immigration Policy in the Fashioning of America*. Cambridge, Mass.: Harvard University Press, 2006

Unsettling the Continent, 1492–1776

Barbara Clark Smith

To look at early North America—the era that began with first contacts among native peoples, Europeans, and Africans on this continent—is to enter a complex and bewildering time. In the past, historians often recounted the era primarily through stories of settlement. Our accounts focused on bands of European migrants, who were animated to leave the Old World in search of adventure or economic gain, with the desire to convert native peoples to Christianity or to find freedom for their own communities to live and worship as they saw fit. These small groups of Europeans came into contact and, oftentimes, conflict with various American Indian tribes. Some of them brought or acquired enslaved Africans, whose labor contributed to the development of New World colonies. Those colonies' particular forms of commerce and agriculture would vary, as would their distinctive social, religious, and political institutions.

In terms of population growth, it was the English migrants whose settlements would flourish, expand, and set the terms for the future. Along the Atlantic coast, English newcomers built new lives in what they saw (quite reasonably, from the standpoint of Europe) as a wilderness—even, in the words of one Pilgrim in seventeenth-century Massachusetts, "a hideous and desolate wilderness."[1] Their fortitude prepared the way for a larger tide of immigrants into British North America in the course of the 1700s, and that tide provided the ground

Figure 1.
Fragment of Plymouth Rock, chipped in 1830, Plymouth, Massachusetts. Although no one present mentioned a rock in their accounts of the Pilgrims' landing, later narrators gave it a prominent place in the national origin story of the United States. A descendant of Governor William Bradford of Plymouth Colony chipped this fragment from a large rock near Plymouth Harbor. National Museum of American History, Smithsonian Institution, gift of Virginia L. W. Fox.

on which the rest of U.S. national history has unfolded. In the context of a museum exhibition, a fragment of "Plymouth Rock"—a souvenir taken in the nineteenth century from the supposed landing site of the Pilgrims—might testify to a lasting attachment to such a settlement story (Figure 1).

There are things that are true in such accounts of settlement, but decades of recent research and rethinking have set historians in search of more fully accurate ways of writing about early America. The experiences and ideas of various bands of Europeans are still critical to the story, of course, but they can no longer be characterized so easily or taken to represent the whole. A narrative built around their projects as "settlement" is simply too narrow for understanding the past. We need a more capacious way of thinking.

Three general areas of research have made this need very clear: First is the exploration of Native American experiences. Before the advent of Europeans, after all, native societies had been in the midst of histories of their own. Their nations were diverse and changing. In some places, such as the Northeast, groups were coming together, as previously disparate peoples combined to build up larger social and political units; in other places, such as the Southeast, once-unified chieftaincies were waning in power and slowly breaking into smaller political groups. Everywhere, different peoples pursued their lives by drawing on established technologies and cultural beliefs, conducting trade and diplomacy with other indigenous nations, and innovating new practices in the face of changing circumstances. Some surviving artifacts bespeak the importance of Native American histories, as does a crest hat representing past events in the lineage of the Eagle Clan of the Tsimshian people of British Columbia, discussed in Christopher Turner's essay in this volume. However various their histories, and however far from static their lives on the continent, native peoples' worlds were nonetheless in many respects long "settled."[2]

For the American Indians, the arrival of strangers from across the ocean brought nothing short of catastrophe. In many areas, European aims of domination and acts of plundering brought violent conflict; nearly everywhere, European microbes carried diseases that would devastate indigenous populations with no acquired immunity to them. Epidemics and warfare led to social disorganization and new conflicts, a cycle of disruption, and an overwhelming story of loss. As the historian Alan Taylor notes, between 1492, when Columbus made landfall, and 1776, when thirteen British colonies declared independence, the human population of the continent did not increase, but declined. This was human tragedy on an extraordinary scale. It does not require much reflection to conclude that these centuries cannot accurately be seen as an age of "settlement" in North America.[3]

Equally important, a simple narrative of settlement does not take into account the experience of the many Africans brought unwillingly both to the West Indies and the continental British colonies. It was true that a first generation of Africans to reach North America came in anomalous ways—sometimes as free traders or sailors, sometimes as bound servants or slaves. These were "Atlantic Creoles," originating in the trading centers that burgeoned along the west coast of Africa in the course of the sixteenth century to engage European commerce. They were familiar with some European cultures, multilingual, and often well traveled within the Atlantic Basin. They played a variety of roles in the fluid, multiethnic port cities of early seventeenth-century North America, where some who arrived as slaves or servants were able to gain freedom and social membership.[4]

Within a short time, however, mainland societies' shift to plantation production changed the prospects for Africans there. With booms in tobacco and then rice production, mainland planters joined proprietors of New World sugar islands in a growing demand for enslaved labor. Over the course of several centuries, hundreds of thousands of Africans, captured from an array of nations in Central

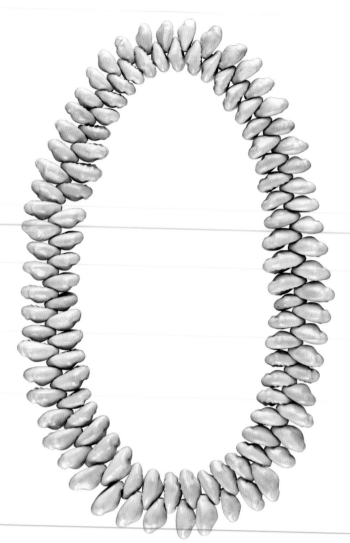

Figure 2.
African cowrie shell necklace, date, artist, and place of origin unknown. The Atlantic slave trade and resulting diaspora of African people profoundly shaped the processes of unsettlement and settlement in the Americas. Cowrie shells like these were used as a form of currency, both in West Africa and in the broader Atlantic triangle of trade. National Museum of American History, Smithsonian Institution, gift of the Chase Manhattan Bank.

and West Africa, were transported to the British continental colonies. A necklace strung of cowrie shells (Figure 2), a common currency in the slave trade between European traders and African suppliers in the Bight of Benin, might symbolize diaspora, the destruction of family and kin ties, or a prelude to the brutal regimentation of plantation slavery, but hardly a history of settlement.[5]

There are two points here: first, the term "settler" will not easily stick to these forcibly transported Americans; second, that term sits uneasily even on the European planters and merchants who based their livelihoods, social systems, and cultural identities on a system of bondage and a construction of racial identity.[6] Indeed, the presence of Africans shaped language, foodways, religious beliefs, and much more; the presence of a system of chattel slavery, moreover, shaped the whole of British North America. Within a common status as chattel slaves, Africans' lives followed different patterns in different regions. Similarly, different colonies felt the impact of slavery in different ways. Northern colonies became "societies with slaves," where the institution of enslaved labor had significant impact, while the southern or plantation colonies became "slave societies," that is, fully reliant on and shaped by the institution.[7]

Even among European Americans, in other words, racial slavery deeply affected everything—material life and concepts of property, of course, but also precious and consequential ideas about "liberty" and "independence." The profoundly unsettling experience imposed on captured Africans was not a tributary to the main current of American events, then, but at the center of the history that followed. And, indeed, the resistances, commitments, innovations, and adaptations of African Americans have defined the nation as thoroughly as have the ideals and institutions of Europeans.

Finally, if narratives of settlement made sense of the lives of some European immigrants to early America, that term does not adequately convey what other colonizers understood themselves to be doing. Some Spanish people certainly settled into new lives on the continent, but Spain's initial project was one of conquest, the forced acquisition of native gold and silver, and command of native labor. Other empires, too, viewed North America less as a place for relocating their own population, and more as an arena for gaining material resources and establishing geopolitical influence in their rivalry with other Atlantic powers. Drawn by the continent's supply of fur-bearing mammals, the Dutch came to New Amsterdam and the French to Quebec intending to establish durable trade relationships with native peoples.

The Dutch West Indies Company founded an outpost on the hilly island of Mannahatta as a shoreline base. They joined the Lenape and other peoples in commerce along the rivers and into the interior. Dutch nationals came to New Amsterdam under the auspices of the company, but the city population also included German Lutherans, French Huguenots, Sephardic Jews, Belgian Walloons, and Africans—anyone who could support the mission of developing the fur trade and protecting Dutch outposts. The city that would become New York, then, was commercial and multiethnic from the outset. Its inhabitants quickly adapted to native forms of diplomacy and standards of exchange—adopting the

Figure 3.
Wampum beads produced in Campbell's Wampum Factory in Park Ridge, New Jersey, 1870 to 1890. Wampum has long been extracted from quahog clamshells and used in commercial and political exchanges among native peoples in the Northeast. These specific beads, produced by a non–Native American business, are an example of how newcomers to the region appropriated the practice. Courtesy of the National Museum of the American Indian, Smithsonian Institution (13/2907).

use of beads made from the shells of quahog (wampum) in their dealings, for example (Figure 3). Although the Dutch brought an established national church, the variety of their city quickly led them toward tolerating other beliefs. If they called their colony New Netherland, only some inhabitants there sought to transplant Dutch society as a primary goal.[8]

The French had broader and more lasting ambitions on the continent. They established cities at Quebec and Montreal, and they conducted agriculture along the Saint Lawrence River for most of two centuries. Still, a limited number of Europeans came to the colony to build lives there. Dedicated to commercial, geopolitical, and religious aims, New France was defined throughout its history by the limited appeal of settlement in the area among potential immigrants from France.[9] As early as the 1630s, French colonial leaders imagined creating a society on other terms. "Our young men shall marry your daughters, and we shall become one people," said Samuel de Champlain to Montagnais and Huron leaders.[10] Here was a vision of French settlement in America, perhaps, one in which immigration of numerous French households would be inessential.

In practice, matters did not unfold strictly as Champlain had imagined they would. The native leaders who heard him did not envision life precisely as the French did, and even French newcomers to the region were sometimes at cross-purposes on whether and how to settle. Thus, Jesuit priests in New France sought to convert native peoples to Catholicism, hoping to bring converts into agricultural households as settled "habitants," attached to the land in a life that the Jesuits considered civil and godly. But fur companies encouraged native peoples not to sedentary lives but to frequent travel into ever more remote areas where furs could be harvested.

Many chose that life over working the land—and so did a good number of Frenchmen. Called *couriers du bois*, these French joined Indians in hunting and trapping in the backcountry, developing a life neither strictly French nor strictly Algonquian. They did often marry native women and had families. Their bilingual children played roles in bridging the divided cultures of their world, as translators, diplomats, and savvy traders with contacts in both worlds (Figure 4). Should we say that Algonquian cultures here unsettled the French, or that settlement simply followed a distinctly unforeseen pattern?[11] Either way, it was through treaties and alliances with native nations, rather than through transfer of European population, that the French laid claim to wide swaths of the continent.

Finally, even the earliest companies of English to land in North America were only "settlers" of a sort. Virginia Company planners chose the Chesapeake region because of the presence there of a sophisticated and prosperous Powhatan society, which it hoped to dominate along the model of what the Spanish had done in Mesoamerica and Peru.[12] Even as the British in Virginia turned to

Figure 4. Illustration decorating a map entitled *Carte Tres Curieuse*, from a 1719 atlas. Beavers are busy at work in this playful illustration set in New France's remote natural environment. Both native peoples and Europeans hunted beaver for their pelts. National Museum of American History, Smithsonian Institution.

Figure 5.
Portrait of Mrs. Charles Lowndes, born Sarah Parker, painted by artist Jeremiah Theus (American, 1716–1774) around 1759. Lowndes was the wife of a wealthy Charleston planter. An expensive portrait such as this was a symbol of high social status in the emerging Charleston elite. Courtesy of the Gibbes Museum of Art/Carolina Art Association, oil on canvas, 30 × 25 inches, 1915.003.0001.

tobacco culture, many displayed more commitment to amassing profits than to settling, per se. Through the seventeenth century, at least, they constructed what historians have called "impermanent architecture"—insubstantial housing soon to be left behind once tobacco crops had exhausted the soil and inhabitants relocated to newer lands.[13]

In South Carolina, Europeans settled rather like the Dutch had done earlier in New Amsterdam, clustering in Charleston and its environs rather than spreading out across the land. They avoided the unhealthy backcountry where they owned rice plantations worked by the enslaved African majority.[14] A genteel portrait of a member of a Charleston planter household bespeaks the emergence of a self-conscious class anxious to see themselves portrayed in a European medium and form indicative of economic and social arrival (Figure 5). By contrast,

Figure 6.
Rice fanner basket made from coils of rush sewn with palmetto leaves in South Carolina, date unknown. Baskets of this type were used in rice production to separate the kernel from the hull. Enslaved Africans combined traditional African agricultural methods with regional materials such as seagrass to innovate the cultivation of rice as a cash crop. National Museum of American History, Smithsonian Institution.

a fanner basket, made by African American hands out of seagrass, emphasizes the role of African knowledge of rice culture and the innovative use of New World materials to produce the tools and technologies that built Carolina society[15] (Figure 6). Together, these artifacts suggest an unsettled world embracing stark disjunctions and profound connections as well.

All these examples militate against viewing the colonial era solely through the lens of European settlement. Might we instead consider describing these centuries as a time of "unsettlement" in North America? That term is both plausible and thought provoking. It captures realities and perspectives that enrich our understanding of the past.[16]

Yet we should hesitate merely to turn the old story on its head. After all, we know that many English, Scots, Irish, and Germans did transplant themselves and their households to the British colonies. Smaller numbers of Spanish, French, Swedes, Dutch, and other groups also made the continent their home. Historians do not need to adopt these groups' perspectives as most essential, but we do need to acknowledge and analyze their extraordinary experience of "planting" themselves in America. Theirs was a form of "settler colonialism," akin to the colonial practices of other Europeans but distinct in its terms and—especially for native peoples, who had no place in settler society—its consequences. Our account of this history has to consider the way that some with origins in Europe, as generations passed and the Native American presence receded from their immediate view, came to identify *themselves* as the "native" population of their regions.[17]

Moreover, the rubric of "unsettlement" can leave the story of Africans and their progeny woefully incomplete. Africans did more than survive under their conditions of New World bondage. They developed new connections and commitments, whether forging new identities with disparate and unknown African others, or combining various African ways with elements of European cultures and responding to resources in the New World environment.[18] Along the coasts of South Carolina and Georgia, for example, they developed a distinctive and new Gullah culture. Across the U.S. South, and through the course of further forced migrations, there is no doubt that generations of Africans and their offspring put down deep roots. They *did* settle, in some sense of that word, becoming Southerners as surely as did European American planters, farmers, artisans, and traders.

Even Native Americans' experience defies simple summary as one of unsettlement. Amidst the devastation brought by contact, native people struggled to recover and regroup, to re-establish meaningful lives that would embody precious traditions even as they departed from the past in critical ways. Everywhere, Native American peoples found resilience and innovative responses to what was, for them as well as for the Europeans and Africans, a "new world."[19]

In New Mexico, to take one example, Tewa, Zuni, Acoma, and other peoples—each with their own language and beliefs—found themselves in a common situation under the rule of conquistadors from the south. With Spanish as a common second language, these different groups devised a new identity as "Pueblo" peoples and together coordinated one of the first great revitalization movements meant to reclaim Native American ways of life. Participants in the Pueblo Revolt of 1680 arose against administrators, priests, and others to push the Spanish hundreds of miles back to the south. When Spanish forces returned, it was on terms of negotiation, part military reconquest and part accommodation.

Material culture can help reveal the complexity of these relationships. Pottery from the Hawikuh mission evokes seventeenth-century Zuni potters

Figure 7.
Seventeenth-century salt cellar from the ruins of the Spanish mission among the Zuni Indians of Hawikuh Pueblo, Cibola County, New Mexico. The maker of this clay vessel decorated it with both Spanish motifs—such as crosses—and Pueblo ones—such as rainbows and upright feathers. Courtesy of the National Museum of the American Indian, Smithsonian Institution (096970).

working with traditional materials and techniques, yet producing nontraditional forms such as candlesticks and soup bowls tailored to European practices and foodways[20] (Figure 7). An architectural bracket, or corbel, bespeaks the mission church at Pecos, New Mexico, established by Spanish Franciscans to convert Pueblo peoples in 1621 and rebuilt after the Pueblo Revolt of 1680 (Figure 8). The corbel stands witness to building and destruction both, reminders of repeated instances of violent conflict between European newcomers and native people.

This was both settlement and unsettlement, then; perhaps most of all, we see a history of lasting but changing *relationship.*[21] Everywhere, indeed, says historian James Axtell, there was "a mutual history of continuous interaction and influence" between native and newcomer, and the phrase can characterize many relationships within and among the varied African and European peoples as well.[22] These groups shaped each other's lives and identities, whether they borrowed or avoided, or sought to connect with or distinguish themselves from one another.

In the context of a museum exhibition, the material artifacts mentioned here can represent some of the wide array of such early American interactions and experiences. Taken separately, such artifacts offer insight into particular

Figure 8.
Corbel, or ceiling bracket, once part of Pecos Mission Church in present day New Mexico. The Pecos Mission Church was established by Spanish missionaries in 1621 and was destroyed during the Pueblo Revolt of 1680. This piece is likely from the rebuilding of the church following the revolt. National Museum of American History, Smithsonian Institution.

occasions or relationships—yet what may challenge most is to recognize that such particularities do not neatly resolve into a single, satisfying story. For the museum visitor, in other words, it is the assemblage and juxtaposition of artifacts that can challenge and, indeed, unsettle. Here is a bewildering range of historical events that both confirm and belie a narrative of "settling" in North America. It is an array undeniably and necessarily incomplete, one that decenters experiences once portrayed as definitive without replacing them with an easily digested alternative account. Beyond including new and often unfamiliar historical agents at the very heart of colonial America, such an array discomfits by intimating the limits of agency as exercised by any one group. Together, these artifacts represent the powerful processes of empire, an underlying logic that shaped lives of individuals and communities in a world not widely open to the free choice implied by some notions of "settlement."

Can we accommodate a messy and multifaceted founding era, one that defies our impulse to untangle and isolate a single thread in order to deem it more essentially American than the others? Such a view will not seamlessly lead us to the history of the US; on the contrary, it may leave unsettled the identity of the "we" and "US" in that history. At the least it should unsettle our language: we need a new word for inhabitants of the United States created in 1776 that lets us use (or encourages us to use) the broader terms "American" and "North American" with greater precision. New language should help us avoid conflating the people and histories proper to the US—we might call them "U.S.-ian"—with the people and histories of the larger continent that are also encompassed in the term "North American," and the people and histories of the larger hemisphere that are also properly denoted by the term "American."

Figure 9.
Creamware pitcher with transfer print, made in England, based on John Fairburn's print *An Emblem of America*, 1795. Here, a women representing America instructs two diminutive Native Americans by pointing to portraits of important European and American figures such as Christopher Columbus and George Washington. National Museum of American History, Smithsonian Institution, gift of Robert H. McCauley.

One telling material artifact suggests the history of the conflation of "American" and "U.S.-ian." In 1798, an English printmaker produced decorative "emblems" of four continents, each represented by a female figure (Figure 9). While the emblems of Asia, Africa, and Europe depicted women indigenous to those continents, the emblem of America depicted a *European American* figure holding a U.S. flag and instructing diminutive native peoples. Soon after the Revolution, then, we see a tendency to reduce America to a single national and racial story. What happens as we seek to undo that reduction? Can we tease apart other American histories from the U.S.-ian ones, and locate the US more accurately in the changing and capacious context of other American histories?

Perhaps the discomfort we and our museum visitors may feel at such changes in both terminology and perspective merely echoes the experiences of Americans past. Early Americans lived in the midst of social and political powers and in pursuit of cultural ideals not entirely comprehensible today. Do we need to

Unsettling the Continent

defend or own such a past, or make it lead to our world as we imagine it today? If so, perhaps we might locate resources in the face of unsettlement—the learning of new languages, openness to new beliefs and new alliances, creative redefinitions of self, resistances both large and small to the imperatives of empire—as a preeminent theme of American (including U.S.-ian) life.

NOTES

1. William Bradford, *Of Plymouth Plantation, 1620–1647,* ed. Samuel Eliot Morison (New York: Alfred A. Knopf, 1979), 62.

2. Neal Salisbury, "The Indians' Old World: Native Americans and the Coming of Europeans," *William and Mary Quarterly,* 3rd ser., 53(1996):435–58. On the Tsimshian Crest Hat, see Christopher Lindsay Turner's essay in this volume.

3. Alan Taylor, *American Colonies: The Settling of North America* (New York: Viking, 2001), xi. Taylor's subtitle retains the term "settling." James H. Merrell, "Some Thoughts on Colonial Historians and American Indians," *William and Mary Quarterly,* 3rd ser., 46 (1989):94–112, points to the inaccuracy of describing European arrivals in the Americas as constituting "peopling" of the hemisphere. Colin G. Calloway, *New Worlds for All: Indians, Europeans, and the Remaking of Early America* (Baltimore: Johns Hopkins University Press, 1997); Daniel K. Richter, *Facing East from Indian Country: A Native History of Early America* (Cambridge, Mass.: Harvard University Press, 2001).

4. Ira Berlin, "From Creole to African: Atlantic Creoles and the Origins of African-American Society in Mainland North America," *William and Mary Quarterly,* 3rd ser., 53 (1996):251–88.

5. David Eltis, "The Volume and Structure of the Transatlantic Slave Trade: A Reassessment," *William and Mary Quarterly,* 3rd ser., 58(2001):17–46. The concentration of cowries in the Bight of Benin trade is noted on page 31. Also, Eltis, "A Brief Overview of the Trans-Atlantic Slave Trade," 2007, http://slavevoyages.org/assessment/essays; John Thornton, *Africa and Africans in the Making of the Atlantic World, 1400–1800* (New York: Cambridge University Press, 1992).

6. Edmund S. Morgan, *American Slavery, American Freedom: The Ordeal of Colonial Virginia* (New York: W. W. Norton & Co., 1975); Nate Huggins, "The Deforming Mirror of Truth: Slavery and the Master Narrative of American History," *Radical History Review*, 49 (Winter 1991):25–48.

7. Ira Berlin, *Many Thousands Gone: The First Two Centuries of Slavery in North America* (Cambridge, Mass.: Harvard University Press, 1998). See also Berlin, *Generations of Captivity: A History of African American Slaves* (Cambridge, Mass.: Harvard University Press, 2003).

8. Oliver A. Rink, *Holland on the Hudson: An Economic and Social History of Dutch New York* (Ithaca: Cornell University Press, 1986); Joyce D. Goodfriend, *Before the Melting Pot: Society and Culture in Colonial New York City 1664–1730* (Princeton: Princeton University Press, 1992).

9. Among populations who left France for North America, Protestant Huguenot communities were unwelcome in orthodox New France. They found a place in various British colonies instead.

10. Denys Delâge and Mathieu d'Avignon, "We Shall Be One People: Quebec," *Common-Place,* 3(4) (July 2003), http://www.common-place-archives.org/vol-03/no-04/quebec-city/.

11. Richard White, *The Middle Ground: Indians, Empires, and Republics in the Great Lakes*

Region, 1650–1815 (Cambridge: Cambridge University Press, 1991).

12. April Lee Hatfield, "Spanish Colonization Literature, Powhatan Geographies, and English Perceptions of Tsenacommacah/Virginia," *Journal of Southern History,* 69(2003):245–82.

13. Cary Carson, Norman F. Barka, William M. Kelso, Garry Wheeler Stone, Dell Upton, "Impermanent Architecture in the Southern American Colonies," *Winterthur Portfolio,* 16(2/3) (Summer–Autumn, 1981):135–96. Carson et al. do emphasize that these immigrants to Virginia came to stay, and that they drew on established English house forms even in building these impermanent structures.

14. S. Max Edelson, *Plantation Enterprise in Colonial South Carolina* (Cambridge, Mass.: Harvard University Press, 2011); Peter H. Wood, *Black Majority: Negroes in Colonial South Carolina from 1670 to the Stono Rebellion* (New York: Knopf, 1974).

15. Judith Anne Carney, *Black Rice: The African Origins of Rice Culture in the Americas* (Cambridge, Mass.: Harvard University Press, 2002); David Eltis, Philip Morgan, and David Richardson, "Agency and Diaspora in Atlantic History: Reassessing the African Contribution to Rice Cultivation in the Americas," *American Historical Review,* 112(2007):1329–58.

16. I first explored this understanding of early America in an exhibition project I co-curated along with James R. Kelly, in collaboration between the Virginia Historical Society and the National Museum of American History, Smithsonian Institution. See James R. Kelly and

Barbara Clark Smith, "Introduction," *Jamestown, Québec, Santa Fe: Three North American Beginnings* (Washington, D.C.: Smithsonian Press, 2007), 10–55.

17. Michael Warner notes European Americans' way of imagining themselves as "the natives," in "What's Colonial About Colonial America?" in *Possible Pasts: Becoming Colonial in Early America,* ed. Robert Blair St. George (Ithaca, N.Y.: Cornell University Press, 2000), 49–72. On settler colonialism, see Lorenzo Veracini, "'Settler Colonialism': Career of a Concept," *Journal of Imperial and Commonwealth History,* 41(2013):313–33.

18. Michael A. Gomez, *Exchanging Our Country Marks: The Transformation of African Identities in the Colonial and Antebellum South* (Philadelphia: University of Pennsylvania Press, 1998).

19. James H. Merrell, "The Indians' New World: The Catawba Experience," *William and Mary Quarterly,* 3rd ser., 41(1984):537–65.

20. Klint Ericson, "From Kitchen to Table: Spatial Practices around Food Preparation and Consumption in a Seventeenth-Century Pueblo Mission," unpublished paper on Hawikuh ceramics in the collection of National Museum of the American Indian, Smithsonian Institution, pp. 12–13.

21. David J. Weber, "Santa Fe," in *Jamestown, Quebec, Santa Fe: Three North American Beginnings,* eds. James C. Kelly and Barbara Clark Smith (Washington, D.C.: Smithsonian Books, 2007), 135–63.

22. James Axtell, "Colonial America without the Indians: Counterfactual Reflections," *Journal of American History,* 73(4)(1987):981–96.

BIBLIOGRAPHY

Axtell, James. "Colonial America without the Indians: Counterfactual Reflections." *Journal of American History,* 73(4)(1987):981–96.

Berlin, Ira. "From Creole to African: Atlantic Creoles and the Origins of African-American Society in Mainland North America." *William and Mary Quarterly,* 3rd ser., (53)(1996):251–88.

_____. *Generations of Captivity: A History of African American Slaves*. Cambridge, Mass.: Harvard University Press, 2003.

_____. *Many Thousands Gone: The First Two Centuries of Slavery in North America*. Cambridge, Mass.: Harvard University Press, 1998.

Bradford, William. *Of Plymouth Plantation, 1620–1647*, ed. Samuel Eliot Morison. New York: Alfred A. Knopf, 1979).

Calloway, Colin G. *New Worlds for All: Indians, Europeans, and the Remaking of Early America*. Baltimore: Johns Hopkins University Press, 1997.

Carney, Judith Anne. *Black Rice: The African Origins of Rice Culture in the Americas*. Cambridge, Mass.: Harvard University Press, 2002.

Carson, Cary, Norman F. Barka, William M. Kelso, Garry Wheeler Stone, and Dell Upton. "Impermanent Architecture in the Southern American Colonies." *Winterthur Portfolio*, 16(2/3) (Summer–Autumn, 1981):135–196.

Delâge, Denys, and Mathieu d'Avignon. "We Shall Be One People: Quebec." *Common-Place*, 3(4) (July 2003). http://www.common-place-archives.org/vol-03/no-04/quebec-city/ (accessed 16 November 2016).

Edelson, S. Max. *Plantation Enterprise in Colonial South Carolina*. Cambridge, Mass.: Harvard University Press, 2011.

Eltis, David. "The Volume and Structure of the Transatlantic Slave Trade: A Reassessment." *William and Mary Quarterly*, 3rd ser., 58(2001):17–46.

_____. "A Brief Overview of the Trans-Atlantic Slave Trade." 2007. http://slavevoyages.org/assessment/essays (accessed 16 November 2016).

Eltis, David, Philip Morgan, and David Richardson. "Agency and Diaspora in Atlantic History: Reassessing the African Contribution to Rice Cultivation in the Americas." *American Historical Review* 112(5) (2007):1329–58.

Ericson, Klint. "From Kitchen to Table: Spatial Practices around Food Preparation and Consumption in a Seventeenth-Century Pueblo Mission." Unpublished paper, National Museum of the American Indian.

Gomez, Michael A. *Exchanging Our Country Marks: The Transformation of African Identities in the Colonial and Antebellum South*. Philadelphia: University of Pennsylvania Press, 1998.

Goodfriend, Joyce D. *Before the Melting Pot: Society and Culture in Colonial New York City, 1664–1730*. Princeton: Princeton University Press, 1992.

Hatfield, April Lee. "Spanish Colonization Literature, Powhatan Geographies, and English Perceptions of Tsenacommacah/Virginia." *Journal of Southern History*, 69(2) (2003): 245–82.

Huggins, Nate. "The Deforming Mirror of Truth: Slavery and the Master Narrative of American History." *Radical History Review*, 49(Winter 1991):25–48.

Kelly, James R., and Barbara Clark Smith. Introduction to *Jamestown, Québec, Santa Fe: Three North American Beginnings*, pp. 10–55. Washington, D.C.: Smithsonian Press, 2007.

Merrell, James H. "The Indians' New World: The Catawba Experience." *William and Mary Quarterly*, 3rd ser., 41(1984): 537–65.

_____. "Some Thoughts on Colonial Historians and American Indians." *William and Mary Quarterly*, 3rd ser., 46(1989):94–112.

Morgan, Edmund S. *American Slavery, American Freedom: The Ordeal of Colonial Virginia*. New York: W. W. Norton & Co., 1975.

Richter, Daniel K. *Facing East from Indian Country: A Native History of Early America*. Cambridge, Mass.: Harvard University Press, 2001.

Rink, Oliver A. *Holland on the Hudson: An Economic and Social History of Dutch New York*. Ithaca, N.Y.: Cornell University Press, 1986.

Salisbury, Neal. "The Indians' Old World: Native Americans and the Coming of Europeans." *William and Mary Quarterly*, 3rd ser., (53) (1996):435–58.

Taylor, Alan. *American Colonies: The Settling of North America*. New York: Viking, 2001.

Thornton, John. *Africa and Africans in the Making of the Atlantic World, 1400–1800.* New York: Cambridge University Press, 1992.

Veracini, Lorenzo. "'Settler Colonialism': Career of a Concept." *Journal of Imperial and Commonwealth History*, 41(2013):313–33.

Warner, Michael. "What's Colonial about Colonial America?" In *Possible Pasts: Becoming Colonial in Early America*, ed. Robert Blair St. George, pp. 49–72. Ithaca, N.Y.: Cornell University Press, 2000.

Weber, David J. "Santa Fe." In *Jamestown, Quebec, Santa Fe: Three North American Beginnings*, eds. James C. Kelly and Barbara Clark Smith, pp. 135–63. Washington, D.C.: Smithsonian Books, 2007.

White, Richard. *The Middle Ground: Indians, Empires, and Republics in the Great Lakes Region, 1650–1815.* Cambridge: Cambridge University Press, 1991.

Wood, Peter H. *Black Majority: Negroes in Colonial South Carolina from 1670 to the Stono Rebellion.* New York: Knopf, 1974.

The geographer Alfred B. Crosby called the cultural processes unleashed by this colonization the "Columbian exchange," a set of reciprocal transfers of ideas, technologies and goods that created an infinite array of blendings and borrowings, of mixings and meldings, of inventions and wholesale appropriations that were often unique and specific to time and place.[2] The New Mexican religious image of Saint Anthony of Padua holding the infant Christ was painted with local pigments on an elk-skin hide in 1725, possibly by an indigenous artisan (Figure 1). For almost a century it adorned the mission church at Santo Domingo Pueblo, a town of indigenous sedentary agriculturalists located some twenty miles south of Santa Fe. There, the town's residents venerated this image, along with that of

Figure 1.
Painting on elk hide of Saint Anthony of Padua with Christ Child, used in the Santo Domingo Mission Church, New Mexico, possibly produced by a Native American neophyte artist around 1725. Franciscan friars set up missions in New Mexico to convert Native Americans to the Catholic faith. The missions used local resources and materials, like this elk hide in place of canvas, in their proselytizing efforts. National Museum of American History, Smithsonian Institution, gift of Dr. J. Walter Fewkes.

Saint Dominic, the town's patron saint, as well as many other images of Christ, the Virgin Mary, and angels and saints that still adorn the church's sanctuary.

The iron spur was cast in the late seventeenth or early eighteenth century in New Mexico (Figure 2). Spurs then, as now, were used to prod horses to move in the direction and at the speed their riders commanded. Horses were of strategic importance to the sixteenth-century conquests of the Aztec and Inca empires, to the seventeenth-century conquest of the Kingdom of New Mexico, to the Pueblo Indians' victory during their 1680 revolt against Spanish rule, and to the terror and pillage the equestrian Comanche and Apache inflicted on the kingdom's residents in the eighteenth century.

Spain's explicit goal in the conquest of the Americas was the Christianization of its newly acquired indigenous subjects, bringing the sweet words of the Gospel and the message of eternal salvation to persons they saw as living in the darkness of the devil. Never far from this ambition was the equally mesmerizing dream of gold that animated Spanish soldiers. Having traveled to the Americas mostly at their own expense, they were intent on profiting from their investments. For this they needed indigenous labor, which technically belonged to the Crown. Mexico's first viceroy, Don Luis Velasco, succinctly explained the situation in 1608 when he wrote, "no one comes to the Indies to plow and to sow, but only to eat and loaf."[3] For such leisure and lordship to become reality, Spaniards had to maximally exploit their indigenous charges even if it meant working them to death. Christianizing the natives and permitting the settlers' personal enrichment were thus always in tension as contradictory imperial goals, pitting clergy against colonists, and together contesting the power of local Crown officials over the distribution of resources produced by indigenous hands. Would the labor of America's natives be put to construct magnificent churches and to tending

Figure 2.
Iron spur, likely of Spanish manufacture and used by Pueblo Indians, produced in the seventeenth or early eighteenth century. Horses and other large beasts of burden were unknown to Native American peoples before European contact. The Pueblo adopted a horse culture from the Spanish, and subsequently used equestrian warfare to successfully expel the Spanish from Pueblo land in a 1680 revolt. National Museum of American History, Smithsonian Institution.

church flocks and crops? Or would it be used creating the wealth and leisure the conquistadors sought? In the Kingdom of New Mexico this debate was particularly shrill and intense in the seventeenth century, creating the conditions that led the Pueblo Indians to rebel violently in 1680, producing the first successful overthrow of Spanish rule in the Americas.

The Kingdom of New Mexico was initially explored on a grand scale in 1540 by Francisco Vásquez de Coronado, but was quickly abandoned as poor in minerals and too costly to settle. When rich veins of silver and gold were discovered in north central Mexico in 1552, in what are now the states of Zacatecas and Guanajuato, Crown resources were channeled to the extraction of this wealth. Several decades passed before the Crown's gaze returned to New Mexico, now at the behest of the Franciscan friars eager to Christianize the souls there. King Philip II's conscience was apparently stirred by these Franciscan pleas and in 1598 he dispatched them with a small group of solider-settlers. While the friars sought to Christianize the Pueblos, the goal of Philip's ministers was to Hispanicize them, to transform them into productive workers, creating the supply chains necessary to provision the mines with food, hides and tallow, cotton and wool cloth, and ceramic vessels. Indeed, to this day Pueblo Indian rugs, blankets, and pottery remain the hallmarks of their craft—sophistication first mastered to satisfy Spanish commercial needs in the seventeenth century.

The image of Saint Anthony of Padua holding the infant Christ on one arm, often with a book of sermons nearby, was but one of the many religious objects the Franciscans took to New Mexico to adorn the mission churches they built. Its function was purely didactic: to teach neophytes through the exemplary lives of the saints the various models of virtuous living and paths to Christian salvation they could emulate. Saint Francis of Assisi started the Franciscan Order in 1209. Saint Anthony joined him in 1220. It is said that he sought membership in the order because he was very deeply moved by seeing the headless bodies of five Franciscans who had been martyred in Morocco while spreading the word of God that year. From this point on, Saint Anthony dedicated his life to the conversion of heretics through simple, eloquent preaching. The book he is often depicted holding is his famous *Sermons for Feast Days*, still used as the inspiration for many Franciscan sermons. Legend holds that thirty years after Anthony's death his body was exhumed. His corpse had turned to dust but his tongue and vocal cords were intact, as vibrant and colorful as if he were still alive. His tongue was placed in a reliquary and displayed in the Padua basilica that bears Anthony's name.

Figure 3.
Iron spur rowel detail. The rowel, used to prod the horse to perform, is designed with a combination of tear drops and hearts. Large rowels, like this one, were common in the New Mexico region. National Museum of American History, Smithsonian Institution.

Traditionally, Saint Anthony's miraculous intercession is petitioned when one wants to recover something lost, be it a thing, person, or even a spiritual good. The Franciscans who went to New Mexico clearly saw the Pueblo Indian as spiritually wayward and lost. The Puebloans were worshiping idols, living debauched lives of sinfulness, practicing incest and sodomy, and obviously under Satan's command, or so the friars said. By cultivating the veneration of Saint Anthony as part of their larger Christianization project, they were sure that through this saint's intercession the Pueblo Indians would be found, baptized, and led to Jesus Christ.

The iron spur we examined at the start finds its meaning in the realm of animal husbandry, in warfare, and in human domination over people and animals (Figure 3). It offers us a small window into the larger objectives of the conquest. This process of domination proceeded exploitatively through the incorporation of native peoples into the polity as tribute-paying royal subjects who were required to toil as virtual slaves. Their Hispanicization would be assured by learning to speak Spanish, by adjusting to a new work regime, by mastering the planting and harvesting of Spanish crops, and the breeding and tending of the animals brought from Spain and central Mexico. By acquiring knowledge of animal husbandry, through the raising of horses, mules, cows, pigs, and sheep, and by using European technology to forge iron plows for planting, and spurs to control horses, the Pueblo Indians someday would become productive Spanish citizens. They would be capable of living by their own wits, entering the market with their hides and tallow, with meat and lard, their donkey caravans packed with salt, ceramics, corn and woven products bound for the commercial mining centers of Mexico, which would yield them personal profit and local reward. In short, this is ideally how they would be Hispanicized.

Nowhere in North or South America had the indigenous peoples domesticated large beasts of burden before 1492. Such animals were acquired through the Columbian exchange. Native Americans had domesticated turkeys, mostly for their feathers, dogs to carry small loads and for meat, and in the Andes there had been some experimenting with the taming of llamas, but that never proved particularly successful nor was it accomplished on the scale that humans in Europe and Asia had when, centuries earlier, they domesticated and corralled horses and cattle.

Don Juan de Oñate, the leader of the expedition that conquered and colonized the Kingdom of New Mexico in 1598, was accompanied by 12 Franciscan friars, representing Christ's 12 original apostles, who were to spread the Gospel, and a party of some 129 soldiers, settlers, and slaves. The Pueblo Indians they conquered were sedentary agriculturalists who had been planting corn, beans, and squash as their dietary mainstays since the thirteenth century. Living without domesticated animals or beasts of burden, what meat entered the Pueblo Indian diet was acquired by hunting larger game animals such as bear, deer, and elk, and smaller ones, such as fish, birds, rodents, and snakes. The early Franciscan friars attested that the Pueblo Indians considered hunting a very precarious masculine activity that required the same skills and entailed the same risks as warfare.

Today in the Euro-American West we think of hunting largely as a sport, a secular activity mostly undertaken by adventurers eager for a mount to place over their home's mantel, and rarely for the meat. But for the pre-Columbian Puebloans, hunting was a necessary and a profoundly religious activity that tied humans with the powerful forces of the natural word in bonds of reciprocity. To successfully capture an elk, for example, required mastery of the prayers, dances, and songs of the hunt that would attract the wild animal, allowing itself to be captured, and, after its death, peaceably consumed to assure that its spirit would not return to wreak havoc and evil. When men prepared for the hunt, just as when they readied for war, they would enter into deep meditative states, fasting and smoking, purifying their bodies by abstaining from sexual contact with women, engaging in emesis and flagellation to prepare their minds and bodies for contact with the animal they hunted. Draping their human bodies with untanned elk hides and adorning their heads with antlers, offering cornmeal and pollen to the spirit of the elk they hoped to kill—through this ritual process, hunters transformed themselves into the hunted. Taking the life of a large game animal required an exchange, an act of human reciprocity. And so the Pueblo Indians offered food to the spirit of the elk, so that the elk would give itself as food. Only through such exchanges between the natural and supernatural, between humans and animals, would the cosmos be kept in balance.[4]

The Spaniards' relationship to large draft animals was fundamentally different: it was one of dominance and mastery. Domesticated animals were beasts of burden, dietary sources of protein, and, particularly with the horse, an essential requisite for the successful waging of war. The iron spur from seventeenth-century New Mexico tells us a much larger European history of biological and technical achievements that proved quite significant in the Spanish conquest of enormous imperial states, such as those of the Aztecs in Mexico and the Incas in Peru, but also of the smaller, less densely populated city-states, such as those of the Pueblo Indians. The spur is an instrument used to forcefully jab a horse's haunches, communicating the direction and clip its rider demands, especially when charging into battle. The horse was the biggest, strongest, and most malleable of Europe's beasts of burden, used first for plowing, logging, and transport, but soon becoming the animal central to the Spanish equestrian culture of warfare that spread to the Americas. Hernán Cortés, whose small and motley army conquered the mighty Aztec Empire in 1521, thought it quite odd and amusing that his indigenous adversaries imagined the horse and its rider not as two distinct entities, but as one gigantic ghastly beast; one so strong, fast, and tall that even the most tested and fearless Aztec warrior cowered before it.[5]

For much of the seventeenth century the Kingdom of New Mexico was in a constant state of turmoil, mostly over the appropriation of indigenous labor. The contestants for it—the Franciscans, the governors, and the colonists—each had very different rationales for who should appropriate its bulk. The end result was a colony governed fitfully between 1598 and 1680, exploiting the indigenous population mercilessly, controlling them with brute force, and, thus, creating the conditions that sparked the Pueblo Revolt of 1680. On 10 August of that year the Pueblo Indians rebelled against their overlords, killing 401 colonists and 21 friars, burning the houses and church compounds in which they lived, desecrating Christian religious images, and sending the survivors packing southward to what became El Paso, Texas. Here the revolt's refugees awaited reinforcements for the kingdom's reconquest. Though several unsuccessful attempts were made over the next 12 years, the Kingdom of New Mexico was reconquered and finally brought back firmly under Spanish rule in 1692.

The reestablishment of Spanish control over New Mexico became imperative to Spain for a number of geopolitical reasons. By 1700, two-thirds of all the world's silver was being produced in the mining towns of northern Mexico. Coveting their colonial neighbor's wealth, the French established outposts in Louisiana in the 1680s. Almost simultaneously the English did likewise, with exploratory forays westward across the Mississippi River. The reassertion of Spanish presence in New Mexico, and soon afterward the colonization of Texas and California, created buffer colonies the Crown hoped would protect its silver fortunes and repel any possible foreign affronts.

In the first century of Spanish presence in New Mexico and Arizona, the Puebloans were indeed Hispanicized. Spanish became their lingua franca and many became dependent on animal husbandry for their dietary protein and their market exchanges, forsaking hunting as a significant masculine activity for several reasons. As we noted above, hunting and warfare were seen by the Puebloans as very similar activities because they each required men to abandon the civility and peaceful ethos that operated in their towns and to enter those "wild" spaces beyond civilization where one could take life, never knowing what the outcome would be. The goal of the Spanish conquest was to completely crush the capacity of the Pueblo Indians to wage war. They did this by prohibiting travel, by outlawing native hunt parties, by replacing the meat captured in hunts with that of domesticated pigs, chickens, sheep, and cattle, and by prohibiting Indians from owning or riding horses. While the Spaniards did momentarily quash Pueblo Indian hunting practices, they failed to fully eviscerate their capacity to wage war. On 10 August 1680, the date the Pueblo Revolt started, the rebels' first strategic act was to steal and kill the principal nerve of warfare, the horses the Spaniards had introduced into the province. Without horses, the vastly outnumbered Spaniards were no match for the now mounted and armed Pueblo warriors.

The Spanish soldiers and Franciscan friars returned to the Kingdom of New Mexico in 1692, chastened and significantly less iconoclastic, allowing the

Puebloans more freedom of movement, more respect for their antique hunting and farming practices, and for their religious beliefs. As part of their Hispanicization, the Pueblo Indians had learned the function of iron spurs. In the eighteenth century much of what became northern Mexico and the American Southwest faced a new set of enemies and an almost perpetual state of war as the nomadic Comanche and Apache entered the region as equestrian warriors par excellence, having captured and tamed the wild Cimarrons the Spaniards first introduced to the land in 1540. Now the tables were turned. Having mastered the use of horses as their own instruments of war, the Comanche and Apaches preyed on Spanish towns and Pueblo villages, raiding and slaving as they wished.[6]

The 1725 picture of Saint Anthony of Padua, painted so carefully and elegantly on an elk-skin hide to adorn the mission church at Santo Domingo Pueblo, retained that reverence for the spirit world that was so fundamental to the Puebloan way of relating to animals on whom they were dependent for their food and for their lives. The Franciscans clearly understood the powerful place of animals in the indigenous cosmology and thus did everything possible to fuse the iconography of the cult of the saints with images of Puebloan animals and their spiritual embodiment, or their hides. What better way to assure that the spirit of the dead elk would not return for nefarious ends than by joining its skin with an image of Saint Anthony? In this way, wayward souls would surely be led to Jesus Christ.

By juxtaposing a seventeenth-century New Mexican elk-skin painting of Saint Anthony and an iron spur, one is able to deeply delve into the history of an area not well known to the American public at large—a history as unique and significant as that of the Eastern Seaboard and its English colonists. Here we explored the Christianization and the Hispanicization of the Pueblo Indians, the contradictory imperial aims that played themselves out in acculturation and resistance, in acquiescence and revolt. We studied Pueblo animism, that belief that animals, just like humans, had souls that had to be appeased if they were to give themselves up to humans as their food. The process of Christianization led us to explore the strategies the Franciscan friars used to convert their charges. And in the elk-skin painting we see the superimposition of one saint's life onto religious dimensions of Puebloan elk-hunting practices. The result of the Columbian exchange here was a fusion of Saint Anthony and an elk into one. The radically transformative power of this exchange is also evident in the iron spur we have returned to so often here from different vectors. Advanced iron-making technology signaled the presence of horses and the impact their introduction had simultaneously on how the Pueblo Indians farmed, hunted, and waged war; the expanse of agricultural production that could now be undertaken with fewer hands; and the predictability of meat in the indigenous diet.

The outcomes of these exchanges of goods, ideas, and technologies was never clear and predictable; the power dynamics between colonizers and the colonized often shifted, always making indigenous people agents of their own histories. Horses, the instruments of war that had been used to conquer the Pueblo Indians in 1598, by 1680 were made their own, and through acute observation the Puebloans learned how to use these horses to gain their liberation and rout Spanish colonists from the kingdom. When colonists returned in 1692, the power dynamics in the province had been turned, the Pueblo Indians becoming more autonomous and more commanding of respect. This is the story two seemingly unrelated objects allow us to reconstruct.

NOTES

1. Ian Woodward, *Understanding Material Culture* (Thousand Oaks, Calif..: SAGE Publications, 2007); Nicole Boivin, *Material Cultures, Material Minds: The Role of the Material World in Human Thoughts, Society, and Evolution* (New York: Cambridge University Press, 2008).

2. The classic work on such cultural transfers remains Alfred W. Crosby's *The Columbian Exchange: Biological and Cultural Consequences of 1492* (Westport, Conn.: Greenwood Press, 1972) and his more recent *Ecological Imperialism: The Biological Expansion of Europe, 900–1900* (New York: Cambridge University Press, 2004).

3. Velasco quoted in Ramón A. Gutiérrez, *When Jesus Came, the Corn Mothers Went Away: Marriage, Sexuality and Power in New Mexico, 1500–1846* (Stanford: Stanford University Press, 1991), 104.

4. Ernest Beaglehole, *Hopi Hunting and Hunting Ritual* (New Haven: Yale University Press, 1936); W. W. Hill, *The Agriculture and Hunting Methods of the Navajo Indians* (New Haven: Yale University Press, 1938); Hamilton A. Tyler, *Pueblo Animals and Myths* (Norman: University of Oklahoma Press, 1975).

5. Hernán Cortés, *Letters from Mexico*, trans. and ed. Anthony Pagden (New Haven: Yale University Press, 1986); Bernal Díaz del Castillo, *The True History of the Conquest of New Spain*, trans. Janet Burke and Ted Humphrey (Indianapolis: Hackett Publishing Co., 2012).

6. Pekka Hämäläinen, *Comanche Empire* (New Haven: Yale University Press, 2009); Karl Jacoby, *Shadows at Dawn: A Borderlands Massacre and the Violence of History* (New York: Penguin, 2008).

BIBLIOGRAPHY

Beaglehole, Ernest. *Hopi Hunting and Hunting Ritual*. New Haven: Yale University Press, 1936.

Boivin, Nicole. *Material Culture, Material Minds: The Role of the Material World in Human Thoughts, Society, and Evolution*. New York: Cambridge University Press, 2008.

Cortés, Hernán. *Letters from Mexico*, trans. and ed. Anthony Pagden. New Haven: Yale University Press, 1986.

Crosby, Alfred W. *Ecological Imperialism: The Biological Expansion of Europe, 900–1900*. New York: Cambridge University Press, 2004.

_____. *The Columbian Exchange: Biological and Cultural Consequences of 1492*. Westport, Conn.: Greenwood Press, 1972.

Díaz del Castillo, Bernal. *The True History of the Conquest of New Spain*, trans. Janet Burke and Ted Humphrey. Indianapolis: Hackett Publishing Co., 2012.

Gutiérrez, Ramón A. *When Jesus Came, the Corn Mothers Went Away: Marriage, Sexuality and Power in New Mexico, 1500–1846*. Stanford: Stanford University Press, 1991.

Hämäläinen, Pekka. *Comanche Empire*. New Haven: Yale University Press, 2009.

Hill, W. W. *The Agriculture and Hunting Methods of the Navajo Indians*. New Haven: Yale University Press, 1938.

Jacoby, Karl. *Shadows at Dawn: A Borderlands Massacre and the Violence of History*. New York: Penguin, 2008.

Tyler, Hamilton A. *Pueblo Animals and Myths*. Norman: University of Oklahoma Press, 1975.

Woodward, Ian. *Understanding Material Culture*. Thousand Oaks, Calif.: SAGE Publications, 2007.

Native American Objects of Memory and Journey from the National Museum of the American Indian

Christopher Lindsay Turner

It is oft cited that Native American people had limited means of recording their histories amid Europeans and other colonial peoples in the earliest years of their interactions, and while aspects of this are true, objects made by native people, of both utility and adornment, often carry a further layer of meaning—that of memory. In one manner, objects made by native people represent their understanding of how they came to be part of the present world, the landscape, and the relationships that define living in it. Objects of native creation may also represent specific types of experiences and their interpretations, and even journeys or migrations taken by native people as a result of their interactions with other peoples, thus critically recording their history after all. And is memory not history unwritten? Three objects from the collections of the National Museum of the American Indian (NMAI) provide a window to explore these questions, with a Native American perspective.

This first object, a Tsimshian crest hat from around 1875 from the Queen Charlotte Islands, an archipelago off the North Coast of British Columbia, Canada, is merely one among many that demonstrate early ways of representing memory

Figure 1.
Tsimshian headdress representing an eagle and its hatchlings, created around 1875 in Port Simpson, British Columbia, Canada. This headdress was created to illustrate the origins of the lineage of Chief Lutguts'amti, one of the founders of the Tsimshian nation. Courtesy of the National Museum of the American Indian, Smithsonian Institution (1/8020), photography by Ernest Amoroso.

and history and a peoples' manner of remembering and celebrating how they came to be in the world (Figure 1). When we consider how unsettling the period of contact was for native people in North America, we must also reconcile the fact that, as contact gave way to conflict over the first century and a half of interactions on the Atlantic coastal region and on the borderlands of the Southwest, native people of regions such as the Pacific coast would have another hundred years of relative isolation within which their traditions thrived, adapted, and advanced.[1] For this reason, it is to those peoples we might look for a perspective on what the land of North America means to them, or rather, how they perceive themselves as fitting into the landscape of creation into which they were placed.

Native people often perceive themselves as having a relationship to the land that is derived from both their relationship with a Creator figure, and their relation to other spirit figures that are responsible for specific physical aspects of their world.[2]

> Just as the spirits surround us in all things, so also we call them into our lives by carving, weaving and painting them on ceremonial objects.[3]

Such is how Tsimshian visitors to the NMAI collections expressed their relationship to these stories and the objects that depict them. The stories native people preserve that recall the roles of these figures also often begin the remembered histories of specific lineages that compose the organizing groups of their lives today: clans. Clan crests are symbolic representations of an ancestral figure, often portrayed in a memorable act of significance to the people: sometimes shaping or introducing an important natural feature or aspect of the world, such as light itself, saving the people from another force of nature, or assisting them through a great trial or journey.[4]

The Tsimshian crest hat has just such a story carved into its features. Though these objects are often masks or hats, used for ceremonies and worn for dances, part of the artistry involves making the figures within move, or seem to move, and become animated through the dance (Figure 2). This hat, however, was crafted specifically to recall the origins of the lineage of chief Lutguts'amti, one of the founders of the Tsimshian nation thousands of years ago. The story

Figure 2.
When the headdress was worn during a dance, the eagle hatchlings moved with the dancer to further animate the retelling of a Tsimshian origin story. Courtesy of the National Museum of the American Indian, Smithsonian Institution (1/8020), photography by Ernest Amoroso.

Figure 3.
Purple wampum and white wampum strung on twine, created between 1750 and 1850, owned by Mahican chief John W. Quinney. While the specific use of this wampum is unknown, some beads strung in this manner carried messages among native peoples, such as collective memories or diplomatic agreements. Courtesy of the National Museum of the American Indian, Smithsonian Institution (23/7862).

involves a specific act of a water spirit in an encounter with Lutguts'amti's people, who appeased the spirit, which appeared to them to have the aspect of many eagles, with a gift and a song and were rewarded with the protection of the spirit on their hunting grounds and from that time forward to be commemorated as the Eagle clan.[5] In this manner, a component story of the formation of a native nation is exemplified, in a specific place in the landscape of North America, and in an embodied way of recalling, giving thanks, and commemorating their incorporation through a useful and beautiful object.

A string of wampum in the NMAI collections, once owned by Mahican Chief John Wannuaucon Quinney (1797–1855) is one that speaks of both memory and journey (Figure 3). Wampum is a form of bead that is produced by drilling out oblong portions of shells found at the Atlantic coast, and was highly valued by native people of the entire region prior to the arrival of Europeans. The Dutch, with their early coastal and riverine trade footholds, were quick to recognize its commercial value in their efforts to engender a vigorous exchange with native people for the furs of the interior.[6] Importantly, wampum had a

Turner

value more significant than its basic decorative and trade purposes. Strings of beads could be used as a messaging device—a way of preserving the memory of a speaker as they communicated—the beads held in their hand for reference between themselves and their audience. For messages of even greater complexity and importance, such as the preservation and recollection of agreements between peoples, the beads were strung more elaborately into belts that conveyed meaning through a rich system of symbolic patterns.[7]

While many things are understood about wampum and its use, we cannot be sure of this item's significance to Quinney and his people. Wampum is, however, durable when cared for and by observing the techniques used to drill out the shells to make the beads, a relative date can be established. The beads in this string are estimated to have been produced as early as 1750. This string of wampum was most certainly made and used on the frontiers of colonial New York, then, but made its way in the hands of its owner Quinney on a long and segmented migration to Wisconsin, where it was collected generations later.[8] The string—possibly at that time in the form of a wampum belt—likely accompanied the Mahicans on what would become a storied and unsettling journey in several stages.[9]

As a people, the Mahicans' original homeland on the Hudson River stretched from Lake Champlain to the Catskills. Although sometimes spelled "Mohican," they are distinct from other Algonquian-speaking peoples such as the "Mohegans" of Connecticuit. By 1738, 150 years of contact with Europeans and changing relations with native neighbors such as the Mohawks had found the Mahicans' population drastically reduced to as few as 500 in their settlement near today's Stockbridge, Massachusetts.[10] Due to a reciprocal acceptance of the succor offered by Christian congregations around them that provided relief in various ways, they largely adopted Christianity. Seeking further protection, they relocated themselves in the late eighteenth century to the central New York region at the invitation of the Oneidas (another tribe that had largely accepted Christianity), where they established a new village called New Stockbridge.

Wannuaucon Quinney came of age in New Stockbridge and inherited a leadership role from his relation and tribal leader, Hendrick Aupaumut. As a community leader during the time, Quinney came to believe, as did the other Mahicans, that their place of relief in New York was unsafe for their particular values—their hosts were larger and more diverse, and various types of Christianity and traditional belief were tolerated.[11] Surrounded by increasingly land- and resource-hungry Americans, who held the belief that the War of Independence had shifted the frontiers considerably, the aging Aupaumut bequeathed to the much younger Quinney the daunting task of moving their people again, this time to Wisconsin, the true new frontier.

Reflecting on the wampum string, it is quite possible that these beads were somehow a part of that passing of leadership and legacy—or a manner of preserving for Quinney some key message pertaining to their history and homeland—that he would need for the next three decades. Native American leaders in the mid-nineteenth century were facing the most deliberate and sustained policy of the American government to obtain full title to the remainder of their lands east of the Mississippi, which were still substantial in the 1830s. Although many Americans are aware of "Indian Removal," as the policy became known, it is far less well understood that it affected dozens of tribes, and not merely those in the Southeast. Also, for many eastern tribes as well as Quinney's Mahicans, the process was a protracted one of migrations in stages, to lands they would occupy only temporarily—periods of great uncertainty and instability where community recovery was difficult.[12] By the time Chief Quinney would settle his people a final time in Shawano County, Wisconsin, in the 1850s, eastern tribes such as the Lenape, the Abenaki, and the Mohawk had collectively lost nearly all of their lands to piecemeal sales or from cessions by treaty with the United States.[13]

For Quinney, this would mean representing his people in a protracted struggle to secure an appropriate land base in Wisconsin and to shape their changing identity amid the ever-shifting frontier. He would visit Washington, D.C. to represent the Mahicans at least three times, receiving a presidential peace medal (also in the NMAI collection); draft the first tribal constitution for them; and ultimately accept U.S. citizenship, along with many of his reluctant people. A final time, they agreed to remove to a tract where they could remain principally Mahican people, rather than U.S. citizens, with a shared landbase. His eloquence as a spokesperson was recognized in speeches such as the one he gave on American Independence Day the year before his death in 1855, and in which he may have been the first to identify himself as a "Native American." He said, "It is curious, the history of my tribe, in its decline, during the last two centuries and a half. Nothing that deserved the name purchase was ever made . . . laws and edicts were subsequently passed, and these laws were said then, and are now called, justice! Oh, what a mockery

Figure 4.
Sewn Glengarry cap with raised beadwork, made by a Tuscaroran artist around 1875 in New York. Named for its Scottish shape, this cap was crafted with both the Tuscarora tradition and the larger American market in mind. Items like these were used by the Tuscarora and also sold to European American tourists. Courtesy of the National Museum of the American Indian, Smithsonian Institution (21/7424).

to confound justice with law."[14] Given that Quinney made this acute observation about America's treatment of native people—even those accepting of aspects of the non-native world, such as Christianity—*before* the largest of the Native American land alienations would occur in the latter part of the nineteenth century,[15] brings some focus to the type of prophetic leader such journeys and tribulations create.

In another manner, objects of native creation may also attempt to represent other peoples encountered in their experience, often not at a primary level of expression (as in a literal view of others) but more likely a recognition of aspects of others' creations that are acknowledged as intrinsically appealing when revealed through their own works of art. One object in the NMAI collection that plays this role is a beaded "Glengarry" cap collected in 1875 among the Tuscarora in New York (Figure 4). The Tuscarora, and the other Haudenosaunee (Iroquois) are noted for their exemplary development of beadwork, particularly in the latter nineteenth century, and for a form of complex beadwork involving a layering of beads for a dramatic visual effect. They are also known for producing a body of artistic works for sale at such places as Niagara Falls, where they sold items they had keenly innovated, often called "whimsies". These were items tourists might use, rather than simply display for exotic appeal, such as tea cozies, purses, and pincushions. Rather different from exotic "collectibles," whimsies subtly and richly represented the persistence and achievements of native people through their presence in the very homes of European Americans (Figure 5).

As the Tuscarora artist and historian Richard W. Hill Sr. has said of this tradition, "For over a century, the men and women from my [Tuscarora] reservation have made beadwork that could be used either in the Iroquois home or the Victorian parlor. In this way, the tiny glass beads are a history of my own people."[16] The Haudenosaunee beadwork style of this period—so colorfully rich and exquisite in its complexity of pattern and technique—was so finely interwoven with Victorian tastes that it seems natural that it peaked during the period, and native artists have long since moved on to other styles and outlets.

Beyond the initial layer of craft, though, there is another way in which native objects of art preserve perspectives on others' lives, and thus invest an item with functions of memory and history. The Glengarry cap is unique, even more so than other whimsies or trade items, in that its form is a nontraditional one that has an apparent derivation from a military style worn by Scottish military personnel.[17] The Tuscarora had the Scots frequently in their periphery, from the inland hill country of the Carolinas, where the Tuscarora had lived until the early eighteenth century. When conflicts with the southern colonies flared, they migrated to a new homeland in the North, to the protection of the Iroquois Confederacy and where Scottish military regiments were nearly always present when British forces were deployed. Over time, Tuscarora beaders appropriated the form for this style of cap. Interestingly, though observed amongst men in the military, the form has become almost exclusively one worn by Haudenosaunee women—though as Richard W. Hill has observed, "whether it was conscious satire cannot be said for sure."[18] What can be said is that this object's appeal, with its animate layers of floral color, is clear even at well over 100 years of age to the Haudenosaunee women who choose today to wear them for social dance.

The potential for an object of art to emerge as a primary way of recognizing migrations made and peoples encountered is an aspect of expression native people share with many others on the American journey. Certainly, the inspiration to record events within the expressive space of an object of beauty that can be admired on artistic levels is not unique; but, for native peoples, telling their stories without these material witnesses to their history would be a most incomplete record. When we represent histories of tribal leaders or heads of clan lineages today, or even unnamable beadworkers, we want to celebrate the fact that

Tuscarora Squaws—Luna Island--Niagara.

Figure 5.

Stereographic print of Tuscaroran whimsy-sellers in Niagara Falls, New York, taken around 1844–1894. Tuscaroran women sold crafts with intricate beadwork, or "whimsies." Very popular among non-native shoppers at this time, beadwork in this style was commonly represented in Victorian households. Courtesy of George Eastman Museum.

native artists recorded the essential events and impressions that moved them, and vividly captured their experiences within their finest artistic forms.

NOTES

1. Sergei Kan, *Memory Eternal* (Seattle: University of Washington Press, 1999), 43.
2. Paul Radin*, The Trickster: A Study in American Indian Mythology* (New York: Knopf, 1972), 181.
3. Lindsay Martin and Susan Marsden, NMAI Community Consultants, *Listening to Our Ancestors* (research notes, NMAI Archives, 2005).
4. Cecile Ganteaume, *Infinity of Nations* (New York: Harper Collins, 2010), 225. For general information on crests in Northwest coast art, see Hilary Stewart, *Looking at Indian Art of the Northwest Coast* (New York: Douglas & McIntyre, 2009).
5. See National Museum of the American Indian, *Listening to Our Ancestors: The Art of Native Life along the Pacific Northwest Coast* (Washington, D.C.: National Geographic, 2005), 112.
6. Ann Rothschild, *Colonial Encounters in a Native American Landscape* (Washington, D.C.: Smithsonian Books, 2003), 197.
7. For more general information about wampum and wampum belts, see Ray Fadden (Tehanetorens), *Wampum Belts of the Iroquois* (Summertown, Tenn.: Book Publishing Company, 1999).
8. The string was passed to Quinney's son, and then through his daughter-in-law's lineage, eventually being acquired at an unknown date by MAI director Dr. Frederick J. Dockstader (Oneida), who was also a relation of the family. (NMAI Collections Database.)
9. See T. J. Brasser, in *Handbook of North American Indians, Vol. 15*, ed. Bruce G. Trigger. (Washington, D.C.: Smithsonian Institution, 1979), 210.
10. T. J. Brasser, *Handbook of North American Indians*, 206.
11. See Laurence Hauptman, "Refugee Havens," in *American Indian Environments,* ed. Christopher Vecsey and Robert W. Venables. (Syracuse: Syracuse University Press, 1980), 132.
12. Prucha, Francis Paul, *The Great Father* (Lincoln: University of Nebraska Press, 1984), I:271.
13. Stuart Banner, *How the Indians Lost their Land: Law and Power on the Frontier* (Cambridge, Mass.: Harvard University Press, 2005), 226.
14. John W. Quinney, quoted in E. F. Jones, *Stockbridge, Past and Present, or, Records of an Old Mission Station* (Springfield, Mass.: S. Bowles, 1854).
15. Banner, *How the Indians Lost their Land,* 257.
16. Richard W. Hill, "Patterns of Expression: Beadwork in the Life of the Iroquois," in *Gifts of the Spirit: Works by Nineteenth Century Contemporary Native American Artists*, ed. Dan Monroe (Salem, Mass.: Peabody Essex Museum, 1996), 44.
17. Tom Hill, *Creation's Journey: Native American Identity and Belief* (Washington, D.C.: Smithsonian Institution Press, 1994).
18. Richard W. Hill, "Patterns of Expression: Beadwork in the Life of the Iroquois," in Monroe, *Gifts of the Spirit*, 52.

BIBLIOGRAPHY

Banner, Stuart. *How the Indians Lost their Land: Law and Power on the Frontier*. Cambridge, Mass.: Harvard University Press, 2005.

Brasser, T. J. "Mahican." In *Handbook of North American Indians, Vol. 15*, ed. Bruce G. Trigger, pp. 198–212. Washington, D.C.: Smithsonian Institution, 1979.

Fadden, Ray (Tehanetorens). *Wampum Belts of the Iroquois*. Summertown, Tenn.: Book Publishing Company, 1999.

Ganteaume, Cecile. *Infinity of Nations*. New York: Harper Collins, 2010.

Hauptman, Laurence. "Refugee Havens." In *American Indian Environments*, ed. Christopher Vecsey and Robert W. Venables, pp. 128–139. Syracuse: Syracuse University Press, 1980.

Hill, Richard. "Patterns of Expression: Beadwork in the Life of the Iroquois," In *Gifts of the Spirit: Works by Nineteenth Century Contemporary Native American Artists*, ed. Dan Monroe. Salem, Mass.: Peabody Essex Museum, 1996.

Hill, Tom. *Creation's Journey: Native American Identity and Belief*. Washington, D.C.: Smithsonian Institution Press, 1994.

Kan, Sergei. *Memory Eternal*. Seattle: University of Washington Press, 1999.

Martin, Lindsay, and Susan Marsden. *Listening to our Ancestors: The Art of Native Life along the Pacific Northwest Coast*. Unpublished research notes. National Museum of American Indian Archives, 2005.

National Museum of the American Indian. *Listening to Our Ancestors: The Art of Native Life along the Pacific Northwest Coast*. Washington, D.C.: National Geographic, 2005.

Prucha, Francis Paul, *The Great Father*. Vol. 1. Lincoln: University of Nebraska Press, 1984.

Quinney, John W. Quoted in E. F. Jones, *Stockbridge, Past and Present, or, Records of an Old Mission Station*. Springfield, Mass.: S. Bowles, 1854.

Radin, Paul. *The Trickster: A Study in American Indian Mythology*. New York: Knopf, 1972.

Rothschild, Ann. *Colonial Encounters in a Native American Landscape*. Washington, D.C.: Smithsonian Books, 2003.

Stewart, Hilary. *Looking at Indian Art of the Northwest Coast*. New York: Douglas & McIntyre, 2009.

Now/Then, We/Them? Toward a More Global U.S. History

John Kuo Wei Tchen

The very idea of myth typifies 'them'—the savages and ancestors 'we' have left behind.

—*Peter Fitzpatrick,* The Mythology of Modern Law *(1992)*

Any "good" student learning the civics lessons of U.S. K–12 education will recall the story of the 1773 Boston Tea Party, in which the Sons of Liberty masquerading as "Mohawks" threw overboard crates of "foreign" British East India Company tea in protest of colonial taxes.[1]

In rejecting foreign tea, American men stood for a "natural law" and local consumption. In the name of "liberty," a sense of fair exchange was powerfully effective in justifying the rebellion against England (Figure 1). The political philosopher John Locke stated approvingly: "Thus in the beginning all the World was America."[2]

Yet, we also know what occurred simultaneous to this European rebellion. American Indians were increasingly pushed off their homelands. With every possession, there was a dispossession. At root? The eighteenth-century liberal ideology's formulation of property and ownership. Who was qualified to "own" the land? And who was not? Anglo-American civilization and law distinguishes "natural" rights: "As much Land as a Man Tills, Plants, Improves, Cultivates, and can use the Product of, so much is his Property. He by his Labour does, as it were, inclose it from the Common."[3] Locke's logic implied that Native Americans lived

Figure 1.
Teapot produced in England around 1766–1770. The phrase "America, Liberty Restored" evokes the era's rhetoric of liberty, freedom, and fairness that fueled the formation of the United States. On the reverse side, "No Stamp Act" commemorates the 1766 repeal of the Stamp Act. National Museum of American History, Smithsonian Institution.

with the land and did not cultivate it (though this was, in fact, not the case)—hence, they forfeited ownership rights to it.

The Sons of Liberty's claim of being "American" was a triple negation—not being European and not consuming foreign "Indies" tea and not becoming indigenous peoples: the American identity dilemma, still ongoing, was born. There have always been many voices and peoples in the making of this place. But have we ever been one America?

Here I propose a curatorial experiment. We pretend for the moment that the powerful don't dominate the writing, classification, collecting, and archiving of the past to justify the present. We take objects caught within certain grand narratives and put them in dialogue with each other in order to loosen up what is known and to momentarily intervene in what was to come.

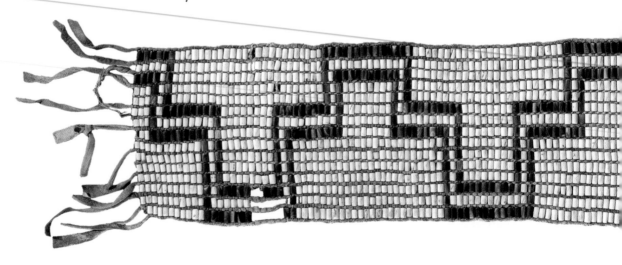

Simply put, might this gleaning of the pre-national American past offer us a way to reimagine what could be now? And as we juxtapose more objects and their contexts in this mix, how might an American story be told that is more accurate and also more globally informed?

WAMPUMPEAG

We turn to the still powerful New York City origin tale (likely embedded in American hearts and minds by satirist Washington Irving) of the Dutch "purchase of Manhattan" for "beads"—or "baubles"—said to be a scant 17 years after Hudson's "discovery." In 1609, Hudson, failing to find the fabled northwest sea route to China, nonetheless entitled the Dutch to stake a claim in the Lenape lands of Manaháhtaan for trading.[4]

Researchers have now documented that among the items exchanged were metal drill bits to enable easier and quicker production of wampum beads. This technology transfer greatly empowered the quantity of beads produced, and wampum became the first North American monetary system, in the European sense.

This Lenape "wampum belt" (Figure 2) was in the possession of the family of William Penn, the Quaker settler and state namesake, at Pennsylvania Castle in

Figure 2.
Wampum belt, made from beads of purple wampum and white wampum, around 1680. This belt is said to be a gift from the Lenape to William Penn. Though some have speculated this belt was a symbol of agreement such as a land sale or treaty, the purpose is unknown. Courtesy of the National Museum of the American Indian, Smithsonian Institution (5/3151), photography by Ernest Amoroso.

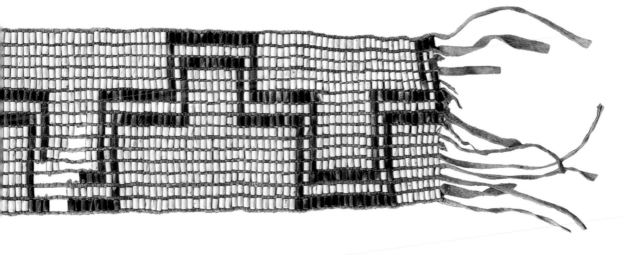

Portland, England. Made by coastal Algonquian peoples living along Long Island Sound, these prized mosaic tapestries wove meticulously hand-carved and drilled beads from the purple of quahog shells and the white of whelks once bountiful in that intertidal zone. The hundreds and thousands of beads that went into the making of each unique piece expressed a range of political, social, and interpersonal relationships among peoples and nations, native and then European. These exchanges created relationships between the makers, the givers, and the receivers. Receivers had the responsibility of keeping true to the spirit of the gift received.

The 2006 reopened National Portrait Gallery core exhibition expressed, in the typical authoritative voice of a curator: "William Penn's Lenape Wampum Belt / Lenape tribal leaders presented this belt to William Penn, the founder of Pennsylvania . . . served as a token of the covenant between the Lenape and Penn. The meandering pattern may refer abstractly to terms of the agreement reached with Penn and his Quaker followers." Critiquing the framing of the wampum, art historian Ruth B. Phillips unpacks the stories North American museums often tell: "because this installation is contained within a section of the gallery's historical narrative entitled 'American Origins, 1600–1900,' it is inevitably subordinated to a teleological account of American continental expansion and dominance, leaving no space for an antiphonal expression of continuing native American claims to sovereign status."[5]

In other words, many Lenape peoples continued claims to sovereignty separate from the "American Origins" story as told by the National Portrait Gallery. These "antiphonal" voices are simply not allowed and effectively silenced. (I wonder, did the text writers and editors even know? Did they give this standard justifying colonizing land claim a second thought?) Those voices, in fact and in the here and now, are actively critiquing this repeated and naive master narrative account of the William-Penn-and-family story. Can a series of curatorial (mis)judgments of placement, conceptual framing, and writing remain oblivious to the larger reality of what truly happened?

Was the National Portrait Gallery interpretation of the wampum belt accurate? The tapestry is said to be symbolic of Lenape "treaties" with Penn over access to Lenape lands, perhaps the 1682 agreement. The actual meaning and history of this "belt" is yet to be determined and possibly lost forever. The geometric pattern, described by European and U.S. collectors and writers included in the Smithsonian documentation, have called it a Greek "meander" pattern[6] (Figure 3). We simply don't know if this is piece is a token of an agreement or not. As new generations of Native American / First Nation artists, writers, scholars, and curators emerge,

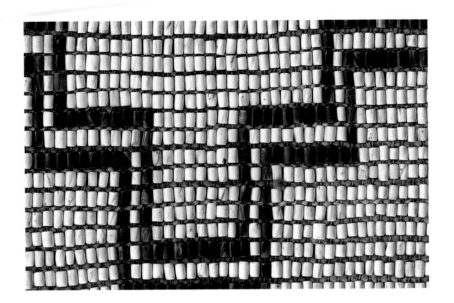

Figure 3.
Different wampum patterns represent tribes, agreements, and laws. Since wampum is considered sacred, the beads are thought to certify agreements. Courtesy of the National Museum of the American Indian, Smithsonian Institution (5/3151), photography by Ernest Amoroso.

an indigenous-based understanding will likely be debated and its meaning and history regenerated.[7]

The Lenape-originated wampum exchange system with Dutch, French, and British colonizers became increasingly reduced solely to money for commercial purposes. These outlanders brought "their own various notions about economic and linguistic exchange. Once [in America], they adopted the local currencies." However, "within a few years, they were also adapting those currencies according to their own traditional practices."[8]

CIQI

This cup could represent all that European explorers sought in their frustrated exploits and in their fervid dreamscapes. Ever since the tales of Marco Polo were retold, few except the European Crown could possess such delicate objects as this Ming Dynasty cup. Such handmade pieces of porcelain still convey a sense of refinement and awe. Its form and surface, its thinness, its fluidity, indeed its sense of time-defying design strikes us even now (Figure 4). We marvel when we look at such an object, hold it, and try to imagine how it was made and with what material. Who made this piece and at what date are not documented. What is documented are the various Western owner-collectors and where the piece has ended up.

This exquisite piece of *ciqi* deriving from kaolinite clay as early as the late sixth–seventh centuries CE. The Jingdezhen potters of Jiangxi Province in southern China

Figure 4.
Porcelain stem bowl, from Jingdezhen, Jiangxi province, China, 1403–1424. This piece of *ciqi*, or Chinese porcelain, was created during the Ming Dynasty. Chinese porcelain was highly valued among the European aristocracy. Courtesy of the Freer Gallery of Art and Arthur M. Sackler Gallery, Smithsonian Institution (F1998.7).

made such pieces. Guilds of artists produced such goods, which were circulated to the Chinese courts and among the European aristocracy. The French term *porcelaine* came to be used by the British, according to the *Oxford English Dictionary*, by 1530. Prior to that ciqi's European name was identical to the land it was made in: "China."

For colonizing European traders, the scouring of North American shorelands into inland forests, and regions beyond the rivers and mountains, were a means to search for "what China wanted." Pelts and ginseng, the white fleshy root used by native peoples as medicine, were in great demand by the merchants of Canton.[9]

In writing about the hard, lustrous surface of ciqi, royal map-maker Samuel de Champlain's *Des Sauvages* (1604) debated whether to call northeast American cowry shells "wampum" or "porcelaine" (later, fake wampum beads were made of porcelain). Across time and space, how would these items be commensurate in terms of value?

This trading quest is what had initially driven "the age of exploration" into *terra incognita*. Italian Cristoforo Colombo died after four trips to the Caribbean believing he had accessed the riches of "the Indies." He claimed the first island of the Bahamas archipelago, believing he was near Cipangu—or Japan—and named the indigenous peoples "Indios."

The complex, rich, cross-cultural interaction of understanding and values always possible in the translation and transvaluation process became increasingly reduced to commodity and land-price logics. Wampum exchanges were already part of an extensive and nuanced system of collaboration, negotiation, and boundary setting. The trade of desired goods from "the East" further complicated the formulation of what it might mean to become an American. When we consider how porcelain (and wampum) were made, with what materials, and by whom, the item returns us to a human hand of great ingenuity and skill, but also a space full of stories yet to be recovered and retold.

REALES

More than pelts and ginseng, Chinese merchants wanted Mexican reales. Trading, via the Dutch and British colonial outposts, was a backwater activity when compared to the vast mining excavations and coin production of Spanish-Conquest America. This one-ounce Mexican dollar circulated globally and became the primary coin of trade. (Hence, also, the creation of its shadowy doppleganger, fake reales. The real reales had to be stamped in the trading process to demonstrate authenticity.) The coin was regularly cut up in pieces for change, giving us the phrase "pieces of eight." This was legal tender in the US until 1857[10] (Figure 5).

In 1493, the year after Columbus bumbled into the Caribbean, Pope Alexander VI decreed the globe divided between Catholic Spain and Catholic Portugal. In 1519–21, Cortés conquered the Aztecs. The Mexican Mint was established in Mexico City. By 1535 it produced reales that were soon circulating widely in the Americas and Asia. In 1546 the silver mines of Zacatecas (Mexico) and Potosi (Peru–Bolivia) were brought into Spanish crown control, and in 1565 the first ship of New Spain left to trade with China via a new Pacific route. In this way,

Figure 5.

Reale minted in Mexico in 1762. Silver was mined in the Spanish colonies of the Americas, and then minted into reales. Accepted in many nations and territories, these coins were the first currency used around the globe. The inscription on this coin reads *utraque unum*, or "both are one," alluding to the merging of the Old and New Worlds. National Museum of American History, Smithsonian Institution.

Columbus's heir and grandson, Luis Colón de Toledo, first Duke of Veragua (a territory on the Isthmus of Panama) witnessed the actual completion of his family patriarch's quest.

In practice, conquistador settlers forced native peoples to harvest the mines of Zacatecas and Potosi, as did their counterparts in the Manila shipyards and docks.[11] The production of such "blood" silver had both local and regional impacts, and reconfigured what oligarchs around the world did and sought. Once again, exchange chains were created—the indigenous silver miner in Potosi became interlinked with a Manila dockhand with a tea-leaf picker in the mountains of Fujian. Each locally produced item entered a global trade linked to other local producers that defied empires and the imagined boundaries of the nation state.

THE GLOBAL TRANS-LOCAL

Let us return to the "Liberty" teapot celebrating the American defeat of the Stamp Act. Is it "American"? The sentiment appears to be. But surfaces are deceiving. It was made by line workers at the Cockpit Hill Factory in Derby, England. The British industrial system, as embodied by the teapot and its marketing, changed the scale and work of English subjects and produced more of these goods for global consumption—even for backwater colonies. Did the owner-designer cheekily sneak this order past the British West India Company? The British Empire had domestic dissenters, clearly. But such was also the nature of capitalist marketing separate from the state's political interests. Simply put, these were teapots for a growing American market.

After the American Revolution, the founding fathers and mothers also sought to gain wealth and power via trade with the world. In 1784, when the *Empress of China*, the first ship of the new U.S. nation, readied to trade with China, workers loaded it with furs, ginseng roots, and Mexican reales. At this moment, being American still also meant being free of the despot King George. But in 1784 it was okay to trade with China for the coveted luxuries.

Separate from these shifting identity politics, a deeper set of relationships can be recovered. Underneath the fickle surface of teapots and accidental discoveries, this brief essay suggests we need to recognize those who made things with their hands and creativity—those who became further linked in a globalizing system of exchanges. And in these exchanges, the local meanings and stories of their work and lives need to be expressed, documented, and appreciated.

The people who dug the mineral-rich clay of southern China for the potters of Jingdezhen workshops and the women who climbed mountains to pick tea leaves were now linked in chains of interaction to the makers of wampum fashioned from the shells of the primordial saltwater estuaries of Long Island Sound, and to the Indios extracting and smelting silver in Zacatecas, and to the factory hand making rebel teapots in Derby. British industrialization, as embodied by this teapot and its marketing, would soon surpass even the power of the Spanish global system of trade, and of the global Chinese tea and teapot system. But what is most valuable, the people-to-people stories and shared connections, are what is missing.

We are told that the desire for profit, a system of the passions and the interests, created this global system. Each item was simply a property operated by a hidden hand increasing the wealth of nations. Yet we know far more was embodied in the processes of wampum making and wampum giving and receiving. And we also know that far more than profit is what kept these exchange relationships meaningful and active. Now more than ever in this shrinking world, we need dialogues, stories, and histories of these relationships that are interlinked in genuine people-to-people cross-cultural communication.

This retelling of the American mythos seeks to complicate and upend the simple tale of American triumph and progress. Each pre-1776 object gleaned from the vast Smithsonian collections is but a fragment of chains of exchanges of meaning and relationships that confound and undercut such grand narratives. Each item collected and processed is often valued only in terms of monetized exchange and as an emblem of cultural distinction. But, to reiterate, when we consider where it was made, with what materials, and by whom, the item returns us to a human hand of great ingenuity and skill, but also a space full of histories and missing decolonizing stories yet to be recovered and retold.[12]

Perhaps this is what James Smithson, the illegitimate son of a duke and a wealthy widow, born in secret in Paris, never marrying and forever rootless, desired. Never having visited the United States, he invested his estate with the ideals of an open institution that would be for "the increase and diffusion of knowledge."[13] This essay's sense of inquiry beyond the bounds of conventional American civic narrative is in keeping the spirit of Smithson's bequest.

Shouldn't it be necessary to look at each of these artifacts at the Smithsonian in a way to offer a new beginning to those stories, to tell them in ways that do not result in a group's silencing, marginalization and/or eradication to the U.S.

self-aggrandizing narrative? Perhaps this has not been possible in the past. In this new era of accelerated globalization, it should be and it must be possible. Issues of basic rights and sovereignty are at stake, as are basic human–global issues. Are "we" not also "them," and "them" "we"?

NOTES

As this essay was being edited, the brilliant, anticolonial scholar of globalization Sir Jack Goody passed away (1919–2015). This essay is dedicated to him and to Juliet Mitchell. My appreciation also goes to Rick Chavolla; Lenape knowledge-bearers Jim Rementer, Brent Stonefish (Lunaapeew Nation of Delaware Nation—Moravian of the Thames), Chief Vincent Mann (Ramapough Lunaape Nation's Turtle Clan), Paula Pechonik (Delaware Tribe of Indians); Joe Baker, Curtis Zunigha, Hadrien Coumans, and Brent Michael Davids of the Lenape Center; Matthew Whitman of the American Numismatics Society; and Bonnie Campbell Lilienfeld of the National Museum of American History. My ongoing thanks, to Tom Bender for his regular rethinking of U.S. history's framings and to Amalia Mesa Bains for her insights into *mestizaje* material cultures. And thanks to Ji Han for his assistance in research, especially in Spanish.

1. For a reinterpretation of the use of the Mohawk identity in the Boston Tea Party, see Donald A. Grinde, Jr. and Bruce E. Johansen, *Exemplar of Liberty: Native America and the Evolution of Democracy* (Los Angeles: UCLA American Indian Studies Center, 1991), 111–40.

2. John Locke, *Two Treatises of Government and A Letter Concerning Toleration* (Stilwell, Kans.: Digireads.com, 2005), 32.

3. Locke, *Two Treatises of Government and A Letter Concerning Toleration*, 81.

4. Ives Goddard, "The Origin and Meaning of the Name 'Manhattan,'" *New York History* 91(4) (Fall 2010), 277–93.

5. Ruth B. Phillips, *Museum Pieces: Toward the Indigenization of Canadian Museums* (Berkeley: University of California Press, 2012), 251. Also see Jean R. Soderlund, *The Lenape Country: Delaware Valley Society before William Penn* (Philadelphia: University of Pennsylvania Press, 2014).

6. Ray Fadden (Tehanetorens), *Wampum Belts of the Iroquois* (Summertown, Tenn.: Book Publishing Company, 1999).

7. For an example of this regeneration process, see Lisa Brooks, *The Common Pot: The Recovery of Native Space in the Northeast* (Minneapolis: University of Minnesota Press, 2008).

8. Marc Shell, *Wampum and the Origins of American Money* (Champaign: University of Illinois Press, 2013), 1, 37–46.

9. John Kuo Wei Tchen, *New York Before Chinatown: Orientalism and the Shaping of America, 1776–1882* (New York: Johns Hopkins University Press, 1999), 25–40.

10. Ellen R. Feingold, *The Value of Money* (Washington, D.C.: Smithsonian Institution Scholarly Press, 2015).

11. Jeffrey A. Cole, *The Postosi Mita, 1573–1700: Compulsory Indian Labor in the Andes* (Stanford: Stanford University Press, 1985).

12. Enrique Dussell, "Agenda for a South-South Philosophical Dialogue," *Human Architecture*, 11(1)(Fall 2013):3–18; and Jack Goody, "Asia and Europe," *History and Anthropology,* 26(3) (2015):263–307.

13. James Smithson's Last Will and Testament, October 23, 1826, Smithsonian Institution Archives, http://siarchives.si.edu/history/exhibits/stories/last-will-and-testament-october-23-1826.

BIBLIOGRAPHY

Brooks, Lisa. *The Common Pot: The Recovery of Native Space in the Northeast.* Minneapolis: University of Minnesota Press, 2008.

Cole, Jeffrey A. *The Postosi Mita, 1573–1700: Compulsory Indian Labor in the Andes.* Stanford: Stanford University Press, 1985.

Dussell, Enrique. "Agenda for a South-South Philosophical Dialogue." *Human Architecture,* 11(1)(Fall 2013):3–18.

Fadden, Ray (Tehanetorens). *Wampum Belts of the Iroquois.* Summertown, Tenn.: Book Publishing Company, 1999.

Feingold, Ellen R. *The Value of Money.* Washington, D.C.: Smithsonian Institution Scholarly Press, 2015.

Goody, Jack. "Asia and Europe." *History and Anthropology,* 26(3)(2015):263–307.

Grinde Jr., Donald A., and Bruce E. Johansen. *Exemplar of Liberty: Native America and the Evolution of Democracy.* Los Angeles: University of California Los Angeles American Indian Studies Center, 1991.

Locke, John. *Two Treatises of Government and a Letter Concerning Toleration.* Stilwell, Kans.: Digireads.com, 2005.

Phillips, Ruth B. *Museum Pieces: Toward the Indigenization of Canadian Museums.* Berkeley: University of California Press, 2012.

Shell, Marc. *Wampum and the Origins of American Money.* Champaign: University of Illinois Press, 2013.

Smithson, James. "Last Will and Testament, October 23, 1826." Smithsonian Institution Archives. http://siarchives.si.edu/history/exhibits/stories/last-will-and-testament-october-23-1826 (accessed August 23, 2016).

Soderlund, Jean R. *The Lenape Country: Delaware Valley Society Before William Penn.* Philadelphia: University of Pennsylvania Press, 2014.

Tchen, John Kuo Wei. *New York Before Chinatown: Orientalism and the Shaping of America, 1776–1882.* New York: John Hopkins University Press, 1999.

Tchen, John Kuo Wei. "New World Displays: *Tornaviaje,* Objects of Desire and the Other Within." In *Return Voyage: The China Galleon and the Baroque in Mexico 1565-1815,* pp. 108-17. Puebla: Museo Internacional del Barroco, 2016.

Creating and Expanding the Nation, 1776–1900

Bonnie Campbell Lilienfeld

Between the founding of the United States of America in 1776 and the dawn of the twentieth century, the nation grew rapidly through the incorporation of land and people. The scope and patterns of growth during this period were neither accidental nor inevitable but the result of countless debates and choices made at all levels of society. Government officials developed ambitious policies to gain territory through settlement, diplomacy, and conquest. Legislators shaped the peopling of the nation through legal and economic policies that managed the processes of immigration, importation, incorporation, slavery, and Indian removal.[1] Receiving communities chose whether or not to accept newcomers who were different from themselves. Individuals decided to immigrate to the United States, to migrate within the nation, or to purchase enslaved people.

Race played an enormous role in shaping the nation. Whites were more able to make choices about where and how they lived, and about how much of their traditional culture they were willing to give up to assimilate into their local community and U.S. society more broadly. In the 1860s the country went to war over the enslavement of Africans and their descendants, challenging the very idea that the United States was a nation with shared ideals. Although the Civil War resulted in the abolition of slavery, people of African descent, as well as Native Americans and Chinese, faced many legal and societal constraints and limitations on their ability to negotiate how they wanted to live in the United States. As the nation continued to transform from a settler republic to a land- and labor-hungry empire, issues such as race and ethnicity shaped national identity as well as geographic and demographic expansion.

E PLURIBUS UNUM

The founders of the United States demonstrated a fundamental intent to create a unified national identity by taking *E Pluribus Unum* (Out of Many, One) as the country's motto (Figure 1). Yet differences in origin, belief, and cultural heritage as well as the racial hierarchy codified by the legal institution of slavery challenged that ideal from the very beginning. That the nation's inhabitants had always been diverse was hinted at by the first U.S. census, mandated by Congress and carried out in 1790 (Figure 2). Although the census did not record inhabitants' ethnicity or country of origin, scholars have studied surnames to infer who resided in the new nation. People of English origin made up just half the population, while people of African descent accounted for almost 20 percent. Roughly a quarter of the population was continental European.[2] While the census may have included some native people along with "all other free persons," most were not counted.[3]

Figure 1.
Eagle with motto *E Pluribus Unum* (Out of many, one), nineteenth century. With the founding of the new nation, patriotic symbols emerged and often promoted themes of unity. This was at odds with the reality that many groups did not enjoy rights and benefits of citizenship. National Museum of American History, Smithsonian Institution, gift of Joel Barlow.

Lilienfeld

At the same time, Congress attempted to define who could be American, and perhaps more consequentially who could not, based on race, status, and perceived moral character. The 1790 Alien Naturalization Act specified that:

> …any alien, being a free white person, who shall have resided within the limits and under the jurisdiction of the United States for a term of two years, may be admitted to become a citizen thereof…in any one of the states wherein he shall have resided for the term of one year at least, and making proof to the satisfaction of the court, that he is a person of good character.[4]

This Act denied citizenship to many of the people whose labor would help sustain the growing economy, including the Chinese, and enslaved and free Africans. Most native peoples also were excluded as members of sovereign American Indian nations.[5] As the United States gained more land, its increasingly diverse peoples had to negotiate their place in the nation. Issues of inclusion and exclusion fueled the struggle for land and equality that would define the United States over the next century and beyond, and transform the definition of who could be American.

Figure 2.
Pitcher commemorating the first United States Census, made in Britain, about 1790. This pitcher is decorated with 1790 census population counts for states and territories, although not all numbers are accurate. The methods of conducting the first census raised questions about who could be considered a member of the new nation. National Museum of American History, Smithsonian Institution.

CONQUERING NEW LAND AND PEOPLING THE NATION

As part of the 1783 Treaty of Paris that concluded the American Revolution, Britain surrendered territory as far west as the Mississippi River to the newly created United States. The treaty recognized the independence of the former British colonies, and divided North American territory among Britain, Spain, and the United States. But the treaty did not take into account the native peoples occupying the land, and it left European powers in control of vast territories beyond the new nation's borders.[6]

The United States almost immediately embarked on the process of obtaining more territory in order to strengthen its power, borders, and wealth and to provide land for its rapidly growing population. In 1787, Congress approved the Northwest Ordinance, which defined the path from territory to statehood and encouraged migration to the area we now know as the Midwest. The intent of the law was that white European Americans would develop the region's natural resources and gradually take over American Indian land.[7] Sixteen years later, the Louisiana Purchase of 1803 led to the acquisition of over 800,000 square miles of land beyond the Mississippi River from France—territory already populated by Western Europeans and native tribes.[8]

As the United States expanded geographically and demographically, issues such as race and ethnicity increasingly determined a person's "suitability" for incorporation into the United States as Americans continued to debate about who should be included. The definition of Americans as "free whites" that was codified in the 1790 Naturalization Act meant most of the Europeans on newly acquired lands were swiftly incorporated into the United States, while native peoples were not. With major acquisitions of land, and U.S. victory over Britain in the War of 1812, many Americans began to embrace a new national identity, symbolized by the patriotic and masculine figure of Uncle Sam (Figure 3). Expansionists promoted the rhetoric of the nation's Manifest Destiny—the belief that the United States was predestined to become a powerful, white Protestant "Empire of Liberty," spreading democracy from the east coast to the west.[9]

As the United States conquered more western territory, the government pursued treaties with American Indian nations in large part to obtain their land and encourage them to give up their traditional ways[10] (Figure 4). As growing numbers of whites pushed west, some native people traded with them or converted to Christianity. But over time, interactions with settlers and a growing demand for land on the part of the United States increasingly led to violence and military action against tribal nations. The Indian Removal Act of 1830 forced almost 100,000

Figure 3.
Uncle Sam figure from National Papier
Mache Works, Milwaukee, Wisconsin,
created in the early 1900s. Uncle Sam first
appeared as a nationalistic symbol during
the War of 1812. He became an American
icon and a paternal representation of U.S.
identity and power that is recognizable
around the world. National Museum of
American History, Smithsonian Institution.

Figure 4.
Silver peace medal presented by Lewis
and Clark to an Osage chief, made in 1801.
Meriwether Lewis and William Clark carried
this medal with them as they explored
newly acquired American territories from
1804 to 1806. Representatives of the United
States often presented medals like this one
to Native American chiefs as diplomatic
gifts. National Museum of American History,
Smithsonian Institution, Government
Transfer, Library of Congress.

Figure 5.
Ledger art drawn at Fort Marion, Florida, between 1875 and 1878 by Koba, a member of the Kiowa tribe. The work, later titled "Indian Discovery of U.S. Calvary," recollects the tradition of resistance to white ways and offers an American Indian account of a previous lifestyle in a warrior and hunter community. National Museum of American History, Smithsonian Institution.

Native Americans to relocate to federal lands west of the Mississippi, and led to the deaths of thousands of Cherokees along the Trail of Tears.[11] Throughout the nineteenth century, U.S. Indian land policy and American Indian wars led to the loss of most native land and ways of life (Figure 5).

By the 1840s, only Mexican territory in the West stood between the United States and the Pacific Ocean. The desire for land outweighed many Americans' concerns over incorporating Catholic Mexicans into the primarily Protestant United States, and President James Polk declared war with Mexico in 1846.[12] Two years later, the United States negotiated its victory over the defeated Mexican government with the Treaty of Guadalupe Hidalgo and the United States acquired land stretching to the California coast, seemingly having fulfilled its "Manifest" destiny. Yet gaining more land created a dilemma. As this land was already home to diverse groups of peoples, the nation grappled with whether and how to incorporate those living there.[13]

INCORPORATING CALIFORNIA:
THE STORY OF THE DEL VALLE FAMILY

The 1848 Treaty of Guadalupe established the southern U.S. border along the Rio Grande River. Mexicans and native peoples had long moved back and forth through this region, and new political configurations did not put a stop to trans-border migration. Although the treaty meant that many Mexicans living north of the border became eligible for U.S. citizenship, even those who had long been established there struggled to retain their culture, property, and political influence.[14] As land-hungry Americans set their sights on California, Mexican land-owners were forced to prove ownership of their land under new U.S. law. Unlike many *Californios*, Ygnacio and Isabel Del Valle succeeded in negotiating the complex and often impossible legal process of establishing claim to their Southern California property (Figure 6). They were able to retain Rancho Camulos, which had belonged to the family since the 1830s.

Having secured their claim, the Del Valles made a success of Rancho Camulos through hard work and ingenuity. They profited from the demand for cattle brought about by the influx of people to California after 1848, and later diversified into citrus, vineyards, and other crops. At the same time, as leaders in the social, cultural, and political life of southern California, the Del Valles helped maintain the *Californio*

Figure 6.
Portraits of Ygnacio and Isabel Del Valle taken in the mid-1800s in Los Angeles, California. The Del Valles were a long-established *Californio* family when the United States acquired California territory in 1848. Unlike many in their position, the Del Valle family was able to certify legal ownership of their land under U.S. law. Courtesy of Seaver Center for Western History Research, Los Angeles County Museum of Natural History.

identity of Mexican Catholics. They chose to preserve their cultural identity through dress, Spanish-language education for their children, and their strong Catholic faith, while also building social bonds and intermarrying with Anglo-Americans. Though the Del Valles chose, and were able, to make the transition from Mexican to Mexican-American, many others felt like foreigners in their own land.

FORCED MIGRATION OF ENSLAVED AFRICANS: THE STORY OF HIRAM WILSON

Incorporation was just one component of the complex pattern of peopling the nation that, along with immigration and importation, brought diverse people from around the world in contact with one another in the United States in the nineteenth century. Not all people came voluntarily, or had any hope of gaining citizenship, owning land, or becoming equal participants in society. More than 10 million Africans were imported by force to provide labor in the New World as part of the transatlantic slave trade between the seventeenth and nineteenth centuries. The majority of those who survived the Middle Passage were taken to the West Indies, but more than 300,000 people were brought to the United States before the end of legal importation in 1808.[15]

The institution of slavery also accounted for the mass movement of people within the nation, as the rise of the labor-intensive cotton economy in the Deep South contributed to the development of a thriving internal slave trade in the United States, documented in legal and business records[16] (Figure 7). As Mississippi, Louisiana, and Alabama joined the Union as slave states, close to a million enslaved people were sent by boat or forced to walk from the Upper South to New Orleans and elsewhere to be sold to owners of cotton and rice plantations in the South and Southwest.[17]

The horrors of slavery have been well documented and cannot be overstated. Much of the antebellum South's economic self-sufficiency and social structure depended on enslaved labor, as did the national economy. Owners often used violence to control the productivity and behavior of enslaved people and tore families apart by selling individuals without regard to kinship. The majority of those enslaved had little power over the type of work they did or the length of their workday. But, as historian Ira Berlin and others have argued, the slave experience differed across time, place, and from one individual to another.[18] A small number of enslaved people were able to negotiate the limited opportunities available to them in order to influence the

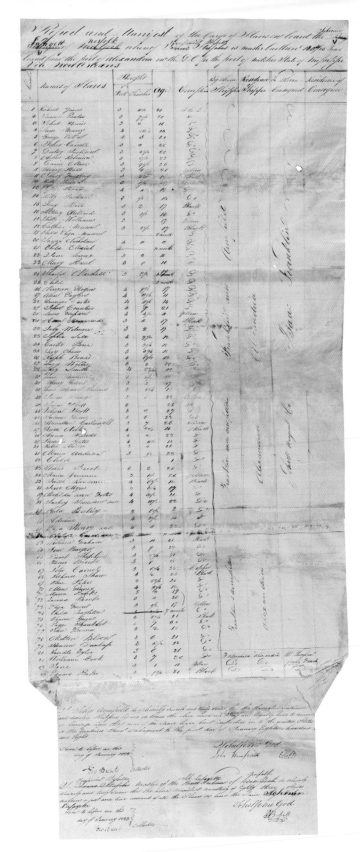

Figure 7.
Slave ship manifest from the schooner *LaFayette*, 1833. This document lists 83 enslaved African American men, women, and children sent from Alexandria, Virginia, to Natchez, Mississippi via the port of New Orleans, Louisiana. The United States ended the legal importation of slaves in 1808, but enslaved people continued to be bought and sold within the country until 1865. National Museum of American History, Smithsonian Institution.

quality of their lives through such practices as hiring-out. When owners hired out their slaves to others it was most often for profit to themselves, but sometimes the enslaved person was able to earn money or learn a new skill (Figure 8).

Some enslaved people, such as Hiram Wilson, were able to use their skills to support themselves as freed people. As land beyond the Mississippi River became available for ownership, many white southerners migrated with their slaves west across the Mississippi River. In 1856, a white North Carolinian Presbyterian minister named James Wilson took 20 slaves to Texas where he established a stoneware pottery, operated by enslaved laborers. After the Civil War, Hiram Wilson and some of the other freed potters established their own successful business, the H. Wilson Pottery (Figure 9). Wilson was then able to pursue an education and founded the freed black community of Capote in Guadalupe County, Texas.[19]

Hiram Wilson's experience as a freed black businessmen was far from typical, and it was not easy for him to accomplish what he did. As freedmen trying to build a life after emancipation, some of his fellow potters were the victims of violence by whites, and the decision to found a black town was likely made in response to racism. As blacks and whites worked to rebuild their lives during postwar Reconstruction, they were forced to navigate the evolving and rocky terrain of race in the United States.

Union victory in the Civil War and the passage of the Thirteenth, Fourteenth, and Fifteenth Amendments in the 1860s led to legal emancipation, and the promise of citizenship and civil and political rights for African Americans.

Figure 8.
Identification tag worn by an enslaved person, Charleston, South Carolina, early 1800s. Some cities instituted badge laws to regulate hired-out slave labor. Hundreds of slave badges survive from Charleston, South Carolina, where they were required intermittently from the 1760s into the nineteenth century. National Museum of American History, Smithsonian Institution, gift of Leon Banoc.

Figure 9.
Stoneware jar made by H. Wilson Pottery in the free black community of Capote, Texas, 1869–1884. As an enslaved man, Hiram Wilson gained marketable skills as a potter. He was able to establish a successful business once he gained his freedom. National Museum of American History, Smithsonian Institution.

But in the decades following the conclusion of the war, many whites came to view the conflict as a force that strengthened the nation they still controlled rather than as a crisis over race that continued to threaten the ideal of *E Pluribus Unum*.[20] Although some whites supported black rights and enfranchisement, most African Americans lived segregated and unequal lives, and had limited access to land and opportunities for work.[21] A century after the Civil War, the United States passed the Civil Rights Act of 1964 and the Voting Rights Act of 1965, but the nation still would continue to struggle with racism and the incorporation of African Americans as equals.

EUROPEAN IMMIGRATION: THE STORY OF PETER GLASS

American expansion was also shaped by massive population movements around the globe in the nineteenth century. Many people left their home countries, propelled by crop failures, rigid class structures, rapid population growth, and political, social, and economic instability fueled in part by industrial and agricultural revolutions.[22] Millions were drawn to the United States by the industrializing nation's demands for labor, the promise of fertile and inexpensive land, and democratic ideals such as liberty, equality, free speech and religious freedom.[23] Throughout the nineteenth century, growing numbers of immigrants were encouraged to

Figure 10.

"Iowa as it is in 1855" booklet for prospective migrants to Iowa. The booklet addresses both United States citizens and new immigrants as potential settlers. While many publications painted an idealistic picture of life in America, this book cautions, "the stern reality of a frontier life will not be all happiness and sunshine." National Museum of American History, Smithsonian Institution.

come to the United States by promises of wealth, letters from family and friends who had migrated, emigration societies, railroads and other employers, and by publications aimed at immigrants (Figure 10). The U.S. government continued to incentivize European immigration and westward movement with the Homestead Act of 1862, which promised 160 acres to those who declared their intent to become citizens and agreed to farm the land for five years.[24]

In the late eighteenth and early nineteenth centuries many immigrants came from Britain, but they increasingly came, too, from the German states. More than five million Germans immigrated to the United States in the 1800s, the largest foreign-language group of the century. Nineteen-year-old Peter Glass was just one of over 19,000 Germans who began their transatlantic journey in the port city of Le Havre, France, in 1844; most had their sights set on the United States.[25] After arriving in New York City and then moving to Massachusetts to work in a piano factory, Glass, like many other German immigrants, migrated to the Midwestern "German Triangle." He and his family purchased a farm in Sheboygan County, Wisconsin in an area heavily populated by both Germans and Irish.[26]

Peter Glass's story suggests the complexity of adaptation for some newcomers. He undoubtedly retained many aspects of his cultural identity by living among Germans, keeping in contact with his family in Bavaria and traveling back to Europe at least once. Glass also used his Old World woodworking skills to create elaborately decorated marquetry furniture. But, Glass became an

American citizen as soon as he could, and clearly embraced the ideals and politics of his adopted land, as evidenced by his use of the American eagle and U.S. military heroes as motifs on his marquetry tables (Figure 11).

By all accounts, Peter Glass seems to have successfully managed the transition from German to German American. On his Wisconsin farm he was less likely to have experienced anti-immigration sentiment, which was so prevalent in U.S. cities but gained less ground in the rural areas of the Midwest.[27] As a white man and a naturalized citizen, Glass was able to make choices about where he lived and worked, and how much of his traditional culture he wished to maintain.

Not all immigrants, even from Europe, were as welcomed and included into American communities. Nearly a million Irish immigrated to the United States in the 1840s and 1850s, in large part due to a potato blight that caused a great famine in Ireland. At the time they were considered less desirable immigrants because they were Catholic, often arrived impoverished, and were perceived as disease-ridden. For many native-born Americans, increasing Irish immigration created tension between the imagined ideal of a homogeneous population and

Figure 11.
Marquetry table made by German immigrant Peter Glass in Wisconsin, 1868. Glass, who lived in a largely German community, illustrated his immigrant identity through his work. He employed European woodworking methods and depicted symbols of U.S. patriotism when he created this elaborate center table. National Museum of American History, Smithsonian Institution, gift of Mrs. Frank A. Vadano.

Figure 12.
Porcelain pitcher with relief-molded decoration, made between 1876 and 1880. "Plain Language from Truthful James," was a poem intended as a rebuke to the ill-treatment of the Chinese, personified by a white miner cheating a Chinese man at cards. Deliberately or not, the maker of this pitcher misunderstood the poem, and illustrates the Chinese man as cheating, too. National Museum of American History, Smithsonian Institution, gift of Jay and Emma Lewis.

the reality of a pluralistic society. Protestant Americans feared that foreign-born Catholics owed their allegiance to a powerful pope, far away in Rome, rather than to the democratically elected leaders of their adopted home. This fear contributed to virulent nativism in the United States, such as anti-Catholic riots against the Irish in the 1830s and 40s, and the formation of the anti-immigrant, anti-Catholic Know Nothing political party in the 1850s.[28] But the Irish were able to naturalize and become citizens. Generations of schooling and increased economic and political power meant that over time the Irish were no longer targeted or perceived as different. For others, acceptance would be more difficult.

EXCLUSION AND INCLUSION CONTINUE

Against the backdrop of geographic expansion, war with Mexico, immigration, and growing tension over slavery, the 1848 discovery of gold at Sutter's Mill drew hundreds of thousands of hopeful prospectors from around the world in search of the rich resources of the newly acquired California territory. Among them were men from southeast China, many of whom hoped to strike gold and return home.[29] They were accepted at first, but as their numbers grew, many poor whites considered the Chinese to be economic competition and responded with hostility (Figure 12). Rising nativism among native-born and immigrant whites ultimately led to the Chinese Exclusion Act of 1882, the first real attempt to regulate immigration to the United States.[30]

At the end of the nineteenth century, with its borders largely established, the United States set its sights on expanding beyond the continent. U.S. military and political intervention led to the incorporation of colonies in Asia and Latin America, including the Pacific islands of Hawaii and the Caribbean island of Puerto Rico in 1898.[31] Although both were of strategic military and commercial importance to the imperial aspirations of the United States, their annexation was fiercely debated, in part over continuing concerns about incorporating diverse, non-white populations into an already pluralistic society.[32]

It is impossible to separate the strands of expansion, race, and ethnicity in the nineteenth-century United States. The nation was able to incorporate land much more easily through force and treaties than it was able to integrate the diverse people already here or crossing the borders. Europeans and their descendants were recognized as having the rights of citizens and landowners and they often restricted these rights to only themselves through legal and social structures, even after the end of slavery. For others these same rights were often out of reach. African Americans were promised citizenship after emancipation but continued to struggle for equality, as did those people incorporated through territorial conquest on the continent. Even as many Americans sought to express a shared national identity, disagreements over who should be included or excluded from the political, social, economic, and cultural life of the United States challenged the unifying ideal of *E Pluribus Unum*. This legacy continues to influence how we negotiate what it means to be American.

NOTES

1. Aristide Zolberg argues that "the absence of federal legislation does not reflect a lack of interest in regulating" immigration. Aristide R. Zolberg, *A Nation by Design: Immigration Policy in the Fashioning of America* (Cambridge, Mass.: Harvard University Press, 2006).

2. Thomas J. Archdeacon, *Becoming American: An Ethnic History* (New York: Simon and Schuster, 1983). About 21 percent of the population were German, Scottish, and Irish—Dutch, French, and Swedish people accounted for 4.5 percent.

3. Russell Thornton, *American Indian Holocaust and Survival: A Population History since 1492* (Norman: University of Oklahoma Press, 1990). Some scholars estimate that there were 600,000 Native Americans living in U.S. territory in 1800, down from more than 5 million before the arrival of Europeans.

4. Library of Congress, "A Century of Lawmaking for a New Nation: U.S. Congressional Documents and Debates, 1774–1875," http://memory.loc.gov/cgi-bin/ampage?collId=llsl&fileName=001/llsl001.db&recNum=226.

5. Martha Menchaca, *Naturalizing Mexican Immigrants: A Texas History* (Austin: University of Texas Press, 2011). Although exceptions were made, language limiting naturalization to white immigrants was in effect until the passage of the Immigration and Nationality Act of 1952.

6. The new nation stretched from the Atlantic Ocean to the Mississippi River, but was surrounded by British territory to the north above the Great Lakes, and Spanish territory to the west and south. Paul Frymer, "'A Rush and a Push and the Land Is Ours': Territorial Expansion, Land Policy, and U.S. State Formation," *Perspectives on Politics* 12(01)(March 2014):119–44, doi:10.1017/S1537592713003745; Stuart Banner, *How the Indians Lost Their Land: Law and Power on the Frontier* (Cambridge, Mass..: Harvard University Press, 2009).

7. James D. Drake, *The Nation's Nature: How Continental Presumptions Gave Rise to the United States of America* (Charlottesville: University of Virginia Press, 2011).

8. Sanford Levinson and Bartholomew H. Sparrow, *The Louisiana Purchase and American Expansion, 1803–1898* (Lanham, Md.: Rowman & Littlefield, 2005).

9. Steven E. Woodworth, *Manifest Destinies: America's Westward Expansion and the Road to the Civil War,* 1st edition (New York: Knopf, 2010).

10. Banner, How the Indians Lost Their Land.

11. John M. Murrin, Paul E. Johnson, James M. McPherson, Alice Fahs, and Gary Gerstle, *Liberty, Equality, Power: A History of the American People, Volume 1: To 1877*, 6th edition (Boston, Mass.: Cengage Learning, 2011); David W. Miller, *The Taking of American Indian Lands in the Southeast: A History of Territorial Cessions and Forced Relocations, 1607–1840* (Jefferson, N.C.: McFarland, 2011).

12. Woodworth, *Manifest Destinies;* John C. Pinheiro, "'Religion without Restriction': Anti-Catholicism, All Mexico, and the Treaty of Guadalupe Hidalgo," *Journal of the Early Republic* 23(1)(1 April 2003):69–96.

13. Archdeacon, *Becoming American: An Ethnic History;* Thornton, *American Indian Holocaust and Survival.*

14. Jeremy Adelman and Stephen Aron, "From Borderlands to Borders: Empires, Nation-States, and the Peoples in between in North American History," *The American Historical Review* 104(3) (1 June 1999):814–41; Menchaca, *Naturalizing Mexican Immigrants.* Although native people, blacks, and those of mixed race obtained Mexican citizenship after independence from Spain in 1821, U.S. racial laws excluded them from citizenship after incorporation of Mexican land; Steven Mintz, *Mexican American Voices: A Documentary Reader* (Chichester, UK: John Wiley & Sons, 2009).

15. James A. Rawley, and Stephen D. Behrendt, *The Transatlantic Slave Trade: A History* (Lincoln: University of Nebraska Press, 2005); Hugh Thomas, *The Slave Trade: The Story of the Atlantic Slave Trade: 1440–1870* (New York: Simon and Schuster, 2013).

16. Ira Berlin, *Many Thousands Gone: The First Two Centuries of Slavery in North America* (Cambridge, Mass.: Harvard University Press, 2000).

17. Damian Alan Pargas, *Slavery and Forced Migration in the Antebellum South* (Cambridge: Cambridge University Press, 2014); Steven Deyle, *Carry Me Back: The Domestic Slave Trade in American Life* (Oxford: Oxford University Press, 2005); Edward E. Baptist, *The Half Has Never Been Told: Slavery and the Making of American Capitalism* (New York: Basic Books, 2014).

18. Ira Berlin, *Generations of Captivity: A History of African-American Slaves* (Cambridge, Mass.: Harvard University Press, 2009).

19. Elmer Joe Brackner Jr., "The Transition from Slave Potter to Free Potter: The Wilson Potteries of Guadalupe County, Texas," in *Texana II: Cultural Heritage of the Plantation South* (Austin: Texas Historical Commission, 1982); Elmer Joe Brackner Jr., "The Wilson Potteries" (master's thesis, University of Texas at Austin, 1981). Like much of the material culture of slavery in the United States, Hiram Wilson's story does not represent the experience of most enslaved people but does serve as a reminder of the diversity of the slave experience in the United States.

20. David W. Blight, *Race and Reunion* (Cambridge, Mass.: Harvard University Press, 2009).

21. Eric Foner, *A Short History of Reconstruction* (New York: Harper Collins, 2015).

22. James M. Bergquist, *Daily Life in Immigrant America, 1820–1870: How the First Great Wave of Immigrants Made Their Way in America,* (2007; repr., Chicago: Ivan R. Dee, 2009).

23. Leonard Dinnerstein and David Reimers, *Ethnic Americans: A History of Immigration*, 5th ed. (New York: Columbia University Press, 2009); David A. Gerber, *American Immigration: A Very Short Introduction* (Oxford: Oxford University Press, 2011).

24. Roger Daniels, *Not Like Us: Immigrants and Minorities in America, 1890–1924* (Chicago: Ivan R. Dee, 1997).

25. Le Havre was one of the major ports of European embarkation before the 1850s, particularly for emigrants from the southern provinces of Germany. Records indicate that 19,600 Germans emigrated from Le Havre in 1844, the majority of them single young men heading to the United States. Emigration from the French city peaked at 54,000 in 1853. Jean Braunstein, "L'émigration Allemande Par Le Port Du Havre Au XIXe Siècle," *Annales de Normandie* 34(1)(1984):95–104, doi:10.3406/annor.1984.6382. Most transatlantic immigrants traveled on cargo ships before regularly scheduled packets, or passenger ships, were introduced in the 1820s. (Bergquist, *Daily Life in Immigrant America*). In Le Havre, Glass and 244 others, mostly Germans and some French, boarded the *Burgundy*, an American-built sailing ship with regularly scheduled passenger service between Le Havre and New York City. Only eight of those on board, six merchants along with a gentleman and his wife, could afford to stay in private cabins. Glass and the other less wealthy immigrants, all of whom listed their occupation as "farming," traveled below deck in steerage. See National Archives and Record Administration, record group 36, rolls 17–19, vol. 2 159: "Naturalization Papers, Court of Common Please, Leominster, Massachusetts, Peter Glass" and "New York, Passenger Lists, 1820–1891," index and images, http://FamilySearch.org, citing NARA microfilm publication M237 (Washington, D.C.: National Archive and Records Administration, n.d.): 399. For information on the *Burgundy*, see "Webb & Allen, William H. Webb," http://www.shipbuildinghistory.com/history/shipyards/719thcentury/webb.htm.

26. National Archive and Records Administration, "New York, Passenger Lists, 1820–1891," index and images, http://FamilySearch.org, citing NARA microfilm publication M237 (Washington, D.C.: National Archive and Records Administration, n.d.): 395–400. Peter Glass and Mary Ann (Mariana) Sthal married 7 October 1845 in Boston, Massachusetts. Ancestry.com, *Massachusetts, Town and Vital Records, 1620–1988*, online database (Provo, Utah: Ancestry.com Operations, Inc., 2011); original data: Town and City Clerks of Massachusetts. *Massachusetts Vital and Town Records*. Provo, Utah: Holbrook Research Institute (Jay and Delene Holbrook). For mention of the "German triangle," see Walter D. Kamphoefner and Wolfgang Helbich, *News from the Land of Freedom: German Immigrants Write Home*, ed. Ulrike Sommer (Ithaca, N.Y.: Cornell University Press, 1993).

27. Roger Daniels, *Coming to America: A History of Immigration and Ethnicity in American Life,* 2nd edition (New York: Harper Collins, 2002).

28. Tyler Gregory Anbinder, *Nativism and Slavery: The Northern Know Nothings and the Politics of the 1850's* (Oxford: Oxford University Press, 1992); Jon Gjerde and S. Deborah Kang, *Catholicism and the Shaping of Nineteenth-Century America* (Cambridge: Cambridge University Press, 2012).

29. While just over 300 Chinese came to California in 1849, by 1852 the number had jumped to 20,000. (Bergquist, *Daily Life in Immigrant America*).

30. Erika Lee, *At America's Gates: Chinese Immigration during the Exclusion Era, 1882–1943*

(Chapel Hill: University of North Carolina Press, 2003).

31. James T. Campbell, Matthew Pratt Guterl, and Robert G. Lee, eds., *Race, Nation, and Empire in American History* (Chapel Hill: The University of North Carolina Press, 2007); Nicholas de Genova, *Racial Transformations: Latinos and Asians Remaking*

the United States (Durham: Duke University Press, 2006).

32. Tom Coffman, *Nation Within: The History of the American Occupation of Hawai`i* (Kāne‘ohe, Hawaii: Koa Books, 2009); Charles R. Venator-Santiago, *Puerto Rico and the Origins of U.S. Global Empire: The Disembodied Shade* (New York: Routledge, 2015).

BIBLIOGRAPHY

Adelman, Jeremy and Stephen Aron. "From Borderlands to Borders: Empires, Nation-States, and the Peoples in between in North American History." *The American Historical Review* 104(3) (1 June 1999):814–41.

Anbinder, Tyler Gregory. *Nativism and Slavery: The Northern Know Nothings and the Politics of the 1850's.* Oxford: Oxford University Press, 1992.

Ancestry.com. *Massachusetts, Town and Vital Records, 1620–1988* [online database]. Provo, Utah: Ancestry.com Operations, Inc., 2011; original data: Town and City Clerks of Massachusetts. *Massachusetts Vital and Town Records.* Provo, Utah: Holbrook Research Institute (Jay and Delene Holbrook).

Archdeacon, Thomas J. *Becoming American: An Ethnic History.* New York: Simon and Schuster, 1983.

Banner, Stuart. *How the Indians Lost Their Land: Law and Power on the Frontier.* Cambridge, Mass.: Harvard University Press, 2009.

Baptist, Edward E. *The Half Has Never Been Told: Slavery and the Making of American Capitalism.* New York: Basic Books, 2014.

Bergquist, James M. *Daily Life in Immigrant America, 1820–1870: How the First Great Wave of Immigrants Made Their Way in America.* Chicago: Ivan R. Dee, 2009. First published 2007 by Greenwood.

Berlin, Ira. *Many Thousands Gone: The First Two Centuries of Slavery in North America.* Cambridge, Mass.: Harvard University Press, 2000.

———. *Generations of Captivity: A History of African-American Slaves.* Cambridge, Mass.: Harvard University Press, 2009.

Blight, David W. *Race and Reunion.* Cambridge, Mass.: Harvard University Press, 2009.

Brackner Jr., Elmer Joe. "The Transition from Slave Potter to Free Potter: The Wilson Potteries of Guadalupe County, Texas." In *Texana II: Cultural Heritage of the Plantation South.* Austin: Texas Historical Commission, 1982.

———. "The Wilson Potteries." Master's thesis, University of Texas at Austin, 1981.

Braunstein, Jean. "L'émigration Allemande Par Le Port Du Havre Au XIXe Siècle." *Annales de Normandie* 34(1)(1984):95–104. doi:10.3406/annor.1984.6382.

Campbell, James T., Matthew Pratt Guterl, and Robert G. Lee, eds. *Race, Nation, and Empire in American History.* Chapel Hill: The University of North Carolina Press, 2007.

Coffman, Tom. *Nation Within: The History of the American Occupation of Hawai`i.* Kāne‘ohe, Hawaii: Koa Books, 2009.

Daniels, Roger. *Coming to America: A History of Immigration and Ethnicity in American Life,* 2nd ed. New York: Harper Collins, 2002.

———. *Not Like Us: Immigrants and Minorities in America, 1890–1924.* Chicago: Ivan R. Dee, 1997.

De Genova, Nicholas. *Racial Transformations: Latinos and Asians Remaking the United States.* Durham, NC: Duke University Press, 2006.

Deyle, Steven. *Carry Me Back: The Domestic Slave Trade in American Life.* Oxford: Oxford University Press, 2005.

Dinnerstein, Leonard, and David Reimers. *Ethnic Americans: A History of Immigration*, 5th ed. New York: Columbia University Press, 2009.

Drake, James D. *The Nation's Nature: How Continental Presumptions Gave Rise to the United States of America*. Charlottesville: University of Virginia Press, 2011.

Foner, Eric. *A Short History of Reconstruction*. New York: Harper Collins, 2015.

Frymer, Paul. "'A Rush and a Push and the Land Is Ours': Territorial Expansion, Land Policy, and U.S. State Formation." *Perspectives on Politics* 12(1)(March 2014):119–44. doi:10.1017/S1537592713003745.

Gerber, David A. *American Immigration: A Very Short Introduction*. Oxford: Oxford University Press, 2011.

Gjerde, Jon, and S. Deborah Kang. *Catholicism and the Shaping of Nineteenth-Century America*. Cambridge: Cambridge University Press, 2012.

Kamphoefner, Walter D., and Wolfgang Helbich. *News from the Land of Freedom: German Immigrants Write Home*. Edited by Ulrike Sommer. Ithaca, N.Y.: Cornell University Press, 1993.

Lee, Erika. *At America's Gates: Chinese Immigration during the Exclusion Era, 1882–1943*. Chapel Hill: University of North Carolina Press, 2003.

Levinson, Sanford, and Bartholomew H. Sparrow. *The Louisiana Purchase and American Expansion, 1803–1898*. Lanham, Md.: Rowman & Littlefield, 2005.

Library of Congress, "A Century of Lawmaking for a New Nation: U.S. Congressional Documents and Debates, 1774–1875." http://memory.loc.gov/cgi-bin/ampage?collId=llsl&fileName=001/llsl001.db&recNum=226 (accessed 23 June 2015).

Menchaca, Martha. *Naturalizing Mexican Immigrants: A Texas History*. Austin: University of Texas Press, 2011.

Miller, David W. *The Taking of American Indian Lands in the Southeast: A History of Territorial Cessions and Forced Relocations, 1607–1840*. Jefferson, N.C.: McFarland, 2011.

Mintz, Steven. *Mexican American Voices: A Documentary Reader*. Chichester, UK: John Wiley & Sons, 2009.

Murrin, John M., Paul E. Johnson, James M. McPherson, Alice Fahs, and Gary Gerstle. *Liberty, Equality, Power: A History of the American People, Volume 1: To 1877*. 6th ed. Boston, Mass.: Cengage Learning, 2011.

National Archives and Record Administration. Record group 36, rolls 17–19, vol. 2.

———. Microfilm publication M237. Washington, D.C.: National Archive and Records Administration, n.d.

Pargas, Damian Alan. *Slavery and Forced Migration in the Antebellum South*. Cambridge: Cambridge University Press, 2014.

Pinheiro, John C. "'Religion without Restriction': Anti-Catholicism, All Mexico, and the Treaty of Guadalupe Hidalgo." *Journal of the Early Republic* 23(1)(1 April 2003):69–96.

Rawley, James A., and Stephen D. Behrendt, *The Transatlantic Slave Trade: A History*. Lincoln: University of Nebraska Press, 2005.

Shipbuilding History. "Webb & Allen, William H. Webb." Last modified March 29, 2012. http://www.shipbuildinghistory.com/history/shipyards/719thcentury/webb.htm (accessed 13 February 2015).

Thomas, Hugh. *The Slave Trade: The Story of the Atlantic Slave Trade: 1440–1870*. New York: Simon and Schuster, 2013.

Thornton, Russell. *American Indian Holocaust and Survival: A Population History Since 1492*. Norman: University of Oklahoma Press, 1990.

Venator-Santiago, Charles R. *Puerto Rico and the Origins of U.S. Global Empire: The Disembodied Shade*. New York: Routledge, 2015.

Woodworth, Steven E. *Manifest Destinies: America's Westward Expansion and the Road to the Civil War*, 1st ed. New York, N.Y.: Knopf, 2010.

Zolberg, Aristide R. *A Nation by Design: Immigration Policy in the Fashioning of America*. Cambridge, Mass.: Harvard University Press, 2006.

Communities of Refuge in Frontier Illinois

Nancy Davis

In October 1817, a swath of western Illinois land bordering the Mississippi River beckoned those with great intentions. In that year the United States government made 5,360,000 acres available there to the War of 1812 veterans in the form of 160- or 320-acre patents, depending on enlistment dates.[1] Of the nearly 17,000 certificates of entitlement conveyed in what was known as the Illinois Military Tract, few were to veterans who actually settled on the land. Most, living far from Illinois, found it impractical to uproot and claim their bounty. Many sold their parcels to speculators for anything they could get, but it was a boon for those who desired cheap land in the West.

The availability of abundant land was one of the foundational aspects in the development of the new nation and the establishment of a capitalistic society. Ownership of such resources devolved to the people rather than to the state, and yet this conception of private ownership was foreign to American Indians who had long lived on this land. The settlers' continual push westward displaced American Indian nations; eventually the U.S. government sought to relocate native tribes west of the Mississippi River. Likely the government's desire to secure these western lands with private settlement bordering the river encouraged a practical solution: to populate it with European Americans.

Within this tract, three very disparate settler communities were established over the next 40 years. They migrated here drawn by affordable property values, the Mississippi River as a nearby transportation system, generally rich soils, a slave-free state, and distance from most regulatory forces. All saw their communities as refuge: from hostile practices, antagonistic groups, and unfair systems of governance. Western Illinois was not the far West, but it was far enough from eastern influence to provide relative isolation and distance from society's distractions.[2] It was here that these settlers came to adjust what they saw wrong in their personal lives, in their religious lives, and in the secular lives of those around them. Their stories provide insights on the variety of motives that stirred numbers of similar groups to seek their own form of sanctuary in the western territories.

THE COMMUNITY OF NEW PHILADELPHIA

In 1830, Free Frank—a free black man who had purchased his freedom and chosen his own name—sold his land in Pulaski County, Kentucky and migrated with some of his family to the Military Boundary Tract in Pike County, Illinois.[3] A man of great entrepreneurial skill, his move was the result of many years of toil: as a slave in frontier South Carolina, as an enslaved farmer in Kentucky, renting himself out as an enslaved miner, and, when free, the owner of a saltpeter operation that provided potassium nitrate for gunpowder.[4] All these efforts, as well as the migration to the frontier free state of Illinois, served the principal purpose of buying his family out of slavery.

Figure 1.
Solomon McWorter, son of Free Frank McWorter, date and location unknown. Free Frank McWorter purchased his son Solomon out of slavery in 1835. Solomon joined his family in New Philadelphia, Illinois, a community of European Americans and free African Americans. Courtesy of the McWorter family.

Figure 2.
Children's rocking chair made by Solomon McWorter, likely for his grandchild, in New Philadelphia, Illinois, date unknown. Both Solomon McWorter and his father, Free Frank McWorter, were entrepreneurial and worked to develop the community of New Philadelphia. As this chair illustrates, Solomon McWorter was a skilled craftsman. Courtesy of the McWorter family.

In Kentucky, Free Frank purchased his wife Lucy in 1817, and his own freedom in 1819. Three of his children were still enslaved in Kentucky when Free Frank, Lucy, and their free children moved to Illinois in 1831. Protecting family members who were free, then pursuing new financial ventures in a distant place to purchase those who were not, was a bold move for the 53-year-old Free Frank. He quickly turned his 160 acres into a cash operation by transporting his saleable farm produce to the Mississippi River. By 1835 he amassed enough capital to return to Kentucky to purchase his 21-year-old son, Solomon (Figure 1).

With the last of his sons now manumitted, Free Frank adopted the last name McWorter and turned his attention to other entrepreneurial efforts. Buying 80 acres in 1836 from the federal government, Free Frank used 45 of them to establish the first known town founded and platted by an African American. He named it New Philadelphia.[5] In the 1850s settlers moving through the area were drawn to this prosperous market town, the only one within the township, with its blacksmith shop, post office, shoemaking shops, a wheelwright, a stagecoach stand, a general store, and a cabinetmaking firm. Solomon McWorter resided within this larger New Philadelphia community on his father's nearby farm. He was a farmer and an inventor of an evaporator to extract syrup from sorghum, as well as a cabinetmaker. Existing business receipts note Solomon's involvement in a cabinetmaking firm. It is possible that the cabinetmaking business listed in the New Philadelphia census was that of Solomon and his white partner, James Pottle. This chair made by Solomon, possibly for his grandchild, is the only known evidence of his craft (Figure 2).

Over time, Free Frank McWorter sold his 144 lots to both African and European Americans who lived side by side in this community that was well located near Mississippi River ports. Eventually, proceeds from the sale of the town lots helped to purchase 12 more family members out of slavery. Yet the McWorters were never free from worry. Slave catchers roamed this area between the Ohio and Mississippi Rivers, kidnapping free blacks and selling them south.

Although there had been other attempts to establish black settlements in western Illinois before the development of New Philadelphia, none existed for any length of time. They were often founded with paternalistic motives, such as Virginian Edward Coles's manumission and resettlement of his slaves on small farms on the Illinois frontier in 1819.[6] More importantly, none had an infrastructure that encouraged their survival. Free Frank McWorter's New Philadelphia had a much longer horizon. His personal intentions to reverse the damage of slavery prompted its founding, but its success stemmed from meeting the needs of a larger settler community. Yet it too eventually suffered when a county road, and then the railroad, bypassed the town in 1869, shifting away the movement of people. This precipitated New Philadelphia's demise. In the early twentieth century only six households remained. Today New Philadelphia is on the National Register of Historic Places and recognized as a National Historic Landmark.

THE MORMON COMMUNITY OF NAUVOO

In 1839 thousands of people from the Church of Jesus Christ of Latter-day Saints fled Missouri when the state governor signed an expulsion order. This was the latest move for a group who had been targeted and run out of several communities for their religious beliefs in the previous seven years. Traveling across the Mississippi River, they purchased affordable lots in the small town of Commerce, situated within the Illinois Military Tract, about 70 miles from New Philadelphia where Free Frank McWorter and his family lived. Renaming the city Nauvoo (Hebrew for Beautiful City), they expected to find refuge here, seeking distance from those who objected to their ways and their forms of worship. With many additional converts arriving from England, the town grew rapidly to 20,000 people, the largest community in Illinois.[7]

As the city developed, the church's founder, Joseph Smith, focused his efforts on constructing a temple that would serve as the center of the Mormon faith. Building began in early 1841 with all able-bodied men laboring to complete the building, which was impressive in size at 128 feet long, 165 feet tall, and 88 feet

Figure 3.
Charles Lambert, one of the designers of the grand temple in Nauvoo, Illinois, photographed in Salt Lake City, Utah, date unknown. When most Mormons abandoned Nauvoo in search of refuge from anti-Mormon vigilantes, Lambert stayed behind for several months to protect the structure. Courtesy of Church History Library, The Church of Jesus Christ of Latter-day Saints, Salt Lake City, Utah.

wide. Timber for the temple came from Mormon-run sawmills in the Wisconsin Territory, while limestone located in nearby quarries was cut by the faithful. Skilled men were needed, however, to carve the elaborate stone capitals.[8]

In 1843 the accomplished English stonecutter Charles Lambert met Mormon missionaries in Louth, England (Figure 3). He quickly accepted the faith and in 1844 sailed to New Orleans, traveled up the Mississippi River, and arrived in Nauvoo that spring. Joseph Smith recognized Lambert's skill and expressed gratitude for his arrival at a propitious time, since Smith had conceived of thirty decorative pilasters with sunstone capitals that might symbolically convey the presence of the celestial kingdom; at its center, a face representing what Joseph Smith had seen in a vision. It is thought that Lambert designed and carved the first prototypical sunstone and likely worked on portions of many, one of which is seen here[9] (Figure 4).

Joseph Smith never saw the finished temple. He was killed by an anti-Mormon mob in the nearby town of Carthage, Illinois in June 1844, six months before the Mormons erected the sunstone capitals on the temple. With their lives threatened once again by suspicious and distrustful local settlers who considered

Figure 4.
Limestone capital carved as a celestial sunstone, Church of Jesus Christ of Latter-day Saints grand temple in Nauvoo, Illinois, around 1845. This 6-foot wide carved sunstone was one of 30 that topped pilasters surrounding the grand temple in Nauvoo, Illinois. The Mormons relocated to Nauvoo to escape persecution, but they abandoned the settlement in 1846 after only seven years. National Museum of American History, Smithsonian Institution.

their practices controversial and their political influence overwhelming, most Mormons fled Nauvoo in early 1846. Lambert stayed behind to protect the temple, not leaving for the far West until the Mormons gave up the city in the fall of 1846. Two years later arsonists burned the structure, leaving little but the four walls. When a tornado struck in 1850, the temple was demolished and only three sunstones—part of Lambert's legacy of devotion—now survive.

Like the McWorters, who ran from the evils of the Kentucky slave state, the Mormons too sought freedom in Illinois. Despite challenges, the McWorter family stayed in Illinois, establishing a community that engaged settlers from the outside. With continued persecution, the Mormons abandoned theirs, eventually forming a settlement in the West's remote Great Basin.

THE ICARIAN COMMUNITY OF NAUVOO

Recognizing an opportunity to reasonably purchase land or rent buildings in Nauvoo from the departing Mormons, the Icarians, a utopian communal society, abandoned a failed venture in Texas and migrated up the Mississippi River. There in 1849–50 with their French founder and leader, Etienne Cabet, they built the Icarian community of Nauvoo. Here in the far frontier of Illinois, they hoped, like the Mormons, to develop their own concept of a perfect community in relative isolation from others.

Cabet's canon, based on his novel *The Voyage to Icaria* and influenced by Thomas More's *Utopia,* stated: "the burdens of labor and the benefits of its results, are shared by all people."[10] Cabet put his philosophy into practice in America because he was forbidden to do so in his home country of France. In Nauvoo he established a community where all members shared property and prosperity equally. Many of the members were artisans and skilled craftspeople from France and elsewhere. Here they developed woodworking shops that made innovatively shaped coat hangers that adjusted to the shape of both men's and women's clothing. These were likely sold to outside markets, helping to keep the community of Icaria solvent. Cabet also insisted that both book-based and vocational education were critical to the success of Icaria. He instituted mandatory schooling for boys and girls and evening classes for adults. Women were considered equal partners in work and marriage, though unable to vote in their communal meetings.

Emile and Annette Baxter of New Jersey, both of French extraction, found Cabet's philosophy compelling. Annette had attended the Sorbonne in France and was a graduate and later teacher at Miss Porter's School in Farmington, Connecticut (Figure 5). Emile, an immigrant, had been well educated in Europe and Scotland, and was engaged in the manufacturing of clothing. The numerous letters exchanged between the Baxters and Cabet indicated the challenge of giving up what they treasured for communal living in Nauvoo—Annette her iron bed, Emile his books and sewing machine—since Cabet insisted that everyone live similarly.[11]

Figure 5.
Annette Baxter, a resident of the Icarian community in Nauvoo, date and location unknown. Baxter believed in Icarian philosophies and participated in the group's communal customs. However, she still struggled to embrace some of the strict guidelines, such as giving up certain luxury possessions. Courtesy of Bob Baxter Family.

Figure 6.

Clothes hanger, from the communal Icarian settlement of Nauvoo, Illinois, mid-eighteenth century. Icarians built a community with shared property, equal division of labor, and relatively equal rights for men and women. Icarian women hung their cloaks on hangers like this one before eating in a communal dining hall. Courtesy of Nauvoo Historical Society and Icarian descendant Bob Baxter and family.

Offering their services and talents to the community, Emile and Annette and their two small children migrated from New Jersey to join the 500 or so in the Colony of Nauvoo in June 1855. There the Baxters participated in Icarian life, Emile as Cabet's secretary and laborer in the workshops, and Annette as a teacher. They lived in a small apartment, ate communally in the dining hall, and wore the simple clothing of the Icarian members. In the dining hall, Annette draped her modest cloak over one of the community's uniquely designed coat hooks, shown here (Figure 6).

Dissent within the community surfaced in 1856 and Cabet left Nauvoo to establish an arm of the colony in St. Louis. Later, other Icarian communities were founded in Iowa and California. It is unclear whether this conflict disillusioned the Baxters, but they returned East in late 1856, only to find how greatly they missed Illinois. The family returned to live among the non-Icarian Nauvoo community in 1857; several Baxter descendants live there still.

All three communities sought to establish a place separate from oppression. Each community's efforts were only partially successful. Despite living in the free state of Illinois and being able to engage in the nearby communities' commercial activities, the McWorters' lives were precarious; slave catchers were nearby and racist attitudes persisted. The Mormon community of Nauvoo rapidly grew to be the largest city in Illinois, but as a result of its growth and power, hostilities with neighbors escalated and overwhelmed it. The Icarians found a place of refuge; though they lived separately from their fellow citizens, their dealings were amicable. Unfortunately, dissension from within was their downfall.

Migration to frontier Illinois provided the inexpensive land and space to forge new communities and create culture. Out of that culture, furniture was built, temple sunstones created, and innovative, everyday implements produced. Very little on the land remains to mark these places, yet these objects stand as records of the ideas and concepts strongly held by these unique communities.

NOTES

1. Siyoung Park, "Land Speculation in Western Illinois Pike County, 1821–1835," *Journal of the Illinois State Historical Society* 77(2)(Summer 1984):115–28; Anne F. Hyde, *Empires, Nations, and Families: A History of the North American West, 1800–1860* (Lincoln: University of Nebraska Press, 2011); Marguerite Jenison Pease, *The Story of Illinois* (Chicago: University of Chicago Press, 1965).

2. Seymour Kesten, *Utopian Episodes: Daily Life in Experimental Colonies Dedicated to Changing the World* (Syracuse, N.Y.: Syracuse University Press, 1993).

3. Free Frank identified himself by this name in the 1820 federal manuscript census, expressing the significance of his purchased freedom. In 1836 he petitioned the state General Assembly to be allowed take the surname McWorter in order to protect his property rights. See Juliet E. K. Walker's *Free Frank: A Black Pioneer on the Antebellum Frontier* (Lexington: University Press of Kentucky, 1983), 48, 106.

4. Walker, *Free Frank*.

5. Paul Shackel, *New Philadelphia: An Archaeology of Race in the Heartland* (Berkeley: University of California Press, 2011).

6. Walker, *Free Frank*, 114.

7. Robert Bruce Flanders, *Nauvoo, Kingdom on the Mississippi* (Champaign: University of Illinois Press, 1965); Roger D. Launius and John E. Hallwas, eds., *Kingdom on the Mississippi Revisited, Nauvoo in Mormon History* (Urbana: University of Illinois Press, 1996).

8. E. Cecil McGavin, *The Nauvoo Temple* (Salt Lake City: Deseret Book Company, 1962).

9. Benson Whittle, "The Sunstones of Nauvoo," *Sunstone Magazine* (July, 2002):17–24.

10. Janet Fischer Palmer, "The Community at Work: The Promise of Icaria," (Ph.D. dissertation., Syracuse University, 1995), 2.

11. Lillian M. Snyder, *The Search for Brotherhood, Peace and Justice: The Story of Icaria* (Deep River, Iowa: Brennan Print 1996), 30.

BIBLIOGRAPHY

Flanders, Robert Bruce. *Nauvoo: Kingdom on the Mississippi*. Champaign: University of Illinois Press, 1965.

Hyde, Anne F. *Empires, Nations, and Families: A History of the North American West, 1800–1860*. Lincoln: University of Nebraska Press, 2011.

Kesten, Seymour. *Utopian Episodes, Daily Life in Experimental Colonies Dedicated to Changing the World*. Syracuse, N.Y.: Syracuse University Press, 1993.

Launius, Roger D., and John E. Hallwas, eds. *Kingdom on the Mississippi Revisited: Nauvoo in Mormon History*. Champaign: University of Illinois Press, 1996.

McGavin, E. Cecil. *The Nauvoo Temple*. Salt Lake City: Deseret Book Company, 1962.

Palmer, Janet Fischer. "The Community at Work: The Promise of Icaria." PhD diss., Syracuse University, 1995.

Park, Siyoung. "Land Speculation in Western Illinois Pike County, 1821–1835." *Journal of the Illinois State Historical Society* 77(2)(Summer 1984):115–28.

Pease, Marguerite Jenison. *The Story of Illinois*. Chicago: University of Chicago Press, 1965.

Shackel, Paul. *New Philadelphia: An Archaeology of Race in the Heartland*. Berkeley: University of California Press, 2011.

Snyder, Lillian M. *The Search for Brotherhood, Peace and Justice: The Story of Icaria*. Deep River, Iowa: Brennan Print 1996.

Walker, Juliet E. K. *Free Frank: A Black Pioneer on the Antebellum Frontier*. Lexington: University Press of Kentucky, 1983.

Whittle, Benson. "The Sunstones of Nauvoo." *Sunstone Magazine*, July 2002.

African American Expression in Antebellum America:
The Story of Dave Drake

Kym Rice

A skilled enslaved artisan named Dave Drake made this deceptively simple-look-ing, nearly two-foot high, pot in Edgefield District, South Carolina, just as the Civil War began (Figure 1). Following years of neglect, museums today study the rare objects that survive from "slavery times" to help us unlock what mattered to the people who made, used, or valued these things in the past and, at the same time, expand our understanding of the distinctive culture created by enslaved African Americans. Boldly signed with his enslaved moniker, "Dave," Drake's pots, like this poetic "verse" pot, not only offer insight into the practices embodied in antebellum plantation and industrial slavery but also suggest ways in which enslaved indi-viduals may have maintained their self-identity and exercised agency despite their challenging circumstances. Although interest in Dave Drake by museums began as early as 1919, experts are still in the process of discovering his work and recovering his story.[1] In order to appreciate this pot's significance, we need to understand what has been uncovered thus far of Dave Drake's life.

Born a slave in about 1800 in the Edgefield District, an area located in up-country South Carolina along the Savannah River bordering Georgia, Dave Drake spent his 70-plus years working around this rural region.[2] Like most slaves, Dave

Figure 1.
Mammoth stoneware storage jar, created by enslaved potter Dave Drake in Edgefield, South Carolina, in 1862. This jar is one of few everyday objects that have survived to tell the story of enslaved artisans in the South. Drake's skill both as a master potter and a poet—extremely rare in a time when teaching literacy to slaves was illegal—is molded into this durable medium. National Museum of American History, Smithsonian Institution.

Drake experienced sale multiple times during his lifetime, but his ability as an "excellent Stone Ware Turner" permitted some security during enslavement and beyond. Even after emancipation in 1865 he remained employed until his death by members of a large extended family who owned several Edgefield pottery factories.[3] Court records indicate that a man named Harvey Drake sold Dave at roughly age 17 to his uncle, Dr. Abner Landrum, to settle a debt. Among his businesses, Landrum established a commercial pottery sometime after 1809 when he first advertised his discovery of "superior quality" clay for making ceramics. Dave Drake, who may have learned his trade from his former owner Harvey Drake (and whose last name he later took in freedom) likely numbered among the five enslaved male "turners" identified as working at "Landrum's Pottery" in 1820.

Located in a community known as "Pottersville," Landrum's manufactory originated the highly fired alkaline-glazed utilitarian stoneware that eventually made Edgefield among the most prolific pottery producers in antebellum

America.[4] Because of the superior kaolin deposits, other potteries creating similar crocks, jugs, pitchers, churns, and pans soon sprang up there.[5] Recently, at a Landrum family site where Dave Drake once worked, archaeologists discovered the remains of a massive kiln that originally stood some 105 feet long as well as a large pug mill used to process the clay.[6] Although Edgefield manufactories distributed their wares throughout the state, their principal customers remained up-country cotton planters who used these durable and inexpensive containers to store the food allowances they supplied to their large workforces.[7] Originally filled by enslaved cooks and kitchen staff with foodstuffs such as meal, lard, preserved pork or beef and then sealed, some pots signed by or attributed to Dave Drake can hold up to 40 gallons of provisions.

As was true for other antebellum Southern industries, Edgefield's workforce was largely enslaved. Stoneware manufacture involved hard physical labor, beginning with digging the clay or chopping wood needed to fire the kiln. Dave Drake and other pottery workers labored long hours, frequently experienced harsh conditions, and suffered brutal treatment. In 1848, after Dave Drake's then-owner Rev. Franklin Landrum whipped a female enslaved worker named Ann for perceived impudence, she hanged herself at the factory within sight of other slaves.[8]

From census data, historians estimate that at their greatest capacity, Edgefield potteries employed more than 100 enslaved workers, mostly men. Like Dave Drake, the potters (called turners) possessed specialized skills that combined strength, coordination, and creative ability.[9] After weighing and preparing the clay through repeated kneading, they turned it round on a pottery wheel, pumping the control wheel with their legs as they shaped the vessel with their hands and added the lug (also called ear) handles distinctive to many Edgefield vessels. Dave Drake, as all the potters did, crafted the larger containers in several parts, beginning with a turned base. His pieces often feature double-collared ring necks, useful for tightly securing the cloth covers over jars after filling. The alkaline glaze applied during firing usually left the pieces a distinctive mottled but glossy tan, brown, or green color, at times made irregular and rough to the touch by the uneven heat.

In his own time, Dave Drake was acknowledged by local residents as a master potter. In 1859, the *Edgefield Advertiser* described white children gathering "to watch old Dave as the clay assumed beneath his magic touch the desired shape of jug, or jar, or crock, or pitcher."[10] During his career, he undoubtedly made thousands of pieces, of which only roughly 170 examples are identified today.[11]

Figure 2.
Dave Drake signed his work with both his name and the initials L.M., for his owner Lewis Miles. National Museum of American History, Smithsonian Institution.

From what remains, it appears that Dave Drake first signed his pots in 1840, using a sharpened stick. He wrote his first name with great flourish in the still wet clay, along with the date, and usually the name or initials of his current owner, Lewis Miles (Figure 2). Sometimes he added a poem or statement on the vessel's shoulders below the rim, leading scholars to refer to them as "verse pots." Experts theorize that the puncture marks Dave Drake usually made correspond to the vessel's gallon-size.[12] From time to time, he applied, as did other enslaved Edgefield potters, further marks—crosses, slashes, circles, Xs—that possibly symbolize a West African cosmogram.[13] Another striking local Africanism is the distinctive "face jug" form, probably transmitted through some 170 enslaved Africans who arrived in Edgefield in 1858, brought illegally to South Carolina from Angola.[14] Inspired by the style, Dave Drake made a large-size face jug (used to hold walking sticks or umbrellas) around 1870, near the end of his career. This is now in the High Museum of Art collections.[15]

Some 30 pots by Dave Drake feature his original poetry, which raises a question—how did he become literate? By the early nineteenth century, most Southern legislatures had enacted strictures against slave literacy, yet in practice many religious slaveholders defied the law. According to family tradition, Abner Landrum taught his slaves to read the Bible.[16] Dave Drake further honed his literacy skills when working, possibly as a typesetter, at Landrum's *South-Carolina Republican* (published in Pottersville, 1824–1827) and its successor, the *Edgefield Hive*, a pro-Unionist newspaper that Landrum owned from about 1827 until 1830, when he relocated to Columbia, South Carolina. Some white citizens of Edgefield so associated Drake with the latter paper that they called him "Dave of the Hive."[17] Perhaps Dave Drake first adopted his poetic stanzas, puns, and inscriptions from his exposure to early newspapers or inexpensive almanacs that published short poems of different kinds.[18] James Miller observes similarities between Drake's use of vernacular language and the rhythmic quality communicated by traditional African American songs.[19] His later poems drew more heavily on the Bible.

"Making this jar," Drake wrote in 1858, "I had all thoughts." Evidently, as he shaped clay with his hands, Dave Drake reflected. He took pride in his craft and on more than one occasion, he described his work product as "A noble jar." While his verses sometimes speak to his enslaved state ("Dave belongs to Mr. Miles/wher the oven bakes & the pot biles" on 31 July 1840), they also register in turn as humorous, clever, and at times, poignant. On 28 June 1854, for instance, Drake stated with a touch of impertinence, "Lm (Lewis Miles) says this handle will crack" (his handles continue intact on the piece today). On 6 December 1858, he considered, "nineteen days before Christmas Eve (a holiday that traditionally included time off for slaves)/lots of people after it's over, how they will grieve."[20] When his former owner Abner Landrum died in 1859, Dave Drake noted, with evident fondness, "Over noble Dr Landrums head/ may guardian angels visit his bed." Missing his family who perhaps were sold away, he observed with palpable sadness on an 1857 pot, "I wonder where is all my relations/ Friendship to all—and every nation."[21] Created by Dave Drake on a Sunday, the traditional day off for enslaved African Americans, this piece represents a rare deeply personal statement.[22]

With habits likely gained during his newspaper work, Dave Drake carefully noted the month, day, and year on many pots. Probably, he had ready access to a calendar, perhaps one he glimpsed hanging on the pottery office wall.[23] Many enslaved individuals formulated their understanding of time by recalling natural phenomena like comet sightings or unusual weather. Yet, like other nineteenth-century Americans, slaves lived in "an increasingly punctilious and hectoring society" where, as Drake did, they expressed a growing awareness of time and understanding of mechanically defined time.[24]

Antebellum whites allowed enslaved individuals precious little autonomy, yet nothing suggests that Dave Drake applied his verses in secret.[25] Indeed, their

Figure 3.
Dave Drake carved this poem into his stoneware storage jar. The inscription reads "I made this jar all of cross/If you don't repent, you will be, lost." National Museum of American History, Smithsonian Institution.

visibility and prominent location together with Drake's use of Lewis Miles's initials seem to indicate the owner's tacit approval.[26] Slaveholders particularly valued their enslaved artisans for their abilities and their monetary worth, and in Drake's case, Michael Chaney attributes his bold signature to a "strategic leniency" policy generally adopted by slaveholders to keep prized slaves in their place.[27] On the other hand, the poems may illustrate Dave Drake's successful negotiations with Miles. The references to cash on several pots ("I made this jar for cash," for example, in 1857) suggest that Miles probably allowed Dave Drake to sell some work himself. His audacious signature, which grew bolder as time went on, together with his rhymes, assert his individual identity powerfully in a way that clearly circumvented his status.

Dave Drake made the skillfully formed pot illustrated here for Miles, and it represents his best work. It also is thought to be his final verse pot. Dated 3 May 1862, Drake begins by proudly proclaiming, "I-made this jar" and continues, "all of cross, if you don't repent you will be lost," which possibly comments on the Civil War, which was just underway (Figure 3). Jill Koverman points out that many slaves were Christians and believed in a final Day of Reckoning and retribution for their enslavement, which undoubtedly helped them deal with intolerable conditions.

While we may never know exactly what Dave Drake intended with any of his poems, conceivably he inscribed his pots as the ultimate act of subversion. His verses were his voice and his pots traveled as messages that eventually reached his fellow slaves, who unpacked them, helped to fill them, carried them to and from storage areas, and opened them in kitchens. As Chaney observes, "he is imparting them (the pottery) with the sign of his identity and rejoicing in their dissemination as vicarious experiences of freedom."[28] It may be, as John Vlach proposes, that enslaved individuals, especially those who were not literate, found encouragement or drew strength from touching Dave Drake's assertive signature or running their hands over the African-inspired marks or the slightly raised verse.[29] Through reading, holding, or touching Dave Drake's inventive missives carried on stoneware, they glimpsed the freedom coming to them right around the corner.

NOTES

1. This article is informed by three major studies of Dave Drake: Cinda K. Baldwin, *Great & Noble Jar: Traditional Stoneware of South Carolina* (Athens: University of Georgia Press for McKissick Museum, 1993); Jill Beute Koverman, ed., *I Made This Jar: the Life and Works of the Enslaved African-American Potter, Dave* (Columbia: University of South Carolina for McKissick Museum, 1998); and Leonard Todd, *Carolina Clay: The Life and Legend of the Slave Potter Dave* (New York: W. W. Norton & Company, 2008). The gift of a very large "Dave pot" to the Charleston Museum in 1919 initiated the museum's research into Edgefield pottery. Later, as part of an oral history project to explore South Carolina pottery in the 1930s, Laura Bragg, then the museum's director, transcribed interviews with several elderly individuals who specifically remembered Dave Drake and his work (Jill Beute Koverman, "Searching for Messages in Clay" in *I Made This Jar*, 19–20). John M. Vlach's 1978 exhibition, *The Afro-American Tradition in the Decorative Arts*, circulated by the Cleveland Museum of Art, was the first modern exhibition to highlight Dave Drake's work (Koverman, *I Made This Jar*, 14).

2. Before emancipation, enslaved individuals frequently were known to whites by their first name. Dave Drake appeared as "Dave" in court records and other documentation. The 1870 South Carolina census identifies him as "David Drake." Because David Drake signed his pots as "Dave," most scholars refer to him by his first name.

3. Description included in the notice for John Landrum's estate, *The Edgefield Advertiser*, 17 February 1846, quoted in Todd, *Carolina Clay,* 96. Dave Drake's complicated ownership history is discussed in Todd, *Carolina Clay*, and also Arthur F. Goldberg and James Witkowski, "Beneath his Magic Touch: The Dated Vessels of the African-American Slave Potter Dave," *Ceramics in America* (2006):2–7, http://www.chipstone.org/article.php/281/Ceramics-in-America-2006/?s=edgefield.

4. For information about Landrum and other Edgefield pottery owners, see John A. Burrison, "South Carolina's Edgefield District: An Early International Crossroads of Clay," *American Studies Journal* 56(2012), www.asjournal.org/56-2012/south-carolinas-edgefield-district-an-early-international-crossroads-of-clay/.

5. Baldwin, *Great & Noble Jar,* observes that most Edgefield pottery related to the storage, preparation, and preservation of food (162).

6. See, for example, Brooke Kenline, "Searching for Enslaved Laborers at the Reverend John Landrum Site (38AK497)," *South Carolina Antiquities* 43(2011):78–79. For more detail concerning the 2011–14 excavations by the University of Illinois in Edgefield, "Archaeology of Edgefield, South Carolina Pottery Communities," http://www.histarch.illinois.edu/Edgefield/.

7. The success of upland cotton made Edgefield the third most populated area in the entire antebellum South. For a detailed portrait of antebellum Edgefield, see Orville Vernon Burton, *In My Father's House Are Many Mansions: Family &*

Community in Edgefield, South Carolina (Chapel Hill: University of North Carolina Press, 1985). The first specific record of Edgefield pottery for sale appears in the *Camden Gazette* in 1819 (Baldwin, *Great & Noble Jar*, 163).

8. Baldwin, *Great & Noble Jar*, 75. Treatment of enslaved individuals by South Carolina slaveholders and other whites is described in Gerald J. Pierson, *The Nature of Resistance in South Carolina's Work Progress Administration Ex-Slave Narratives,* Dissertation.com (2002), www.bookpump.com/dps/pdf-b/1121598b.pdf.

9. Dave Drake lost a leg around 1835, in an accident when he reportedly "got drunk and layed on the railroad track." During his later career, he presumably worked with a helper who moved the wheel (Koverman, *I Made This Jar*, 20). Two Dave pieces are cosigned—both in 1859, one with "Baddler" and another with "Mark" (possibly Mark Jones, in whose household Dave Drake lived in at the end of his life).

10. Quoted in Goldberg and Witkowski, "Beneath his Magic Touch," 4.

11. We can only guess how and why particular pieces survive to the present day. Weight and size may be a factor. Examples of Dave Drake's work are still being discovered. Eve M. Kahn, "Slave Potter's Presence Emerges in Fragments," *New York Times* (31 August 2012), http://www.nytimes.com/2012/08/31/arts/design/pottery-by-david-drake-a-slave-craftsman-in-edgefield-sc.html.

12. The first vessel attributed to Dave Drake dates to 1829 and is marked only with holes called punctates. See the list, "Known Dated Vessels Signed by or Attributed to the Slave Potter Dave," in Goldberg and Witkowski, "Beneath his Magic Touch," 9–12. Lewis Miles owned Dave from 1840–43 and 1849–65 (Goldberg and Witkowski, 4–6).

13. J. W. Joseph and Nicole Isenbarger, "Marks in Common: Current Research of African American Marks on Colonoware and Edgefield Stoneware, "*South Carolina Antiquities*, 43(2011):80. See also Grey Gundaker, "The

Kongo Cosmogram in Historical Archaeology and the Moral Compass of Dave the Potter," *Historical Archaeology* 45(2)(2011):176–83. Scholars debate the marks' origins and meanings, which apparently traveled without slaveholders' notice from the coastal region to Edgefield. Similar cosmogram designs also appear on colonoware, the low-fired earthenware associated with eighteenth-century enslaved potters in South Carolina as well as elsewhere on other pottery linked to slavery. For examples and discussion of African-derived influences, see Leland Ferguson, *Uncommon Ground: Archaeology and Early African America, 1650–1800* (Washington, D.C.: Smithsonian Books, 2004) and Mark P. Leone, *The Archaeology of Liberty in an American Capital: Excavations in Annapolis* (Berkeley: University of California Press, 2005).

14. An African named Romeo (who came to South Carolina via the *Wanderer*) likely worked at the Thomas Davies pottery in Edgefield (Todd, *Carolina Clay*, 128). See also Mark M. Newell with Peter Lenzo, "Making Faces: Archaeological Evidence of African American Face Jug Production," *Ceramics in America* (2006), http://www.chipstone.org/article.php/287/Ceramics-in-America-2006/Making-Faces:-Archaeological-Evidence-of-African-American-Face-Jug-Production.

15. Acc. 1997.190. Published in Todd, *Carolina Clay*, illustration 15.

16. Throughout the antebellum South, pious slaveholders schooled their slaves, despite growing legal restrictions. Free blacks, who largely were literate, may have instructed some enslaved individuals; still others taught themselves to read and write. Frederick Douglass, for example, surreptitiously looked at his owners' children's schoolbooks and practiced his letters while they were away at church. For more about slave literacy, see Heather Andrea Williams, *Self-Taught: African American Education in Slavery and Freedom* (Chapel Hill: University of North Carolina Press, 2005), 7–30.

17. Others remembered him for his creative skill as "Dave the Potter" or "Dave Pottery" (Koverman, *I Made This Jar*, 22).

18. Newspaper publishers printed and sold almanacs; itinerant traveling peddlers also sold them.

19. James A. Miller, "Dave the Potter and the Origins of African-American Poetry" in Koverman, *I Made This Jar*, 57.

20. Lists of Dave Drake's verse pots are included in Todd, *Carolina Clay*, 229–52 and Goldberg and Witkowski, "Beneath his Magic Touch", 28–30.

21. Koverman, "Searching for Messages in Clay: What Do We Really Know about Dave?" in *I Made This Jar*, 24.

22. Although few former slaves succeeded in locating their lost relatives after the Civil War, Dave Drake's biographer speculates that he did reunite with a daughter and lived his final years with her family (Todd, *Carolina Clay*, 162–66). In July 2016, almost 30 descendants of Drake gathered in Edgefield to celebrate "Dave Day." Dede Biles, "Descendants of famous potter David Drake introduced on Dave Day!" *Aiken Standard* (9 July 2016), http://www.aikenstandard.com/20160709/160709481/descendants-of-famous-potter-david-drake-introduced-on-dave-day.

23. Regular mail delivery and scheduled stagecoach and train trips all contributed to antebellum Americans' growing "time awareness." See Carlene Stephens, "'The Most Reliable Time': William Bond, the New England Railroads, and Time Awareness in 19th-century America," *Technology and Culture*, 30(1)(January 1989):4–7. The town of Edgefield with its courthouse stood at the intersection of four major roads used by stagecoaches. In the early 1830s, the South Carolina Railroad constructed a passenger line from Charleston to the Savannah River port of Hamburg at the District's lower edge. Roads, post offices, and other transportation features in the Edgefield District are illustrated on S. Augustus Mitchell, "Map of the States of North Carolina, South Carolina, and Georgia," 1835 (hmap1835m5), Hargrett Rare Book & Map Library, University of Georgia.

24. Mark Michael Smith, *Mastered by the Clock: Time, Slavery, and Freedom in the American South* (Chapel Hill: University of North Carolina Press, 1997): 135, 138 (quote).

25. Examinations of the dates that appear on Dave Drake's pots reveal no particular pattern. Based on the dates he recorded, it appears Drake made them on every day of the week, throughout the year. No Dave pieces are identified for the period 1844–1849, when he worked for Rev. John Landrum and his son, B.F. Landrum, who had a reputation for cruelty (Todd, *Carolina Clay*, 107–12).

26. The largest number of Dave pots survive from the time he worked for Lewis Miles, Abner Landrum's son-in-law, at the Miles Pottery located at Stoney Bluff, outside the town of Edgefield (Goldberg and Witkowski, "Beneath his Magic Touch," 15–17).

27. Michael A. Chaney, *Fugitive Vision: Slave Image and Black Identity in Antebellum Narrative* (Bloomington: Indiana University Press, 2007), 89.

28. Chaney, *Fugitive Vision*, 192.

29. Vlach, *The Afro-American Tradition in the Decorative Arts*, 76–77. See also Aaron de Groft, "Eloquent Vessels / Poetics of Power: The Heroic Stoneware of 'Dave the Potter,'" *Winterthur Portfolio* 33(4)(Winter 1998):249–60.

BIBLIOGRAPHY

Baldwin, Cinda K. *Great & Noble Jar: Traditional Stoneware of South Carolina*. Athens: University of Georgia Press for McKissick Museum, 1993.

Biles, Dede. 2016. "Descendants of famous potter David Drake introduced on Dave Day!" *Aiken Standard*, 9 July 2016. http://www.aikenstandard.com/20160709/160709481/descendants-of-famous-potter-david-drake-introduced-on-dave-day (accessed 10 July 2016).

Burrison, John A. "South Carolina's Edgefield District: An Early International Crossroads of Clay." *American Studies Journal* 56(2012). http://www.asjournal.org/56-2012/south-carolinas-edgefield-district-an-early-international-crossroads-of-clay (accessed 30 June 2015).

Burton, Orville Vernon. *In My Father's House Are Many Mansions: Family & Community in Edgefield, South Carolina*. Chapel Hill: University of North Carolina Press, 1985.

Chaney, Michael A. *Fugitive Vision: Slave Image and Black Identity in Antebellum Narrative*. Bloomington: Indiana University Press, 2007.

de Groft, Aaron. "Eloquent Vessels / Poetics of Power: The Heroic Stoneware of 'Dave the Potter." *Winterthur Portfolio* 33(4)(Winter 1998):249–60.

Ferguson, Leland. *Uncommon Ground: Archaeology and Early African America, 1650–1800*. Washington, D.C.: Smithsonian Books, 2004.

Goldberg, Arthur F., and James Witkowski. "Beneath his Magic Touch: The Dated Vessels of the African-American Slave Potter Dave." *Ceramics in America* (2006):2–7, http://www.chipstone.org/article.php/281/Ceramics-in-America-2006/?s=edgefield (accessed 28 June 2015).

Gundaker, Grey. "The Kongo Cosmogram in Historical Archaeology and the Moral Compass of Dave the Potter." *Historical Archaeology* 45(2)(2011):176–83.

Joseph, J. W., and Nicole Isenbarger. "Marks in Common: Current Research of African American Marks on Colonoware and Edgefield Stoneware." *South Carolina Antiquities*, 43(2011):80.

Kahn, Eve M. 2012. "Slave Potter's Presence Emerges in Fragments." *New York Times*, 31 August 2012. http://www.nytimes.com/2012/08/31/arts/design/pottery-by-david-drake-a-slave-craftsman-in-edgefield-sc.html (accessed 1 May 2015).

Kenline, Brooke. "Searching for Enslaved Laborers at the Reverend John Landrum Site (38AK497)." *South Carolina Antiquities*, 43(2011):78–79.

Koverman, Jill Beute, ed. *I Made This Jar: The Life and Works of the Enslaved African-American Potter, Dave*. Columbia: University of South Carolina for McKissick Museum, 1998.

Leone, Mark P. *The Archaeology of Liberty in an American Capital: Excavations in Annapolis*. Berkeley: University of California Press, 2005.

Map of the States of North Carolina, South Carolina, and Georgia. Philadelphia: S. Augustus Mitchell (publisher), 1835. Hmap1835m5, Hargrett Rare Book & Manuscript Library, University of Georgia Libraries. http://dlg.galileo.usg.edu/hmap/id:hmap1835m5.

Miller, James A. "Dave the Potter and the Origins of African-American Poetry." In *I Made This Jar: The Life and Works of the Enslaved African-American Potter, Dave*, ed. Jill Beute Koverman, pp. 53–61. Columbia: University of South Carolina for McKissick Museum, 1998.

Newell, Mark M., and Peter Lenzo. "Making Faces: Archaeological Evidence of African American Face Jug Production." In *Ceramics in America 2006*. Milwaukee, Wisc.: Chipstone Foundation, 2006. http://www.chipstone.org/article.php/287/Ceramics-in-America-2006/Making-Faces:Archaeological-Evidence-of-African-American-Face-Jug-Production (accessed 28 June 2015).

Pierson, Gerald J. *The Nature of Resistance in South Carolina's Work Progress Administration Ex-Slave Narratives*. Dissertation.com, 2002, www.bookpump.com/dps/pdf-b/1121598b.pdf (accessed 11 November 2016).

Smith, Mark Michael. *Mastered by the Clock: Time, Slavery, and Freedom in the American South.* Chapel Hill: University of North Carolina Press, 1997.

Stephens, Carlene. "'The Most Reliable Time': William Bond, the New England Railroads, and Time Awareness in 19th-century America." *Technology and Culture* 30(1)(January 1989):1–24.

Todd, Leonard. *Carolina Clay: The Life and Legend of the Slave Potter Dave.* New York: W. W. Norton & Company, 2008.

University of Illinois in Edgefield. "Archaeology of Edgefield, South Carolina Pottery Communities." http://www.histarch.illinois.edu/Edgefield/ (accessed 9 May 2015).

Vlach, John Michael. *The Afro-American Tradition in the Decorative Arts.* Cleveland: Cleveland Museum of Art, 1978.

Williams, Heather Andrea. *Self-Taught: African American Education in Slavery and Freedom.* Chapel Hill: University of North Carolina Press, 2005.

Lady in the Harbor:
The Statue of Liberty as American Icon

Alan M. Kraut

The Statue of Liberty towers above New York Harbor, at the gateway to the United States, welcoming the "huddled masses" to America's shores, their few worldly possessions crammed into battered suitcases and trunks. Immigrants on board ship glance worshipfully at the statue as they prepare to disembark and begin a new life. This tableau has become iconic in American culture, sustaining the national mythology that the statue was by design a welcoming beacon of liberty and altruistic sanctuary for the oppressed and impoverished of other lands. Of course the history of the Statue of Liberty is considerably more complicated. It was, at its inception, hardly linked to voluntary immigration at all; rather it was a symbol of slavery's abolition and slave emancipation as well as Franco-American friendship. In the Smithsonian Institution's collection is a *maquette*, a small model of the Statue of Liberty created by French sculptor Frédéric Auguste Bartholdi (ca. 1884) preliminary to construction of the mammoth statue that stands in the Hudson River (Figure 1).

A replica of Lady Liberty raises the question of precisely how the gift from the people of France to the people of the United States became symbolic of America's peopling, from the involuntary migration that transported Africans

Figure 1.
Statue of Liberty terra-cotta and tin model, created by sculptor Frédéric Auguste Bartholdi around 1884. The Statue of Liberty was designed to celebrate the end of American slavery. Soon after the statue's construction, its meaning evolved to symbolize the United States more broadly and the promise of the American dream. National Museum of American History, Smithsonian Institution, gift of Richard Butler.

from freedom into bondage to a voluntary migration that brought to the United States the oppressed of other lands in search of prosperity. And, how did this statue, originally called "Liberty Enlightening the World," instead become the preeminent icon of the United States of America?

Maquettes were made into small models to reward donors who contributed their francs or dollars to the Franco-American Union for construction of the statue in the 1880s.[1] The story goes that the idea of having the French people bestow upon the American people a statue celebrating the end of slavery in the United States emerged during an 1865 dinner conversation between one man devoted to the emancipation of all in bondage, or denied liberty any way, and another man passionate about very large statuary, especially figures paying homage to high ideals such as universal human liberty. The former was Édouard-René Lefebvre de Laboulaye. The latter was Frédéric Auguste Bartholdi.[2] (Figure 2)

Laboulaye was an eminent nineteenth-century French scholar of political and legal institutions. Keenly interested in the United States, he authored a

Figure 2.
Portrait of Auguste Bartholdi, French sculptor who created the Statue of Liberty maquette in preparation for the construction of the larger monument, date unknown. Bartholdi envisioned his statue would represent the common ideal of liberty shared by the French and American people. Courtesy of the Statue of Liberty National Monument, National Park Service.

three-volume history of the United States (*Histoire des Etats-Unis*) between 1855 and 1866. He was riveted by the American Civil War, joyous that the United States endured and abolished slavery after the war as France had in 1794, and shattered by President Abraham Lincoln's assassination. Although he never visited the United States, Laboulaye received an honorary doctorate from Harvard University in 1864 and the following year hosted a dinner party at which guests animatedly exalted the martyred Lincoln and criticized France's Second Empire's imperfect commitment to individual liberty.[3]

Whether or not it is true that Laboulaye and Bartholdi first discussed creating their statue at this dinner, by 1871 the two had agreed upon a project to create a monument to the Union's triumph and commitment to liberty expressed in the abolition of slavery with an allegorical representation of liberty on a grand scale. It would embody the common aspirations for freedom shared by the French and American peoples. According to Laboulaye, the gift should be "a common work of both nations," celebrating the shared belief in liberty that had brought the Marquis de Lafayette to the other side of the Atlantic to aid in the American Revolution. Moreover, it would not be the gift of one government to another, but of one people to another.[4]

Bartholdi embraced this monumental expression of liberty whole-heartedly. Born in 1834 in Colmar, near the border with Germany in the Alsace region, he was raised and educated in Paris. Trained as a sculptor, Bartholdi was increasingly attracted to public statuary, especially the very large representations then in vogue. Even before Laboulaye formally offered him the commission, Bartholdi visited the United States in 1871 to scout potential sites, eventually deciding upon Bedloe's Island (renamed Liberty Island in 1956) in New York Harbor, location of a military installation. President Ulysses S. Grant personally promised the site to Bartholdi for his statue.

Fund-raising, planning, and construction did not proceed smoothly or rapidly, but by the summer of 1880 the Franco-American Union had collected approximately 400,000 francs ($250,000), along with in-kind contributions such as copper donated for the statue's exterior. Completed, the Statue of Liberty was indeed magnificent. With her pedestal, Lady Liberty stood 305 feet 11 inches in height above mean low water level, higher than the office buildings that towered above Manhattan Island. The statue's copper exterior was suspended from an iron support frame that had arrived disassembled from France in over 200 wooden crates. Yet there were no fears she might collapse. The assembled statue had been put on display in France for over six months prior to its journey to the United States. Likewise, parts of the statue, including the right arm holding the torch and the crown, had been shown even earlier for fund-raising at the United States' Centennial in Philadelphia in 1876 and in Paris at the Universal Exposition of 1878.[5]

Lady Liberty was rife with symbolism. She carried in her left arm a tablet of law branded with the date of the Declaration of Independence. Her right hand held high the torch of enlightenment. Her left foot crushed the broken chain of bondage, a reference to the Thirteenth Amendment to the Constitution, which ended slavery throughout the nation. *The New York Times* described the excitement leading up to the 28 October 1886 dedication, presided over by President Grover Cleveland, in glowing terms: "All day yesterday people came to the city in droves to participate in today's celebration. Extra heavily loaded trains, much behind schedule time, were the rule on every railroad entering the city. Every hotel was crowded to its utmost capacity last night, and there was hardly one of the better known hotels which did not have to turn away hundreds of would be guests."[6]

By contrast, the African American community of the late nineteenth and early twentieth centuries responded to the Statue of Liberty much more ambivalently. African American newspapers in several states had published news stories about the statue and printed solicitations from the American Committee for the Statue of Liberty to raise money for the statue's pedestal. American Committee fund-raising materials made a direct linkage between the statue and African

American Liberty. Beginning in April 1885, the African American *Cleveland Gazette* ran a series of advertisements placed by the American Committee. Those that appeared in the 25 April, 2 May, and 4 July editions offered contributors a six-inch nickel-plated miniature of the Statue for a $1.00 donation and a 12-inch bronze replica for a $5.00 contribution.[7]

And some definitely thought the statue worth celebrating. Among those who marched in the parade held the day that the statue was dedicated, 28 October 1886, was the Twentieth Regiment of U.S. Colored Troops, which had been sponsored by the Union League of New York in 1863–64.[8] Ironically, the only attendees to actually voice dissent on the day of the ceremony were members of the New York State Women's Suffrage Association who were aboard a boat in the harbor near Bedloe's Island protesting women's exclusion from the political liberties the statue was intended to symbolize. How could liberty, personified by the statue as a woman, be celebrated when the "unalienable rights" proclaimed by the Declaration of Independence still excluded women? They "denounced the ceremonies just witnessed as a farce."[9]

Yet there is considerable evidence that many in the African American community saw the statue and its message as hypocritical in the light of American racism and discrimination. An editorial in the *Cleveland Gazette,* published on 27 November 1886, insisted that

> It is proper that the torch of the Bartholdi statue should *not* be lighted until this country becomes a free one in reality. 'Liberty Enlightening the World,' indeed! The expression makes us sick. This government is a howling farce. It can not or rather *does not* protect its citizens within its *own* borders. . . . The idea of the 'liberty' of this country, 'enlightening the world,' or even Patagonia, is ridiculous in the extreme.[10]

In 1906, three African Americans were lynched by a white mob in Springfield, Missouri. Two of them had been charged with raping a white woman. After they were hanged, the bodies were burned. The mob took a model of the Statue of Liberty from the town center and placed it on top of the tower from which the men had been hanged. There was a riot and only the Missouri militia finally restored peace.[11] One of the most renowned African American newspapers, the *Chicago Defender,* published an image of the statue in July 1917 with the words, "'Liberty, Protection, Opportunity, Happiness, For all White Men' and 'Humiliation, Segregation, Lynching, for all Black Men,'"[12] The statue that had been conceived as a celebration of emancipation was, in the eyes of slavery's descendants, a specter of racial hypocrisy.

Figure 3.
"Liberty enlightening the world," a lithographic print created in 1883, from the Travelers Insurance Co. in Hartford, Connecticut. This print illustrated the Statue of Liberty at its future site in New York Harbor. Using the statue's original title, "Liberty enlightening the world," the Travelers Insurance Company immediately employed the symbolism of the new statue to equate its company with far-reaching ideals. Courtesy of the American Antiquarian Society.

African American writers rarely referred to the Statue of Liberty in a positive way. In his 1968 autobiography, African American leader W. E. B. Du Bois recalled that, when he returned from Europe in 1894, his ship passed the Statue of Liberty, "I know not what multitude of emotions surged in the others, but I had to recall that mischievous little French girl [on the ship's deck] whose eyes twinkled as she said: 'Oh yes the Statue of Liberty! With its back toward America, and its face toward France.'" In his campaign for equal rights, Du Bois likely often felt that Lady Liberty had turned her back on his people.[13]

It was another migration, a voluntary migration from many regions of the globe, women and men pursuing economic opportunity and in flight from oppression in their homelands, with which the Lady in the Harbor ultimately became synonymous (Figure 3). American poet Emma Lazarus was the one who forged the link between the Statue of Liberty and voluntary immigration. The daughter of an affluent German-Jewish family living in New York, Lazarus was an activist seeking to facilitate the emigration of Jewish victims of Russian pogroms. She authored "The New Colossus" in 1883 as a donation to an auction of art and literature organized by the American Committee at the National Academy of Design in New York to raise money for the Statue of Liberty's pedestal. Five lines of Lazarus's poem made especially clear the connection between migration and the new statue. In the poem, the "Mother of Exiles" speaks and requests of "ancient lands":

> Give me your tired, your poor,
> Your huddles masses, yearning to breathe free,
> The wretched refuse of your teeming shore.
> Send these, the homeless, tempest-tost to me,
> I lift my lamp beside the golden door!

The Statue of Liberty, her torch raised high, seemed to Lazarus to be a beacon of freedom, welcoming the foreign-born.[14]

Certainly, many foreign-born seemed to be heeding the statue's call in the decades following its construction. Between the 1880s and the 1920s, 23.5 million immigrants arrived in the United States, most from southern and eastern Europe, as well as China, Japan, and Mexico.[15] In 1901, Georgina Schuyler, a poetry-loving descendant of old New York aristocracy, began a campaign to memorialize her friend Emma Lazarus, who had died in 1887. Thus it was that in 1903, during a peak period of migration, Lazarus's poem and its moving reference to the immigrant was inscribed on a bronze tablet mounted on a wall in the statue's pedestal.[16] Now Lazarus's poem was fastened to the Statue of Liberty even as she had fastened the statue to the American immigration experience.

Whatever the original intent of the French gift, the letters and oral histories of those immigrants, mostly European, who arrived in the port of New York, suggest that they saw and remembered the Statue of Liberty, even if these newcomers did not always know precisely what it was. Some thought the statue was the tomb of Christopher Columbus. Theodore Spako from Greece, who emigrated in 1911 at the age of 16, recalled a question from another boy: "What's the statue?" The lad's father responded, "That [sic] Christopher Columbus." However, young Theodore disagreed. "Listen, this don't look like Christopher Columbus. That's a lady there."[17]

A Polish immigrant, Celia Rypinski, saw the "lady with the torch" and began to pray.[18] Ten-year-old Larry Edelman arriving from Russia in 1910, recalled, "When we were told, on a Saturday morning, we would be passing the Statue of Liberty we all lined the deck. The thrill of seeing that Statue there. And the tears in everybody's eyes, which as a child, got me the same feeling."[19] Rota Fischbach, arriving from Germany in 1926 recalled her mother saying in German, "Rota, we're in America. There's the big lady."[20] Another German, Marie Kunert, age 15 when she arrived, recalled, "Seein' [sic] the Statue of Liberty, that was impressive . . . everybody crowded on the railing. We all wanted to see that wonderful Amerika [sic] and the Statue."[21]

Many newcomers saw the Statue of Liberty as embodying their own aspirations for liberty in their new home. Morry Helzner from Russia recalled, "When the [ship's] horn started to blow and when we saw the Statue of Liberty, I thought I was in heaven . . . She's up there and saying, 'Come on in. From now on you are a free person. You do as you please. And long as you behave yourself, you're coming to a country where you can—if you want to make a success, it's up to you.'"[22] Helen Nitti from Italy recalled her impressions as an 11-year-old arrival, "Yeah. We heard about the statue in the old country. Yeah. Yeah. But then when the ship got—just before we could see the statue, it slowed down just to a crawl. And then we got right in front of it. And it seemed like it was standing still. And then we all looked, of course . . . and I heard these women sayin' [sic], 'We are free.' *'Siamo liberi.'*"[23] Recognizing the impact of the statue on newcomers, the ships' crews would alert immigrants to the visual treat in store for them. Dr. Aelyas Kassab of Syria recalled that in 1899 when she arrived, "They [the crew] told us the night before to be sure to get up early in the morning so that we—can see the Statue of Liberty . . . We all got up—oh, before daylight—went up on the—the deck was full of the passengers. Everybody was up. The morning was beautiful. And we knew that the—the Statue of Liberty . . . we all cried."[24]

Not every newcomer was awestruck or moved to tears. Angelo Rucci, who arrived as an eight-year-old from Italy in 1923, recalled barely giving the statue a thought. "Well. One of the things—everybody was making a big thing about the Statue of Liberty but I didn't think that much about it at the time. We saw it and it looked like a great big building in the middle of the ocean to us. Some—for some reason, it didn't impress any member of my family [laughs] at that time."[25]

Unfortunately, the immensity of liberty symbolized by the statue remained beyond the grasp of many arrivals and their descendants. Racism, nativism, and economic exploitation contradicted the promise of a better life that the statue in the harbor embodied. Ironically, even while Lady Liberty's promise at times remained unfulfilled, her iconic significance expanded, often beyond America's borders. By the end of the twentieth century and the dawn of the twenty-first, the Statue of Liberty had become a transnational symbol of liberty that political dissidents around the world embraced, such as the Chinese students who stood with their papier-mâché Statue of Liberty outside the Chinese Embassy in Washington, D.C. at the time of the Tiananmen Square protest in 1989.

Why did Lady Liberty evolve into arguably the most popular iconic representation of the United States, at least partially supplanting Uncle Sam, the bald eagle, the American flag, and other iconography of nation? As the twentieth century aged, Americans increasingly embraced the ideals of ethnic and racial pluralism, if, at times, only rhetorically. This amplified the relevance of the Statue of Liberty's twin heritage celebrating the slave's emancipation and the immigrant's quest. Freedom and pluralism increasingly emerged as the cornerstones of America's self-identification, an identity that those of all political persuasions could embrace.

After signing the Immigration and Nationality Act of 1965 on Liberty Island beneath the gaze of the statue which he knew "welcomed so many to our shores," Democratic President Lyndon Johnson observed, "The land flourished because it was fed from so many sources—because it was nourished by so many cultures and traditions, and peoples."[26] And when he spoke at the dedication of the newly renovated Statue of Liberty on 3 July 1986, Republican President Ronald Reagan referred to Lady Liberty as "everybody's gal," who was "still giving life to the dream of a new world where old antagonisms could be cast aside and people of every nation could live together as one."[27]

Still, the Statue of Liberty has hardly been an uncontested icon. Some scholars have objected to the statue as too triumphal, a symbol that fails to reflect the patterns of prejudice and discrimination that remain embedded in the national legacy. From 1972 until 1991 the National Park Service's American Museum of Immigration was housed in the Statue of Liberty's pedestal.[28] One cultural critic, while allowing that the statue is "one of the central shrines of American culture," regarded the museum's interpretation as uncritically upbeat, while a second exhibit on a separate floor in the monument's base was narrowly confined to the statue's origins, addressing not at all the peopling of the United States.[29] The latter purpose is today well served by a museum across the harbor from the Statue of Liberty, the Ellis Island National Immigration Museum, which provides a nuanced and complex tale of the experience of newcomers throughout American history. A new, state-of-the-art museum is planned for Liberty Island.

Activists have periodically repurposed the statue. Some have occupied the statue to protest the contradictions they perceive between American policies and the high ideals that Lady Liberty was intended to embody. On the afternoon of 26 December 1971, fifteen members of the Vietnam Veterans Against the War

Figure 4.
Demonstrators protest the Vietnam War at the Statue of Liberty, 1971. Members of Vietnam Veterans Against the War believed the statue was a symbol of American freedom that provided a stark contrast to U.S. military action in Vietnam. Courtesy of Photograph Collection of the American Museum of Immigration, Liberty Island, U.S. Department of the Interior, National Park Service.

organization remained on the island after the last tour boat departed and occupied the statue for two days, demanding that President Richard Nixon end the war in Southeast Asia (Figure 4). After a judge issued a restraining order, the protesters left with clenched fists held high. Their press release said, "The reason we chose the Statue of Liberty is that since we were children, the statue has been analogous in our minds with freedom and the America we love. . . . Until this symbol again takes on the meaning it was intended to have, we must continue our demonstration." Two years later the same group occupied the statue for a day to protest the inadequate treatment of veterans of the war.[30]

While today some Americans deplore the use of the Lady in the Harbor as a commercial symbol deployed to sell goods, or look coldly upon it as uncritical fanfare to American freedom, many others continue to regard the Statue of Liberty with reverence as an icon of what the nation aspires to be at its best.[31] Those whose families prospered in the United States are especially warm in their expressions of feeling for the American icon. Working on the renovation of the statue in the 1980s, Tony Soraci, "a tool belt around his waist, balanced on a narrow metal rod of scaffolding," was photographed leaning over to proudly place a kiss on the forehead of Miss Liberty. The grandson of immigrant Italians, he planned to describe that kiss to his own grandchildren someday.[32] Lady Liberty, with the chains of bondage underfoot and her torch lighting the way to greater human dignity, remains for Soraci and so many others a paean to global freedom like no other. For Americans of every race, religion, and ethnicity the Lady in the Harbor will always embody the tale of two migrations.

NOTES

1. Yasmin Sabina Khan, *Enlightening the World: The Creation of the Statue of Liberty* (Ithaca, N.Y.: Cornell University Press, 2010), 137.

2. Khan, *Enlightening the World*, 47. Evidence that the Statue of Liberty was born at a dinner party is thin. It may be a legend traceable to a single source, an 1885 fund-raising pamphlet written by Bartholdi, after Laboulaye's death. See Executive Summary of *The Black Statue of Liberty Rumor: An Inquiry into the History and Meaning of Bartholdi's Liberté éclairant le Monde.* The report was compiled in 2000 by independent consultant Rebecca M. Joseph with Brooke Rosenblatt and Carolyn Kinebrew for the National Park Service in response to persistent rumors that the Statue of Liberty was intended to depict a black woman. The author of this article was among those scholars asked by the historian of the Park Service, Dwight Pitcaithely, to review a draft of the report. http://www.nps.gov/stli/learn/historyculture/black-statue-of-liberty.htm.

3. Joseph, Rosenblatt, and Kinebrew, *The Black Statue of Liberty Rumor*, 10, 14.

4. Laboulaye, as quoted in Khan, *Enlightening the World*, 15.

5. Khan, *Enlightening the World*, 1, 123, 137. A more recent and excellent account of the Statue of Liberty's construction is Elizabeth Mitchell, *Liberty's Torch: The Great Adventure to Build the Statue of Liberty* (New York: Atlantic Monthly Press, 2014). Still valuable is Marvin Trachtenberg, *The Statue of Liberty* (New York: Penguin Books, 1977).

6. *New York Times*, 28 October 1886.

7. *Cleveland Gazette*, 25 April, 2 May, 4 July 1885.

8. *New York Times*, 28 and 29 October 1886.

9. Khan, *Enlightening the World*, 181.

10. *Cleveland Gazette*, 27 November 1886. The quotation is also cited in Lynn Pohl, *The Changing Face of the Statue of Liberty* (Washington, D.C.: National Park Service, 2009), 44. This publication is based on a Historic Resource Study for the National Park Service by John Bodnar, Laura Burt, Jennifer Stinson, and Barbara Truesdale.

11. Pohl, *The Changing Face of the Statue of Liberty*, 45–46.

12. Pohl, *The Changing Face of the Statue of Liberty*, 46.

13. W. E. B. Du Bois, *The Autobiography of W. E. B. Du Bois, A Soliloquy on Viewing My Life from the Last Decade of Its First Century* (New York: International Publishers, Inc., 1968), 182.

14. Esther Schor, *Emma Lazarus* (New York: Schocken, 2006), 188–95. Also on the transformation of the Statue of Liberty into a symbol for voluntary immigration, see John Higham, "The Transformation of the Statue of Liberty," in *Send These to Me: Jews and Other Immigrants in Urban America* (New York: Atheneum, 1975), 78–88.

15. The figure is an approximation based on U.S. Census data. See N. Carpenter, "Immigrants and Their Children," *U.S. Bureau of the Census Monograph 7* (Washington, D.C., 1927), 324–25. See also, Alan M. Kraut, *The Huddled Masses: The Immigrant in American Society, 1880–1921,* 2nd ed. (Wheeling, Ill.: Harlan Davidson, Inc., 2001), 2–3, 34–35, 40.

16. Schor, *Emma Lazarus,* 250. Also, Higham, *Send These to Me,* 80.

17. Theodore Spako, interview in Peter Morton Coan, ed. *Ellis Island Interviews: In Their Own Words* (New York: Checkmark Books, 1997), 278.

18. Celia Rypinski interview in David M. Brownstone, Irene M. Franck, and Douglass L. Brownstone, *Island of Hope, Island of Tears: In Their Own Words, the Story of Those Alive Today Who Made the Great Migration Through Ellis Island from the Old World to the New* (New York: Rawson, Wade Publishers, Inc., 1979), 141.

19. Larry Edelman in Coan, *Ellis Island Interviews,* 155.

20. Rota Fichbach in Coan, *Ellis Island Interviews,* 188.

21. Marie Kunert, oral history in National Park Service, Statue of Liberty National Monument Oral History Archives, Keck #12. Keck is one of several interview series that make up the oral history collection at Ellis Island. The author wishes to profusely thank George D. Tselos, National Park Service Supervisory Archivist in the Archives/Oral History Reference Library at the Statue of Liberty–Ellis Island National Monument, who compiles quotations from immigrant oral histories about the Statue of Liberty. I also wish to thank Barry Moreno, National Park Service Librarian at Ellis Island.

22. Morry Helzner in National Park Service, Statue of Liberty N.M. Oral History Archives, Keck #55.

23. Helen Nitti in National Park Service, Statue of Liberty N.M. Oral History Archives, Keck #78.

24. Dr. Aeylas Kassab, in National Park Service, Statue of Liberty N.M. Oral History Archives, Keck #89.

25. Angelo Rucci, in National Park Service, Statue of Liberty N.M. Oral History Archives, Keck #83.

26. President Lyndon B. Johnson's remarks at the signing of the Immigration Bill, Liberty Island, New York, 3 October 1965, http://www.lbjlib.utexas.edu/johnson/archives.hom/speeches.hom/651003.asp.

27. Reagan's remarks at the Statue of Liberty Centennial Celebration, 3 July 1986, http://www.reagan.utexas.edu/archives/speeches/1986/70386d.htm.

28. Barbara Blumberg, *Celebrating the Immigrant: An Administrative History of the Statue of Liberty National Monument, 1952–1982,* Cultural Resource Management Study 10 (Washington, D.C.: National Park Service, 1985), https://www.nps.gov/parkhistory/online_books/stli/adhi.htm.

29. Mike Wallace, *Mickey Mouse History and Other Essays on American Memory* (Philadelphia: Temple University Press, 1996), 62. Many of the complexities concerning precisely what the Statue of Liberty represents or should represent were addressed at the time of the renovation of the statue in the 1980s. The best account of that process and the central role played by historians is described in F. Ross Holland, *Idealists, Scoundrels, and the Lady: An Insider's View of the Statue of Liberty–Ellis Island Project* (Urbana: University of Illinois Press, 1992).

30. Blumberg, *Celebrating the Immigrant,* Chapter 1, https://www.nps.gov/parkhistory/online_books/stli/adhi1.htm.

31. Pohl, *Changing Face of the Statue of Liberty,* 53–59.

32. The elegant description of Soraci is from President Ronald Reagan's remarks at the opening ceremonies of the Statue of Liberty Centennial Celebration in New York, 3 July 1986. As a member of the Statue of Liberty–Ellis Island Foundation's History Committee, the author was privileged to be present at the ceremony. https://reaganlibrary.archives.gov/archives/speeches/1986/70386d.htm.

BIBLIOGRAPHY

Blumberg, Barbara. *Celebrating the Immigrant: An Administrative History of the Statue of Liberty National Monument 1952–1982*. Cultural Resource Management Study 10. Washington, D.C.: National Park Service, 1985.

Brownstone, David M., Irene M. Franck, and Douglass L. Brownstone. *Island of Hope, Island of Tears: In Their Own Words, the Story of Those Alive Today Who Made the Great Migration Through Ellis Island from the Old World to the New*. New York: Rawson, Wade Publishers, Inc., 1979.

Carpenter, N. "Immigrants and Their Children." *U.S. Bureau of the Census Monograph 7*. Washington, D.C.: United States Government Printing Office, 1927.

Coan, Peter Morton, ed. *Ellis Island Interviews: In Their Own Words*. New York, Checkmark Books, 1997.

Du Bois, W. E. B. *The Autobiography of W. E. B. Du Bois: A Soliloquy on Viewing My Life from the Last Decade of Its First Century*. New York: International Publishers, Inc, 1968.

Higham, John. *Send These To Me: Jews and Other Immigrants in Urban America*. New York: Atheneum, 1975.

Holland, F. Ross. *Idealists, Scoundrels, and the Lady: An Insider's View of the Statue of Liberty–Ellis Island Project*. Urbana: University of Illinois Press, 1992.

Johnson, Lyndon B. "President Lyndon B. Johnson's Remarks at the Signing of the Immigration Bill, Liberty Island, New York, October 3, 1965." Lyndon Baines Johnson Library and Museum, Austin, Tex. http://www.lbjlib.utexas.edu/johnson/archives.hom/speeches.hom/651003.asp (accessed 11 March 2015).

Joseph, Rebecca M., Brooke Rosenblatt, and Carolyn Kinebrew. *The Black Statue of Liberty Rumor: An Inquiry into the History and Meaning of Bartholdi's Liberté éclairant le Monde*. Northeast Ethnography Program, National Park Service. (Last modified September 2000.) http://www.nps.gov/stli/learn/historyculture/black-statue-of-liberty.htm (accessed 11 March 2015).

Khan, Yasmin Sabina. *Enlightening the World: The Creation of the Statue of Liberty*. Ithaca, N.Y.: Cornell University Press, 2010.

Kraut, Alan M. *The Huddled Masses: The Immigrant in American Society, 1880–1921*. 2nd ed. Wheeling, Ill.: Harlan Davidson, Inc., 2001.

Mitchell, Elizabeth. *Liberty's Torch: The Great Adventure to Build the Statue of Liberty*. New York: Atlantic Monthly Press, 2014.

Pohl, Lynn. *The Changing Face of the Statue of Liberty*. Washington, D.C.: National Park Service, 2009.

Reagan, Ronald. "Remarks at the Opening Ceremony of the Statue of Liberty Centennial Celebration in New York, New York, July 3, 1986." Ronald Reagan Presidential Library and Museum, Simi Valley, Calif. https://reaganlibrary.archives.gov/archives/speeches/1986/70386d.htm (accessed 11 March 2015).

Schor, Esther. *Emma Lazarus*. New York: Schocken, 2006.

Statue of Liberty National Monument and Ellis Island. Oral History Archives. National Park Service.

Trachtenberg, Marvin. *The Statue of Liberty*. New York: Penguin Books, 1977.

Wallace, Mike. *Mickey Mouse History and Other Essays on American Memory*. Philadelphia: Temple University Press, 1996.

Contesting the Nation, 1900–1965

Fath Davis Ruffins

In 1903, when the African American scholar and activist W. E. B. Du Bois wrote that "the problem of the Twentieth Century is the problem of the color-line," he was in the middle of a very long life.[1] Du Bois was born in 1868, the same year that the Fourteenth Amendment to the U.S. Constitution was passed[2] (Figure 1). He spent his childhood in a society reeling from the Civil War. After the war he lived through deeply oppressive years when the nation became segregated by law and by custom. Violence against people of color rose to new heights of brutality. He also witnessed some of the bittersweet triumphs of the modern civil rights movement.[3] Du Bois died in Ghana, West Africa on 28 August 1963, the same day as the historic March on Washington, and his passing was announced from the podium. His prediction about the color line turned out to be completely correct.

In 1900, most native-born white Americans believed that an Anglo-Protestant white supremacist racial hierarchy was crucial for national stability and identity, and that all immigrants should assimilate as soon as possible. These views restricted all people of color to limited social, economic, and educational spheres. The related political movement meant to protect the interests of native-born or long-established inhabitants against those of immigrants was called "nativism," and nativist elected officials developed new laws to restrict the number of immigrants from certain parts of the world. Yet by the end of Du Bois's lifetime, enough

Figure 1.
Portrait of Dr. W. E. B. Du Bois, photographed in Washington, D.C. in 1911. A prolific author and activist, W. E. B. Du Bois helped shape twentieth-century debates about race both in the United States and globally. Among his many contributions, Du Bois co-founded the National Association for the Advancement of Colored People in 1909. Scurlock Studio Records, ca. 1905–1994, Archives Center, National Museum of American History.

white Americans had changed their views such that the nation passed new civil rights laws and courts at all levels decided cases meant to guarantee equal rights to all Americans. These were rights that had been promised earlier, but discriminatory laws such as those levying poll taxes, which required everyone who voted to pay a special tax, were passed to prevent Americans of color from exercising them.[4] In 1965, after decades during which federal laws severely limited immigration, a new law opened the possibility of immigration to the wider world, increasing the diversity of the American populace—sometimes in unexpected ways. By the 1970s, a leading national metaphor suggested that the United States was "a nation of nations," in which the importance of immigrant contributions and diversities could be celebrated.[5] While "cultural pluralism" had developed into a mainstream ideology shared by many liberals and centrists, other Americans clung to long-held racial views and practices. Massive resistance to the modern civil rights movement characterized not only the South but many parts of the urban and suburban North as well.

This essay highlights some of the principal factors that led to these cultural shifts. The unanticipated shocks of World War II and the Cold War were key causal elements. People of color and sympathetic whites formed advocacy organizations, pushed for new laws, published books and articles, and created new elementary and secondary school curricula that emphasized the social and economic advantages of diversity. By the mid-1960s, these coalitions led by African Americans gained enough political and social power to challenge key elements of a centuries-old system of white racial hierarchy, in legislatures, courts, universities, religious settings, and in the streets. This essay investigates the significant movements, organizations, and individuals as well as the tremendous obstacles they faced in striving for a nation that came closer to living up to its long-stated ideals.

COMPETING BELIEFS ABOUT RACE AND ETHNICITY

By 1920, the United States had emerged as a world power with widely scattered territories (e.g., Puerto Rico, Hawaii, the U.S. Virgin Islands, American Samoa, and Guam) and unacknowledged colonies (e.g., Cuba, the Philippines).[6] Rapid industrialization and urbanization beckoned southern and eastern Europeans seeking social mobility, freedom from conscription, religious tolerance, and greater economic opportunity.

Early twentieth-century images reflected common ideas about the appropriate hierarchy of the different "races." Ordinary trade cards, magazine illustrations, and illustrated sheet music were filled with images of Uncle Sam (Figure 2), and later the Statue of Liberty, welcoming all newcomers—even some who by law could not immigrate or become naturalized citizens, such as those from Asia. People emigrated from places such as Italy, Poland, the Balkans, and Russia because they were pushed out of their homelands by poverty, wars, revolutions, and religious intolerance. The United States was remarkably easy to get into,

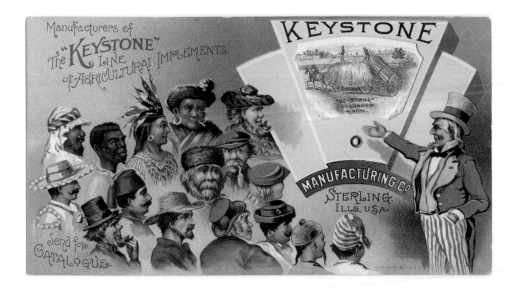

Figure 2.
Trade card for the Keystone Manufacturing Company in Sterling, Illinois, 1892. In this illustration, Uncle Sam presents Keystone Manufacturing Company's agricultural implements to different peoples of the world. Each figure is associated with a specific racial or ethnic group, specified by stereotypical facial features, clothing, and adornments. Archives Center, National Museum of American History, Smithsonian Institution.

compared to western Europe and Japan. Before the 1920s, there was no such thing as an illegal alien. If a person could get to American shores, he or she could stay or go back and forth many times, unless convicted of a crime.[7]

Not all who came here settled here. For example, many Italian and Polish men often went back and forth, spending some years in the United States, then returning home temporarily or even permanently. Yet enough of these new people did stay that some Americans began to worry whether the "national character" would change. Political, social, and religious leaders often invoked this term as a nod to the widespread understanding that "national character" depended upon the maintenance not only of white supremacy in relation to all people of color, but also the unchallenged notion that British and northern European laws, customs, language, and religious traditions had always been, and should always be, the fundamental organizing element of American society. Even other Europeans, such as those from the south, central, and eastern regions, were viewed as coming from lesser cultures. In the 1990s, scholars such as Theodore Allen and David Roediger began to use the term "whiteness" to describe this constellation of socio-political attitudes.[8]

Newer arrivals hailed from cultures quite different from the earlier British and other Northern European immigrants, who often called themselves "natives."[9] Jewish, Polish, Irish, and Italian communities also broadened and complicated what it meant to be "white" because although they were not people of color, they did not fit the normative Anglo-Saxon Protestant archetype of the time.[10] Each new wave of international immigrants and internal migrants encountered some prejudice and discrimination. Social anxieties about immigration also served to harden explicitly racial hierarchies that segregated all people of color as outside the national mythology of equality and freedom for all. By the time Du Bois died, the nation was only just beginning to enforce the anti-discrimination laws that challenged white supremacy and create more inclusive definitions of what it meant to be American. However powerful, these laws and judicial rulings could not quickly eliminate the customs and values contained in white supremacy. Debates over the relevance of past prejudices and symbols continue into the twenty-first century, for example in the discussion over states and public institutions flying Confederate flags.

As immigration increased, many native-born whites wondered whether it was possible to have social order with so many culturally dissimilar people. Anxieties about the growing population of southern and eastern Europeans sparked the passage of the Immigration Act of 1924. This law limited new immigrants from those regions to a very small percentage, based on their presence in the population in 1890. According to the U.S. Department of State Office of the Historian, the purpose of the act was "to preserve the ideal of American homogeneity."[11]

"Old stock" Americans of northern European, Protestant descent wondered how to preserve their traditions, values, and the nation's "Anglo-dominant" character. By 1920, an "Americanization movement" had emerged involving public school officials, the YMCA and YWCA, groups such as the Sons and Daughters of the American Revolution, veterans' groups, especially the Grand Army of the Republic and the American Legion, and many local governments. They developed public school curricula, sponsored historical pageants about the Founding Fathers and the Revolutionary era, worked towards English-only instruction, and actively developed patriotic celebrations for Independence Day (4 July) and George Washington's birthday (22 February).

Many scholars, educators, elected officials, and opinion leaders posited that assimilation was the only way to inculcate normative Anglo-Protestant values and produce good citizens. In 1909, a play entitled *The Melting Pot*, written by Jewish immigrant Israel Zangwill, first popularized the notion that it was just a matter of time before all newcomers would give up any distinctive cultural traits in order to blend together into "Americanness." For example, businessman Henry Ford organized English schools and pageants for his workers where

The Ford English School graduating class as they emerged from the "Melting Pot

Figure 3.

"Melting Pot" graduation ceremony from the Ford English School, 1916. Aligned with the popular melting pot philosophy of the time, the Ford Motor Company offered English and Americanization classes to its workers. Upon graduation, the melting pot ideal was literally acted out in a ceremony where graduates passed through a large "melting pot" and emerged in uniform Americanized clothing. Courtesy of the collections of The Henry Ford, Dearborn, Michigan. Object ID P.O.5167.

they literally acted out the "melting pot" ideal. Participants started with their original ethnic clothing and flags, then passed through a symbolic cauldron, and emerged wearing similar sober suits and waving American flags. In particular, Jewish, Slavic, Greek, and other eastern European immigrant groups experienced some discrimination in economic opportunities and education, but not nearly to the same extent as did people of color. As in the case of Henry Ford's program, tremendous economic and social pressures were exerted to force the acceptance of this Protestant, Anglo dominant superiority (Figure 3).

Not all resistance to immigration was so genteel. In the 1920s the Ku Klux Klan (KKK) was reorganized in Indiana, home to many southerners who had migrated from Kentucky and Tennessee. Klan parades in broad daylight, nighttime meetings where crosses were burned, and violent intimidation worked to terrorize Catholic immigrants and communities of color (Figure 4). As a result of redlining,

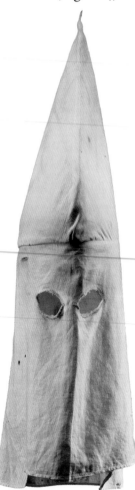

Figure 4.
White pointed hood worn by a member of the Ku Klux Klan, 1920s. Employing tactics of mass violence and fear, the Ku Klux Klan terrorized minority communities throughout the twentieth century. Members wore hoods like this one to conceal their identities. National Museum of American History, Smithsonian Institution, gift of Mr. Hoffman.

Ruffins

prejudice, and the threat of violence, most cities were made up of neighborhoods defined by ethnic/racial boundaries of language, national origin, religion, and other customs, making them easily identifiable targets.

Thousands of African American men and women were lynched in the South and elsewhere. Photographs of gleeful white mobs crowding around the broken body of a colored person appeared in newspapers and were sometimes sent as postcards. Such mob actions rarely received any judicial sanctions or even public criticism.[12] Typically, newspapers reported that such acts were committed by "persons unknown."[13] This violence against black and brown people (including Native Americans and those of Mexican descent), against immigrants (even those who would eventually identify as white, such as Italians and Jews), and against labor organizers (who were often foreign-born) reinforced Anglo-Protestant conformity and white racial supremacy.

While the Klan was a grassroots national organization, academic eugenicists Madison Grant and Harry Laughlin offered "scientific" rationales for segregation, and reinforced fears of "mongrelization" or "race mixing." This trade card in an ordinary printer's sample book was offered routinely as one option for illustrating a business enterprise (Figure 5). While this image is more explicit than others, such ideas were commonplace.[14]

Espousing a competing vision for American society, Progressivist reformers believed that national harmony could be created through viewing all cultures as offering some distinct gift or contribution to American life.[15] Founding settlement houses to work with the urban poor, Jane Addams and other reformers wanted to build

Figure 5.

"Professor Darwin" design offered for use on cigar labels by printing firm F. Heppenheimer's Sons in New York, around 1879. Everyday objects such as this trade card reinforced the application of Charles Darwin's scientific theory to racial hierarchies of people. Archives Center, National Museum of American History, Smithsonian Institution.

cultural bridges that would support immigrant families and cushion their entrance into American life. Philosopher and educator John Dewey joined W. E. B. Du Bois as a founding member of the interracial, interfaith advocacy organization the National Association for the Advancement of Colored People (NAACP).[16] Dewey and like-minded others were concerned with fighting ethnic prejudices, especially through education, creating children's toys, books, and curricula to teach tolerance. They believed that if children were taught to be prejudiced, then they also could be taught to be open-minded and accepting of cultural diversity.[17] For example, this "teaching tolerance" chart was amended by African American writer Langston Hughes and used during the many lectures he gave around the country (Figure 6).

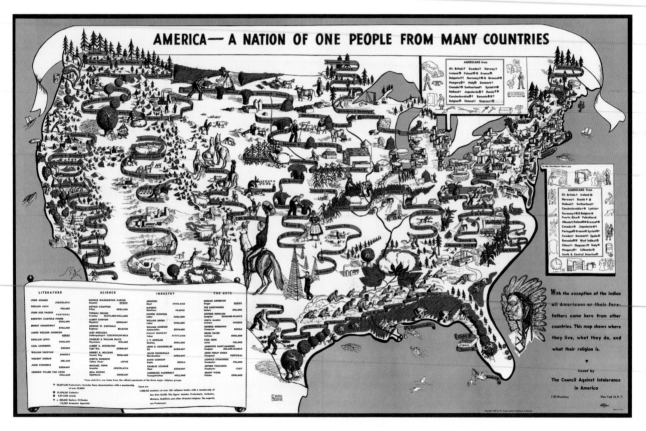

Figure 6.

"America—A nation of one people from many countries," created by Emma Bourne for The Council Against Intolerance in America in 1940. This illustration mapped the United States by ethnic group, profession, and religion. Meant to promote tolerance and unity, materials like these were printed for educational use. The poet Langston Hughes used a red pen to add his own commentary to this map, including an illustration of a burning cross in the American South. Courtesy of Beinecke Rare Book and Manuscript Library, Yale University and by permission of Harold Ober Associates Incorporated.

Grassroots campaigns across the nation, which historian Diana Selig has termed "the cultural gifts movement," organized interfaith groups such as the National Conference of Christians and Jews (NCCJ) with a specific goal of "teaching tolerance."[18] By holding interfaith (and sometimes in the North, interracial) meetings, conferences, symposia, teaching seminars and other events, groups such as the NCCJ sought to counteract white supremacy ideologies of the interwar years.

In 1915, German Jewish immigrant philosopher Horace Kallen coined the term "cultural pluralism" as a new way of thinking about American diversity.[19] He wrote that the diversity of the United States was the strength of the nation and its economy, which was in direct contrast to the notions of "Nordic" superiority. Kallen rejected the idea of the "melting pot" where every difference would dissolve. Rather, he proposed the metaphor of a "symphony" where different groups played distinct instruments and each had a special role to play in the creation of the American nation. Kallen influenced generations of liberal scholars and leaders. His views about so-called "hyphenated Americans" grew more influential after World War II. By 1951, the notion that American cultural diversity was a positive strength began to take hold. Historian Oscar Handlin, the child of Russian Jewish immigrants, opened his Pulitzer Prize–winning book *The Uprooted* with the statement: "Once I thought to write a history of the immigrants in America. Then I discovered that the immigrants *were* American history."[20]

Nonetheless, all groups could not be accommodated by Handlin's benign view of immigration. The nation included millions of formerly enslaved African Americans, who had been unwillingly imported. The United States had also forcibly incorporated highly diverse Indian peoples, and the mixed-race populations of lands that were formerly part of the Spanish empire in the Caribbean and Mexico, and the island populations in the Pacific.

As a result of this complicated history of peopling, the United States developed laws and customs to privilege white people and to control and contain distinct populations of nonwhite peoples. Between the 1880s and 1950s, many state laws mandated racial segregation: the separation of people by color from cradle to beyond the grave.[21] In 1896, the Supreme Court issued the Plessy v. Ferguson decision which declared that "separate could be equal" under the Fourteenth Amendment to the Constitution. After this decision, most states in the South and elsewhere passed highly detailed segregation laws. Definitions of "whiteness" were especially important; the notion that "one drop of colored blood" made a person "nonwhite" was enshrined in law.[22]

By the 1950s, national customs and state laws enforced racial divisions in public and private life. Throughout much of the nation, virtually all colored children were legally or customarily prevented from attending public school with white children. Churches, private clubs, hotels, and restaurants were segregated by custom in most places and in some states by law. Public facilities were segregated by law as well (Figure 7). Even cemeteries had black, white, and "Spanish" sections.[23] In some places, mailmen delivered "colored mail" and "white mail" in separate pouches.

Nevertheless, ironies abounded. While colored people were legally separate and unequal, colored women raised white children, cooked and cleaned in white homes, and nursed white people through illness and old age. Present in many private spaces as servants, colored people could not enter those same spaces as equals. Du Bois's color line was indeed the fundamental problem of the nation.

The key ideological problem with both mainstream and alternative theories of immigration is that they justified continuing discrimination against African Americans and other people of color and did not acknowledge that historically slavery and segregation were just as "American" as ideals of freedom and equality.[24] Many whites viewed African Americans and other ethnic groups such as Puerto Ricans as "unmeltable," singularly unable to be included in the growing ideology of a "nation of immigrants." In many ways, the massive immigrations that occurred from 1880 to 1920 served to harden racial lines, because even those Europeans previously considered to be "lesser" were legally and socially considered to be designated white and favorably compared to nonwhite people. The contradictions between these newer pluralistic ideals and older prejudicial realities accompanied Americans as they entered the maelstrom of World War II.

THE IRONIES OF WORLD WAR II AND THE COLD WAR

The generation who struggled through the Depression and the war years certainly made many sacrifices, but most also perpetuated racial segregation. Consequently, the nostalgic consensus that has grown up about this generation bears little relationship to the historical experiences of many minority Americans of that same generation.[25] The U.S. Armed Forces had been segregated since the mid-nineteenth century. African Americans and darker-skinned Mexicans, Puerto Ricans, and other Latinos served in colored units, while European Americans and sometimes lighter-skinned Latinos served in white units. Most Asian Americans served in separate units as well.

The ironies of fighting against the racist, anti-Semitic Third Reich with segregated troops were clearly visible to many.[26] For the first time, the United States government released patriotic posters, documentary films, and other images of heroic African Americans, such as this poster of Doris "Dorie" Miller[27] (Figure 8). The African American newspaper the *Pittsburgh Courier* supported this notion that African Americans had to fight on two fronts. They supplied their own propaganda through the popular "Double V" campaign—to win victory in the war abroad, then to achieve victory in the war against racism and discrimination at home[28] (Figure 9). Civil rights activists such as A. Philip Randolph and Mary

Figure 8.
Color photolithographic poster of Dorie Miller, designed by Office of War Information art director, David Stone Martin, 1943. Navy messman Dorie Miller was serving on the *U.S.S. West Virginia* when Japan attacked Pearl Harbor in 1941. He rescued a wounded officer and manned an antiaircraft gun to defend the ship. This poster honoring Miller was meant to inspire the black community to participate in the war effort. Courtesy of National Portrait Gallery, Smithsonian Institution.

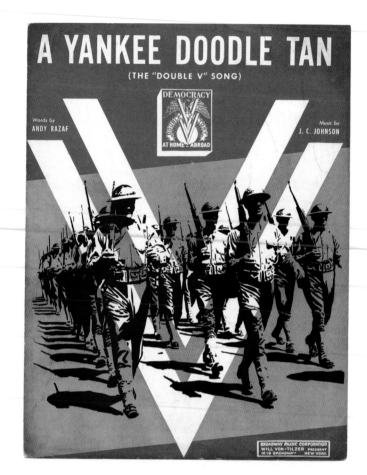

Figure 9.

"A Yankee Doodle Tan (The 'Double V' Song)," words by Andy Razaf and music by J. C. Johnson, published by the Broadway Music Corporation in 1942. As part of the civil rights campaign to gain equal rights for African Americans, this song referred to a war being waged on two fronts: against the Axis powers in World War II, and against an established racial hierarchy at home. Archives Center, National Museum of American History, Smithsonian Institution.

Figure 10.

Christmas Card from World War II soldier Ken Nihei to a resident of the Topaz Relocation Center in Utah. Nihei was a solder in the 442nd Combat Team, a segregated all-Japanese American division of the U.S. Army that served in World War II. While fighting abroad, he sent this card to family members or friends held at the Japanese internment camp in Topaz, Utah. National Museum of American History, Smithsonian Institution, gift of Takako Tsuchiya Endo, Tama Tsuchiya Koda, Keyko Tsuchiya Hall, and Takenori Tsuchiya.

McLeod Bethune campaigned to have jobs in the war industries open to everyone, not just whites.[29]

Many other racial ironies abounded during World War II. While a very small number of German or Italian immigrants (and sometimes their families) were detained, about 120,000 Japanese-born and Japanese American families were forced into internment camps. Meanwhile, the 442nd Regimental Combat Unit, composed entirely of Japanese Americans, served in Europe and became one of the most highly decorated units (Figure 10). Native American "Code Talkers," often from remote, impoverished reservations, sent secret messages for the military in their native language.[30] Minority groups who suffered prejudice and discrimination were critical to the Allied victory abroad as well as the war industries at home.

The war also underscored a newly shared "Americanness," dependent upon a shared "whiteness" of Italians, Jews, Poles, and others whose relatives had immigrated before 1924. In Army platoons and Navy ships, white ethnic groups served alongside "old-stock" Americans from across the country, cementing battle-tested friendships across ethnic lines. Both during and after the war, numerous movies and comic books celebrated ethnically diverse platoons.[31] Immigrant men also volunteered for the Armed Forces in large numbers, including Chaim (later Harold) Kempner. In the 1920s, Kempner immigrated with his Jewish family from

Figure 11.
Uniform Jacket of United States Army Lieutenant Chaim Kempner, an immigrant from Russia, World War II (pictured as donated). Military service and related industries brought diverse people from cities, towns, and rural areas across the nation to live, work, and fight together. In the 1940s every segment of the population mobilized to fight in World War II. National Museum of American History, Smithsonian Institution.

the Pale of Settlement within Russia as a young child and grew up in the United States. When the war came and the Jews of Europe were threatened with extinction, Chaim Kempner volunteered (Figure 11). Because he could speak several languages, he served as a writer and journalist for a number of Army publications.[32] After growing up in an ethnically Jewish community, working for the Army papers enabled him to meet and interview powerful figures such as General Dwight Eisenhower as well as to roam around the region and converse with refugees and others displaced by the war.[33] And like many others, Kempner's military service in a multiethnic unit during the war helped him develop relationships with other Americans that continued after military service.

After the deprivations of the Depression and the dislocations of the war, many Americans retreated to home and family as a sanctuary against an uncertain future during the increasing tensions and rivalries between the United States and the Soviet Union that came to be known as the Cold War. These young veterans and their wives left behind crowded multigenerational households in urban ethnic neighborhoods, defined by language, religion, foodways, and other customs from their homelands, and moved to new homes in the suburbs. In the years between 1944 and 1960, 60 million new Americans were born, creating a vast new group of consumers, especially of baby and child products, toys, games, family sedans, and all manner of goods[34] (Figure 12). Transistor radios, portable record players, and powerful new alternative radio stations provided this generation of "baby boomers" with access to previously segregated music such as

Figure 12.
Thirteen-fluid-ounce can of Gerber baby formula, 1964–1973. Baby formula and other infant- and child-rearing goods flooded the growing consumer market during the post–World War II baby boom. National Museum of American History, Smithsonian Institution, the Fournet Drugstore Collection.

rhythm and blues, early rock and roll, and other cultural forms that may also have helped shift cultural dynamics in the post-war years.

As planned neighborhoods, nicknamed "Levittowns" after real-estate developments in the Northeast, were built all across the nation, many white people established their "nuclear families" in the segregated suburbs. As housing covenants that discriminated against Jews were declared illegal, Jewish people also joined all-white suburbs.[35] African Americans and other people of color, in contrast, were usually excluded by restrictive covenants, government policies, and "redlining" by insurance companies, banks, and the federal government, thereby losing crucial opportunities to own homes and build wealth as many white Americans were doing.[36]

At the same time, many African American, Puerto Rican, Mexican American, and Asian American veterans came home and organized against segregation and racist prejudices.[37] The NAACP brought a slew of new legal cases to local and federal courts. New organizations, such as the Southern Christian Leadership Conference (SCLC), the Student Nonviolent Coordinating Committee (SNCC), and others sponsored boycotts, marches, and protests to argue that "separate" was inherently unequal, unconstitutional, and immoral.[38]

During the Cold War, the United States sent propaganda materials and news media worldwide to proclaim American democracy. The Soviet Union and other communist governments pointed out episodes of American hypocrisy, such as black churches being bombed, and interracial, interfaith marchers being attacked by police and mobs. These events were covered on television and in newspapers around the world, giving other countries reason to balk at American claims of moral superiority.[39]

In response to a new direct action movement and the history of service during the war by all minority groups, a series of court decisions ultimately reinforced the civil rights of all Americans. The most famous of these is the Supreme Court rulings in Brown v. Board of Education (1954, 1955), which declared segregated public schools unconstitutional.[40] These court cases were followed by the passage of the Civil Rights Act (1964) and the Voting Rights Act (1965), which marked the beginning of a legally desegregated society and what many hoped would be a new "equal opportunity society."[41] While these efforts began the process of desegregation, both in the South and the North there was profound violence against civil rights workers, the bombing of churches, and massive resistance which resulted in the closing of whole school systems, the paving over of public pools, and the constant surveillance by police and government officials of people deemed to be suspect.

All these postwar changes created cracks in the strict legal walls barring most immigration from all of Asia, Africa, and southern and eastern Europe. Exemptions and special laws were passed in the 1940s and 1950s to allow in various new kinds of refugees, exiles, special excepted categories, and asylum seekers. Congress found an increasing number of ways to let in people fleeing Communist oppression in eastern Europe, the Soviet Union, and Cuba.[42] These new forms of access even extended to previously banned immigrants from Asia, including military allies China, Taiwan, and Korea. As Section Four of this volume details, in 1965 Democratic Representative Emanuel Celler from New York and Democratic Senator Philip Hart from Michigan sponsored a successful new Immigration and Nationality Act that opened the nation to the entire world for the first time in 80 years.[43]

Nonetheless, white supremacist values remained powerful. Many Southern states mounted massive resistance to these changes. When the Rev. Martin Luther King led an attempted march in the suburbs of Chicago, he encountered unmitigated racism and resistance that matched, if not exceeded, the response of Southern communities. In 1968, Richard Nixon was elected to the presidency through a coalition of what he called the "silent majority" of Northern working-class whites who had previously voted for the Democratic party but were now disillusioned and the "Southern strategy" that attracted white Democrats to join the Republican party by appealing to their beliefs that segregation should continue as a matter of states' rights. Meanwhile, the difficulties and violence of the Vietnam War reinforced many older prejudices about Asians and Asian Americans. For example, the lingo of the men fighting the war and characterizing their enemy as "gooks" entered the language of popular culture through news broadcasts and films.[44]

Today, years later, we live in a time when civil rights advances are being reinterpreted and arguably weakened by recent Supreme Court decisions. Nonetheless, this earlier socio-political activism widened the definition of what it meant to be American, including and embracing the contributions of African Americans and others whose historical and cultural experiences had also been ignored. Many schools, businesses, and governments now celebrate Black History Month each February. This holiday was established by Carter G. Woodson as Negro History Week in Chicago in 1926 (Figure 13). In 1976, during the Bicentennial of the Declaration of Independence, the month-long celebration was officially recognized by President Gerald R. Ford.[45]

Figure 13.
Portrait of Dr. Carter Woodson, Washington, D.C., in 1915. Woodson was a scholar and activist who advocated for wider acceptance and appreciation of African American history. He established Negro History Week in 1926, which later was officially recognized and expanded to Black History Month, celebrated each February. Scurlock Studio Records, ca. 1905-1994, Archives Center, National Museum of American History, Smithsonian Institution.

Black History Month paved the way for the celebration of the histories and cultures of other people of color, such as Hispanic Heritage Month (mid-September to mid-October), Native American History Month (November), Asian and Pacific American History Month (May), and others.[46] Though the full history of these cultural shifts has not yet been written, the musical preferences, fashion sensibilities, language, and aesthetic concerns of many young white Americans swung away from middle-class Anglo-conformity and normativity. This teenage generation began to seek out encounters with those cultural expressions, such as music and dance, which had been created in the colored enclaves of American society. All of these nonmaterial, intangible aspects of the American experience may also have contributed to the greater acceptance of a wider notion of cultural diversity.

CRACKS IN THE COLOR LINE

In 1900, the Americanization project was in full swing. But, after the challenges and sacrifices of World War II, the stories of more recently arrived Americans were recognized and celebrated as the authentic American experience.[47] In 1960,

John F. Kennedy, a war hero, was elected as the first Irish Catholic president and considered to be the first of "immigrant stock." In the years since Du Bois's death, numerous alternative metaphors have been offered to replace "melting pot," including "salad bowl," "mosaic," tapestry," and "quilt." During the 1990s, the term "multiculturalism" became widely used. Each of these efforts embodied a crucial but not total change in cultural attitudes. Each seismic alteration produced a furious response from those who still clung to nativist ideas and who had remained powerful in American society.

In the twenty-first century, many Americans, though far from all, would agree that the nation is now made up of ethnically and racially diverse people who are nonetheless fully American.[48] While racial and religious prejudices remain present, and violence is still possible, Kallen's ideas about cultural pluralism have become widely accepted among both liberal sectors and younger generations. While Americans who can remember a segregated nation are now passing into history, their stories and struggles remain relevant. All Americans living today exist in a nation shaped by these earlier prejudices, conflicts, ironies, and changing ideas about how to live in a diverse nation.

NOTES

1. W. E. B. Du Bois, *The Souls of Black Folk* (Chicago: A. C. McClurg and Co., 1903), vii–viii.

2. The Fourteenth Amendment redefined citizenship by asserting that the term "citizen" includes all people who were born or naturalized in the United States. The Amendment also states that all citizens are deserving of "equal protection before the law." To read the amendment visit "Primary Documents in American History," Library of Congress, last modified 20 April 2015, http://www.loc.gov/rr/program/bib/ourdocs/14thamendment.html.

3. For more information about this time period see Eric Foner, *Reconstruction: America's Unfinished Revolution, 1863–1877* (New York: Harper & Row, 1988).

4. Laws were passed in many southern states that required people to pay a tax, known as a "poll tax" to vote. In other words, if you wanted to vote, you had to make a payment of $1.00 or $1.50 in order to vote. These taxes were cumulative, so that if you had tried to vote ten years ago and now wanted to vote again, your tax was not $1.00, but $10.00. Everyone had to pay the tax to vote, but in practice only poor people had difficulty paying the tax. Poll taxes were declared unconstitutional in 1964 by the 24th amendment to the U.S. Constitution.

5. Werner Sollors, *Beyond Ethnicity: Consent and Descent in American Culture* (New York: Oxford University Press, 1986); Werner Sollors, ed., *The Invention of Ethnicity* (New York: Oxford University Press, 1989).

6. The people in these unacknowledged colonies were never declared citizens of the United States. Even when people in the territories did receive citizenship, as Puerto Ricans did in 1917, often the full rights of citizens as outlined in the U.S. Constitution were ruled by various courts not to apply to them. For more on this, see

Bartholomew H. Sparrow, *The Insular Cases and the Emergence of American Empire* (Lawrence: University Press of Kansas, 2006).

7. Under the Naturalization Act of 1790 the law limited full citizenship to free white men. Although this law had been on the books since 1790, there was no federal government agency to police the borders until 1924. Newly constituted, the Border Patrol focused their attention on the United States–Mexico border nearly exclusively. It was originally set up to prevent Chinese immigrants from crossing illegally into the United States, since their immigration had been largely banned since 1882. On the term "illegal alien," see Mae M. Ngai, *Impossible Subjects: Illegal Aliens and the Making of Modern America* (Princeton: Princeton University Press, 2004).

8. For more on this topic, see Theodore Allen, *The Invention of the White Race* (London, Verso Press, 1994). See also Peter Kolchin, "Whiteness Studies: The New History of Race in America," *The Journal of American History* 89(1)(June 2002):154–73, doi:10.2307/2700788; David Roediger, *The Invention of Whiteness: Race and the Making of the American Working Class* (London, Verso Press, 1991).

9. Only native people can be considered indigenous to the Americas. These earlier immigrants were predominantly from Great Britain, including the English, Scottish, Welsh, and the Protestant Irish, though they often called themselves "natives." Northern European groups were predominantly German and Dutch, with a small number of Scandinavians. Saying "My ancestors came on the Mayflower" was a way of expressing the notion that these were the original, native, Americans. Irish Catholic immigration is somewhat different because that group had a distinct history of subjugation by the British on the island of Ireland. Significant numbers of Irish Catholics began to arrive in the 1840s and the early 1850s as a result of famine and extreme poverty. For more on earlier racial designations, see Thomas A. Guglielmo, *White on Arrival: Italians, Race, Color,* and *Power in Chicago, 1890–1945* (New York: Oxford University Press, 2003).

10. For more on this topic of Anglo-dominance, see Desmond S. King, *Making Americans: Immigration, Race, and the Origins of the Diverse Democracy* (Cambridge, Mass.: Harvard University Press, 2000).

11. Helene Hayes, *U.S. Immigration Policy and the Undocumented* (Westport, Conn.: Praeger Publishers, 2001). For more on this topic: Steven G. Koven and Frank Götzke, *American Immigration Policy: Confronting the Nation's Challenges* (New York: Springer, 2010); Stuart J. Wright, *An Emotional Gauntlet: From Life in Peacetime America to the War in European Skies* (Madison: University of Wisconsin Press, 2004); Aristide R. Zolberg, *A Nation by Design: Immigration Policy in the Fashioning of America* (Cambridge, Mass.: Harvard University Press, 2006). See also the essay in this volume by Alan Kraut.

12. For more on the history of violent white supremacist organizations and their connections with police in many states, see Kenneth T. Jackson, *The Ku Klux Klan in the City 1915–1930* (Chicago: I. R. Dee, 1992). Other sources include: Diane McWhorter, *Carry Me Home: Birmingham, Alabama: The Climactic Battle of the Civil Rights Revolution* (New York: Simon & Schuster, 2001); Leonard J. Moore, *Citizen Klansmen: The Ku Klux Klan in Indiana, 1921–1928* (Chapel Hill: University of North Carolina Press, 1991); Allan W. Trelease, *White Terror: The Ku Klux Klan Conspiracy and Southern Reconstruction* (Baton Rouge: Louisiana State University Press, 1995); Wyn Craig Wade, *The Fiery Cross: The Ku Klux Klan in America* (Oxford: Oxford University Press, 1998). For groups other than the KKK, see: Colin Flint, *Spaces of Hate: Geographies of Discrimination and Intolerance in the USA* (New York: Routledge, 2004); George Fredrickson, *White Supremacy* (London: Oxford University Press, 1981).

13. For more on the history of lynching, see: Bruce Baker, *This Mob Will Surely Take My Life:*

Lynchings in the Carolinas, 1871–1947 (London: Continuum, 2008); W. Fitzhugh Brundage, ed., *Under the Sentence of Death: Lynching in the South* (Chapel Hill: University of North Carolina Press, 1997); Paul Ortiz, *Emancipation Betrayed: the Hidden History of Black Organizing and White Violence in Florida from Reconstruction to the Bloody Election of 1920* (Berkeley: University of California Press, 2005). Some of the most infamous race riots include Springfield, Illinois (1908); St. Louis, Missouri (1917); Chicago, Illinois (1919); Tulsa, Oklahoma (1921); Rosewood, Florida (1923).

14. Madison Grant was a leading conservationist who supported the establishment of national parks and was a vocal advocate of the Boy Scouts and other examples of "muscular Christianity" which would keep the Aryan population strong. Though today his work would be called "pseudoscience," in his lifetime he was seen as a prominent scientist who justified inequality based on race. His several books include *The Passing of the Great Race or the Racial Basis of European History* (New York: C. Scribner's Sons, 1921), *The Founders of the Republic on Immigration, Naturalization, and Aliens* (New York: C. Scribner's Sons, 1928), and *Conquest of a Continent or the Expansion of Race* (New York: C. Scribner's Sons, 1934). Other noted "race scientists" include Harry H. Laughlin, *Eugenical Sterilization in the United States* (Chicago: Psychopathic Laboratory of the Municipal Court of Chicago, 1922). Laughlin thought that sterilization based on scientific principles would prevent the inferior from propagating and thereby debasing the national character with their progeny.

15. For more on this, see Eric. P. Kaufmann, *The Rise and Fall of Anglo-America.* (Cambridge, Mass.: Harvard University Press, 2004). For more information on Jane Addams, who won the Nobel Peace Prize in 1931, see James Weber Linn, *Jane Addams: A Biography* (Champaign: University of Illinois Press, 2000) and Louise W.

Knight, *Citizen: Jane Addams and the Struggle for Democracy* (Chicago: University of Chicago Press, 2005). For a sample of Dewey's writing, see John Dewey, *Democracy and Education: An Introduction to the Philosophy of Education* [1916] (New York: WLC Books, 2009). For more information on Dewey, see Nathan Crick, *Democracy & Rhetoric: John Dewey on the Arts of Becoming* (Columbia: University of South Carolina Press, 2010); Stephen M. Fishman and Lucille McCarthy, *John Dewey and the Philosophy and Practice of Hope* (Champaign: University of Illinois Press, 2007).

16. The NAACP was founded in 1909 in response to a violent white race riot in Springfield, Illinois in 1908 (seen as very symbolic, as this was the hometown and burial place of Abraham Lincoln). W. E. B. Du Bois was another founding member. He became the founding editor of the NAACP magazine, *The Crisis.* For more on the history of the NAACP, see Patricia Sullivan, *Lift Every Voice: The NAACP and the Making of the Civil Rights Movement* (New York: The New Press, 2009).

17. For more on theories of education as a pathway to develop tolerance, see Diana Selig, *Americans All: The Cultural Gifts Movement* (Cambridge, Mass.: Harvard University, 2008). In her book, Selig includes analyses of key figures of this "cultural gift" movement of many different organizations, including Everett R. Clinchy of the National Conference of Christians and Jews, Rachel Davis DuBois, a Quaker educator and activist, and philosopher and educator John Dewey, as well as Horace Kallen, the best-known philosopher of cultural pluralism.

18. For more information on this movement, see Selig, *Americans All.* For more on the history of Highlander, see the history section of the group's web page: www.highlandercenter.org.

19. See Horace Kallen, "Democracy Versus the Melting Pot," *The Nation* (25 February 1915), available online at http://www.exp098.msu.edu/people/kallen.htm. See also Kallen, *Culture and*

Democracy in the United States [1924] (New York: Arno Press, 1970). For more on Kallen, see Sidney Ratner, "Horace Kallen and Cultural Pluralism," *Modern Judaism* 4(2)(May 1984):185–200, http://www.jstor.org/stable/1396461.

20. Oscar Handlin, *The Uprooted: The Epic Story of the Great Migrations that Made the American People* (New York: Grosset and Dunlap, 1951).

21. For more on the laws of segregation, see Paul Finkleman, ed*., Lynching, Racial Violence, and the Law* (New York: Garland Press, 1992).

22. A foundational text on American segregation and its justifications is C. Vann Woodward, *The Strange Career of Jim Crow* (New York: Oxford University Press, 1974). See also Woodward, *The Burden of Southern History* (Baton Rouge: Louisiana State University Press, 1993). Additional sources include Paul Finkelman, *Encyclopedia of African American History, 1896 to the Present: From the Age of Segregation to the Twenty-First Century* (New York: Oxford University Press, 1964) and Douglas Massey and Nancy Denton, *American Apartheid: Segregation and the Making of the Underclass* (Cambridge, Mass.: Harvard University Press, 1993).

23. The contemporary term "Latinos" was not widely used before the 1980s. In areas such as South Texas, the Southwest, and Southern California, people of Mexican descent named themselves *Tejanos, Hispanos,* or *Californios* as well as *Mexicanos.* When signs were put up to keep the "colored Mexicans" out of white establishments during these years, the term "Spanish" was frequently used, along with ethnic slurs.

24. These key historical connections are raised by Michelle Alexander in *The New Jim Crow: Mass Incarceration in the Age of Color Blindness* (New York: New Press, 2010) and Douglass A. Blackmon in *Slavery by Another Name: The Re-Enslavement of Black Americans from the Civil War to World War II* (New York: Anchor Books, 2009).

25. The World War II generation has become widely referred to in popular culture as "the greatest generation" of Americans, following the lead of television journalist Tom Brokaw, *The Greatest Generation* (New York: Random House, 1981).

26. In 1944, the United States Army released a documentary film, *The Negro Soldier,* about the service of African American men in the nation's wars (tactfully leaving out the Civil War). Directed by Frank Capra, this was a follow up to his film series, *Why We Fight.* Initially, the Army officials feared that the film would be controversial, but it was widely popular among black and white servicemen. It was so popular that after the war it was released stateside and is credited with changing some people's opinions of African Americans' service to the nation. See Thomas Cripps and David Culbert, "The Negro Soldier (1944): Film Propaganda in Black and White," *American Quarterly* 31(5) (Winter 1979):616–40. http://www.jstor.org/stable/2712429.

27. For more information, see Richard E. Miller, *The Messman Chronicles: African Americans in the U.S. Navy, 1932–1943* (Annapolis, Md.: Naval Institute Press, 2004).

28. For more information on the Double V campaign and the agitation for the desegregation of the U.S. Armed Forces, see: James Rawn Jr., *The Double V: How Wars, Protest, and Harry Truman Desegregated America's Military* (New York: Bloomsbury, 2013); Ronald Takaki, *Double Victory: A Multicultural History of America in World War II* (New York: Little, Brown, 2000); Jon E. Taylor, *Freedom to Serve: Truman, Civil Rights, and Executive Order 9981* (New York: Routledge, 2013).

29. For more on this, see: Andrew E. Kersten and Clarence Lang, eds., *Reframing Randolph: Labor, Black Freedom, and the Legacies of A. Philip Randolph* (New York: New York University Press, 2015); David Welky, *Marching Across the Color Line: A. Philip Randolph and Civil Rights in the World War II Era* (New York: Oxford University Press, 2013). For additional information on Mary McLeod Bethune, see: Rackham Holt,

Mary McLeod Bethune: A Biography (Garden City, N.Y.: Doubleday and Co., 1964); Audrey Thomas McCluskey and Elaine M. Smith, eds., *Building a Better World: Essays and Selected Documents* (Bloomington: Indiana University Press, 1999).

30. The technique of using Native American language speakers to send secret tactical messages was pioneered in World War I by Cherokee and Choctaw men. For more information on this, see: Salley McClain, *Navajo Weapon: The Navajo Code Talkers* (Tucson: Rio Nuevo Publishers, 2001); William C. Meadows, *The Comanche Code Talkers of World War II* (Austin: University of Texas Press, 2002).

31. Examples of such films include: John Wayne, *Sands of Iwo Jima,* directed by Allan Dwan (Los Angeles: Republic Pictures, 1949), John Wayne and Robert Ryan, *Flying Leathernecks,* directed by Nicholas Ray (Burbank, Cal.: RKO Radio Pictures, 1951), John Wayne and Henry Fonda, *The Longest Day,* produced by Darryl F. Zanuck (Burbank, Cal.: Twentieth Century Fox, 1962), and Burt Lancaster, Montgomery Clift, and Frank Sinatra, *From Here to Eternity,* directed by Fred Zinnemann (Burbank, Cal.: Columbia Pictures, 1963), based on the James Jones novel of the same name: Jones, *From Here to Eternity* (New York: Charles Scribner's Sons, 1951).

32. Chaim Kempner could speak Hebrew, German, Yiddish, Lithuanian, and Russian, according to his daughter, Aviva Kempner. Conversation with Aviva Kempner, daughter and donor, 24 July 2016, and excerpts from Chaim Kempner's writings sent by e-mail to author from Ms. Kempner.

33. Conversation with Aviva Kempner, daughter and donor, 24 July 2016, and excerpts from Chaim Kempner's writings sent by e-mail to author from Ms. Kempner. In Berlin, while writing for *The Grooper,* Kempner met and married Hanka Ciesla. Ciesla was a Polish Jewish woman who had survived the war passing as a Catholic in a work camp. Both of them lost most of their European family members in the death camps, although Ciesla's younger brother Dudek survived Auschwitz. Their daughter, Aviva Kempner, donated her father's military jacket to the National Museum of American History in 2015.

34. For more information on the formation of the American suburbs, see: James A. Jacobs, *Detached America: Building Houses in Postwar Suburbia* (Charlottesville: University of Virginia Press, 2015); Kenneth T. Jackson, *Crabgrass Frontier: The Suburbanization of the United States* (New York: Oxford University Press, 1985). For more on these families and the baby boom, see Elaine Tyler May, *Homeward Bound: American Families in the Cold War Era* (New York: Basic Books, 1988); Jessica Weiss, *To Have and to Hold: Marriage, the Baby Boom, and Social Change* (Chicago: University of Chicago Press, 2000).

35. For more on this process of change, see Hasia R. Diner, *The Jews of the United States 1654–2000* (Oakland: University of California Press, 2006).

36. For additional information specifically on African American suburbs, see Andrew Wiese, *Places of their Own: African American Suburbanization in the Twentieth Century* (Chicago: University of Chicago Press, 2004). See also the essay by Davarian Baldwin in this volume.

37. A brief list of the many veterans involved in the postwar civil rights movement include Medgar Evers (NAACP), Amzie Moore and Aaron Henry of the Regional Council of Negro Leadership (RCNL), Dr. Hector P. Garcia, founder of the American G.I. Forum, and Daniel K. Inouye, who was first elected to the House of Representatives from Hawaii after it became a state in 1959. In 1962, he was elected to the U.S. Senate where he served for nearly 50 years.

38. Other important interracial, interfaith civil rights organizations of this era included the Congress of Racial Equality (CORE), the Urban League, and the National Council of Negro Women (NCNW). There were numerous other

local and regional organizations across the country, such as the Mississippi Democratic Freedom Party.

39. For additional information on the bombings in Birmingham and the civil rights movement, see McWhorter, *Carry Me Home* and Charles E. Connerly, *"The Most Segregated City in America": City Planning and Civil Rights in Birmingham, 1920–1980* (Charlottesville: University of Virginia Press, 2005).

40. There was an important case prior to Brown v. Board of Education. In 1947, a federal appeals court in California rendered a decision in the Mendez et al. v. Westminster School District of Orange County. In its ruling, the United States Court of Appeals for the Ninth Circuit held that the segregation of Mexican and Mexican American students into separate "Mexican schools" was unconstitutional. However, because this was a California-specific case, it did not affect schools across the nation as did the Brown v. Board cases in 1954 and 1955.

41. Robert Dallek, *Flawed Giant: Lyndon Johnson and His Times, 1961–1973* (New York: Oxford University Press, 1998). For additional information on Nixon's "Southern Strategy," see Earl Black and Merle Black, *The Rise of Southern Republicans* (Cambridge, Mass.: Harvard University Press, 2003). For more on the Voting Rights Act, see Gary May, *Bending toward Justice: The Voting Rights Act and the Transformation of American Democracy* (New York: Basic Books, 2013).

42. For more information on immigration to the United States from Communist countries after World War II, see: Maria Cristina Garcia, *Havana USA: Cuban Exiles and Cuban Americans in South Florida, 1959–1994* (Berkeley: University of California Press, 1996) and Ngai, *Impossible Subjects*. See also the essay in this volume by Sojin Kim.

43. Bill Ong Hing, *Defining America: Through Immigration Policy* (Philadelphia: Temple University Press, 2012), 95; Lyndon B. Johnson's remarks at the signing of the Immigration Bill, Liberty Island, New York, 3 October 1965, http://www.lbjlib.utexas.edu/Johnson/archives.hom/speeches.hom/651003.asp.

44. For more on how the Vietnam War reinforced old stereotypes of Asian Americans, see Erika Lee, *The Making of Asian America: A History* (New York: Simon and Schuster, 2015).

45. For more on Woodson, see: Claire Corbould, *Becoming African Americans: The Public Life of Harlem 1919–1939* (Cambridge, Mass.: Harvard University Press, 2009); Jacqueline Anne Goggin, *Carter G. Woodson: A Life in Black History* (Baton Rouge: Louisiana State University Press, 1993).

46. During the late 1960s and early 1970s, many historically black universities were attempting to expand Black History Week into a full month. According to some sources, the first celebration of Black History Month took place at Kent State University in 1970. In 1976, during the United States Bicentennial, Black History Month was formally recognized by the federal government. For more on how certain aspects of African American culture came to be incorporated into a liberal mainstream, see Gary Gerstle, *American Crucible: Race and Nation in the Twentieth Century* (Princeton: Princeton University Press, 2001).

47. Robert L. Fleegler, *Ellis Island Nation: Immigration Policy and American Identity in the Twentieth Century* (Philadelphia: University of Pennsylvania Press, 2013).

48. Since 11 September 2001, some of the most urgent contemporary religious prejudices in the United States seem to be focused on Muslim followers and the Islamic faith. Numerous violent incidents have occurred around the country and mosques have been defaced. At the same time, violence against African Americans remains high throughout the nation.

BIBLIOGRAPHY

Alexander, Michelle. *The New Jim Crow: Mass Incarceration in the Age of Color Blindness.* New York: New Press, 2010.

Allen, Theodore. *The Invention of the White Race.* London: Verso Press, 1994.

Baker, Bruce. *This Mob Will Surely Take My Life: Lynchings in the Carolinas, 1871–1947.* London: Continuum, 2008.

Black, Earl, and Merle Black. *The Rise of Southern Republicans.* Cambridge, Mass.: Harvard University Press, 2003.

Blackmon, Douglas A. *Slavery by Another Name: The Re-Enslavement of Black Americans from the Civil War to World War II.* New York: Anchor Books, 2009.

Brokaw, Tom. *The Greatest Generation.* New York: Random House, 1981.

Brundage, W. Fitzhugh, ed. *Under the Sentence of Death: Lynching in the South.* Chapel Hill: University of North Carolina Press, 1997.

Connerly, Charles E. *"The Most Segregated City in America": City Planning and Civil Rights in Birmingham, 1920–1980.* Charlottesville: University of Virginia Press, 2005.

Corbould, Claire. *Becoming African Americans: The Public Life of Harlem 1919–1939.* Cambridge, Mass.: Harvard University Press, 2009.

Crick, Nathan. *Democracy & Rhetoric: John Dewey on the Arts of Becoming.* Columbia: University of South Carolina Press, 2010.

Cripps, Thomas, and David Culbert. "The Negro Soldier (1944): Film Propaganda in Black and White," *American Quarterly* 31(5) (Winter 1979):616–40. http://www.jstor.org/stable/2712429 (accessed 11 November 2016).

Dallek, Robert. *Flawed Giant: Lyndon Johnson and His Times, 1961–1973.* New York: Oxford University Press, 1998.

Dewey, John. *Democracy and Education: An Introduction to the Philosophy of Education.* New York: WLC Books, 2009.

Diner, Hasia R. *The Jews of the United States 1654–2000.* Oakland: University of California Press, 2006.

Du Bois, W. E. B. *The Souls of Black Folk.* Chicago: A. C. McClurg and Co., 1903.

Finkleman, Paul, ed. *Encyclopedia of African American History, 1896 to the Present: From the Age of Segregation to the Twenty-First Century.* New York: Oxford University Press, 1964.

———, ed. *Lynching, Racial Violence, and the Law.* New York: Garland Press, 1992.

Fishman, Stephen M., and Lucille McCarthy. *John Dewey and the Philosophy and Practice of Hope.* Champaign: University of Illinois Press, 2007.

Fleegler, Robert L. *Ellis Island Nation: Immigration Policy and American Identity in the Twentieth Century.* Philadelphia: University of Pennsylvania Press, 2013.

Flint, Colin. *Spaces of Hate: Geographies of Discrimination and Intolerance in the USA.* New York: Routledge, 2004.

Flying Leathernecks. Directed by Nicholas Ray. Burbank, Cal.: RKO Radio Pictures, 1951.

Foner, Eric. *Reconstruction: America's Unfinished Revolution, 1863–1877.* New York: Harper & Row, 1988.

Fredrickson, George. *White Supremacy.* London: Oxford University Press, 1981.

From Here to Eternity. Directed by Fred Zinnemann. Burbank, Cal.: Columbia Pictures, 1963.

Garcia, Maria Cristina. *Havana USA: Cuban Exiles and Cuban Americans in South Florida, 1959–1994.* Berkeley: University of California Press, 1996.

Gerstle, Gary. *American Crucible: Race and Nation in the Twentieth Century.* Princeton: Princeton University Press, 2001.

Goggin, Jacqueline Anne. *Carter G. Woodson: A Life in Black History.* Baton Rouge: Louisiana State University Press, 1993.

Grant, Madison. *Conquest of a Continent or the Expansion of Race*. New York: C. Scribner's Sons, 1934.

———. *The Founders of the Republic on Immigration, Naturalization, and Aliens*. New York: C. Scribner's Sons, 1928.

———. *The Passing of the Great Race or the Racial Basis of European History*. New York: C. Scribner's Sons, 1921.

Guglielmo, Thomas A. *White on Arrival: Italians, Race, Color, and Power in Chicago 1890–1945*. New York: Oxford University Press, 2000.

Handlin, Oscar. *The Uprooted: The Epic Story of the Great Migrations that Made the American People*. New York: Grosset and Dunlap, 1951.

Hayes, Helene. *U.S. Immigration Policy and the Undocumented*. Westport, Conn.: Praeger Publishers, 2001.

Highlander Research and Education Center. "History". Last modified 2012. http://highlandercenter.org/about-us/history/ (accessed 11 November 2016).

Hing, Bill Ong. *Defining America: Through Immigration Policy*. Philadelphia: Temple University Press, 2012.

Holt, Rackham. *Mary McLeod Bethune: A Biography*. Garden City, N.Y.: Doubleday and Co., 1964.

Jackson, Kenneth T. *Crabgrass Frontier: The Suburbanization of the United States*. New York: Oxford University Press, 1985.

———. *The Ku Klux Klan in the City 1915–1930*. Chicago: I. R. Dee, 1992.

Jacobs, James A. *Detached America: Building Houses in Postwar Suburbia*. Charlottesville: University of Virginia Press, 2015.

Johnson, Lyndon B. "President Lyndon B. Johnson's Remarks at the Signing of the Immigration Bill, Liberty Island, New York, October 3, 1965." Lyndon Baines Johnson Library and Museum, Austin, Tex.. http://www.lbjlib.utexas.edu/johnson/archives.hom/speeches.hom/651003.asp (accessed 11 November 2016).

Jones, James. *From Here to Eternity*. New York: Charles Scribner's Sons, 1951.

Kallen, Horace. "Democracy Versus the Melting Pot," *The Nation*, 25 February 1915. Available online at http://www.exp098.msu.edu/people/kallen.htm (accessed 11 November 2016).

———. *Culture and Democracy in the United States*. New York: Arno Press, 1970.

Kaufmann, Eric P. *The Rise and Fall of Anglo-America*. Cambridge, Mass.: Harvard University Press, 2004.

Kersten, Andrew E. and Clarence Lang, eds., *Reframing Randolph: Labor, Black Freedom, and the Legacies of A. Philip Randolph*. New York: New York University Press, 2015.

King, Desmond S. *Making Americans: Immigration, Race, and the Origins of the Diverse Democracy*. Cambridge, Mass.: Harvard University Press, 2000.

Knight, Louise W. *Citizen: Jane Addams and the Struggle for Democracy*. Chicago: University of Chicago Press, 2005.

Kolchin, Peter. "Whiteness Studies: The New History of Race in America," *The Journal of American History*. 89(1)(June 2002):154–73. doi:10.2307/2700788.

Koven, Steven G., and Frank Götzke. *American Immigration Policy: Confronting the Nation's Challenges*. New York: Springer, 2010.

Laughlin, Harry H. *Eugenical Sterilization in the United States*. Chicago: Psychopathic Laboratory of the Municipal Court of Chicago, 1922.

Lee, Erika. *The Making of Asian America: A History*. New York: Simon and Schuster, 2015.

Library of Congress. "Primary Documents in American History." Washington, D.C., 2015. http://www.loc.gov/rr/program/bib/ourdocs/14thamendment.html (accessed 11 November 2016).

Linn, James Weber. *Jane Addams: A Biography*. Champaign: University of Illinois Press, 2000.

Massey, Douglass, and Nancy Denton. *American Apartheid: Segregation and the Making of the*

Underclass. Cambridge, Mass.: Harvard University Press, 1993.

May, Elaine Tyler. *Homeward Bound: American Families in the Cold War Era*. New York: Basic Books, 1988.

May, Gary. *Bending Toward Justice: The Voting Rights Act and the Transformation of American Democracy*. New York: Basic Books, 2013.

McClain, Salley. *Navajo Weapon: The Navajo Code Talkers*. Tuscon, Ariz.: Rio Nuevo Publishers, 2001.

McCluskey, Audrey Thomas, and Elaine M. Smith, eds. *Building a Better World: Essays and Selected Documents*. Bloomington: Indiana University Press, 1999.

McWhorter, Diane. *Carry Me Home: Birmingham, Alabama: The Climactic Battle of the Civil Rights Revolution*. New York: Simon & Schuster, 2001.

Meadows, William C. *The Comanche Code Talkers of World War II*. Austin: University of Texas Press, 2002.

Miller, Richard E. *The Messman Chronicles: African Americans in the U.S. Navy, 1932–1943*. Annapolis, Md.: Naval Institute Press, 2004.

Moore, Leonard J. *Citizen Klansmen: The Ku Klux Klan in Indiana, 1921–1928*. Chapel Hill: University of North Carolina Press, 1991.

Ngai, Mae M. *Impossible Subjects: Illegal Aliens and the Making of Modern America*. Princeton: Princeton University Press, 2004.

Ortiz, Paul. *Emancipation Betrayed: The Hidden History of Black Organizing and White Violence in Florida from Reconstruction to the Bloody Election of 1920*. Berkeley: University of California Press, 2005.

Ratner, Sidney. "Horace Kallen and Cultural Pluralism," *Modern Judaism* 4(2)(May 1984):185–200. http://www.jstor.org/stable/1396461 (accessed 11 November 2016).

Rawn, James Jr. *The Double V: How Wars, Protest, and Harry Truman Desegregated America's Military*. New York: Bloomsbury, 2013.

Roediger, David. *The Invention of Whiteness: Race and the Making of the American Working Class*. London: Verso Press, 1991.

Sands of Iwo Jima. Directed by Allan Dwan. Los Angeles: Republic Pictures, 1949.

Selig, Diana. *Americans All: The Cultural Gifts Movement*. Cambridge, Mass.: Harvard University Press, 2008.

Sollors, Werner. *Beyond Ethnicity: Consent and Descent in American Culture*. New York: Oxford University Press, 1986.

_____, ed. *The Invention of Ethnicity*. New York: Oxford University Press, 1989.

Sparrow, Bartholomew H. *The Insular Cases and the Emergence of American Empire*. Lawrence: University Press of Kansas, 2006.

Sullivan, Patricia. *Lift Every Voice: The NAACP and the Making of the Civil Rights Movement*. New York: The New Press, 2009.

Takaki, Ronald. *Double Victory: A Multicultural History of America in World War II*. New York: Little, Brown, 2000.

Taylor, Jon E. *Freedom to Serve: Truman, Civil Rights, and Executive Order 9981*. New York: Routledge, 2013.

The Longest Day. Produced by Darryl F. Zanuck. Burbank, Cal.: Twentieth Century Fox, 1962.

The Negro Soldier. Produced by Frank Capra. Washington, D.C.: United States Government, 1944.

Trelease, Allan W. *White Terror: The Ku Klux Klan Conspiracy and Southern Reconstruction*. Baton Rouge: Louisiana State University Press, 1995.

Wade, Wyn Craig. *The Fiery Cross: The Ku Klux Klan in America*. Oxford: Oxford University Press, 1998.

Weiss, Jessica. *To Have and to Hold: Marriage, the Baby Boom, and Social Change*. Chicago: University of Chicago Press, 2000.

Welky, David. *Marching Across the Color Line: A. Philip Randolph and Civil Rights in the World War II Era*. New York: Oxford University Press, 2013.

Why We Fight. Film series directed by Frank Capra. Washington, D.C.: United States Government, 1942–1945.

Wiese, Andrew. *Places of their Own: African American Suburbanization in the Twentieth Century*. Chicago: University of Chicago Press, 2004.

Woodward, C. Vann. *The Burden of Southern History*. Baton Rouge: Louisiana State University Press, 1993.

_____. *The Strange Career of Jim Crow*. New York: Oxford University Press, 1974.

Wright, Stuart J. *An Emotional Gauntlet: From Life in Peacetime America to the War in European Skies*. Madison: University of Wisconsin Press, 2004.

Zangwill, Israel. *The Melting-Pot: Drama in Four Acts*. New York: Macmillan, 1909.

Zolberg, Aristide R. *A Nation by Design: Immigration Policy in the Fashioning of America*. Cambridge, Mass.: Harvard University Press, 2006.

Education and Americanization:
The Language of Community

Joan Fragaszy Troyano and
Debbie Schaefer-Jacobs

Schools are important arenas where political and cultural debates multiply and manifest. By the early twentieth century, the American public school system had developed from its simple common school roots into a national ecosystem led by local communities and states but increasingly connected by shared ideologies and methodologies, structures, professional teachers, and a dramatically growing and diversifying student population.[1] An alternative system of private schools catered to linguistic, racial, ethnic heritage, or religious groups. The largest of these were parochial schools administered by regional Catholic dioceses. Immigrant children, mostly from Europe and the Americas and unfamiliar with English, joined overflowing classrooms in both public and parochial schools. As a result, language—both linguistic and rhetorical—was a major point of contention, reflecting institutional and local conflicts.

Influential civic leaders and social reformers in the urban Northeast and Midwest who wanted to "Americanize" recent immigrants prioritized learning of the English language. Largely focused on public schools, these reformers believed that mastering American English also required the adoption of Anglo-Protestant values and the language of patriotism (Figure 1). Parochial schools, based in linguistic and ethnic communities, had more flexibility to offer instruction in the native language of the students, retain heritage traditions, and teach

Figure 1.

Poster from the Americanization Committee of the Cleveland Board of Education, Cleveland, Ohio, 1917. Written in six languages (English, Italian, Hungarian, Slovenian, Polish, and Yiddish), the text invites parents of Cleveland public school students to attend free English classes. National Museum of American History, Smithsonian Institution.

courses with religious values. Yet the Catholic leadership often was more concerned with unifying the religious community and creating patriotic American Catholics. For scholars, there is an abundance of archival evidence for these approaches, including teacher training, administrative communications, legal cases, and policies. Material culture of the classroom, on the other hand, provides insight into student experiences and educational practices. A small savings bank and a report card reveal how the public and parochial school systems attempted to develop shared communities amid linguistic and cultural diversity.

Originating from the common schools of the Northeast, American public schools were designed to educate youth socially, culturally, and intellectually to become productive citizens. Although there were no national requirements for continuity across the states in the nineteenth century, public school curricula typically included basic reading and writing of standardized American English, patriotic study of history and civics, science, and math. The most universal experience for students across the country was the use of two particular text-books to teach English literacy: various editions of Webster's *Blue-Back Speller*, first published in the 1780s, and the *McGuffey Reader*, first released in 1836. These two texts developed basic grammar and reading skills through literary passages, including Protestant prayers and morality tales, and were used in homes and schools of all sizes.[2]

The most extreme application of these educational priorities was the federal American Indian boarding school system initiated in the 1870s. This national educational system removed tens of thousands of Native American children from their homes and sent them to government-run boarding schools across the nation for cultural and vocational training. To force assimilation, the boarding schools used military-like schedules and disciplinary methods, imposed English-only language, and forbid native languages, customs, and dress.[3] In contrast, localized administration of public schools across the country resulted in less uniform curricula and student experiences.

The national Centennial celebrations of 1876 prompted a patriotic fervor that manifested in the development of classroom supplies, materials, and practices. Students used slate pencils wrapped in American flags, learned patriotic songs, and recited a variety of pledges to the nation. The influential magazine *Youth's Companion* encouraged student-led direct sales to put a "flag over every school house" and by the fall of 1892, to perform the Pledge of Allegiance in classrooms across the country.[4]

In the decades following the Centennial, elite Americans in New York and Boston turned their attention to their own urban neighbors and became increasingly concerned that the influx of immigrants from southern and eastern Europe would destroy their carefully cultivated Protestant, Anglo-American identity. In an attempt to assimilate the newcomers, veteran and civic groups including the Grand Army of the Republic, the Masons, the Daughters of the American Revolution, and various temperance organizations supplemented the efforts of politicians and the federal Bureau of Education in the "Americanization movement" to foster a shared American culture among the student population.[5]

Together these educators and civic groups developed school programs that encouraged patriotic rituals and ceremonies, with private groups often underwriting contests, school plays and pageants, and other inspirational activities.[6] They promoted Protestant values through the use of the King James Bible and the *McGuffey Reader*, and the removal or sanitizing of Catholic Spanish and Portuguese

Figure 2.
"Little Red School House Savings Bank," distributed by Jos. D. Lowe Company in Boston, Massachusetts, around 1900. This small bank takes the form of a one-room schoolhouse. Messages on the bank aligned with the Americanization movement's nostalgia for an imagined, homogeneous United States. National Museum of American History, Smithsonian Institution, gift of Dr. Richard Lodish American School Collection.

conquest of North American lands in textbooks.[7] As their efforts spread west and south, classrooms, teaching tools, and writing equipment began to showcase nationalistic symbols such as eagle and flag imagery and images of the Founding Fathers.[8] Surrounding the curriculum of language literacy was a variety of visual materials and experiential learning activities for how to be an American.

This small "Little Red School House Savings Bank" in the style of a one-room schoolhouse placed the Americanization movement's platform of assimilation, patriotism, and self-reliance directly into the hands of schoolchildren (Figure 2). Distributed by the Boston-based Jos. D. Lowe Company around 1900 and at a cost of 25 cents, the bank included a small slot for coins and a latch to open the bottom.[9] Functional banks such as this were distributed to encourage students to develop habits of saving and thrift.[10] In this case, the small bank made of wood, cardboard, and paper also provided a venue to circulate the patriotic imagery and language that characterized the Americanization movement.

In addition to representing the single-room schoolhouse of a small town—a nostalgic image in an era of rapid urban growth—the images and words on the bank provide a patriotic rhetoric that encourages holders to commit themselves to the nation. Dedications identify the first school in Dorchester, Massachusetts, from 1630, and there is an ode on the roof to "The dear country schoolhouse/America's schoolhouse/The little red schoolhouse/The pride of our land." George Washington and "Mrs. Elizabeth (Betsey) Ross" are credited with the "Stars and

Troyano and Schaefer-Jacobs

Stripes" national flag in 1777.[11] In addition, three statements decorate the bank, each using the first-person voice to connect the reader with the conviction of the statement:

On the rooftop, the original version of the Pledge of Allegiance:

> I pledge allegiance to my flag/and the Republic, for which it stands/one nation, indivisible, with liberty and justice for all.

Under the eaves, the "Balch Pledge," named for George Thatcher Balch, who led patriotic and civic programs in New York City schools and wrote his own pledge prior to the adoption of the national pledge:[12]

> I give my heart and my hand to my country—one country, one language, one flag.

On the side, a modification of the Balch Pledge, turned into a rousing motto of the tenets of the Americanization movement (Figure 3):

> On These We Insist: *One Nation, One Flag, One Language, One School.*

For the child receiving this bank as a gift, or motivated to sell it in order to gain further rewards, the schoolhouse and its message are familiar: *one school* and *one flag*. Perhaps more important for the adults leading this wing of the Americanization movement was the insistence on *one language* and *one nation*.

Debates and court cases over the language of classroom instruction had occurred frequently on the local, state, and national level since the origins of tax-supported schools. Around 1900, when this savings bank was produced, bilingual and multilingual schools existed across the country. In some communities

Figure 3.

An Americanization pledge is printed on the bank, revealing the importance many placed in a single language and education system that reflected white Anglo-Saxon Protestant ideals. National Museum of American History, Smithsonian Institution, gift of Dr. Richard Lodish American School Collection.

there were organized courses, classroom lessons, or informal programs tied to the cultural heritage of their residents. Not all educators, parents, or Americans agreed with this varied approach, however.[13] Former president Theodore Roosevelt vocalized the opinion of many native-born Americans, saying "We have room for but one language here and that is the English language, for we intend to see that the crucible turns our people out as Americans, and American nationality, and not as dwellers in a polyglot boarding house."[14] This bank, with its references to colonial legends, its promotion of Americanization rhetoric included in the two pledges, and its stance on the linguistic path to social unity, reflects a specific and powerful version of assimilation at work at the turn of the twentieth century. The bank also demonstrates why some might want to develop different options for their own community.

Alternatives to public schools developed either from a community's desire to control the education of its children or out of necessity. Prejudices against immigrants, non-Anglo, and non-European Americans resulted in uneven access to public schools at all levels. When public schools intimidated, or often intentionally excluded, students based on race, the affected community had to organize its own teachers and classes. Chinese, Mexican, and Japanese Americans often did this in the West, as did African Americans throughout the South and across the country. White ethnic groups such as German Lutherans and Jews, who were not specifically excluded from their local public schools but preferred to control the language of instruction or the religious interpretation of curricula, also established schools to meet their own communities' needs.[15]

The largest network of alternative schools was the American parochial school system, which developed in the 1830s in response to the Nativist movement of anti-Catholic sentiment, disagreements over curricula and the use of the King James Bible in public schools, and disputes over financial support of schools. As the number and distribution of Catholics increased, parochial schools associated with a neighborhood church outnumbered the older mission-based schools organized by religious orders. Catholics began to arrive in increasing numbers in the 1880s, and particularly from southern and eastern Europe. From approximately ten percent of the population in the 1860s, by the 1930s roughly 30 million Catholics were nearing one quarter of the American population, and were the single largest religious denomination.[16] While the vast majority of Catholic children attended public schools, religious schools offered the option to learn in a native language that in many places was specifically denied in public schools.

Troyano and Schaefer-Jacobs

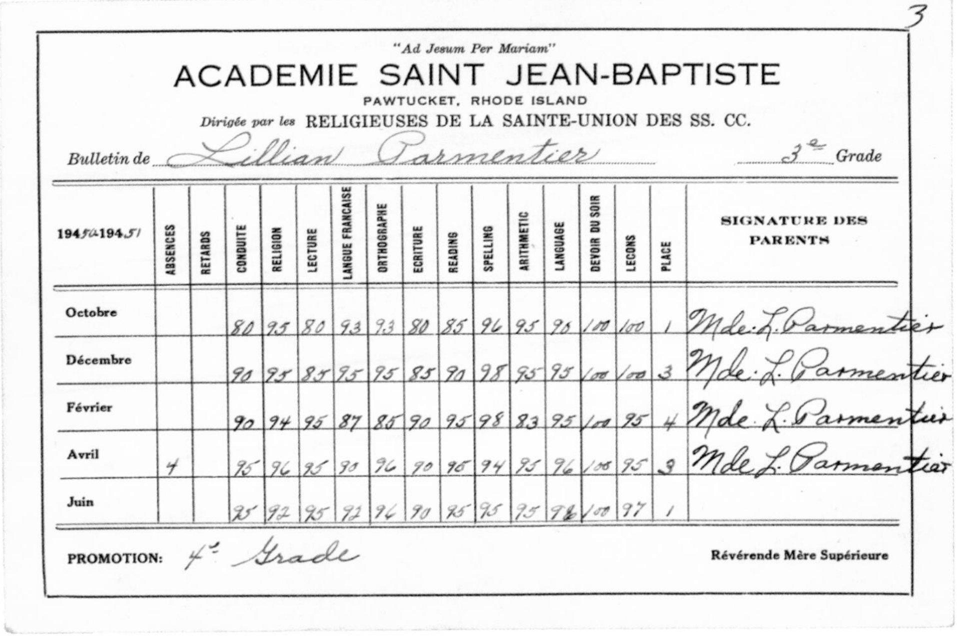

"Ad Jesum Per Mariam"

ACADEMIE SAINT JEAN-BAPTISTE
PAWTUCKET, RHODE ISLAND
Dirigée par les RELIGIEUSES DE LA SAINTE-UNION DES SS. CC.

Bulletin de *Lillian Parmentier* — 3ᵉ Grade

1945-1946	ABSENCES	RETARDS	CONDUITE	RELIGION	LECTURE	LANGUE FRANCAISE	ORTHOGRAPHE	ECRITURE	READING	SPELLING	ARITHMETIC	LANGUAGE	DEVOIR DU SOIR	LECONS	PLACE	SIGNATURE DES PARENTS
Octobre			80	95	80	93	93	80	85	96	95	95	100	100	1	Mde. L. Parmentier
Décembre			90	95	85	95	95	85	90	98	95	95	100	100	3	Mde. L. Parmentier
Février			90	94	95	87	85	90	95	98	83	95	100	95	4	Mde. L. Parmentier
Avril	4		95	96	95	90	96	90	96	94	95	96	100	95	3	Mde. L. Parmentier
Juin			85	92	95	92	96	90	85	95	95	96	100	97	1	

PROMOTION: *4ᵉ Grade* — Révérende Mère Supérieure

Figure 4.

Lillian Parmentier's fourth-grade report card from Saint Jean-Baptiste parochial school in Pawtucket, Rhode Island, 1951. Most of the students at the school were the children of French-speaking Canadian immigrants. This bilingual report card reflects the community's adoption of some American customs and simultaneous preservation of their French Canadian heritage, particularly language. Courtesy of the Catholic School Archives in the Museum of Work and Culture at the Rhode Island Historical Society, Woonsocket, Rhode Island.

Yet because multiple parishes serving different linguistic groups coexisted within the regional diocese structure of the Catholic Church, particularly in the urban North, localized communities still faced challenges to retaining their linguistic and cultural heritage in the face of Americanization rhetoric.

This bilingual report card from the Academie Saint Jean-Baptiste parochial school in 1951 represents a single child's experience within the broader legacy of an immigrant community attempting to retain a linguistic and cultural heritage (Figure 4). Like other French-speaking Canadians living in New England, the parishioners who founded Saint Jean-Baptiste as a girls' school at the turn of the twentieth century wanted the option to retain a distinct community—*la survivance*—or acclimatize into American society on their own terms.[17] Academie Saint Jean-Baptiste in Pawtucket, Rhode Island, was in the diocese of Providence, yet parishioners maintained lasting relationships with their compatriots left behind in Quebec.[18] The documentation on the report card, as well as the school's curriculum, was bilingual. Lillian Parmentier and her classmates learned "Religion," "Conduct lessons," "French," and "Devotions" in French, while their core classes such as History, Civics, Geography, Math, Spelling, Reading, and English grammar were taught in English. Combined with parish leadership brought from Quebec, French Canadians in the Providence diocese could have the bulk of

Figure 5.
Second-grade play at Academie Saint Jean-Baptiste, around 1948. Lillian Parmentier is standing on the far left in the front row. Students in this image, mostly of Catholic French Canadian descent, appear in their First Communion dresses, which were often worn for special school events. Courtesy of Lillian Parmentier Rivet and the Catholic School Archives in the Museum of Work and Culture at the Rhode Island Historical Society, Woonsocket, Rhode Island.

their cultural and spiritual training in their native language[19] (Figure 5). By 1951 a bilingual report card was less common than in 1900, around the time when the savings bank was produced. Across the country, the number of bilingual parochial schools had decreased due to pressure from English-speaking Irish clergy ministering to non-English-speaking parishioners, from the surrounding communities, and increasing scrutiny by the state. Conflicts over language were further complicated by battles over who would have financial and political control over the schools within each diocese.[20] In Rhode Island the 1920s was the pivotal decade for bilingual, and particularly French, curricula. The state's Peck Education Act of 1922 required that private schools use English to teach coursework that paralleled public schools.[21] Although the Peck Act was struck down as unconstitutional the following year, it immediately preceded a diocese-wide fight over English language instruction and control of parish schools.

In addition to French-speaking schools such as Academie Saint Jean-Baptiste, the diocese also included Italian, Polish, Lithuanian, Portuguese, and English-speaking parishes. In an attempt to create a more unified community, the Providence-based church leadership decided to tax parishes to fund several English-only high schools.[22] They also supported the assimilation curriculum in the *Catechism of Catholic Education* issued by the Irish-American bishops. The

Troyano and Schaefer-Jacobs

Franco-American parishioners had been saving money for their own bilingual high school and refused to fall in line with the diocese's plans. Inspired by the newspaper *La Sentinelle*, an estimated 10,000 Franco-Americans sued the English-speaking episcopate over financial support for English-only high schools. The conflict lasted several years, involved the Church hierarchy, and resulted in the excommunication of several activists within the French Canadian community.[23] Undeterred, the community continued to support French bilingual schools such as Saint Jean-Baptiste until budget cuts, rising teacher salaries, and declining enrollment forced the school to close in 1975.[24] Ironically, many of its students transferred to St. Raphael Academy, one of the English-only schools founded in the 1920s.

Even within a shared religious community, debates about language could prove divisive. The upper levels of Church leadership supported the tenets of the Americanization movement, believing that it would unify Catholics and improve their standing in the larger national community. Moreover, central administrative procedures forced on local, community-based schools run by bilingual or multilingual parish priests and nuns often were led by English-only advocates. Vocal bishops insisted that they had the right to approve curricula and use of language. To appease politicians while distancing himself from Rome, Bishop John Ireland claimed, "Ours is the American Church, and not Irish, German, Italian, or Polish."[25] The bishop's appeal to fellow Catholics, and his support for English as the language of instruction, is similar to the motto on the bank, with a simple addition: "*one church*." For both appeals, the inclusive rhetoric prioritized belonging to a national whole—whether a church or a country—that used a shared language.

Although bilingual schools usually developed from the desire and efforts of an immigrant community to retain traditions, bilingual instruction often eased the process of adaptation and assimilation. Over the past 100 years, language and heritage schools that started out teaching in a language of the student's country of origin then moved to bilingual instruction, and eventually became schools for English speakers to learn the language and culture of their ancestors. Report cards like this one from Academie Saint Jean-Baptiste are testaments to the priorities and political debates of generations of non-English speaking immigrant communities, representing the constituency of past and present students.

The tension between cultural pluralism and assimilation in education has been fought on many fronts. The manufactured children's bank and a single child's report card reflect different attitudes toward language and Americaniza-tion in the first part of the twentieth century. The public schools largely adopted a custom of assimilation. Parochial schools could provide an alternative option that began with bilingual instruction. In keeping with centuries of debate, the multiplicity of approaches to contemporary schooling and continuous immigra-tion from around the globe means that the issue of language use in schools re-mains as contentious as ever.

NOTES

1. Thomas J. Schlereth, *Victorian America: Trans-formations in Everyday Life 1876–1915* (New York: Harper Collins, 1991), 247. The dramatic increase went from 2,526 schools in 1890 to 14,326 schools in 1920.

2. On Webster's *Blue-Back Speller*, see Stephen Prothero, *The American Bible: How Our Words Unite, Divide, and Define a Nation* (New York: HarperOne, 2012), 102–04; E. Jennifer Monaghan, *A Common Heritage: Noah Webster's Blue-Back Speller* (Hamden, Conn.: Archon Books, 1983). On *McGuffey*, see John H. Wester-hoff, *McGuffey and His Readers: Piety, Morality, and Education in Nineteenth-Century America* (Nashville: Abingdon, 1978). The *McGuffey* readers remain popular in the twenty-first century.

3. Native American tribes resisted the school-ing and worked to change policies, but it took decades for classroom lessons to reflect the diversity of native cultures. K. Tsianina Lomawaima, Brenda J. Child, and Margaret L. Archuleta, eds., *Away from Home: American Indian Boarding School Experiences, 1879–2000* (Phoenix: Heard Museum, 2000); David Wallace Adams, *Education for Extinction: American Indians and the Boarding School Experience, 1875–1928* (Lawrence: University Press of Kansas, 1995).

4. The *Youth's Companion* magazine led the schoolhouse flag movement and the adop-tion of the Pledge of Allegiance by developing patriotic activities and supplying premium rewards that also helped boost magazine sales. The September 1892 issue included the Pledge of Allegiance, written by Francis Bellamy. The pledge was published one month before the Columbus Day 400th anniversary ceremony at the Columbian Exposition and the magazine encouraged its recitation in schools through-out the country. Richard J. Ellis, *To the Flag: The Unlikely History of the Pledge of Allegiance* (Lawrence: University Press of Kansas, 2005).

5. The South had proportionally fewer immigrants and the public school system was less univer-sal, with African Americans largely dependent on charity and community-driven schools. White elites wanted to retain a stark racial division, so civic groups often led by women, such as the United Daughters of the Confeder-acy, promoted their particular interpretations of patriotic history through reading materials, toys and games, and the building and unveiling of thousands of public monuments. See Karen L. Cox, *Dixie's Daughters: The United Daugh-ters of the Confederacy and the Preservation of Confederate Culture* (Gainesville: University Press of Florida, 2003); Mary S. Hoffschwelle, *The Rosenwald Schools of the American South* (Gainesville: University Press of Florida, 2006). On the impact of childhood play, see Robin Bernstein, *Racial Innocence: Performing Ameri-can Childhood from Slavery to Civil Rights* (New York: New York University Press, 2011).

6. Eric P. Kaufmann, *The Rise and Fall of Anglo-America*, (Cambridge, Mass.: Harvard University Press, 2004); Desmond S. King, *Making Americans: Immigration, Race, and the Origins of the Diverse Democracy* (Cambridge, Mass.: Harvard University Press, 2000); Joseph Moreau, *Schoolbook Nation: Conflicts Over American History Textbooks from the Civil War to the Present* (Ann Arbor: University of Michigan Press, 2003). Immigrant communities themselves also were involved in nurturing American patriotism, although not necessarily to replace their own cultural heritage; see Jeffrey E. Mirel, *Patriotic Pluralism: Americanization Education and European Immigrants* (Cambridge, Mass.: Harvard University Press, 2010); Paula S. Fass, *Outside in: Minorities and the Transformation of American Education* (New York: Oxford University Press, 1989).

7. The celebration of American founders and heroes led Catholics and other ethnic groups to promote their own heroes in books, monuments, and other arenas of public culture. See Moreau, *Schoolbook Nation*; Sheila Brennan, *Stamping American Memory: Collectors, Citizens, Commemoratives, and the Post* (Ann Arbor: University of Michigan Press, 2014) (digital; print forthcoming), http://stampingamericanmemory.org.

8. H. H. Wheaton, "New Possibilities in Education," *The Annals of the American Academy of Political and Social Science* 67(Sep. 1916):274–280; Bernard J. Weiss, ed., *American Education and the European Immigrant: 1840–1940* (Chicago: University of Illinois Press, 1982), xiv.

9. Jos. D. Lowe Co. was a relatively new business in Boston, catering to women, according to advertisements in local newspapers of the period. An 1863 graduate of Mount Holyoke Female Seminary, the financially comfortable Josephine Dwyer Lowe advocated for women, as is indicative of her bank's advertisements in Boston during the late 1890s and early 1900s. This was probably when this bank was manufactured.

10. Savings banks were popular among immigrants, particularly women and children. Boston Provident, founded in 1816, noted that 71 percent of its early depositors were women and children. Public school banking developed in New York in the late 1870s and by 1885 had spread throughout the country. Philanthropist and social reformer Charles Loring Brace created a savings bank in 1854 for the boys he was assisting in vocational schools for the Children's Aide Society in New York. Sara Louisa Oberholtzer, "School Savings Banks," *The Annals of the American Academy of Political and Social Science* 3(1)(1892):14–29, http://www.jstor.org/stable/1008744; Ashley Cruse, "A History of Progressive-Era School Savings Banking 1870 to 1930," Working Paper 01-3 (St. Louis: Center for Social Development, Washington University, August 2001), 1–2. This bank may have been distributed as a reward, or "premium," for student-led direct sales, as was common in this period.

11. Whether Dorchester, Massachusetts, was in fact the location of the first public school remains debated.

12. George Thatcher Balch, a Civil War veteran, was appointed by the New York City mayor to inspect the schools for health issues, which led to a preoccupation with the teaching of patriotism within the schools.

13. Paul J. Ramsey, *Bilingual Public Schooling in the United States: A History of America's "Polyglot Boardinghouse"* (New York: Palgrave Macmillan, 2010). Ironically, sometimes linguistically diverse communities also insisted on English-only schools to prevent the domination of a European language that was enforced in their homeland (most often German over another Central European language). See Mirel, *Patriotic Pluralism*, 105–47.

14. Theodore Roosevelt as quoted in John Bartlett, *Familiar Quotations: A Collection of Passages, Phrases, and Proverbs Traced to Their Sources in Ancient and Modern Literature* (Boston: Little, Brown, 1982). Contemporary readers would

have seen this quote reprinted in newspapers, including the 7 January 1919 edition of the *Chicago Daily Tribune*.

15. Ramsey, *Bilingual Public Schooling in the United States*.

16. Timothy Walch, *Parish School: American Catholic Parochial Education from Colonial Times to the Present* (Washington, D.C.: National Catholic Education Association, 2003); James J. Hennesey, *American Catholics: A History of the Roman Catholic Community in the United States* (Oxford: Oxford University Press, 1983).

17. Richard S. Sorrell, "The *survivance* of French Canadians in New England (1865–1930): History, Geography and Demography as Destiny," *Ethnic and Racial Studies* 4(1)(January 1981):90–109.

18. Sorrell, "The *survivance* of French Canadians in New England."

19. Jason Peters, "Emerging Voices: 'Speak White': Language Policy, Immigration, Discourse, and Tactical Authenticity in a French Enclave in New England," *College English* 75(6)(July 2013):563–81.

20. Marvin Lazerson, "Understanding American Catholic Educational History," *History of Education Quarterly* 17(3)(Autumn 1977):306–09.

21. There is a long history of localized legislation covering the language of instruction in the schools. These include the 1839 Bilingual Law in Ohio that authorized German–English instruction at a parent's request and similar laws such as the 1847 French/English Bilingual Curriculum Act in Louisiana and the 1850 New Mexico Territory Act authorizing Spanish and English. By the late 1880s, however, legislation requiring instruction in English became more prevalent at local levels and included Wisconsin's Bennett Law of 1888 and the Edwards Law in Illinois in 1889. Although the Wisconsin and Illinois laws were repealed within a few years, they were indicative of the new trend towards English-only instruction. See Ramsey, *Bilingual Public Schooling in the United States*.

22. The celebration of Mass in Latin also provided some continuity of experience for Catholics. The 1884 Third Plenary Council of Baltimore recommended a Catholic school for every parish. Walch, *Parish School*.

23. Jason Peters, "Emerging Voices: 'Speak White.'"

24. In the twenty-first century, St. Jean Baptiste Church continues to be bilingual, with regular mass in English and Spanish, in place of French.

25. Walch, *Parish School*, 80–83.

BIBLIOGRAPHY

Adams, David Wallace. *Education for Extinction: American Indians and the Boarding School Experience, 1875–1928*. Lawrence: University Press of Kansas, 1995.

Bartlett, John. *Familiar Quotations: A Collection of Passages, Phrases, and Proverbs Traced to Their Sources in Ancient and Modern Literature*. Boston: Little, Brown, 1982.

Bernstein, Robin. *Racial Innocence: Performing American Childhood from Slavery to Civil Rights*. New York: New York University Press, 2011.

Brennan, Sheila. *Stamping American Memory: Collectors, Citizens, Commemoratives, and the Post*. Ann Arbor: University of Michigan Press, 2014 (digital; print forthcoming). http://stampingamericanmemory.org (accessed 5 August 2016).

Cox, Karen L. *Dixie's Daughters: The United Daughters of the Confederacy and the Preservation of Confederate Culture*. Gainesville: University Press of Florida, 2003.

Cruse, Ashley. "A History of Progressive-Era School Savings Banking 1870 to 1930." In Working Paper 01–3. St. Louis: Washington University Center for Social Development, 2001.

Ellis, Richard J. *To the Flag: The Unlikely History of the Pledge of Allegiance*. Lawrence: University Press of Kansas, 2005.

Troyano and Schaefer-Jacobs

Fass, Paula S. *Outside in: Minorities and the Transformation of American Education.* New York: Oxford University Press, 1989.

Fraser, James W. *Between Church and State: Religion and Public Education in Multicultural America.* Baltimore: Johns Hopkins Press, 2016.

Hennesey, James J. *American Catholics: A History of the Roman Catholic Community in the United States.* Oxford: Oxford University Press, 1983.

Hoffschwelle, Mary S. *The Rosenwald Schools of the American South.* Gainesville: University Press of Florida, 2006.

Kaufmann, Eric P. *The Rise and Fall of Anglo-America.* Cambridge, Mass.: Harvard University Press, 2004.

King, Desmond S. *Making Americans: Immigration, Race, and the Origins of the Diverse Democracy.* Cambridge, Mass.: Harvard University Press, 2000.

Lazerson, Marvin. "Understanding American Catholic Educational History." *History of Education Quarterly* 17(3)(Autumn 1977):306–09.

Lomawaima, K. Tsianina, Brenda J. Child, and Margaret L. Archuleta, eds. *Away from Home: American Indian Boarding School Experiences, 1879-2000.* Phoenix: Heard Museum, 2000.

Mirel, Jeffrey E. *Patriotic Pluralism: Americanization Education and European Immigrants.* Cambridge, Mass.: Harvard University Press, 2010.

Monaghan, E. Jennifer. *A Common Heritage: Noah Webster's Blue-Back Speller.* Hamden, Conn.: Archon Books, 1983.

Moreau, Joseph. *Schoolbook Nation: Conflicts Over American History Textbooks from the Civil War to the Present.* Ann Arbor: University of Michigan Press, 2003.

Oberholtzer, Sara Louisa. "School Savings Banks." *The Annals of the American Academy of Political and Social Science* 3(1)(1892):14–29. http://www.jstor.org/stable/1008744 (accessed 5 August 2016).

Peters, Jason. "Emerging Voices: 'Speak White': Language Policy, Immigration, Discourse, and Tactical Authenticity in a French Enclave in New England." *College English* 75(6)(July 2013):563–81.

Prothero, Stephen. *The American Bible: How Our Words Unite, Divide, and Define a Nation.* New York: HarperOne, 2012.

Ramsey, Paul J. *Bilingual Public Schooling in the United States: A History of America's "Polyglot Boardinghouse."* New York: Palgrave Macmillan, 2010.

Schlereth, Thomas J. *Victorian America: Transformations in Everyday Life, 1876–1915.* New York: Harper Collins, 1991.

Sorrell, Richard S. "The *survivance* of French Canadians in New England (1865–1930): History, Geography and Demography as Destiny." *Ethnic and Racial Studies* 4(1)(January 1981):90–109.

Walch, Timothy. *Parish School: American Catholic Parochial Education from Colonial Times to the Present.* Washington, D.C.: National Catholic Education Association, 2003.

Weiss, Bernard J., ed. *American Education and the European Immigrant: 1840–1940.* Chicago: University of Illinois Press, 1982.

Westerhoff, John H. *McGuffey and His Readers: Piety, Morality, and Education in Nineteenth-Century America.* Nashville: Abingdon, 1978.

Wheaton, H. H. "New Possibilities in Education." *The Annals of the American Academy of Political and Social Science* 67(Sep. 1916):274–80.

Chicago's "Concentric Zones": Thinking Through the Material History of an Iconic Map

Davarian L. Baldwin

The city…is a product of nature.

—Robert Park, *The City* (1925)

At the turn of the twentieth century, Chicago's smokestacks, skyscrapers, railways, and immigrants came to represent the promise of a modern America. Yet with this promise also came the perils of overcrowded tenements, political corruption, violent labor unrest, and bloody race riots. In the face of such disparities between industrial prosperity and urban poverty, the journalist-turned-social-scientist Robert Park made the bold claim that the city "is something more than a congeries of individual men and of social conveniences…it is a product of nature." Reformers like Jane Addams at Chicago's famed Hull House settlement worked tirelessly to address the challenges faced by new immigrants adjusting to the city. In sharp contrast, University of Chicago scholar Park argued that the efforts of city planners, reformers, and politicians failed to modify urban conditions because the "city has a life quite its own," an underlying pattern of growth and organization made visible by the new science of sociology.[1]

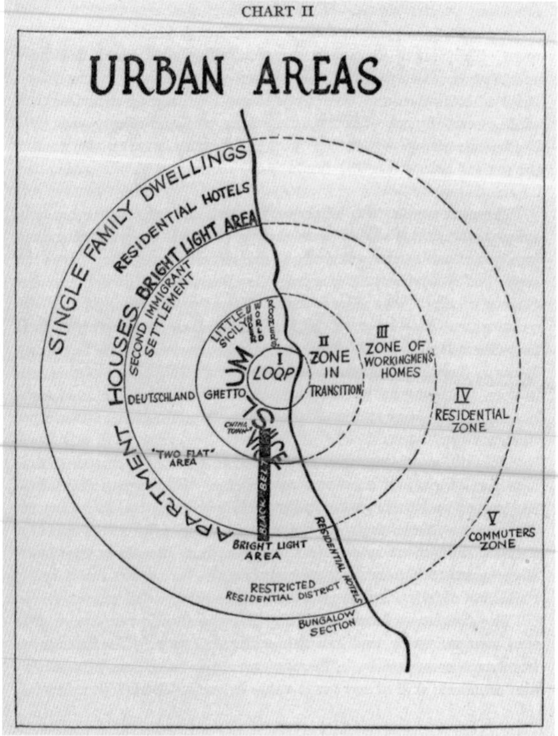

Figure 1.
Concentric zones map of Chicago, created by Dr. Ernest Burgess, a sociologist at the University of Chicago, 1925. Dr. Burgess and his colleagues created new theories to explain and map urban growth, using Chicago as a case study. This map and its corresponding theories justified racial inequality in urban development as a natural byproduct of immigration, new industries, and city growth. Courtesy of the University of Chicago Library, Chicago, Illinois.

Park's theories helped to propel the "Chicago School" of sociology to academic prominence, but it was the "concentric zones" diagram created by his colleague Ernest Burgess that literally put the abstract theory of a "natural" city on the map. The map presents the city divided into five circular zones (Figure 1). At the core is the downtown business area, teeming with skyscrapers occupied by the white-collar headquarters of industry, finance, and trade. A "zone in transition" surrounds the core, where immigrants were packed into overcrowded tenements built on top of each other, with residents overwhelmed by the toxic waste, soot-filled air, and mind-numbing noise of nearby factories and slaughtering houses. The next zone contains the two-family homes of second-generation immigrants with the economic means to escape the slums. The residential hotels and single-family-housing districts in the residential zone of middle-class citizens follow, until the map finally reaches the low-rise bungalows of the affluent commuter zone.[2]

Hailed by scholars as arguably "the most famous single visual document" of the modern city, the concentric zones map was created by Burgess and made popular in the landmark 1925 book *The City*, coauthored by University of Chicago scholars Park, Burgess, and Roderick McKenzie. Burgess gathered his data from the local geography of Chicago, but the concentric zones imagery here was used for understanding cities across the country where city leaders were trying to make sense of new migrants, new industries, and new ways of life. This concentric zones framework departed from the earlier maps presented by the 1895 *Hull House Maps and Papers*. The *Hull House* maps detailed an immigrant city shaped by unjust economic conditions, with the hopes that such visual evidence would inspire drastic reforms in housing and labor relations. In contrast, the concentric zonal design presented social inequalities as a natural part of urban growth patterns, to explain that there were predictable, unalterable, and hence scientific laws governing city life. Ultimately, the Chicago School's concentric zones map eclipsed the earlier *Hull House* model to give visual form to an emerging set of standards for the management of the modern city. This visual document helped strengthen sociology's claim to be the "science of society" and became a design model used to justify residential segregation in the process.

WHY CHICAGO? WHY A "CHICAGO SCHOOL"?

One might first ask, how did the specific details of Chicago's urban landscape come to serve as a model for the general study and design of American city life? Chicago served as a manufacturing gateway between the well-established cities of finance in the east and the abundant resources from an expanding western frontier. Home to large-scale manufacturing (International Harvester, Armour, Swift, U.S. Steel), transportation (Illinois Central Railroad and Pullman), and conspicuous consumption (Marshall Field & Co), Chicago became known as the "City of the Big Shoulders." Rapid industrialization helped make Chicago the fastest-growing city in the country, with a population of one million by 1890, 80 percent of whom were either born abroad or the children of immigrants. Aging tenements became overcrowded Towers of Babel brimming with "foreign" languages and customs. Workers grew increasingly frustrated with 100-hour work weeks; some followed the Chicago legacy of the Haymarket bombing and Pullman strike by joining organized labor protests. African Americans fled the Jim-Crow South in search of expanded freedoms, but faced new forms of racial segregation culminating in the bloody race riots of 1919.[3]

Chicago's cultural landscape was changing. To those at the top, the teeming streets, schoolhouses, and shop floors looked like chaos in need of order. Famed German sociologist Max Weber described Chicago as being "like a man whose skin has been peeled off and whose entrails one sees at work." But where this European social scientist saw a dying organism, the upstart Chicago School of sociology saw a vibrant "sociological laboratory" of experimentation, a "living textbook." Where reformers identified race riots or immigrant poverty as "social problems" to be solved, the Chicago School instead saw phases within an "inevitable" process of urban growth. The concentric zones model showed all social forces ultimately coming into peaceful coexistence, or what the sociologists called "assimilation."[4]

"…NEITHER DESIGNED NOR CONTROLLED"

The concentric zones map provided an image of order and stability in cities, like Chicago, where conflicts and inequalities were daily reminders that the social order remained far from settled. The zonal design used Park's theory of "human ecology" to explain that, like species in the plant ecosystem, various social groups—then called races—were dispersed across the city, not simply according to "occupation interests or economic conditions" but also distributed by "personal tastes" and "temperaments." This use of a biological metaphor helped identify the dynamic influx and physical location of new migrants but also rationalized the dramatic inequalities in their living and work conditions.[5]

A great semicircular zone of tenements cut through immigrant neighborhoods on the city's Near West Side, where over 20 different ethnic groups were jammed into overcrowded buildings meant as holding pens for a cheap labor force. The average tenement flat held five family members in three rooms without water or plumbing, adequate light, or sufficient ventilation. Just outside, residents endured a stench-filled landscape of horse-stable manure, dilapidated outhouses, and uncovered piles of garbage. Poverty restricted immigrant workers to the dangerous tenements. But whether rich or poor, African Americans were forced to live in the segregated Black Belt district on the city's South Side. Racial segregation was maintained by white violence or restrictive covenants—legally binding agreements between white homeowners to not rent, sell, or lease to nonwhites, with threat of civil action. Racial restrictions and subsequent overcrowding increased kitchenette-style housing, where older homes long abandoned by Chicago's white residents were now cut up into single room apartments with a communal bath and rented without a lease or even a kitchen. Housing in the growing Black Belt was deemed worst in the city, where landlords could extract the highest rents from the poorest residents. How could such poor conditions exist in a city of prosperity?[6]

Through his theory of human ecology, Park deployed the notion of temperaments—group-specific behaviors—to suggest that the urban population "segregate[s]

Figure 2.
Dr. Ernest Burgess, sociologist and creator of the concentric zones map, date unknown. Dr. Burgess is shown here in front of a Social Research Map of Chicago. Courtesy of the University of Chicago Library Special Collections Research Center, Chicago, Illinois.

itself," elite enclaves "spring up," and slums simply "grow up" in ways that are "neither designed nor controlled."[7] He recognized that dilapidated tenements became the home of poor and working class immigrants while African Americans were segregated into the Black Belt. But Park concluded people would not live in these areas "unless they were perfectly fit for the environment in which they are condemned to exist." Burgess took these popular ideas about upward mobility and segregation and plotted them directly within the concentric design, suggesting a scientific link between race, culture, and geography[8] (Figure 2).

Burgess used the concentric design not only to define where specific racial groups existed in space but also to give physical space a distinctly racial meaning. In this context, segregated populations are no longer moved and isolated by public policy or powerful groups, but are seen as biologically suited to "natural areas," where each physical space has its "own peculiar selective and cultural characteristics."[9] A year earlier Park observed, "The Negro is 'all right in his place' and the same is probably true of every other race, class, or category of persons." Burgess also calls the map's "zone in transition" one of "deterioration," where the slums coexist with the unassimilated immigrant colonies of Chinatown, Little Sicily, and the Jewish Ghetto, all dwelling in a region of poverty and "decay." He also suggested that even occupational choices such as "Irish policemen, Greek ice-cream parlors, Chinese laundries, Negro porters [and] Belgian janitors," were *more* a result of "racial temperament" than education or training.[10]

Burgess reserves special distinction for residents of the "Black Belt." The persistence of a segregated black community challenged the human ecological claim that assimilation was inevitable. But by mapping the "Black Belt" as a "natural area," then African American isolation in the city became a product of racial temperament instead of white violence or restrictive covenants. As a visual complement, the Black Belt punctures the white map of concentric circles from zones II through IV, represented as an intrusive and monolithic black strip separate from the rest of the social order. The concentric zones map explained that physical separation within the built environment was naturally caused by racial difference. Linking urban segregation to nature not only justified social inequalities but also helped secure the Chicago School's desire for professional authority as a science of society.[11]

"IN MORE GRAPHIC AND MINUTE FORM"

The concentric zones map became the visual paradigm for managing modern American cities, but at the expense of other geographic interpretations of city

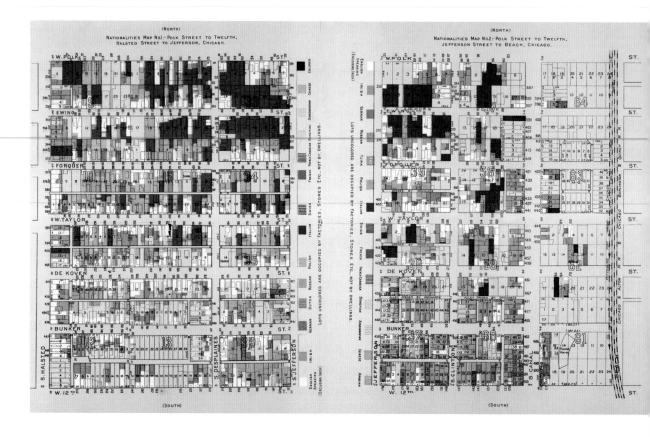

life. The maps in the 1895 *Hull House Maps and Papers* "had a monumental influence on Chicago sociology and, in turn, American sociology."[12] The *Hull House* maps actually pioneered the Chicago tradition of urban studies and the use of mapmaking as a method for displaying the demographic information of urban residents according to geography. Charles Booth's "Descriptive Map of London Poverty" had been the preeminent urban map of the day, with its landmark appraisal of economic conditions across the entire city. The *Hull House* maps were certainly influenced by Booth, but they focused on the third of a square mile directly to the east of Hull House "in more graphic and minute form"[13] (Figure 3).

Figure 3.

Nationality map, created by Hull House residents and published in *Hull House Maps and Papers*, 1895. A team of Hull House residents conducted door-to-door household surveys to map communities for demographic, social, and cultural factors. The Hull House team hoped that by exposing troubling conditions, they would inspire Americans to advocate for social reform. Courtesy of University of Illinois at Chicago Library [HV4196C4H761895c505, HV4196C4H761895c506, HV4196C4H761895c507, HV4196C4H761895c508].

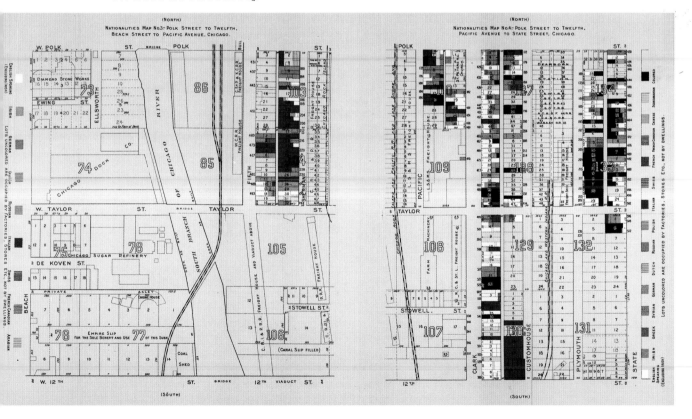

Mapmaking in Chicago was a product of the political culture of the Hull House settlement, bringing together the editorial leadership of Hull House Head Resident Jane Addams, Florence Kelley's training in statistical analysis, and the teams of residents organized to conduct extensive door-to-door household surveys. Unlike the "Chicago School," the largely female corps of Hull House researchers did not put forward an abstract racial model of urban form to explain the causes of poverty. The *Hull House* maps offered a detailed visual portrait of nationality, wages, and occupations of residents to "present conditions rather than to advance theories"[14] (Figure 4).

On opening the book, the reader saw pockets at the front and back of the volume, each containing a multicolored map labeled "Map of Wages" and "Map of Nationalities" respectively. According to historian Alice O'Conner, these maps "offered a distinctive way to *look* at poverty."[15] The text of *Hull House Maps and Papers* put forward the idea of socially homogenous and racially distinct "natural areas" later found in the concentric zones diagram. But the actual *Hull House* maps challenged the notion of ethnically distinct natural areas by offering a "photographic reproduction" of one small section of Chicago's nineteenth ward that included a residential intermingling of 18 nationalities in the same space.[16]

Instead of Park's naturally segregated "immigrant and racial colonies," we see the "greater minuteness" of racial hierarchy within a single slum where "colored" residents are pushed to the "least desirable" blocks in the northeast corner,

Figure 4.
Jane Addams with children at Hull House in Chicago, Illinois, 1933. Hull House, founded by Jane Addams and Ellen Gates Starr in 1889, revolutionized the field of social work by offering practical assistance, vocational training, and social and cultural activities to struggling Chicago residents. Courtesy of University of Illinois at Chicago Library [JAMC 0000 00030 0058].

the Chinese are confined to basement laundries, and Jews and Italians are overwhelmingly cordoned off in the rear of tenement buildings.[17] Hull House residents knocked on doors and went into homes and sweatshops to collect the information that animated these maps. But the book's authors were emphatic that the goal was not "sociological investigation" or research simply for the pursuit of knowledge. For these women, poverty was a problem that needed to be solved. The maps were meant to arouse a public outcry about the conditions of the "most inert and long suffering citizens of the commonwealth." Yet the Hull House focus on "constructive work" also signaled the relegation of *Hull House Maps and Papers*, and its female scholars, to the margins of social science research.[18]

THE CHICAGO TRADITION

While the concentric zones design was directly influenced by the mapping methods of *Hull House Maps and Papers*, Chicago School scholars began to establish a harsh distinction between academic sociology and what was now being dismissed as the applied sociology associated with largely women reformers. The concentric zones map became a physical artifact of the Chicago School's ambition to claim scientific legitimacy and discard the influence of the Hull House legacy. Park and Burgess denounced the action-oriented, reform-focused research of places like Hull House as tainted by the biased advocacy of "do-goodism." Ideas about gender differences were used to mark objective, scientific research as a man's domain. By 1920, female social scientists and their applied approach were largely removed from sociology. In turn, academia pushed these women pioneers to the emerging field of "social work" and the University of Chicago's new School of Social Service Administration. The concentric zones design also bolstered the assertion that there were observable and predictable patterns of urban growth and development. The structure of the map provided visual legitimacy to the Sociology Department's claim that the field could operate like a natural science. Ultimately, the Chicago School's mapping of unalterable natural laws, especially concerning racial segregation, gained the interests of both private industry and public policymakers.[19]

The concentric zones map suggested that segregation was an ecological characteristic of natural areas, and this model of urban growth was immediately picked up by the fledgling real estate industry. The National Association of Real Estate Boards (NAREB) had to stimulate demand for a consumer product (land) that was in ample supply. NAREB argued that their more limited supply of all-white properties guaranteed a better economic investment. In their amended 1924 code of ethics, in pamphlets, real estate education classes, and textbooks, NAREB argued that "colored people" carry an "economic disturbance" and therefore neighborhoods must be kept racially homogenous to secure profitable land sales and increase neighborhood value. When the Federal Housing Authority (FHA) passed the 1934 National Housing Act, the criteria for mortgage insurance shifted from a

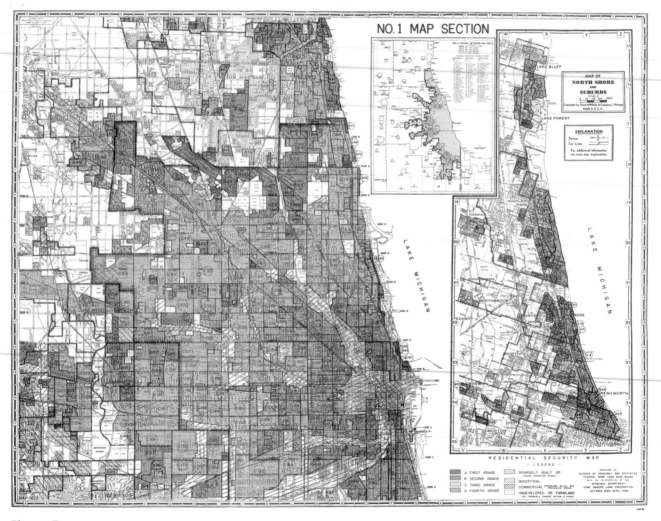

Figure 5:
Residential Security Map of Chicago, Northern Section, October 1939–April 1940. The Home Owner's Loan Corporation (HOLC), along with local assessors, created these maps to evaluate residential areas for their mortgage insurance and lending risks by considering not only housing conditions but also the race and class of residents. Black and poor neighborhoods were bound by red lines to highlight areas of financial risk, which initiated the discriminatory practice of "redlining." Courtesy of the National Archives and Records Administration.

strict economic assessment of property value to include an evaluation of the borrower's character. Successive editions of the FHA's *Underwriting Manual* warned that locations considered for new mortgage loans must be in areas protected against "inharmonious racial groups." At the same time, the federally-sponsored Home Owners' Loan Corporation created "residential security maps" for cities across the country where the investment potential of a neighborhood was largely measured by the race of its inhabitants (Figure 5). Ultimately, if an area was mapped as racially black it also became a zone of financial divestment.[20]

By the end of the twentieth century, decades of divestment from African American and, increasingly, Latino neighborhoods turned into a targeted investment in economically vulnerable communities. Peddlers of the disastrous sub-prime mortgages (also called "ghetto loans") pursued communities that had been historically denied access to financial services, exclusively offering high interest rates in black and brown neighborhoods without regard for wealth, housing stock, or credit score. The infamous concentric zones map cemented a geographic linkage between race and land value that continues.[21]

NOTES

1. Robert E. Park, Ernest W. Burgess, and Roderick D. McKenzie, *The City* [1925] (Chicago: University of Chicago Press, 1970), 1, 4.

2. Andrew Abbott and Jolyon Wurr, "Chicago Studied: Social Scientists and Their City," in Janice Reiff, Ann Durkin Keating, and James Grossman, eds., *The Electronic Encyclopedia of Chicago* (Chicago: Chicago Historical Society, 2005), http://www.encyclopedia.chicagohistory.org/pages/1213.html; and Park, Burgess, and McKenzie, *The City*, 56.

3. Walter Nugent, "Demography: Chicago as a Modern World City," in Reiff, Keating, and Grossman, *The Electronic Encyclopedia of Chicago*; Cameron McWhirter, *Red Summer: The Summer of 1919 and the Awakening of Black America* (New York: St. Martin's Griffin, 2012); Robin Bachin, *Building the South Side: Urban Space and Civic Culture in Chicago, 1890–1919* (Chicago: University of Chicago Press, 2003); Carl Smith, *Urban Disorder and the Shape of*

Belief: The Great Chicago Fire, The Haymarket Bomb, and the Model Town of Pullman (Chicago: University of Chicago Press, 1996); William Cronon, *Nature's Metropolis: Chicago and the Great West* (New York: Norton, 1991); James Gilbert, *Perfect Cities: Chicago's Utopias of 1893* (Chicago: University of Chicago Press, 1991); and William Tuttle, *Race Riot: Chicago in the Red Hot Summer of 1919* (New York: Atheneum, 1970).

4. Quoted from Max Weber, *From Max Weber: Essays in Sociology* (London: Routledge, 2013), 15; Albion Small, "Scholarship and Social Agitation," *American Journal of Sociology* 1(5)(March 1896):581; Louis Menand, *The Metaphysical Club* (New York: Farrar, Straus, and Giroux, 2001), 319.

5. Park, Burgess, and McKenzie, *The City*, 5 and 43; Daniel Breslau, "The Scientific Approach of Social Research: Robert Park's Human Ecology and American Sociology," *Theory and Society* 19(4)(Aug. 1990):417–46; and J. Nicholas Entrikin, "Robert Park's Human Ecology and

Human Geography," *Annals of the Association of American Geographers* 70(1)(Mar. 1980):43–58.

6. Thomas Philpott, *The Slum and the Ghetto: Immigrants, Blacks, and Reformers in Chicago, 1880–1930* (Belmont, Cal.: Wadsworth Publishing, 1991); and Davarian L. Baldwin, "Black Belts and Ivory Towers: The Place of Race in U.S. Social Thought, 1892–1948," *Critical Sociology* 30(2)(2004):397–450.

7. Park, Burgess, and McKenzie, *The City*, 43, 6, and 5.

8. Park, Burgess, and McKenzie, *The City*, 9 and 5, and Baldwin, "Black Belts and Ivory Towers."

9. Park, Burgess, and McKenzie, *The City*, 1 and 77.

10. Robert Park, "The Concept of Social Difference," *Journal of Applied Sociology* 8(1924):340; Park, Burgess, and McKenzie, *The City*, 56 and 57. Also see: Henry Yu, *Thinking Orientals: Migration, Contact, and Exoticism in Modern America* (New York: Oxford University Press, 2001); Mabel O. Wilson, "Making a Civilization Paradigm: Robert Park, Race, and Urban Ecology," unpublished seminar paper (6 December 1996); and Andrew Ross, *The Chicago Gangster Theory of Life: Nature's Debt to Society* (London: Verso, 1994), 117.

11. Baldwin, "Black Belts and Ivory Towers."

12. Mary Jo Deegan, *Jane Addams and the Men of the Chicago School, 1892–1918* (New Brunswick, N.J.: Transaction Books, 1998), 55.

13. Residents of Hull House, *Hull House Maps and Papers* (New York and Boston: Thomas Y. Crowell & Co. 1895), 9.

14. Residents of Hull House, *Hull House Maps and Papers*, 13; Menand, *The Metaphysical Club*; and Deegan, *Jane Addams and the Men of the Chicago School.*

15. Alice O'Conner, *Poverty Knowledge: Social Science, Social Policy, and the Poor in Twentieth-Century U.S. History* (Princeton: Princeton University Press, 2001), 28.

16. Residents of Hull House, *Hull House Maps and Papers*, 9.

17. Park, Burgess, and McKenzie, *The City*, 9; Residents of Hull House, *Hull House Maps and Papers*, 11; and O'Conner, *Poverty Knowledge*, 29.

18. Residents of Hull House, *Hull House Maps and Papers*, vii–viii and 14.

19. Deegan, *Jane Addams and the Men of the Chicago School*, 143; Ira Harkavy and John Puckett, "Lessons from Hull House for the Contemporary Urban University," *Social Service Review* 68(3)(Sep. 1994):299–321.

20. Kevin Gotham, *Race, Real Estate, and Uneven Development: The Kansas City Experience, 1900–2000* (Albany: State University of New York Press, 2002), 35; Jennifer Light, *The Nature of Cities: Ecological Visions and the American Urban Profession, 1920–1960* (Baltimore: Johns Hopkins University Press, 2009), 11–17, 70–81; and Henrika Kuklick, "Chicago Sociology and Urban Planning Policy: Sociological Theory as Occupational Ideology," *Theory and Society* 9(6) Nov. 1980):821–45.

21. Michael Powell, "Bank Accused of Pushing Mortgage Deals on Blacks," *New York Times*, 6 June 2009; Dorceta Taylor, *Toxic Communities: Environmental Racism, Industrial Pollution, and Residential Mobility* (New York: New York University Press, 2014); and Gregory Squires, "Predatory Lending: Redlining in Reverse," *National Housing Institute* 139 (Jan./Feb. 2005), http://www.nhi.org/online/issues/139/redlining.html.

BIBLIOGRAPHY

Abbott, Andrew and Jolyon Wurr. "Chicago Studied: Social Scientists and Their City." In *The Electronic Encyclopedia of Chicago*, ed. Janice Reiff, Ann Durkin Keating, and James Grossman. Chicago: Chicago Historical Society, 2005. http://www.encyclopedia.chicagohistory.org/pages/1213.html (accessed 5 February 2015).

Bachin, Robin. *Building the South Side: Urban Space and Civic Culture in Chicago, 1890–1919.* Chicago: University of Chicago Press, 2003.

Baldwin, Davarian L. "Black Belts and Ivory Towers: The Place of Race in U.S. Social Thought, 1892–1948." *Critical Sociology* 30(2)(2004): 397–450.

Breslau, Daniel. "The Scientific Appropriation of Social Research: Robert Park's Human Ecology and American Sociology." *Theory and Society* 19(4)(Aug. 1990): 417–46.

Cronon, William. *Nature's Metropolis: Chicago and the Great West.* New York: Norton, 1991.

Deegan, Mary Jo. *Jane Addams and the Men of the Chicago School, 1892–1918.* New Brunswick, N.J.: Transaction Books, 1998.

Entrikin, J. Nicholas. "Robert Park's Human Ecology and Human Geography." *Annals of the Association of American Geographers* 70(1)(Mar. 1980):43–58.

Gilbert, James. *Perfect Cities: Chicago's Utopias of 1893.* Chicago: University of Chicago Press, 1991.

Gotham, Kevin. *Race, Real Estate, and Uneven Development: The Kansas City Experience, 1900–2000.* Albany: State University of New York Press, 2002.

Harkavy, Ira, and John Puckett. "Lessons from Hull House for the Contemporary Urban University." *Social Service Review* 68(3)(Sep. 1994):299–321.

Kuklick, Henrika. "Chicago Sociology and Urban Planning Policy: Sociological Theory as Occupational Ideology." *Theory and Society* 9(6)(Nov. 1980):821–45.

Light, Jennifer. *The Nature of Cities: Ecological Visions and the American Urban Profession, 1920–1960.* Baltimore: Johns Hopkins University Press, 2009.

McWhirter, Cameron. *Red Summer: The Summer of 1919 and the Awakening of Black America.* New York: St. Martin's Griffin, 2012.

Menand, Louis. *The Metaphysical Club.* New York: Farrar, Straus, and Giroux, 2001.

Nugent, Walter. "Demography: Chicago as a Modern World City." In *The Electronic Encyclopedia of Chicago*, J. L. Reiff, A. D. Keating, and J. R. Grossman, eds. Chicago: Chicago Historical Society, 2005. http://www.encyclopedia.chicagohistory.org/pages/962.html (accessed 5 February 2015).

O'Conner, Alice. *Poverty Knowledge: Social Science, Social Policy, and the Poor in Twentieth-Century U.S. History.* Princeton: Princeton University Press, 2001.

Park, Robert. "The Concept of Social Difference." *Journal of Applied Sociology* 8(1924):339–44.

Park, Robert E., Ernest W. Burgess, and Roderick D. McKenzie. *The City.* 1925. Reprint, Chicago: University of Chicago Press, 1970.

Philpott, Thomas. *The Slum and the Ghetto: Immigrants, Blacks, and Reformers in Chicago, 1880–1930.* Belmont, Cal.: Wadsworth Publishing, 1991.

Powell, Michael, 2009. "Bank Accused of Pushing Mortgage Deals on Blacks." *New York Times*, 6 June 2009.

Residents of Hull House. *Hull House Maps and Papers.* New York and Boston: Thomas Y. Crowell & Co., 1895.

Ross, Andrew. *The Chicago Gangster Theory of Life: Nature's Debt to Society.* London: Verso, 1994.

Small, Albion. "Scholarship and Social Agitation." *American Journal of Sociology* 1(5)(Mar. 1896):564–82.

Smith, Carl. *Urban Disorder and the Shape of Belief: The Great Chicago Fire, The Haymarket Bomb, and the Model Town of Pullman.* Chicago: University of Chicago Press, 1996.

Squires, Gregory. "Predatory Lending: Redlining in Reverse." *National Housing Institute* 139 (Jan./Feb. 2005). http://www.nhi.org/online/issues/139/redlining.html (accessed 5 February 2015).

Taylor, Dorceta. *Toxic Communities: Environmental Racism, Industrial Pollution, and Residential Mobility.* New York: New York University Press, 2014.

Tuttle, William. *Race Riot: Chicago in the Red Hot Summer of 1919.* New York: Atheneum, 1970.

Weber, Max. *From Max Weber: Essays in Sociology.* London: Routledge, 2013.

Wilson, Mabel O. "Making a Civilization Paradigm: Robert Park, Race, and Urban Ecology." Unpublished seminar paper, New York University, last modified 6 December 1996.

Yu, Henry. *Thinking Orientals: Migration, Contact, and Exoticism in Modern America.* New York: Oxford University Press, 2001.

Pulling at the Threads:
A Korean American Diptych

Sojin Kim

ARRIVALS

Leading the way from the plane that had just landed on an Oregon tarmac, Bertha Holt carried eight-month-old Betty Rhee Holt, one of eight children whom she and her husband Harry were adopting (Figure 1). In celebration of the momentous occasion, the four girls were clad in *hanbok*, a traditional Korean dress.

It was October 1955 and dozens of media outlets documented the homecoming of this group of mixed-race babies from Korean orphanages.[1] They were the offspring of U.S. servicemen and Korean women, and they were bound for American families—among the earliest international transracial adoptees to enter this country. The forces behind this effort, Bertha and Harry Holt, were devout Christians who lived with their six biological children in Creswell, Oregon. They were moved by a sense of charity and divine calling to respond to the suffering wrought by the Korean War. To bring their eight new children to the United States, they worked successfully with their senator to introduce a special bill that made possible the issuing of non-quota immigrant visas beyond the two-per-family limit permitted under the 1953 Refugee Relief Act. They subsequently

Figure 1.
Bertha and Harry Holt arriving in Portland, Oregon, with their eight adoptive children, 14 October 1955. Media and humanitarian attention to the plight of the tens of thousands of children orphaned as a result of the partitioning and militarization of the Korean peninsula focused the sympathies and curiosity of an American public who had been relatively unfamiliar with the region and the reasons for U.S. intervention in the Korean War. Courtesy of Holt International Children's Services.

established a private adoption agency, which to date accounts for roughly 50 percent of all Korean adoptees placed in American homes and contributed to launching an international adoption movement.

PULLING AT THE THREADS

There is a Korean saying, "clothes are the wings"—they have the power to carry us beyond where we currently stand. It instructs that impressions of vital consequence are formed around the clothes we wear.

Betty Rhee Holt's hanbok is a striking, accessible vehicle for storytelling (Figure 2). Its tiny scale makes it precious. After more than half a century, the colors are still vibrant. And it is displayed on a mount that skillfully suggests human volume. It is one of several items in a collection related to the Holt family at the Smithsonian National Museum of American History. Other materials include the kid-sized cowboy boots and immigration documents of Nathan, another of the eight adoptees.[2]

Figure 2.

Hanbok, a traditional Korean dress, worn by Betty Rhee Holt, 1955. Betty Rhee Holt was one of eight Korean children adopted by the Holt Family in 1955. The Holts chose to dress their adopted daughters in Korean ceremonial clothing to mark the occasion of their arrival to the United States. National Museum of American History, Smithsonian Institution, gift of Betty Holt Blankenship.

In context of the current discourse on Korean international adoption—which includes scholarship by adoptees themselves—Rhee Holt's hanbok is also a loaded and fraught symbol. Since the early 2000s, scholars have used transnational and interdisciplinary frameworks to formulate new analysis of the history of transracial adoption and Korean immigration. This includes a growing body of critical adoption studies,[3] as well as research elaborating the relationships between religion and migration[4] and popular culture and "Cold War Orientalism."[5] This work offers a counterpoint to narratives of American exceptionalism and immigrant integration by reckoning with the legacies of U.S. neocolonialism in Asia and by underscoring the persistence of race in defining identities and shaping experiences.

At the Smithsonian, we grapple with subjective and historical accountabilities in our collecting and exhibition endeavors. The Rhee Holt hanbok reflects a precise moment and specific personal interactions, which were themselves the products of historical events and geopolitics. Like any artifact, it is multivalent and available to many shifting points of reference. Consideration of the Holt artifacts inspires different sorts of inquiry, including those that reframe other collections inside and outside the Smithsonian. These tell optimistic stories but also raise troubling questions that draw together many strands woven into this country's history, including those related to race, gender, class, religion, immigration, foreign policy, the U.S. military, family life, and social welfare.

In the next paragraphs, I tug at the threads of Betty Rhee Holt's dress, unraveling some related moments and broader contexts that conditioned Korean migration to the United States from the period of Japanese colonialism through liberation, after the partitioning of the Korean peninsula, and in the immediate Cold War aftermath. In the process, I introduce a second point of reference—a photo and hanbok from my own family—examining how the forces of empire, war, and religion connect experiences across geography and generations. In locating these resonances, I suggest the layered, imperfect, and roomy project of interpretation—the tensions between the particular and the general, the personal and the public, the artifact and its representation, and the practical versus symbolic meaning of things.

A CHANGE OF CLOTHES

The hanbok is a distinctively Korean outfit dating back centuries. It is made from silk, hemp, or cheaper synthetic materials. The form and component pieces typical of both men's and women's hanbok were standardized in the early twentieth century and continue to be modified and reinterpreted—even entering the world of couture. People now differentiate between "traditional" and "modern" hanbok, with the "traditional" mostly worn on special occasions by small children or elderly women. Along with the Republic of Korea flag, the female hanbok serves as one of the most telegraphic visual symbols of Korean culture.

In Korean tradition, children are dressed in colorful hanbok for their 100-day celebrations and first birthdays. Both occasions represent milestones in a child's progress—the first marking survival beyond the vulnerable months of infancy, and the next casting attention toward a fortuitous future. The adults who dressed Betty Rhee Holt and her new sisters presumably did so to celebrate the important threshold that these children were crossing—they were embarking on a new start, leaving behind the tumult and tragedy of their early lives. The gesture of dressing the Holt daughters in hanbok—documented and reproduced through many media outlets—also visually highlighted the transnational, transracial nature of the arrival: foreign babies from a distant country welcomed into white American families.

Clothes are a significant means through which identities are projected. They contribute to the "optics of identity" and difference.[6] Thus they often function in public narratives about immigration to generically signal cultural distinctiveness. It is worth considering then how ethnic clothing such as the Rhee Holt hanbok—both the representation and the artifact—contributes to reinforcing a problematic assumption about cultural and social assimilation: that it is straight-forward, simply a matter of will, or an inevitable process whereby immigrants shed their origins as naturally as a child outgrows a garment.

There was enormous press coverage of the Holt adoption. *Life* magazine published photo spreads of the children in the Korean orphanage, arriving in the United States, and at home in the following days and months. These "before" and "after" images measured the successful incorporation of the children into American life. They contributed to American popular interest in the plight of Korean orphans, which, as many scholars have described, emerged from and replicated the contradictions and interdependency of the U.S.–Korea Cold War relationship—affirming a sense of obligation to Korea, framing this in terms of rescue, and celebrating notions of a human family that could transcend national and racial distinctions.[7] Indeed, hundreds of people subsequently wrote the Holts to learn how they might also adopt Korean orphans.

PROVIDENTIAL PATHWAYS

Against this image of arrival, I consider another from two decades earlier; a personal artifact, a photo from my grandmother's album (Figure 3). This formal portrait

Figure 3.
Sura Kang with her godmother Charlotte Brownlee in Seoul, Korea, early 1930s. Like other American Christian missionaries in Korea, Brownlee worked as an educator and formed lasting relationships with her students and their families. These relationships sometimes provided pathways for future emigration from Korea to the United States. Courtesy of the family of Hui-Sung Youn.

taken in Seoul in the early 1930s shows my mother, Sura Kang, then a young child, with her godmother Charlotte Brownlee, an American Methodist missionary. Brownlee was from Munfordville, Kentucky. She arrived in Korea in 1913, where she worked as a kindergarten teacher, focusing her efforts on children's education, in particular for girls. My grandmother directly benefited from this calling. Though she had never gone to primary school, she learned to read and write in her late teens while attending a Methodist girls' high school, where she met Brownlee.

There is an immediate visual analogy between this and the Holt homecoming photos: both document kinship between European American women and Korean girls—accentuated visually through the age of the women, their associated roles as guardians or protectors, and in the juxtaposition of Western and Korean clothing. Though distinct in the ways they initially functioned—one was a public representation of arrival, the other a personal memento during a departure—both materialize the deep and complex involvement of Protestant Christianity in the peninsula, a dynamic that has been in overlapping degrees productive and patronizing.

The occasion for the photo was Brownlee's imminent departure from Korea for a furlough year back in the States. With escalating instability for Christians and foreigners in Japanese-occupied Korea, the future was uncertain. During her absence, her copy of this keepsake would encourage and remind Brownlee of her work and personal obligations in Korea. For my grandmother, the photo was reassuring evidence of her family's relationship with an advocate and Christian role model.

Today this photo also serves as an artifact representing how the Cold War context of the Holt adoptions extends back before World War II to earlier generations of foreign interventions in the region. Brownlee was part of a movement of Protestant women who embarked on missions in Korea beginning as early as 1884, just after the "hermit kingdom" was forcibly opened through treaty agreements, first by Japan, then by the United States. As a consequence of several intersecting conditions—including a medical missionary's close relationship with the royal family, the struggle for territorial dominance in East Asia, and the subsequent emergence of Japan's colonial claim on Korea—Christianity took firm root and grew. By 1910, the year Korea was annexed by Japan, there were more than 800 Presbyterian and Methodist educational institutions in Korea. By the early 1930s, there were some 300,000 practicing Christians.[8]

Facing rapid change and repression, Koreans found meaningful associations between Christianity and modernization, social reform, and their movement for independence. Through religion, they made enduring relationships with Americans and American institutions. And accordingly, Christianity directly shaped Korean immigration aspirations and opportunities over many generations, in the process creating new forms of privilege and access.[9] For instance, 40 percent of the first Korean laborers who arrived to work in Hawaii's plantations in 1903 were Christian congregants recruited by their ministers. Many of the independence leaders in exile were Methodist or Presbyterian. After liberation, a significant amount of material relief was funneled into the peninsula through Protestant denominations. And as Christian missionaries established the country's earliest orphanages in the late 1800s, faith-based organizations were among the first to facilitate Korean adoption after the Korean War. Missionaries played a major role in promoting and supporting the adoption of Korean children by American families. The Holts themselves were introduced to the orphan "crisis" by Dr. Bob Pierce, founder of the Christian mission service World Vision, which promoted "sponsorship" of Korean orphans. The adoption agency they subsequently established was explicit about their goal to place adoptees into Christian families.

These evangelical endeavors inevitably reinforced American political, economic, and military projects. And relationships of the types documented in the Holt–Rhee and Brownlee–Kang photographs were leveraged to serve the secular imperatives of expansionist foreign policy and the changing racial order in the United States between World War II and the 1960s. Visually, the two images support then-emergent national narratives about the general threat of communism, the specific necessity of American trusteeship over the Korean peninsula to stem this threat, and the dependency of weaker foreign bodies on protective American ones. What's more, the specific bodies in the photographs signal the process through which some Asians were recast as suitable and desirable immigrants during a period of U.S. history otherwise characterized by Asian exclusion.

The stakes of the United States' political realignments and concerns in Asia during and after World War II directly affected domestic immigration policy. As a champion of freedom internationally, the U.S. was pressed to demonstrate its commitment to equality at home. And as certain Asians were reclassified as helpful or in need of help, their potential as citizens improved. Thus, for instance, had the 1943 Magnuson Act ended Chinese exclusion (legislatively) when China was allied with the U.S. in the war against Japan.

My mother was among a very small number of Koreans who came to the United States just after World War II. She and the others who arrived between 1945 and the early 1960s were a wave of "exceptions" more or less equally constituted by three categories: adoptees, brides of U.S. servicemen, and students or professionals with existing ties to the military or religious institutions. Landing in 1949—just after separate governments were established in the two Koreas—my mother enrolled in college, as would her siblings, through the sponsorship of American missionaries such as Charlotte Brownlee.

The Holt children and other adoptees from Korea who would follow in the 1950s and early 1960s were the beneficiaries of legislative changes enabling the non-quota immigration of political refugees, orphans, and war brides. Though the numbers of these post–World War II Asian immigrants were small compared to what would follow after the Immigration and Nationality Act of 1965 (the Hart-Celler Act), they were symbolically important to the ideals the United States projected to itself and the world during the 1950s and 1960s. They, along with my mother's cohort of classmates, embodied the possibility of recovery and redemption after war. At a time when the country's enduring social inequities were being challenged, they were proof of American opportunity. They would appear to demonstrate how diverse peoples could be domesticated and integrated into the national family.[10]

DEPARTURES

Clothes are the wings. They are the basis for lasting impressions, and as such they facilitate our progress and promotion. We also wear specific clothes as we maneuver through the distinct stages of our lives—as did Betty Rhee Holt and her sisters, flying that last leg of their journey between Hawai`i and Oregon, dressed in their bright hanbok.

The things we choose to carry through life with us are significant—doing so takes physical effort. It reflects a valuation—choice of this over that. For over five decades, Betty Rhee Holt's family held onto a dress that she probably outgrew shortly after arriving in the United States. My mother kept certain things—including hanbok—as she migrated through four countries—five, if one figures in her passage south across the 38th parallel in 1945. Occasionally dusted off and aired for a special occasion or portrait, these were otherwise packed away. And over time, they came to be regarded—as with Rhee Holt's baby hanbok—as mementos, not unlike the bronzed shoes and locks of hair that people hold on to as touching, almost unbelievable evidence of who they once were.

My grandmother, Hui-Sung Youn, immigrated to the United States in 1972 through the family reunification preference of the Hart-Celler Act. Prior to this, she had been able to visit her children by accompanying Holt adoptees on their flights from Korea to the USA—an arrangement related to her involvement in Christian churches and schools. When she departed Korea for good, my grandmother left behind a kindergarten she founded in Brownlee's name. She brought with her many hanbok. But she was old school, and these were her daily attire—they were a functional part of her wardrobe. She had some for church and other formal occasions. She also brought from Korea the garment in which we were instructed to bury her. In the meantime, it was stored in our basement amid trunks of baby clothes, boxes of schoolbooks, souvenirs of our American childhoods. When she died in 1992, we dressed her in the hanbok, a plain dress of off-white fabric, a traditional contrast to the bright colors worn for birthdays and weddings. I remember my mother carefully tying the sash to fasten the top jacket, a simple gesture acknowledging that departures, like arrivals, are thresholds of great significance and that the substance of clothes is both material and immaterial.

NOTES

Thanks to Stephen Callis, Lawrence-Minh Bùi Davis, William Estrada, Veronica Jackson, Eric Kang, Somi Kim, Valerie Matsumoto, Shelley Nickles, and David Yoo for their feedback and assistance on this chapter.

1. There were a total of 12 children in this group of adoptees. Eight were adopted by the Holts, four were adopted by other families.

2. In the early 2000s, the National Museum of American History undertook a project on the subject of Korean adoption in the United States. See Shelley Nickles, "Korean Adoption: An American Story" and "Proposal: Children of the Korean War," two documents that framed the research and collecting efforts (Washington, D.C.: National Museum of American History Collections, 2003).

3. Tobias Hübinette, *Comforting an Orphaned Nation: Adoption and Adopted Koreans in Korean Popular Culture* (Stockholm: Stockholm University, 2005); Jane Jeong Trenka, Julia Chinyere Oparah, and Sun Yung Shin, eds. *Outsiders Within: Writing on Transracial Adoption* (Campbridge, MA: South End Press, 2006). Dong Soo Kim, "A Country Divided: Contextualizing Adoption from a Korean Perspective," in *International Korean Adoption: A Fifty-Year History of Policy and Practice*, eds. Kathleen Ja Sook Bergquist, M. Elizabeth Vonk, Dong Soo Kim, and Marvin D. Feit (Binghamton, N.Y.: The Haworth Press, 2007), 3–17; Rebecca Hurdis, "Lifting the Shroud of Silence: A Korean Adoptee's Search for Truth, Legitimacy, and Justice," in Bergquist et al., *International Korean Adoption*, 171–78; Jae Ran Kim, "Waiting for God: Religion and Korean American Adoption," in *Religion and*

Spirituality in Korean America, eds. David K. Yoo and Ruth H. Chung (Urbana: University of Illinois, 2008), 83–99; Eleana J. Kim, *Adopted Territory: Transnational Korean Adoptees and the Politics of Belonging* (Durham, N.C.: Duke University Press, 2010); Catherine Ceniza Choy, *Global Families: A History of Asian International Adoption in America* (New York: New York University Press, 2013); Soojin Pate, *From Orphan to Adoptee: U.S. Empire and Genealogies of Korean Adoption* (Minneapolis: University of Minnesota Press, 2014); and David K. Yoo and Eiichiro Azuma, eds., *The Oxford Handbook of Asian American History* (New York: Oxford University Press, 2016).

4. Yoo and Chung, eds., *Religion and Spirituality in Korean America;* David K. Yoo, *Contentious Spirits: Religion in Korean American History, 1903–1945* (Stanford: Stanford University Press, 2010); Albert L. Park and David K. Yoo, eds., *Encountering Modernity: Christianity in East Asia and Asian America* (Honolulu: University of Hawai`i Press, 2014).

5. Sean Metzger, *Chinese Looks: Fashion, Performance, Race* (Bloomington: Indiana University Press, 2014); and Christina Klein, *Cold War Orientalism: Asia in the Middlebrow Imagination, 1945–1961* (Berkeley: University of California Press, 2003).

6. Diana Baird N'Diaye, "The Will to Adorn and the Optics of Identity," *Talk Story: Culture in Motion,* December 2014, http://www.folklife.si.edu/talkstory/2014/the-will-to-adorn-and-the-optics-of-identity/.

7. It is also important to recognize the connection between such popular media campaigns and Time Life publisher Henry R. Luce, whose family was well connected to missionary projects in Asia and who was a very vocal advocate of American anti-communism intervention in Asian countries, including Korea. Kim, "Waiting for God," and Klein, *Cold War Orientalism.*

8. Yoo, *Contentious Spirits* and Elizabeth Underwood, *Challenged Identities: North American Missionaries in Korea, 1884–1934* (Seoul: Royal Asiatic Society, Korea Branch, 2003).

9. For an explanation of the shifting role of Protestant Christianity in Korean society—from serving as a force for social reform and the independence movement to being a more socially and politically conservative agent of the establishment after liberation and the Korean War—see Chung-Shin Park, *Protestantism and Politics in Korea* (Seattle: University of Washington Press, 2003) and Robert E. Buswell Jr. and Timothy S. Lee, eds., *Christianity in Korea* (Honolulu: University of Hawaii Press, 2006).

10. For discussion of the "Cold War imperative" that informed the transformation of Asians from inassimilable into model minorities, see Robert G. Lee, *Orientals: Asian Americans in Popular Culture* (Philadelphia: Temple University Press, 1999); Klein, *Cold War Orientalism*; Madeline Y. Hsu, *The Good Immigrants: How the Yellow Peril Became the Model Minority* (Princeton: Princeton University Press, 2015); Ellen D. Wu, *The Color of Success: Asian Americans and the Origins of the Model Minority* (Princeton: Princeton University Press, 2014); and Simeon Man, "Empire and War in Asian American History" in Yoo and Azuma, eds., *The Oxford Handbook of Asian American History,* 253–66.

BIBLIOGRAPHY

Bergquist, Kathleen Ja Sook, M. Elizabeth Vonk, Dong Soo Kim, and Marvin D. Feit, eds. *International Korean Adoption: A Fifty-Year History of Policy and Practice.* Binghamton, N.Y.: The Haworth Press, 2007.

Buswell Jr., Robert E., and Timothy S. Lee, eds. *Christianity in Korea.* Honolulu: University of Hawaii Press, 2006.

Choy, Catherine Ceniza. *Global Families: A History of Asian International Adoption in America*. New York: New York University Press, 2013.

Hsu, Madeline Y. *The Good Immigrants: How the Yellow Peril Became the Model Minority*. Princeton: Princeton University Press, 2015.

Hübinette, Tobias. *Comforting an Orphaned Nation: Adoption and Adopted Koreans in Korean Popular Culture*. Stockholm: Stockholm University, 2005.

Hurdis, Rebecca. "Lifting the Shroud of Silence: A Korean Adoptee's Search for Truth, Legitimacy, and Justice." In *International Korean Adoption: A Fifty-Year History of Policy and Practice*, ed. Kathleen Ja Sook Bergquist, M. Elizabeth Vonk, Dong Soo Kim, and Marvin D. Feit, pp. 171–78. Binghamton, N.Y.: The Haworth Press, 2007.

Kim, Dong Su. "A Country Divided: Contextualizing Adoption from a Korean Perspective." In *International Korean Adoption: A Fifty-Year History of Policy and Practice*, ed. Kathleen Ja Sook Bergquist, M. Elizabeth Vonk, Dong Soo Kim, and Marvin D. Feit, pp. 3–17. Binghamton, N.Y.: The Haworth Press, 2007.

Kim, Eleana J. *Adopted Territory: Transnational Korean Adoptees and the Politics of Belonging*. Durham, N.C.: Duke University Press, 2010.

Kim, Jae Ran. "Waiting for God: Religion and Korean American Adoption." In *Religion and Spirituality in Korean America*, ed. David K. Yoo and Ruth H. Chung, pp. 83–99. Urbana: University of Illinois, 2008.

Klein, Christina. *Cold War Orientalism: Asia in the Middlebrow Imagination, 1945–1961*. Berkeley: University of California Press, 2003.

Lee, Robert G. *Orientals: Asian Americans in Popular Culture*. Philadelphia: Temple University Press, 1999.

Man, Simeon. "Empire and War in Asian American History." In *The Oxford Handbook of Asian American History*, ed. David K. Yoo and Eiichiro Azuma, pp. 253–66. New York: Oxford University Press, 2016.

Metzger, Sean. *Chinese Looks: Fashion, Performance, Race*. Bloomington: Indiana University Press, 2014.

N'Diaye, Diana Baird. "The Will to Adorn and the Optics of Identity." *Talk Story: Culture in Motion* (blog). 17 December 2014. http://www.folklife.si.edu/talkstory/2014/the-will-to-adorn-and-the-optics-of-identity/ (accessed 7 November 2016).

Nickles, Shelley. "Korean Adoption: An American Story" and "Proposal: Children of the Korean War." Washington, D.C.: National Museum of American History Collections, 2003.

Park, Albert L. and David K. Yoo, eds. *Encountering Modernity: Christianity in East Asia and Asian America*. Honolulu: University of Hawai`i Press, 2014.

Park, Chung-Shin. *Protestantism and Politics in Korea*. Seattle: University of Washington Press, 2003.

Pate, Soojin. *From Orphan to Adoptee: U.S. Empire and Genealogies of Korean Adoption*. Minneapolis: University of Minnesota Press, 2014.

Trenka, Jane Jeong, Julia Chinyere Oparah, and Sun Yung Shin, eds. *Outsiders Within: Writing on Transracial Adoption*. Cambridge, MA: Sound End Press, 2006.

Underwood, Elizabeth. *Challenged Identities: North American Missionaries in Korea, 1884–1934*. Seoul: Royal Asiatic Society, Korea Branch, 2003.

Wu, Ellen D. *The Color of Success: Asian Americans and the Origins of the Model Minority*. Princeton: Princeton University Press, 2014.

Yoo, David K. *Contentious Spirits: Religion in Korean American History, 1903–1945*. Stanford: Stanford University Press, 2010.

Yoo, David K. and Eiichiro Azuma, eds. *The Oxford Handbook of Asian American History*. New York: Oxford University Press, 2016.

Yoo, David K., and Ruth H. Chung, eds. *Religion and Spirituality in Korean America*. Urbana: University of Illinois, 2008.

New Americans, Continuing Debates, 1965–2014

Margaret Salazar-Porzio

After 1965, immigration patterns significantly shifted with the passage of the Immigration and Nationality Act (Hart-Celler Act). At the same time, jet planes made immigration and migration easier and cheaper, while new technologies for information sharing and communication became increasingly part of everyday life in the United States. Discourses about race and nation changed with political advances in civil and human rights and as new sociocultural intersections shaped our local, national, and transnational identities. Cultural identities have been shaped by global exchanges for centuries, but after 1965 new immigration policies coupled with advancements in transportation and communication technologies allowed for more constant flows of people, ideas, and goods. These movements sparked a kind of cultural globalism that challenges our assumptions around race and nation.[1] Visual and material culture reflects these changes and offers ways to rethink enduring inequalities and the possibilities for alliance toward social justice amid accelerating globalization.

This essay puts into historical context a few examples of visual and material representations from our recent past to demonstrate how communities exist in complex relationships within global circuits of exchange. First, the essay provides a chronological overview of how policies put into place in 1965 have affected our nation. Then, the essay takes a thematic approach, examining representations that reflect national trends and popular notions of race and nation in the post-1965 era. Finally, it suggests how we might look to these kinds of representations as a way to understand our shared future.

At one level, these visual and material artifacts suggest the boundaries of race might be transcended through a multicultural discourse. But they can also provide a deeper look into inter-group relations in the United States. These representations and the stories behind them situate notions of race, ethnicity, and class within historically shaped axes of power and inequality.[2]

Our current moment calls for a visual and material look that takes into consideration both changing demographics and how communities interact in an increasingly connected and globalized world. This section explores some of the rich crossings of race and place in the recent past. Post-1965 visual and material culture can help us reimagine communities, urban histories, political borders, and new migrations by thinking about their intersections.

THE CHANGING FACE OF AMERICA

The civil rights movements of the 1950s spurred many American liberal activists and politicians into action, and they initiated bold new government policies to advance racial equality. This progressive agenda soon included women's rights, new social programs for the poor and elderly, job training, environmental laws, and educational and other social benefits for the middle class. In fact, Congress passed more progressive legislation between 1964 and 1972 than in any period since the New Deal of the 1930s.[3]

In May 1964, the nation still reeling from John F. Kennedy's assassination the year before, President Lyndon Baines Johnson delivered a commencement address at the University of Michigan outlining his vision for the future. Barely six months in office, Johnson stated, "We have the opportunity to move not only toward the rich society and the powerful society, but upward to the Great Society."[4] Johnson successfully advanced his ambitious Great Society liberal reform program, securing not only civil rights legislation but also an array of policies in education, medical care, transportation, environmental protection, poverty reduction, immigration reform, and programs to revitalize the arts and humanities.[5] It even became possible, at this moment of reform zeal, to tackle the nation's discriminatory immigration policy with the Immigration and Nationality Act of 1965, also known as the Hart-Celler Act.[6]

Figure 1.
President Lyndon B. Johnson speaking to a crowd on Liberty Island, New York City, New York, to mark the signing of the Immigration and Nationality Act, 1965. The Immigration and Nationality Act (Hart-Celler) transformed immigration policy by abolishing the previous quota system, focusing on family reunification, and supporting skilled labor. Courtesy of the Lyndon B. Johnson Presidential Library, photograph by Yoichi Okamoto.

The events of 1965 would have profound implications for the nation in the late twentieth and early twenty-first centuries. In this one year, the civil rights revolution reached its apex and a new immigration policy was put into place. At the same time, urban unrest bubbled up in big cities from Los Angeles to New York. Despite public policy advances, fissures in Johnson's Great Society widened and deepened as the US embarked on a major war in Vietnam and anti-war youth movements and urban rebellions across the nation were broadcast in the news media. In the decades after 1965, the nation would see new and renewed struggles for rights and justice, the resurgence of political and religious conservatism, the end of the Cold War, the globalization of economies and communications, and the development of new technologies for transportation and information.[7] An extraordinary flow of new immigrants after the Hart-Celler Act also led to new intergroup dynamics. Material culture of the era reflects these new demographic shifts and the limits and contradictions of contemporary racial discourses.

The Hart-Celler Act abandoned a quota system that favored northern European immigrants, replacing it with numerical limits for countries across the globe. President Johnson signed the law at the base of the Statue of Liberty and said simply that immigrants would be admitted "on the basis of their skills and their close relationship to those already here"[8] (Figure 1). American residents from Latin America and the Caribbean were best positioned to take advantage of this family reunification provision. Millions of Mexican immigrants came to the United States to join their families, and U.S. residents from El Salvador, Guatemala, and the Dominican Republic brought their families to join them. Tens of thousands of immigrants from El Salvador and Guatemala arrived seeking sanctuary or asylum during the civil wars of the 1980s and were now able to be reunited with family. While many were able to seek asylum, others were denied refugee status. Considering their great numbers, relatively few were able to be legally reunited with family even though it was U.S. intervention in Latin America that had displaced them.[9] Despite various difficulties in immigrating to the United States from Latin America, in just a few decades Latinos began outnumbering African Americans in a notable demographic shift.[10]

Yet, if the abolition of national origins quotas in 1965 was an inclusionary reform, Hart-Celler also continued numerical restriction, imposing it on the entire world. Countries in the Western Hemisphere that previously had no numerical limits now faced significant restrictions. The global nature of equal restrictions on all countries, regardless of size, need, or relationship to the United States, demonstrated a civil rights–era ethos of formal legal equality.[11] Ironically, as Mae Ngai has shown, Hart-Celler has also been the single most important reason for undocumented migration since 1965.[12]

Between 1970 and 2000, the Census Bureau reported that the population of the United States grew by 77 million. Of this population increase, immigrants accounted for 28 million, with legal entrants numbering 21 million and undocumented entrants estimated at about seven million. Relatively few immigrants came from Europe, which had dominated immigration to the United States since colonial times. The overwhelming majority—some 25 million—now came from Latin America (16 million) and East Asia (nine million). During these decades, Asian immigrants came largely from China, the Philippines, South Korea, India, and Pakistan. In addition, 700,000 refugees came to the United States from Southeast Asia (Vietnam, Laos, and Cambodia) after the

Vietnam War. This immigration signaled more than new flows of people into the United States. At the same time immigration from Asia increased, Japan and China were also growing more influential economically, and more transnational trade crossed the Pacific.[13] Throughout much of its history, the US had oriented itself toward the Atlantic. Now economic, political, and immigration patterns would turn toward the Pacific.

During this time, unmistakable immigration and migration trends resulted in renewed debates over ethnic and racial identity and public policies, which looked a great deal like conflicts in the early decades of the century. Then, many native-born white Protestants worried that the largely Catholic and Jewish immigrants from southern and eastern Europe, along with African American migrants leaving the South, could not assimilate and threatened the imagined "purity" of the nation. Although the conflicts looked the same, the cultural paradigm had shifted. In the early twentieth century, the "melting pot"—a term borrowed from the eponymous 1908 play—became a metaphor for how American society could accommodate diversity.[14] The melting pot idea required ethnic groups to assimilate to a generic European American model. Many native-born Americans found solace in this melting pot concept because it implied that a single "American" culture existed and would predominate once all newcomers assimilated into the so-called mainstream.

Others envisioned a pluralistic American society that would eventually replace the "melting pot" assimilationist discourse. By the 1990s, concepts like transnationalism, multiculturalism, and hybridity became widely used. Each overlaps in different ways and has particular political implications, and all fall short of truly describing the complicated processes of "becoming American" that are part and parcel of living in the United States.

FROM NATIONAL TO TRANSNATIONAL

As new transportation technologies like the Boeing 747 airplane allowed for people to travel easily across oceans, transnational identities became more common and easily maintained. Religion and spirituality are a prime location in culture to find evidence of change and cultural blendings. The Hindu Temple of North America, established in 1971 in Queens, New York, by a group of newly arrived Indian professionals, created an ecumenical symbol as their logo that captured this transnational experience (Figure 2). The symbol and the temple provide a

Figure 2.
Prototype religious symbol for the Hindu Temple Society building in Flushing, Queens, New York, created around 1970. It incorporates symbols for five of the world's faiths: (clockwise from top) Hinduism, Buddhism, Christianity, Judaism, and Islam. They surround a central symbol representing the lamp of knowledge and the sixth religion of Universalism. National Museum of American History, Smithsonian Institution, gift of Hindu Temple Society of North America.

dynamic material record of transnational relationships that cross cultural and political borders. Both were designed and built by artisans from India and composed of largely imported materials. The construction process became a transnational exchange of ideas, people, materials, and religious beliefs—made possible by advances in transportation and communication.

The prototype of the temple's religious symbol, once carved into the building's original facade, also represents a new kind of transcultural identification[15] (Figure 3). The symbol features five of the world's major faiths—Hinduism, Buddhism, Christianity, Judaism, and Islam. They are illuminated by the lamp of knowledge and Universalism in the center. This ecumenical symbol invites us to consider the creative weavings of religious practice as transcultural alliance. Queens, arguably the most diverse borough of New York City with proponents of religious freedom dating back to colonial times, provides an important space for blending traditions. The religious iconography featured in this singular transcultural, transnational symbol brings multiple faiths together and reveals connections between new immigrant and migrant populations and their receiving communities in the United States. The ecumenical symbol welcomes practitioners of all faiths into the space for worship, community, and sustenance; a dining hall in the lower level serves traditional Indian dishes. In this story of intersections, the United States is not a clearly demarcated or homogeneous nation made up of assimilated or assimilating immigrants. Instead, this is a story of fluidity

Figure 3.
The Hindu Temple Society of North America temple in Queens, New York, photographed around 1990. This temple building was opened in 1977. The ecumenical symbol, representing six of the world's religions, was originally carved into the facade to the right of the entrance. Courtesy of the Hindu Temple Society of North America.

that allows for difference, coexistence, and coming together—a transcultural and transnational process that is ongoing.

FROM MELTING POT TO MULTICULTURAL

In the 1980s and 1990s, the concept of "multiculturalism" emerged as a popular way to define the complexities of social diversity. Americans, this concept suggested, were not a single people into whom others melded; rather, they comprised a diverse set of ethnic and racial groups living and working together or at least in close proximity.[16] The definition of "American" could change, rather than requiring the burden of change to be shouldered only by ethnic "others." In the end, however, multiculturalism was a power-evasive, celebratory framework that depended on a unified nation.

Posters of interracial labor coalitions demonstrate the importance of this multicultural discourse to campaigns for equality and better conditions in the workplace. A poster from the International League of Garment Workers Union (ILGWU) in New York City illustrates how diverse racial and socioeconomic groups came together with common goals in the struggles for better labor conditions and pay (Figure 4). Eventually, through strike activity and pressure tactics, the largely female membership, as well as union officials, became vital players in industry negotiations.[17] This poster commemorates a 1982 victory won by the union's diverse constituency and features two hands clasped at the forefront; one is covered by a red sleeve with white lace at the cuff, the other is clothed in a traditional white dress shirt peeking out from under a navy-blue coat sleeve. The handshake is meant to represent an agreement between the mostly female garment workers and predominantly male garment manufacturer executives.

In the background, hands of various skin tones uphold the ILGWU's insignia. Garment workers in New York City in the 1980s were frequently Chinese or Central or South American immigrants who faced long hours under stressful, unhealthy conditions with no opportunities for advancement. They understood the importance of coming together in common cause despite their different backgrounds and languages. Chinese writing at the right side of the poster is translated below the image to repeat the bilingual message: "There is strength in unity." In the center of the poster is the flowing word "Victory" heralded by a dragon in the shape of the letter "V" to symbolize cultural traditions in New York City's Chinatown. This poster reveals how a particular union embraced a kind of stereotypical cultural diversity, while also suggesting that uniting across races and ethnicities would allow all to succeed together.

A second poster from the 1980s combines a host of important interracial civil and human rights organizations: the SEIU, or Service Employees International Union, which unites workers in healthcare, property services (building cleaning and security), and public services (state government workers, public school employees, bus drivers, and childcare); NOW, the National Organization for Women, a feminist advocacy group that focuses on achieving full equality for women through education and litigation; the NAACP, or National Association for the Advancement of Colored People, which played an integral role in the fight for African American civil rights and currently ensures "political, educational, social, and economic equality of rights for all persons;"[18] and MALDEF, the Mexican American Legal Defense and Educational Fund, a leading Latino legal civil rights organization (Figure 5).

Figure 4.
Poster from the 23–25 International Ladies Garment Workers Union, AFL-CIO, 1982. The poster from the local union chapter in New York City's Chinatown celebrates rallies and strike mobilization that involved over 10,000 Chinese women immigrants. National Museum of American History, Smithsonian Institution, gift of the International Ladies Garment Workers Union.

Figure 5.
"Together Against Discrimination" poster, from around 1987. The poster urges equal treatment regardless of gender, ethnicity, race, and religious faith. It celebrates a partnership between the Service Employees International Union, the National Organization for Women, the National Association for the Advancement of Colored People, and the Mexican American Legal Defense and Education Fund. National Museum of American History, Smithsonian Institution, gift of Service Employees International Union.

The poster features four faces of different races and genders under the bold stanza: "We are male and female / Young and old / People of all races / And religious faiths. / We are America / And we are together / Against discrimination." The poster links these four groups to struggles for rights and justice while redefining American identity in a way that reflects racial diversity within a multicultural discourse. Multicultural coalitions like these certainly focused on cross-racial and intergroup relations, but, as NOW's inclusion demonstrates, gender was another important dimension that cut across struggles for social justice. Although the discrimination experiences of women, especially women of color, were and are frequently the product of intersecting patterns of racism and sexism, these experiences tended not to be represented within multicultural discourses of the time.[19]

While mainstream multiculturalism often depoliticized labor rights campaigns, clearly organizations interested in better conditions for working people found strength in cross-gender and interracial coalition building. These posters suggest there was room within multiculturalism to create antidiscrimination movements for justice and equality.

A decade later, in the fall of 1993, *Time* magazine published a cover that provides an important entry point from which to understand post-1965 demographic change and debates over multiculturalism[20] (Figure 6). The cover features a computer-generated multiracial woman. The image represented an imagined U.S. future of both racial synthesis and cutting-edge technology. At the time, this rendering was seen as a revolutionary computer design based on the projected future racial and ethnic composition of the U.S. population. An attractive feminine "mix" of "Anglo Saxon, Middle Eastern, African, Asian, Southern European, and Hispanic," she was to be "The New Face of America," an example of "How Immigrants are Shaping the World's First Multicultural Society."[21]

When *Time* magazine published its multiracial cover girl, the ideology of multiculturalism was already an integral part of popular culture. The concept was widely accepted because it could emphasize the pleasant aspects of ethnic diversity without engaging the challenge of cultural differences and the existence of racial hierarchies. Multicultural images like this one ignore the importance of historical, geographic, and cultural inequalities in determining racialization in the United States. At the same time, gender plays an important role in making this multicultural representation palatable to a broad American public. Using the metaphor of the multicultural society, *Time* author Danzy Senna updated the melting pot cliché by featuring a depoliticized multicultural woman whose

Figure 6.
Time magazine special issue, 18 November 1993. Post-1965 immigration to the United States changed the racial and ethnic composition of the nation. *Time* and other magazines illustrated these demographic shifts on their covers. From *Time* Magazine (Volume 142 Number 22) © Time Inc., used under license.

existence celebrated racial mixture through a computer-rendered racial synthesis that ignores the long history of antimiscegenation laws, gender dynamics, and sexist customs in the United States.[22] The attractive, multiracial woman personified a nonthreatening future *Time* thought its readers would accept.

These decades also included culture wars raging over family values, federal and state laws, global warming, immigration, sexuality, separation of church and state, censorship, and the political economy, among other issues.[23] Many believed a shared set of public values could hold a multicultural U.S. society together, despite ideological differences and even as various groups maintained unique cultural traditions. Proponents of multiculturalism likened this view of American culture to a "stew" or "salad bowl"—metaphors that allow for the survival of ethnic differences while assuming individuals would and could still be part of a national whole.

Critics of multiculturalism have argued the discourse is a highly simplistic way of understanding racial and ethnic differences. Others have contended that multiculturalism perpetuated ethnic chauvinism and conferred preferential treatment on "undeserving" minority groups. Anxieties about a multicultural nation have further resulted in anti–affirmative action campaigns and English-only language mandates.[24] Nativist movements also resurfaced in the late twentieth century. Legislation like California's Proposition 187 (1994), which punished "illegal immigrants by restricting their access to schools, medical care, and other social services," revealed a new kind of anti-immigrant sentiment.[25] Like the nativism based on ideas of racial superiority that appeared in the early twentieth century at the height of Southern and Eastern European immigration to the United States, nativism in the late twentieth century also was deeply connected to racism.[26] With the increase of immigration from Asia and Latin America in the post-1965 era, nativists could direct their frustration toward immigrant groups who did not look European.[27] Over the years, immigrants themselves responded to these attacks by increasing political activity, forming communities and alliances such as the Coalition of Immokalee Workers, featured in the next pages.

FROM POLAR OPPOSITES TO A THIRD SPACE

By the mid-1990s, as the so-called culture wars reached new levels of polarization, it became clear our social and cultural lives existed outside of multiculturalist or binary ways of thinking. The notion of hybridity became popular as a cultural process (a scientific notion borrowed from biology and horticulture) that provided an alternative to polar opposites along the spectrum of political debate. Many in the United States and across the globe found the concept provided a third possibility.[28] Hybridity refers to sociocultural transformation in which different groups generate new fusions out of existing cultural traditions.[29] This is distinct from the idea of a "melting pot," which refers to assimilation into a singular American mainstream culture—one that by this time seemed no longer possible and at best highly fractured. Hybridity provided another possibility and a way out of binary thinking that allows for agency and even a restructuring and destabilizing of power.[30] Although scholars are skeptical about the validity of an exuberant kind of hybridity that challenges oppressive forces, the following example illustrates how this might just be possible.

Like the interracial labor organizations featured in earlier posters, the story of the Coalition of Immokalee Workers (CIW) is about intergroup collaborations. The representations they produce for social justice campaigns reveal a kind of hybridization of cultures and identities. The CIW, founded in 1993, is a loose-knit cross-racial coalition of agricultural workers, foodies, environmentalists, and even celebrities that advocates for better conditions for agricultural workers as well as local and independent alternatives to the industrial food system.[31]

Figure 7.
The March for Dignity, Dialogue, and a Fair Wage, Florida, 2000. The Coalition of Immokalee Workers and partner activists marched from Fort Myers to Orlando, Florida, to advocate for improved working conditions and higher wages in the agricultural industry. Courtesy of Kat Rodriguez.

Our entry point to this story is a sculpture of the Statue of Liberty, made by Latina artist and community organizer Kat Rodriguez and carried on a two-week, 230-mile "March for Dignity, Dialogue, and a Fair Wage" from Fort Myers to Orlando, Florida, in early 2000 (Figure 7). This sculpture represents more than liberty. In the statue's left arm is a bucket of tomatoes; her right hand extends into the air to offer up a single tomato, and on the pedestal reads a simple message borrowed from the Harlem Renaissance poet Langston Hughes: "I, too, am America!"[32] Rodriguez painted the statue's bronze skin tone to reflect the racial diversity of the mostly Mexican, Haitian, Mayan, and Guatemalan agricultural workers and CIW labor organizers. The statue combines the recognizable green patina of Lady Liberty with a skin color that reflects current U.S. demographics. Part national symbol and part agricultural worker, this sculpture allows for grassroots action as it confronts power relations (Figure 8).

New Americans, Continuing Debates

Figure 8.
Immokalee Statue of Liberty, created by Kat Rodriguez, 2000. This rendition of the Statue of Liberty is holding a tomato in her right hand instead of a torch, and a tomato basket in her left hand instead of a tablet. The papier-mâché and mixed-media sculpture linked the struggles of migrant farm workers with a powerful symbol of immigration to the United States. National Museum of American History, Smithsonian Institution, gift of Coalition of Immokalee Workers.

The Florida march displayed new strength and momentum for organized labor. In the postwar period's McCarthyist and anti-union atmosphere, labor union membership and effectiveness significantly declined. Many industries, in particular the garment industry, responded to union strength by moving work from cities to other areas and then overseas. In the 1980s, union busting became particularly intense.[33] In fact, since the labor movements of the 1950s and 1960s, many organizers' gains have been few and far between. But the CIW has found ways to be successful. A diverse base of support and new strategies for targeting large corporations in this era of global capitalism have made it possible for the coalition to win battles for higher pay and better working conditions. Here the Statue of Liberty is a national symbol made more powerful by its hybrid representation that highlights persistent issues of inequality. Representations like this can challenge a nationalistic melting pot story by calling attention to the unequal distribution of resources and payment for labor.

SHIFTING DEMOGRAPHICS

The fundamental demographic shifts in American society after Hart-Celler have led to striking changes in intergroup relations and the identification of new cultural processes like transnationalism, multiculturalism, and hybridization. Clearly, individual and group identities and experiences in the United States could not be contained in or understood through a singular sociocultural framework. The mixing, crossing, and defying of categories manifest in different material ways. The *Many Voices, One Nation* exhibition uses artifacts of cross-racial collaboration, coalition, and exchange to help visitors recognize assumptions about identity as well as the contradictions present in everyday life. These representations will become even more important as demographics shift in dramatic ways over the next decades of the twenty-first century.

The Pew Research Hispanic Trends Project has projected that by 2050 the nation's racial and ethnic mix will be majority nonwhite. Latino and Asian communities are two of the fastest-growing populations in this demographic shift. Pew's research suggests that by 2050, numbers of Latinos or Hispanics will rise to 29 percent, and people of Asian descent will rise to 9 percent of the overall population. African Americans were 13 percent of the population in 2005 and will likely be around the same proportion in 2050, while non-Hispanic whites, who made up 67 percent of the population in 2005, will be only 47 percent in 2050.[34] These numbers indicate that within the next 50 years, almost half of the United States will be of Asian and Latino descent, a trend that has already significantly disrupted and will continue to disrupt the color line that W. E. B. Du Bois so famously articulated at the turn of the twentieth century in his seminal work *The Souls of Black Folk*.[35] As this essay has detailed, especially in the post-1965 era, much of this demographic change is the direct result of large-scale Asian and Latino immigration and settlement, which has become a fundamental dimension of many spaces and their cultural politics.

Ideas are powerful and complicated. Their material forms, like those featured in this essay, move us beyond melting-pot or multiculturalist ideologies toward a more complex understanding of identities shaped by forces of racism, classism, capitalism, and geopolitics. As a curator, the challenge is to present these objects in a way that invites visitors to read the political implications of human experiences beyond celebrations of simplistic notions of multiculturalism—and in less than 100 words for each museum label.

After 1965, many throughout the United States realized our assumptions and beliefs about identities were inadequate and imprecise in the face of new migrations. When our intellectual concepts are measured against the material world, it becomes apparent we require an expansion of our social imaginaries to better understand ourselves in relation to each other. Material culture can offer a critical framework that might allow us to imagine our different communities through intersections instead of limitations.

NOTES

1. Globalism refers to a world characterized by networks of connections spanning multiple continents. It is a way of understanding the interconnections of our contemporary world as well as patterns that underlie and explain these processes. For a deep and broad look at these processes, see Michael Hardt and Antonio Negri, *Empire* (Cambridge, Mass.: Harvard University Press, 2000). Literatures on identification, hybridity, and *mestizaje* are all useful in this essay in different ways. Selected key texts on these issues include: Diana Fuss, *Identification Papers: Readings on Psychoanalysis, Sexuality, and Culture* (New York: Routledge, 1995); Judith Butler, *The Psychic Life of Power Theories in Subjection* (Stanford: Stanford University Press, 1997) and *Gender Trouble: Feminism and the Subversion of Identity* (New York: Routledge, 1989); Homi Bhabha, *The Location of Culture* (London: Routledge, 1994); Pnina Webner and Tariq Modood, eds., *Debating Cultural Hybridity* (London: Zed Books, 1997); Robert Young, *Colonial Desire: Hybridity in Theory, Culture, and Race* (London: Routledge, 1995); Nestor García-Canclini, *Hybrid Cultures: Strategies for Entering and Leaving Modernity* (Minneapolis: University of Minnesota Press, 1995); Gloria Anzaldúa, *Borderlands/La Frontera* (San Francisco: Spinsters/Aunt Lute, 1987). George Lipsitz, *The Possessive Investment in Whiteness* (Philadelphia: Temple University Press, 1998), documents numerous historical instances of alliance, identification, and tension among people of color in traditional politics. Gary Okihiro, *Margins and Mainstreams: Asians in American History and Culture* (Seattle: University of Washington Press, 1994), specifically cites instances of such cross-identifications and collaborations between Asian Americans and African Americans. See Wendy Cheng, *The Changs Next Door to the Díazes: Remapping Race in Suburban California* (Minneapolis: University of Minnesota Press, 2013); John Horton, *The Politics of Diversity: Immigration, Resistance, and Change in Monterey Park, California* (Philadelphia: Temple University Press, 1995); Leland Saito, *Race and Politics* (Urbana: University of Illinois Press, 1998); Mary Pardo, *Mexican-American Women Activists: Identity and Resistance in Two Los Angeles Communities* (Philadelphia: Temple University Press, 1998) for coalitions and tensions among Anglos, Asian Americans, and Chicano/Latinos in Monterey Park, California. A burgeoning literature examines interracial alliances, affiliations, and conflicts, often revealing the historically unstable and contingent nature of race and the intersection with gender and class, among other social forces. For historical works, see Ronald Takaki, *Iron Cages: Race and Culture in 19th Century America* (Oxford: Oxford University Press, 1979); and Neil Foley, *The White Scourge:*

Mexicans, Blacks, and Poor Whites in Texas Cotton Culture (Berkeley: University of California Press, 1997), for example.

2. Here I primarily refer to Michael Omi and Howard Winnant, *Racial Formation in the United States* (New York: Routledge, 1986; third edition published 2015) and Louis Althusser, *Lenin and Philosophy and Other Essays,* trans. Ben Brewster (New York: Monthly Review Press, 2001).

3. For documentation on the shift from civil rights to human rights, see: Thomas F. Jackson, *From Civil Rights to Human Rights: Martin Luther King, Jr., and the Struggle for Economic Justice* (Philadelphia: University of Pennsylvania Press, 2007).

4. Lyndon B. Johnson, "Remarks at the University of Michigan," 22 May 1964, in *Public Papers of the Presidents of the United States: Lyndon B. Johnson, 1963–64,* Vol. 1 (Washington, D.C.: Government Printing Office, 1965), 704–7.

5. Scholarly accounts of Johnson's work show that his motives were complex. As a southerner who previously opposed civil rights for African Americans, Johnson wished to make a mark on history in memorial to his slain predecessor, and to make a name for himself as a president of all the people through his Great Society initiatives. See Michael L. Gillette, *Launching the War on Poverty: An Oral History* (Oxford: Oxford Oral History Series, 2010); and Annelise Orleck and Lisa Gayle Hazirjian, eds., *The War on Poverty: A New Grassroots History, 1964–1980* (Athens: University of Georgia Press, 2011) for strong background and analysis. For more information on the Great Society see: Gareth Davies, *From Opportunity to Entitlement: The Transformation and Decline of Great Society Liberalism* (Lawrence: University Press of Kansas, 1996); Sidney M. Milkis and Jerome M. Mileur, eds., *The Great Society and the High Tide of Liberalism* (Boston: University of Massachusetts Press, 2005). And for a traditional account of Johnson's presidency: Vaughn Davis Bornet, *The Presidency of Lyndon B. Johnson* (Lawrence: University Press of Kansas, 1983).

6. Aristide R. Zolberg, *A Nation by Design: Immigration Policy in the Fashioning of America* (Cambridge, Mass.: Harvard University Press, 2006) has chronicled the development of American immigration policy from its early roots in the decade preceding the Declaration of Independence through its development in the nineteenth and twentieth centuries, up through current (2000) immigration reform issues. Zolberg and others demonstrate how the 1965 immigration reform policies were considered as much a triumph in American society as was civil rights legislation. In particular, the book describes how issues of immigration returned to the forefront of American politics in 1965 and have been a lightning rod since.

7. The recent past is a challenge to interpret without the luxury of hindsight to guide us in weighing the significance of events and determining which developments will have lasting effects and which are more fleeting. Nevertheless, the period between 1965 and our current moment is only recently starting to emerge in the minds of historians with some clarity. Scholarly insights about the current era are reflected here.

8. See Mae Ngai, *Impossible Subjects: Illegal Aliens and the Making of Modern America* (Princeton: Princeton University Press, 2004); Zolberg, *A Nation by Design*; and Howard Zinn, *A People's History of the United States* (New York: Harper Collins Publishers, 2003). The legislation included provisions that eased the entry of immigrants who were professionals, scientists, and artists "of exceptional ability," or who possessed skills in high demand in the United States. To promote family reunification, the law also stipulated that close relatives of legal residents in the US could be admitted outside the numerical limits, an exception that especially benefited immigrants from Asian and Latin American countries.

9. See, for example, Cecilia Menjívar, *Fragmented Ties: Salvadoran Immigrant Networks in America* (Berkeley: University of California Press, 2000);

Nora Hamilton and Norma Stolz Chinchilla, *Seeking Community in a Global City: Guatemalans and Salvadorans in Los Angeles* (Philadelphia: Temple University Press, 2001); Ana Patricia Rodríguez *Dividing the Isthmus: Central American Transnational Histories, Literatures, and Cultures* (Austin: University of Texas Press, 2010); and Arturo Arias and Claudia Milian, eds., *Latino Studies, Special Issue: U.S. Central Americans: Representations, Agency and Communities* 11(2)(Summer 2013). For important works about U.S. involvement in Latin America, see among others: Allan Burns, *Maya in Exile: Guatemalans in Florida* (Philadelphia: Temple University Press, 1993); Aviva Chomsky and Aldo Lauria-Santiago, *Identity and Struggle at the Margins of the Nation-State: The Laboring Peoples of Central America and the Hispanic Caribbean* (Durham, N.C.: Duke University Press, 1998); Jason Colby, *The Business of Empire: United Fruit, Race, and U.S. Expansion in Central America* (Ithaca, N.Y.: Cornell University Press, 2011); José Luis Falconi and José Antonio Mazzotti, eds., *The Other Latinos: Central and South Americans in the United States* (Cambridge, Mass.: David Rockefeller Center for Latin American Studies, Harvard University, 2008); Elizabeth Ferris, *The Central American Refugees* (New York: Praeger, 1987); Lisa García Bedolla, *Fluid Borders: Latino Power, Identity, and Politics in Los Angeles* (Berkeley: University of California Press, 2005); María Cristina García, *Seeking Refuge: Central American Migration to Mexico, the United States, and Canada* (Berkeley: University of California Press, 2006); and Michel Gobat, *Confronting the American Dream: Nicaragua under U.S. Imperial Rule* (Durham, N.C.: Duke University Press, 2005).

10. Analysis of the U.S. Census population figures for the 20 largest cities for 1970, 1980, 1990, and 2000. See U.S. Department of Commerce, Bureau of the Census, *1970 Census of Population, Characteristics of the Population*, Vol. 1, Pts. 1–52 (Washington, D.C., 1973); U.S. Department of Commerce, Bureau of the Census, *2000 Census of Population and Housing, Summary Population and Housing Characteristics*, Pt. 1, PHC-1-1, Table 10 (Washington, D.C., 2002). See also U.S. Census Bureau website, http://factfinder.census.gov.

11. Mae Ngai, *Impossible Subjects.*

12. Mae Ngai, *Impossible Subjects,* xxv. Although outside the purview of this essay, it is important to note that early guest worker programs as well as a shared economy set the stage for large-scale migration between Mexico and the United States. The Bracero Program in particular brought Mexicans in as guest workers and many of them settled in the Southwest. Decades later, given the provisions of the Hart-Celler Act, many former Braceros and their families (those who were not repatriated during the 1930s) could more easily reunite with family members across the border. Like the Braceros, many guest workers who have since engaged in circular migration have decided to stay in the US or were forced to stay because of the tightening of border enforcement in the mid-twentieth century. For more on this history, see: Ana Elizabeth Rosas, *Abrazando el Espíritu: Bracero Families Confront the U.S.–Mexico Border* (Berkeley: University of California Press, 2014); Anna Pegler-Gordon, *In Sight of America: Photography and the Development of U.S. Immigration Policy* (Berkeley: University of California Press, 2009); and Mireya Loza, *Defiant Braceros: How Migrant Workers Fought for Racial, Sexual, and Political Freedom* (Chapel Hill: University of North Carolina Press, 2016).

13. See Steven Masami Ropp, "Secondary Migration and the Politics of Identity for Asian Latinos in Los Angeles," *Journal of Asian American Studies* 3(2)(2000):219–29; David Gutierrez, "The New Normal? Reflections on the Shifting Politics of the Immigration Debate," *International Labor and Working Class History* 78(2010):118–22; Mae M. Ngai, "The Civil Rights Origins of Illegal Immigration," *International Labor and Working Class History* 78(2010):93–99.

14. Israel Zangwill, *The Melting Pot*, 1908. For more on the melting pot concept and its expression in public life, see Fath Davis Ruffins's essay in this volume.

15. The term "transculturalism" is attributed to Brazilian sociologist Gilberto Freyre and Cuban legal and social critic Fernando Ortiz, who used the term to provide a framework for analyzing global racial and cultural mixtures. The symbol was originally carved into the building's facade, where it could be seen for decades, until destroyed during the Temple's renovation that was completed in 2009.

16. Desmond S. King, *Making Americans: Immigration, Race, and the Origins of the Diverse Democracy* (Cambridge, Mass.: Harvard University Press, 2000); Eric P. Kaufmann, *The Rise and Fall of Anglo-America* (Cambridge, Mass.: Harvard University Press, 2004); Diana Selig, *Americans All: The Cultural Gifts Movement* (Cambridge, Mass.: Harvard University Press, 2008).

17. In the 1980s, membership in the ILGWU was 90 percent female, but the leadership was still primarily male. For more information on the garment industry, see Peter Liebhold and Harry Rubenstein, *Between a Rock and a Hard Place* (Los Angeles: University of California Los Angeles, Asian American Studies Center, 1999); Elizabeth Weiner and Hardy Green, "A Stitch in Our Time: New York's Hispanic Garment Workers in the 1980s," in Joan Jensen and Sue Davidson, eds., *A Needle, A Bobbin, A Strike: Women Needle Workers in America* (Philadelphia: Temple University Press, 1984), 278–96; and Janet Zandy, "'Women Have Always Sewed': The Production of Clothing and the Work of Women," *Women's Studies Quarterly* 23(1/2) Working-Class Studies (Spring–Summer, 1995):162–68.

18. See the NAACP website for more information: http://www.naacp.org/pages/our-mission.

19. Kimberlé W. Crenshaw's groundbreaking work details the concept of intersectionality. See, for example, her book *On Intersectionality: Essential Writings* (New York: New Press, 2016) and her earlier article "Mapping the Margins: Intersectionality, Identity Politics, and Violence against Women of Color," *Stanford Law Review* 43(6) (July 1991):1241–99.

20. Of course, the claim that the late-twentieth-century United States is the world's first multicultural society is patently false, and over 20 years later the racial composition of U.S. society is rather different from *Time*'s anticipated numbers, with Latino and Asian-origin populations comprising the largest groups.

21. To be exact, Danzy Senna of *Time* magazine stated the ratio of racial mixing was to reflect a one-to-one ratio of the projected future racial makeup of the United States. At the time, they believed the country's demographics would be "15% Anglo Saxon, 17.5% Middle Eastern, 17.5% African, 7.5% Asian, 35% Southern European, and 7.5% Hispanic." Danzy Senna, "The New Face of America: How Immigrants Are Shaping the World's First Multicultural Society," *Time*, 18 November 1993. Of course, as of the 2010 census, we know people of Latino and Asian descent are the largest and fastest-growing groups.

22. Caroline A. Streeter, "The Hazards of Visibility: 'Biracial' Women, Media Images, and Narratives of Identity" in *New Faces in a Changing America: Multiracial Identity in the 21st Century*, Loretta I. Winters and Herman L. DeBose, eds. (New York: SAGE Publications, 2003).

23. See James Davison Hunter, *Culture Wars: The Struggle to Define America* (New York: Basic Books, 1991).

24. A good look at affirmative action debates is included in David Roediger, *Towards the Abolition of Whiteness: Essays on Race, Politics, and Working Class History* (New York: Verso, 1994). For a look at the difference between multicultural and multiracial, see Winters and DeBose, eds., *New Faces in a Changing America*.

25. George J. Sanchez, "Face the Nation: Race, Immigration, and the Rise of Nativism in Late

Twentieth Century America," *The International Migration Review* 31(4) Special Issue: Immigrant Adaptation and Native-Born Responses in the Making of Americans (Winter 1997):1009–30, 1012.

26. Racial nativism arose across the nation in ebbs and flows throughout the twentieth century. In the early years of the twentieth century, many Americans accepted and propagated theories of race that supported racial nativism. During the 1920s, nativism ran rampant with immigration restriction legislation and the activities of the Ku Klux Klan. And in 1930, during the height of the Great Depression, Labor Secretary William Doak promised to rid the country of "four hundred thousand illegal aliens" whom he believed were taking jobs away from American citizens. See Abraham Hoffman, *Unwanted Mexican Americans in the Great Depression: Repatriation Pressures, 1929–1939* (Tempe: University of Arizona Press, 1974), 36–37; also, John Higham, *Strangers in the Land: Patterns of American Nativism, 1860–1925* (New York: Antheneum, 1974). For a more accessible, poignant commentary, see Ira Katznelson, *When Affirmative Action Was White: An Untold History of Racial Inequality in Twentieth-Century America* (New York: W. W. Norton & Company, 2006).

27. For an important discussion about the connections between late-twentieth-century nativism and racism across the political spectrum, see Sanchez, "Face the Nation" .

28. See Bhabha, *The Location of Culture*. The writings of Bhabha, a postcolonial theorist, are the most prominent about hybridity. The concept of hybridity has also come into play as another word for mixing. Hybridity, when carefully considered in its social reality, has been a history of slavery, rape, and racial mixing that is the result of unequal power relations, colonialism, and conquest. It is a painful history of interracial identity. But scholars like Homi Bhabha, Stuart Hall, and Francoise Lionnet write about it as the triumph of the postcolonial or the subaltern over the hegemonic. In work around hybridity over the past decade, a rather loose set of related terms have also proliferated and gone unproblematized. It is no longer clear what is being suggested when referring to processes that are understood to be hybrid or hybridizing like diaspora, creolization, intercultural encounters and interaction, transculturation, *meztisaje*, or syncretism. Each demonstrates and implicates different political ideologies and for this reason they should not be used interchangeably without defining or problematizing.

29. Gary Gerstle, "Thoughts on the Americans All Exhibit," unpublished memo to Smithsonian National Museum of American History, dated 19 May 2012.

30. Bhabha, *The Location of Culture*. In postcolonial theory, Homi Bhabha contends that a new hybrid identity or subject-position can emerge from the interweaving of elements of the colonizer and colonized, challenging the validity and authenticity of any essentialist cultural identity.

31. For more information on the CIW, visit their website: http://ciw-online.org/. Also, see Orlando Serrano, "Colonial Brews: Cafe and Power in the Americas," (Ph.D. diss., University of Southern California, 2014), 128–32. Serrano's dissertation provides a brief account of how the CIW launched its Fair Food Campaign with the aim of improving conditions for Florida agricultural workers by having "major fast-food and supermarket corporations agree to a four-point program: pay one penny more per pound of tomatoes; abide by an enforceable code of conduct for suppliers; market incentives for agricultural suppliers that respects workers' human rights even when those rights are not guaranteed by law; and 100% transparency for tomato purchases in Florida" (128).

32. Langston Hughes, "I, Too, Sing America," *The Collected Poems of Langston Hughes* (New York: Knopf and Vintage Books, 1994).

33. One of the most significant blows to organized labor in recent memory came in 1981, when President Ronald Reagan claimed that the striking Professional Air Traffic Controllers Organization (PATCO) union was in violation of the Taft-Hartley Act's prohibition against such actions by government workers. The Taft-Hartley Act (1947) severely restricted the power of unions and the actions labor could take in its defense. Reagan ordered all air traffic controllers back to work within 48 hours, subsequently fired the more than 11,000 workers who had disobeyed his order, and then barred them from federal service for life. This executive action had a severe negative impact on labor unions across the nation. For important works on organized labor in the US in the twentieth century, see for example: Lizabeth Cohen, *Making a New Deal: Industrial Workers in Chicago, 1919–1939*, 2nd ed. (Cambridge: Cambridge University Press, 2014); James R. Green, *The World of the Worker: Labor in Twentieth-Century America* (Champaign: University of Illinois Press, 1998); and Jack Metzgar, *Striking Steel: Solidarity Remembered* (Philadelphia: Temple University Press, 2000). For an important work connecting civil rights and labor rights struggles, see Zaragosa Vargas, *Labor Rights Are Civil Rights: Mexican American Workers in Twentieth-Century America* (Princeton: Princeton University Press, 2007).

34. Jeffrey S. Passel and D'Vera Cohn, "U.S. Population Projections: 2005–2050," Pew Research Center, Social & Demographic Trends, http://www.pewsocialtrends.org/2008/02/11/us-population-projections-2005-2050/ (2008) and Pew Research Center, Hispanic Trends http://www.pewhispanic.org/.

35. Many important works have come out in relation to how Latino and Asian communities have disrupted the color line. In particular, see Shawn Michelle Smith, *Photography on the Color Line: W. E. B. Du Bois, Race, and Visual Culture* (Durham, N.C.: Duke University Press, 2005), for a detailed description of how visual culture has contributed to this history of race and identity; also Adrian Burgos, *Playing America's Game: Baseball, Latinos, and the Color Line* (Berkeley: University of California Press, 2007), takes a very poignant look at how Latino, Native American, and Hawaiian baseball players crossed the color line well before Jackie Robinson; other important histories of interracial collaboration, collision, and coalition include Laura Pulido's *Black, Brown, Yellow, and Left: Radical Activism in Los Angeles* (Berkeley: University of California Press, 2006), and Tomás Almaguer's *Racial Fault Lines: The Historical Origins of White Supremacy in California* (Berkeley: University of California Press, 2008). Claire Jean Kim's work on Racial Triangulation and Manuel Pastor's work on black–brown relations in Los Angeles also add important dimensions to this literature on inter-group relations that move beyond simple racial categorization. See Claire Jean Kim, "The Racial Triangulation of Asian Americans," *Politics & Society* 27(1)(March 1999):105–38; Manuel Pastor and Laura Pulido, "Where in the World is Juan—and What Color is He? The Geography of Latino Racial Subjectivity in Southern California," *American Quarterly* 65(2) (June 2013):309–41; Manuel Pastor and Vanessa Carter, "Conflict, Consensus, and Coalition: Economic and Workforce Development Strategies for African Americans and Latinos," *Race and Social Problems* 1(3)(2009):143–56; and Manuel Pastor, *Latinos and the L.A. Uprising: The Economic Context* (Claremont, Cal.: Tomás Rivera Center, 1993).

Almaguer, Tomás. *Racial Fault Lines: The Historical Origins of White Supremacy in California.* Berkeley: University of California Press, 2008.

Althusser, Louis. *Lenin and Philosophy and Other Essays.* Trans. Ben Brewster. New York: Monthly Review Press, 2001.

Anzaldúa, Gloria. *Borderlands/La Frontera.* San Francisco: Spinsters/Aunt Lute, 1987.

Arias, Arturo and Claudia Milian, eds. *Latino Studies, Special Issue: U.S. Central Americans: Representations, Agency and Communities,* 11(2) (Summer 2013).

Bedolla, Lisa García. *Fluid Borders: Latino Power, Identity, and Politics in Los Angeles.* Berkeley: University of California Press, 2005.

Bhabha, Homi. *The Location of Culture.* London: Routledge, 1994.

Bornet, Vaughn Davis. *The Presidency of Lyndon B. Johnson.* Lawrence: University Press of Kansas, 1983.

Burgos, Adrian. *Playing America's Game: Baseball, Latinos, and the Color Line.* Berkeley: University of California Press, 2007.

Burns, Allan. *Maya in Exile: Guatemalans in Florida.* Philadelphia: Temple University Press, 1993.

Butler, Judith. *The Psychic Life of Power Theories in Subjection.* Stanford: Stanford University Press, 1997.

_____. *Gender Trouble: Feminism and the Subversion of Identity.* New York: Routledge, 1989.

Cheng, Wendy. *The Changs Next Door to the Díazes: Remapping Race in Suburban California.* Minneapolis: University of Minnesota Press, 2013.

Chomsky, Aviva and Aldo Lauria-Santiago. *Identity and Struggle at the Margins of the Nation-State: The Laboring Peoples of Central America and the Hispanic Caribbean.* Durham, N.C.: Duke University Press, 1998.

Cohen, Lizabeth. *Making a New Deal: Industrial Workers in Chicago, 1919–1939.* 2nd ed. Cambridge: Cambridge University Press, 2014.

Colby, Jason. *The Business of Empire: United Fruit, Race, and U.S. Expansion in Central America.* Ithaca, N.Y.: Cornell University Press, 2011.

Crenshaw, Kimberlé W. *On Intersectionality: Essential Writings.* New York: New Press, 2016.

_____. "Mapping the Margins: Intersectionality, Identity Politics, and Violence against Women of Color." *Stanford Law Review* 43(6)(July 1991):1241–99.

Davies, Gareth. *From Opportunity to Entitlement: The Transformation and Decline of Great Society Liberalism.* Lawrence: University Press of Kansas, 1996.

Falconi, José Luis and José Antonio Mazzotti, eds. *The Other Latinos: Central and South Americans in the United States.* Cambridge, Mass.: David Rockefeller Center for Latin American Studies, Harvard University, 2008.

Ferris, Elizabeth. *The Central American Refugees.* New York: Praeger, 1987.

Foley, Neil. *The White Scourge: Mexicans, Blacks, and Poor Whites in Texas Cotton Culture.* Berkeley: University of California Press, 1997.

Fuss, Diana. *Identification Papers: Readings on Psychoanalysis, Sexuality, and Culture.* New York: Routledge, 1995.

García, María Cristina. *Seeking Refuge: Central American Migration to Mexico, the United States, and Canada.* Berkeley: University of California Press, 2006.

García-Canclini, Nestor. *Hybrid Cultures: Strategies for Entering and Leaving Modernity.* Minneapolis: University of Minnesota Press, 1995.

Gerstle, Gary. "Thoughts on the Americans All Exhibit." Unpublished memo to Smithsonian National Museum of American History. 19 May 2012.

Gillette, Michael L. *Launching the War on Poverty: An Oral History.* Oxford: Oxford Oral History Series, 2010.

Gobat, Michel. *Confronting the American Dream: Nicaragua under U.S. Imperial Rule.* Durham, N.C.: Duke University Press, 2005.

Green, James R. *The World of the Worker: Labor in Twentieth-Century America*. Champaign: University of Illinois Press, 1998.

Gutierrez, David. "The New Normal? Reflections on the Shifting Politics of the Immigration Debate." *International Labor and Working Class History* 78(2010):118–22.

Hamilton, Nora and Norma Stolz Chinchilla. *Seeking Community in a Global City: Guatemalans and Salvadorans in Los Angeles*. Philadelphia: Temple University Press, 2001.

Hardt, Michael and Antonio Negri. *Empire*. Cambridge, Mass.: Harvard University Press, 2000.

Higham, John. *Strangers in the Land: Patterns of American Nativism, 1860–1925*. New York: Antheneum, 1974.

Hoffman, Abraham. *Unwanted Mexican Americans in the Great Depression: Repatriation Pressures, 1929–1939*. Tempe: University of Arizona Press, 1974.

Horton, John. *The Politics of Diversity: Immigration, Resistance, and Change in Monterey Park, California*. Philadelphia: Temple University Press, 1995.

Hughes, Langston. "I, Too, Sing America." *The Collected Poems of Langston Hughes*. New York: Knopf and Vintage Books, 1994.

Hunter, James Davison. *Culture Wars: The Struggle to Define America*. New York: Basic Books, 1991.

Jackson, Thomas F. *From Civil Rights to Human Rights: Martin Luther King, Jr., and the Struggle for Economic Justice*. Philadelphia: University of Pennsylvania Press, 2007.

Johnson, Lyndon Baines. "Remarks at the University of Michigan," 22 May 1964, in *Public Papers of the Presidents of the United States: Lyndon B. Johnson, 1963–64*, Vol. 1, pp. 704–7. Washington, D.C.: Government Printing Office, 1965.

Katznelson, Ira. *When Affirmative Action Was White: An Untold History of Racial Inequality in Twentieth-Century America*. New York: W. W. Norton & Company, 2006.

Kaufmann, Eric P. *The Rise and Fall of Anglo-America*. Cambridge, Mass.: Harvard University Press, 2004.

Kim, Claire Jean. "The Racial Triangulation of Asian Americans." *Politics & Society* 27(1) (March 1999):105–38.

King, Desmond S. *Making Americans: Immigration, Race, and the Origins of the Diverse Democracy*. Cambridge, Mass.: Harvard University Press, 2000.

Liebhold, Peter and Harry Rubenstein, *Between a Rock and a Hard Place*. Los Angeles: University of California Los Angeles, Asian American Studies Center, 1999.

Lipsitz, George. *The Possessive Investment in Whiteness*. Philadelphia: Temple University Press, 1998.

Loza, Mireya. *Defiant Braceros: How Migrant Workers Fought for Racial, Sexual, and Political Freedom*. Chapel Hill: University of North Carolina Press, 2016.

Menjívar, Cecilia. *Fragmented Ties: Salvadoran Immigrant Networks in America*. Berkeley: University of California Press, 2000.

Metzgar, Jack. *Striking Steel: Solidarity Remembered*. Philadelphia: Temple University Press, 2000.

Milkis, Sidney M. and Jerome M. Mileur, eds. *The Great Society and the High Tide of Liberalism*. Boston: University of Massachusetts Press, 2005.

Ngai, Mae M. "The Civil Rights Origins of Illegal Immigration." *International Labor and Working Class History* 78(2010):93–99.

_____. *Impossible Subjects: Illegal Aliens and the Making of Modern America*. Princeton: Princeton University Press, 2004.

Okihiro, Gary. *Margins and Mainstreams: Asians in American History and Culture*. Seattle: University of Washington Press, 1994.

Omi, Michael and Howard Winnant. *Racial Formation in the United States*. New York: Routledge, 1986. 3rd ed. 2015.

Orleck, Annelise and Lisa Gayle Hazirjian, eds. *The War on Poverty: A New Grassroots History, 1964–1980*. Athens: University of Georgia Press, 2011.

Pardo, Mary. *Mexican-American Women Activists: Identity and Resistance in Two Los Angeles*

Communities. Philadelphia: Temple University Press, 1998.

Passel, Jeffrey S. and D'Vera Cohn. "U.S. Population Projections: 2005–2050," Pew Research Center, Social & Demographic Trends. 2008. http://www.pewsocialtrends.org/2008/02/11/us-population-projections-2005-2050/ (accessed 19 April 2015).

Pastor, Manuel. *Latinos and the L.A. Uprising: The Economic Context*. Claremont, Cal.: Tomás Rivera Center, 1993.

Pastor, Manuel and Vanessa Carter. "Conflict, Consensus, and Coalition: Economic and Workforce Development Strategies for African Americans and Latinos." *Race and Social Problems* 1(3) (2009):143–56.

Pastor, Manuel and Laura Pulido, "Where in the World is Juan—and What Color is He? The Geography of Latino Racial Subjectivity in Southern California." *American Quarterly* 65(2) (June 2013):309–41.

Pegler-Gordon, Anna. *In Sight of America: Photography and the Development of U.S. Immigration Policy*. Berkeley: University of California Press, 2009.

Pew Research Center. Hispanic Trends. http://www.pewhispanic.org/ (accessed 19 April 2015).

Public Papers of the Presidents of the United States: Lyndon B. Johnson, 1963–64, Vol. 1. Washington, D.C.: Government Printing Office, 1965.

Pulido, Laura. *Black, Brown, Yellow, and Left: Radical Activism in Los Angeles*. Berkeley: University of California Press, 2006.

Rodríguez, Ana Patricia. *Dividing the Isthmus: Central American Transnational Histories, Literatures, and Cultures*. Austin: University of Texas Press, 2010.

Roediger, David. *Towards the Abolition of Whiteness: Essays on Race, Politics, and Working Class History*. New York: Verso, 1994.

Ropp, Steven Masami "Secondary Migration and the Politics of Identity for Asian Latinos in Los Angeles." *Journal of Asian American Studies* 3(2) (2000):219–29.

Rosas, Ana Elizabeth. *Abrazando el Espíritu: Bracero Families Confront the U.S.-Mexico Border*. Berkeley: University of California Press, 2014.

Saito, Leland. *Race and Politics*. Urbana: University of Illinois Press, 1998.

Sanchez, George J. "Face the Nation: Race, Immigration, and the Rise of Nativism in Late Twentieth Century America." *The International Migration Review* 31(4) Special Issue: Immigrant Adaptation and Native-Born Responses in the Making of Americans (Winter 1997):1009–30.

Selig, Diana. *Americans All: The Cultural Gifts Movement*. Cambridge, Mass.: Harvard University Press, 2008.

Senna, Danzy. "The New Face of America: How Immigrants Are Shaping the World's First Multicultural Society." *Time*, 18 November 1993.

Serrano, Orlando. *Colonial Brews: Cafe and Power in the Americas*. Ph.D. diss., University of Southern California, 2014.

Smith, Shawn Michelle. *Photography on the Color Line: W. E. B. Du Bois, Race, and Visual Culture*. Durham, N.C.: Duke University Press, 2005.

Streeter, Caroline A. "The Hazards of Visibility: 'Biracial' Women, Media Images, and Narratives of Identity." In *New Faces in a Changing America: Multiracial Identity in the 21st Century*, eds. Loretta I. Winters and Herman L. DeBose, pp.301–322. New York: SAGE Publications, 2003.

Takaki, Ronald. *Iron Cages: Race and Culture in 19th Century America*. Oxford: Oxford University Press, 1979.

U.S. Department of Commerce, Bureau of the Census, *1970 Census of Population, Characteristics of the Population*, Vol. 1, Pts. 1–52. Washington, D.C., 1973.

U.S. Department of Commerce, Bureau of the Census, *2000 Census of Population and Housing, Summary Population and Housing Characteristics*, Pt. 1, PHC-1-1, Table 10. Washington, D.C., 2002.

Vargas, Zaragosa. *Labor Rights Are Civil Rights: Mexican American Workers in Twentieth-Century America*. Princeton: Princeton University Press, 2007.

Webner, Pnina and Tariq Modood, eds. *Debating Cultural Hybridity.* London: Zed Books, 1997.

Weiner, Elizabeth and Hardy Green. "A Stitch in Our Time: New York's Hispanic Garment Workers in the 1980s." In *A Needle, A Bobbin, A Strike: Women Needle Workers in America*, eds. Joan Jensen and Sue Davidson, pp. 278–96. Philadelphia: Temple University Press, 1984.

Winters, Loretta I. and Herman L. DeBose, eds. *New Faces in a Changing America: Multiracial Identity in the 21st Century.* New York: SAGE Publications, 2003.

Young, Robert. *Colonial Desire: Hybridity in Theory, Culture, and Race.* London: Routledge, 1995.

Zandy, Janet. "'Women Have Always Sewed': The Production of Clothing and the Work of Women." *Women's Studies Quarterly* 23(1/2) Working-Class Studies (Spring–Summer, 1995):162–68.

Zangwill, Israel. *The Melting-Pot: Drama in Four Acts.* New York: Macmillan, 1909.

Zinn, Howard. *A People's History of the United States.* New York: Harper Collins Publishers, 2003.

Zolberg, Aristide R. *A Nation by Design: Immigration Policy in the Fashioning of America.* Cambridge, Mass.: Harvard University Press, 2006.

Old South, New Migrations

L. Stephen Velasquez

As I was turning off of Ponce de Leon Boulevard onto Indian Creek Drive outside of Clarkston, Georgia, two women walked in front of me wearing white and red Burmese sarongs with gold embroidery. I was struck by seeing these women in suburban Atlanta, a place that is not historically associated with migrants from around the globe. Yet over the past 50 years Southern communities, especially suburban towns connected to major cities, have been transformed as global migrations have profoundly changed the long-standing racial and cultural politics of the South.[1]

As a curator for the National Museum of American History, I went to the South to collect objects that could help tell the story of the impact of this migration and how existing communities and newcomers have negotiated changing demographics and increasing cultural diversity. I was specifically interested in how these negotiations played out on the sports field. Sports have long been arenas where tensions about rapidly changing cultural and racial differences and American identities have been defined and contested.[2] Objects I've collected from refugee and migrant children who formed soccer teams reflect debates about community identity and belonging in two small towns in the South: Clarkston, Georgia, and Siler City, North Carolina.

In 2004 a group of refugee kids newly arrived to Clarkston from war-torn countries of Africa, Europe, and Asia came together under Coach Luma Mufleh to form a recreational soccer league called The Fugees, short for "Refugees."[3]

Two years earlier in Siler City, a group of Latino teens gathered on the high-school practice football field with Coach Paul Cuadros to start the first Jordan Matthew High School soccer team, Los Jets.[4] The Fugees and Los Jets are just two examples in a trend that has repeated itself across the South and elsewhere in the United States, as global migrations have required communities to adapt to new ways of life brought by new immigrants. In both cases, the persistence of the coaches and the enthusiasm and talent of the players helped cultivate a rich and diverse network of local support.

The growth in popularity of youth soccer in urban and suburban areas since the 1970s has been the result of more television coverage and marketing, but also of changing demographics.[5] The 1965 Immigration and Nationality Act, commonly known as the Hart-Celler Act, enabled immigrants from Asia, Africa, and Latin America to migrate to the United States in larger numbers.[6] Though Southern states have seen a rapid and major increase in immigration, faster than the national average, the actual amount of growth still remains small by national standards.[7] In 2000 about seven percent of Atlanta's population was foreign born. More importantly, in suburban towns like Clarkston and Siler City rapid immigrant settlement resulted in an even higher percentage, at 15 percent or more, of the population being foreign born.[8]

For Siler City and Clarkston, as well as many other Southern towns in the United States in the late twentieth century, a soccer ball was seen as a symbol of foreignness and difference.[9] Playing sports like baseball, football, and basketball marked players and fans as "all American" and immigrants often play these sports to become "more American" and ease assimilation.[10] But with the rise of new immigrant groups following 1965 immigration laws, and a widening interest in soccer, players have been challenging the dominance of baseball and football and finding new audiences across the U.S. South.[11]

The material culture we collect and exhibit can help us understand the journey of migrants and how migrants shape local history. What objects do curators collect to represent contemporary migration? What can a green soccer jersey and well-used cleats from The Fugees or a soccer ball and a team chain from Los Jets tell us about the immigrant and migrant experience? These items may only seem to speak to us about youth soccer, team sports, or the history of soccer in the United States. But they tell a more compelling and complex story about kids struggling to play soccer, tensions brought about by changing demographics in the rural South, and about assimilation and diversity in the nation. These objects also speak to the unity, strength, and success of these teams—not only on the field but also within the community.

THE FUGEES

For a museum exhibit, a jersey is an object with a strong visual draw, one that can also be an entry point that represents the community from which it came. Team jerseys are the uniforms that identify players or mark fans. The green Fugees jersey is critical to the story of a group of refugee grade-school children, newly arrived to Clarkston from war-torn countries such as Somalia, Congo, Bosnia, Kosovo, and Afghanistan (Figure 1). In 2004 Coach Luma Mufleh, a young Jordanian immigrant, formed The Fugees as a recreational soccer team to help engage young refugees in something they were passionate about, and to help them "figure out what they have in common."[12] Playing soccer was an opportunity for them to come together. At the same time, the sport set the players apart from the rest of the town and created tensions between established residents and these

Figure 1.
Fugees soccer team jersey, Clarkston, Georgia, around 2012. The Fugees (short for "Refugees") was made up of refugee children from all over the world. Despite their diverse backgrounds and past experiences, the student athletes became united when they wore their team jerseys. National Museum of American History, Smithsonian Institution, gift of the Fugees family.

Figure 2.
Fugees team photograph, Clarkston, Georgia, 2014. Soccer has been a popular sport played in many parts of the world, but when the Fugees first established their team, the game was not yet common in the Southern community of Clarkston, Georgia. Coach Luma Mufleh is in the center of the photograph. Courtesy of Luma Mufleh on behalf of Fugees Family.

newcomers. This green jersey united a number of diverse refugee children regardless of ethnic or racial differences (Figure 2).

In addition to being the new kids in a small school, wearing a soccer jersey marked the young team members as different from those wearing more popular baseball or football jerseys. The YMCA and the Clarkston Community Center collaborated in helping Coach Mufleh establish the team. The YMCA rented the soccer field behind the Community Center and became a hub for the refugees. After only two years, several of the center's board members, who openly criticized the refugee community for not contributing more to the center's upkeep, severed its relationship with the YMCA. The decision forced Mufleh to find other spaces. Clarkston Mayor Lee Swaney argued that the town's large park was designated only for baseball—even though Clarkston had not had a team in many years.[13] Instead, the town offered The Fugees a pitted field studded with broken glass.

Although Clarkston was a government-sanctioned refugee relocation site, in an effort headed by such organizations as the International Rescue Committee and World Relief, new refugees were dropped into the central-Georgia town with limited assistance and were packed into limited English courses offered by community organizations. In the 1980s and 1990s, refugee resettlement organizations picked Clarkston as an ideal place to relocate refugees because it was only a few miles from downtown Atlanta, it was on the commuter rail, it had abundant affordable housing, and it was a cheap place to live. Even though some organizations, churches, and individuals welcomed them, members of the refugee community felt harassed and discriminated against by local law enforcement and believed they were singled out for small driving infractions.[14] Clarkston residents also were experiencing a major shift. Over the previous 30 years the immigrant population in the town, including refugees from Africa, Asia, and Europe, had grown to roughly 30 percent of the total population—very different than it was in the 1970s.[15]

When I visited Clarkston and Coach Luma Mufleh for the first time, I was searching for objects that would represent the players' experiences of migration and making a home in a new place. My research pointed me toward a player nicknamed "One Shoe," an eight-year-old boy who came to practice, took out the one soccer shoe he had from his pack, and put it on his right foot.[16] I did not track down "One Shoe," his pack, or his single shoe, but I collected a pair of hand-me-down cleats, used by several different players throughout the years (Figure 3). The shoes help illustrate the struggles of the migrant kids, and the determination and resourcefulness of the refugee community. In many cases the refugee families could not afford the equipment. The players relied on boosters or donations for shoes and jerseys, which are reused and handed down to players until they can no longer be used.

Figure 3.
Fugees team soccer cleats, Clarkston, Georgia, about 2012. These well-used soccer cleats were worn by several Fugees team members. They were handed down to younger players who were unable to purchase their own cleats. National Museum of American History, Smithsonian Institution, gift of the Fugees family.

I do not know how many players have worn these shoes, but these shoes help us understand not just the poverty or perseverance of the children, but also how some in the community reacted to these newcomers with kindness. Over time. Tensions have dissipated enough that families can use the Community Center, there are programs for education, language, and business, and the students have facilities to play and practice. The Fugees story is not unique; another youth soccer team in neighboring North Carolina also ignited debates about newcomers to their community.

LOS JETS

This photo of Los Jets shows us another team similar to the Fugees (Figure 4). The group of Latino boys called themselves *Los Jets*, the Spanglish version of the high-school team name "The Jets."[17] Coach Paul Cuadros, a journalist born in Michigan to Peruvian immigrant parents, also wanted to help a group of kids struggling to fit in.[18] Siler City, a self-described American "football town," where everyone would turn out on Friday nights to watch the Jets football team, was

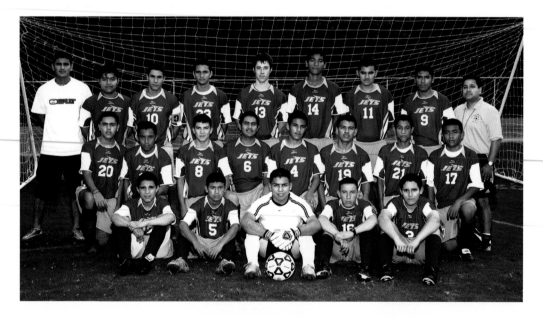

Figure 4.
Los Jets team photo, Siler City, North Carolina, 2004. Though soccer was not traditionally played in Siler City, a new influx of Latino families and their soccer-playing teens caused the sport's local popularity to grow. Coach Paul Cuadros is on the right. Courtesy of Paul Cuadros.

shifting from a predominately white and black Southern population to a town with a large Latino population migrating both from elsewhere in the United States and Central America.

In the 1980s and early 1990s Siler City had lost many manufacturing jobs and the younger population, both white and black, left for the more urban centers around Raleigh-Durham. In the 1990s the poultry industry started expanding, drawing in workers from across the United States as well as seasonal migrant workers, who often were Latino. Many Latino families moving to the area were fleeing inner-city violence and seeking new economic opportunities in agriculture and the expanding processing plants in and around town. By the late 1990s, the population of Latinos grew enough to strain schools, community services, and housing. As in other small communities in the South, growth of foreign-born population was beginning to be noticed. Even though the numbers of immigrants and rate of growth were small by comparison to California or New York, North Carolina's immigrant population still grew faster than the national average.[19] In 2010 approximately 50 percent of Siler City identified as "Hispanic" in the census.[20]

In Siler City many believed the arrival of the refugees and migrants put a strain on city services that were ill prepared for this influx of diverse newcomers. They argued that language programs were inadequate and teachers were spending too much time helping the newcomers. Many longtime residents complained that city services like trash collecting and housing were stretched to the maximum. An increase in anti-immigrant sentiment strained the relationship between arrivals and the white community in particular. For instance, in Siler City in 2000, an anonymous tip led to a federal Immigration and Naturalization Service raid of a local plant, in which several immigrants were arrested. This event sent fear throughout the Latino community. Later that same year, anti-immigrant activist and Ku Klux Klan leader David Duke led a rally organized by the local chapter of the white supremacist group National Alliance, further causing resentment and tension between the newcomers and longtime town residents.[21]

School administrators initially denied that students had enough interest in starting a soccer team at the high school, even though there was sizeable interest from many of the Latino students who made up half the school.[22] After the team formed in 2002, during games with neighboring towns and teams, Los Jets players were heckled with racist comments such as "stupid Mexicans" and snickering at the pronunciation of their names.[23]

In Siler City, I was drawn to a chain and signed soccer ball because of what they could tell us about the team, the town, and the role of sports. The simple hardware-store chain was used by Cuadros at the start of his third and winning season in a game against a rival high school (Figure 5). Caudros had the players hold the chain during an inspirational speech to physically and emotionally unite them. The tight-knit team of kids that rallied around this chain went on to win the state championship in 2004. This ball was signed by players from that year (Figure 6). The team's success led to increased support and acceptance from the school and community.

These objects remind us that sport is not just a leisure activity but is wrapped up in how personal, cultural, and national identities are expressed and constructed.[24] The sports field became the epicenter of where the towns of Clarkson and Siler City grappled with changing demographics and community acceptance.

GAME CHANGERS

The struggles the newcomers faced in Clarkston and Siler City represent some of the continuing challenges of living in a globalized and increasingly diverse United States. Some longtime residents of these towns found the migrant populations to be in conflict with their daily lives and traditions: strange new foods appeared in the grocery store, increasing numbers of foreign-language signs went up around town, and local interest in soccer exceeded that in baseball or football.[25] For some longstanding citizens in small Southern towns, placing blame for real or perceived problems, imposing barriers to civic participation, or denying

Figure 5.
Chain used as a team-building aid for Los Jets soccer team, Siler City, North Carolina, around 2004. Members of Los Jets held this chain in huddles and team-building exercises. It was used as a metaphor for cohesion on the field. Courtesy of Paul Cuadros.

Velasquez

Figure 6.
Soccer ball used by Los Jets soccer team, Siler City, North Carolina, 2004. Los Jets won the North Carolina State Championship just two years after starting the soccer team. This ball is signed by all team members to commemorate their victory. Courtesy of Paul Cuadros.

services outright, are deliberate strategies often deployed against newcomers to resist changes. Having places to play sports or music, having the opportunity to buy or sell particular foods, and the ability to hold religious services is about more than making a home—it also is about who is included in a community.[26]

For teams like Los Jets and the Fugees, sports offered a way for newly arrived migrants to come together and define themselves where in other areas of life their agency would be limited.[27] As Mike Cronin and David Mayall explain, "Sport has been used by the nation state for different purposes… The most common practical embodiment of this has been amongst immigrants as they seek either to preserve the cultural separateness of their own ethnic group, or as they strive to assimilate themselves into their host community."[28] Thus, sport can compel established communities to confront diversity directly.

Los Jets and the Fugees illustrate how soccer provided a physical and social outlet and a way for kids to come together in a new community despite all the tensions that surrounded them as migrants and foreigners.[29] Kids shared knowledge of the game and the common experience of being migrants while helping each other to adjust to their new communities. As I searched for material culture to talk about migration, I was struck by how the chain used by Los Jets might be seen as a representation of oppression and restriction, but they used it for strength and unity. Just as each player of the team makes up a link and makes the chain stronger, every migrant group that comes in contributes to what makes the United States stronger.

The rich diversity of our cities and towns that comes from migrations can be seen on the sports field. In the U.S. South, the changing demographics and the tensions brought about by this change have played out on the soccer field. Towns like Siler City and Clarkston have experienced a significant change from majority black and/or white to majority foreign born, changing the character and makeup of communities. Teams like Los Jets and the Fugees, formed by the children of migrants, wanted to play soccer but met resistance and difficulty.

As I left the offices of Coach Mufleh and Coach Cuadros I looked around at all the soccer awards and trophies for first place in tournaments and finals. But my gaze lingered a bit more on awards and plaques given by the city, sponsors, and other organizations for dedication to improving the community, on humanitarian awards given for improving the lives of children, and for exemplary dedication to improving the lives of newcomers to the community. Despite early tensions, the Clarkston and Siler City communities eventually came together to give the kids the space and support they needed to practice and become successful soccer players, students, and members of the community. These objects and stories help document and interpret changing communities in the United States. They remind us that sports are a critical component of daily life, local communities, and national history.

NOTES

1. For more information on the changing U.S. South, see Mary E. Oden and Elaine Lacy, *Latino Immigrants and the Transformation of the U.S. South* (Athens: University of Georgia Press, 2009); Julie Weise, "Dispatches from the 'Viejo' New South: Historicizing Recent Latino Immigration," *Latino Studies* 10(1–2)(2012):41–59.

2. For more information about sports, race, and cultural identity, see Mike Cronin and David Mayall, *Sporting Nationalisms: Identity, Ethnicity, Immigration and Assimilation* (London: F. Cass, 1998) and Douglas Hartmann, "Rethinking the Relationship Between Sport and Race in American Culture: Golden Ghettos and Contested Terrain," *Sociology of Sport Journal* 17(2000):229–53.

3. Warren St. John, *Outcasts United: A Refugee Team, an American Town* (New York: Spiegel and Grau, 2009).

4. Paul Cuadros, *A Home on the Field: How One Championship Team Inspires Hope for the Revival of Small Town America* (New York: Rayo, 2006).

5. Andrei S. Markovits and Steve L. Hillerman, *Offside: Soccer and American Exceptionalism* (Princeton: Princeton University Press, 2001).

6. Aristide R. Zolberg, *A Nation by Design: Immigration Policy in the Fashioning of America* (Cambridge, Mass.: Harvard University Press, 2008); Donna Gabaccia, *Immigration and American Diversity: A Social and Cultural Reader* (Malden, Mass.: Blackwell, 2002). Another driver of migration is refugee resettlement. The 1980 Refugee Resettlement Act standardized resettlement of refugees with a cap at 50,000 per year. For an overview of the 1965 Hart-Celler Act and its impact,

see Margaret Salazar-Porzio's essay in this volume. For more information about changing demographics brought about by immigration and refugee resettlement see Roger Daniels and Otis L. Grahm, *Debating American Immigration, 1882–Present* (Lanham, Md.: Rowman and Littlefield, 2001); Leon F. Bouvier and John L. Martin, "Shaping Georgia: The Effects of Immigration, 1970–2020," Center for Immigration Studies, 1995, http://cis.org/GeorgiaImmigrants-19702020.

7. Bouvier and Martin, *Shaping Georgia*.

8. United States Census Bureau, 2000 Census, http://factfinder.census.gov.

9. Markovits and Hillerman, *Offside*; Andrei Markovits and Steven L. Hillerman, "Soccer in America: A Story of Marginalization," *Entertainment and Sports Law Review* 13(2) (1995–96):225–55.

10. Loring M. Danforth, "Is the 'World Game' an 'Ethnic Game' or an 'Aussie Game'? Narrating the Nation in Australian Soccer," *American Ethnologist* 28(May 2001):363–87; Gerald Gems and Gertrud Pfister, *Understanding American Sports* (London, New York: Routledge. 2009); Markovits and Hillerman, *Offside*. Matti Goksøyr, "Nationalism" in *Routledge Companion to Sports History*, eds. S. W. Pope and John Nauright (London and New York: Routledge, 2010), 268–94.

11. From about 1972, when the Title IX policy was implemented, through 2000, marking the 1999 Women's and Men's Worlds Cup, there has been an increase in U.S. youth sports participation in general and soccer in particular. The total registration for youth soccer in 1980 was 888,705; by 2001, it had increased to 3,884,423. For more information, see Markovits and Hillerman, *Offside*; Andrei S. Markovits and Steven L. Hellerman, "Women's soccer in the United States: yet another American 'exceptionalism,'" *Soccer and Society* 4(2) (2003):14–29.

12. St. John, *Outcasts United*, 60.

13. For more information about the fight for fields see St. John, *Outcasts United*, 51–98.

14. For more about how the refugee community and longtime residents felt about changes, see St. John, *Outcasts United*, 35–45.

15. For more information about refugee resettlement policy, see Roger Daniels, *Guarding the Golden Door: American Immigration Policy and Immigrants since 1882* (New York: Hill and Wang, 2004). See also United States Census Bureau, 2000 Census.

16. St. John, *Outcasts United*, 56.

17. For more on the use and creation of Spanglish see Ana Celia Zentella, *Growing Up Bilingual: Puerto Rican Children in New York* (New York, Blackwell,1997) and "'José, can you see?' Latin@ Responses To Racist Discourse," in *Bilingual Games: Some Literary Investigations*, ed. Doris Sommer, (New York: Palgrave MacMillian, 2003), 51–66

18. Cuadros, *A Home on the Field*.

19. Steven A. Camarota, "A Record-Setting Decade of Immigration: 2000–2010," Center for Immigration Studies, 2011, http://cis.org/2000-2010-record-setting-decade-of-immigration.

20. United States Census Bureau, 2010 Census.

21. For more about local reaction to the Latino populations and the Duke rally, see Cuadros, *A Home on Field*, 43–57.

22. For more on school makeup and the school tensions, see Cuadros, *A Home on the Field*, 36–57.

23. Cuadros, *A Home on the Field*, 86.

24. S. W. Pope and John Nauright, eds., *Routledge Companion to Sports History* (London and New York: Routledge, 2010); Steven W. Pope, "Negotiating the 'Folk Highway' of the Nation: Sport, Public Culture, and American Identity, 1870–1940," *Journal of Social History* 27(2) (1993):327–40; John Hargreaves, *Sports, Power and Culture: A Social and Historical Analysis of Popular Sport in Britain* (New York: St. Martin's Press, 1986). For more about diverse Latino and immigrant groups creating a "third space," a familiar cultural and social space,

see Marie Price and Courtney Whitworth, "Soccer and Latino Cultural Space" in *Hispanic Spaces, Latino Places: Community and Cultural Diversity in Contemporary America*, ed. Daniel D. Arreola (Austin: University of Texas Press, 2004), 167–86.

25. St. John, *Outcasts United*; Cuadros, *A Home on the Field*.

26. For a few examples of immigrants negotiating public space, see Sean Basinski, "Hot Dogs, Hipsters, and Xenophobia: Immigrant Street Food Vendors in New York," *Social Research: An International Quarterly* 81(2)(Summer 2014): 397–408; Pierrette Hondagneu-Sotelo and José Miguel Ruiz, "Illegality and Spaces of Sanctuary: Belonging and Homeland Making in Urban Community Gardens," in *Constructing Immigrant 'Illegality': Critiques, Experiences, and Responses*, eds. Cecilia Menjívar and Daniel Kanstroom (New York: Cambridge University Press, 2014): 246–71; Fazila Bhimji, "Struggles, Urban Citizenship, And Belonging: The Experience Of Undocumented Street Vendors And Food Truck Owners In Los Angeles," *Urban Anthropology and Studies of Cultural Systems and World Economic Development*, 39(4)(Winter 2010):455–92.

27. Chris Kennett, "Sport, immigration and multiculturality," *Centre d'Estudis Olímpics: Universitat Autònoma de Barcelona*, 2005, http://olympicstudies.uab.es/pdf/wp103_eng.pdf.

28. Cronin and Mayall, *Sporting Nationalisms*, 4.

29. Joan G. DeJaeghere and Kate S. McCleary, "The Making of Mexican Migrant Youth Civic Identities: Transnational Spaces and Imaginaries," *Anthropology and Education Quarterly* 41(3)(2010):228–44; José Alamillo, "Playing Across Borders: Transnational Sports and Identities in Southern California and Mexico, 1930–1945," *Pacific Historical Review* 79(3) (2010):360–92.

BIBLIOGRAPHY

Alamillo, José. "Playing Across Borders: Transnational Sports and Identities in Southern California and Mexico, 1930–1945." *Pacific Historical Review*, 79(3)(2010):360–92.

Basinski, Sean. "Hot Dogs, Hipsters, and Xenophobia: Immigrant Street Food Vendors in New York." *Social Research: An International Quarterly*, 81(2)(Summer 2014):397–408.

Bhimji, Fazila. "Struggles, Urban Citizenship, And Belonging: The Experience of Undocumented Street Vendors And Food Truck Owners In Los Angeles." *Urban Anthropology and Studies of Cultural Systems and World Economic Development*, 39(4) (Winter 2010):455–92.

Bouvier, Leon F. and John L. Martin, "Shaping Georgia: The Effects of Immigration, 1970–2020." Center for Immigration Studies, 1995. http://cis.org/GeorgiaImmigrants-19702020 (accessed 19 June 2016).

Camarota, Steven A. "A Record-Setting Decade of Immigration: 2000–2010." Center for Immigration Studies, 2011. http://cis.org/2000-2010-record-setting-decade-of-immigration (accessed 19 June 2016).

Cronin, Mike and David Mayall. *Sporting Nationalisms: Identity, Ethnicity, Immigration and Assimilation*. London: F. Cass, 1998.

Cuadros, Paul. *A Home on the Field: How One Championship Team Inspires Hope for the Revival of Small Town America*. New York: Rayo, 2006.

Danforth, Loring M. "Is the 'World Game' an 'Ethnic Game' or an 'Aussie Game'? Narrating the Nation in Australian Soccer." *American Ethnologist*, 28 (May 2001):363–87.

Daniels, Roger. *Guarding the Golden Door: American Immigration Policy and Immigrants Since 1882*. New York: Hill and Wang, 2004.

Daniels, Roger and Otis L. Grahm. *Debating American Immigration, 1882–Present*. Lanham: Rowman and Littlefield, 2001.

DeJaeghere, Joan G. and Kate S. McCleary. "The Making of Mexican Migrant Youth Civic Identities: Transnational Spaces and Imaginaries." *Anthropology and Education Quarterly*, 41(3)(2010):228–44.

Gabaccia, Donna. *Immigration and American Diversity: A Social and Cultural Reader*. Malden, Mass.: Blackwell, 2002.

Gems, Gerald and Gertrud Pfister. *Understanding American Sports*. London, New York: Routledge, 2009.

Goksøyr, Matti. "Nationalism." In *Routledge Companion to Sports History*, eds. S. W. Pope and John Nauright, pp. 268–94. London and New York: Routledge, 2010.

Hargreaves, John. *Sports, Power and Culture: A Social and Historical Analysis of Popular Sport in Britain*. New York: St. Martin's Press, 1986.

Hartmann, Douglas. "Rethinking the Relationship Between Sport and Race in American Culture: Golden Ghettos and Contested Terrain." *Sociology of Sport Journal*, 17(2000):229–53.

Hondagneu-Sotelo, Pierrette and José Miguel Ruiz. "Illegality and Spaces of Sanctuary: Belonging and Homeland Making in Urban Community Gardens." In *Constructing Immigrant 'Illegality': Critiques, Experiences, and Responses*, eds. Cecilia Menjívar and Daniel Kanstroom, pp. 246–71. New York: Cambridge University Press, 2014.

Kennett, Chris. "Sport, immigration and multiculturality." *Centre d'Estudis Olímpics: Universitat Autònoma de Barcelona*. 2005. http://olympicstudies.uab.es/pdf/wp103_eng.pdf (accessed 6 June 2015.

Markovits, Andrei S. and Steve L. Hillerman. *Offside: Soccer and American Exceptionalism*. Princeton: Princeton University Press, 2001.

_____. "Soccer in America: A Story of Marginalization." *Entertainment and Sports Law Review*, 13(2)(1995–96):225–55.

_____. "Women's soccer in the United States: yet another American 'exceptionalism.'" *Soccer and Society*, 4(2)(2003):14–29.

Oden, Mary E. and Elaine Lacy. *Latino Immigrants and the Transformation of the U.S. South*. Athens: University of Georgia Press, 2009.

Pope, S. W. and John Nauright, eds. *Routledge Companion to Sports History*. London and New York: Routledge, 2010.

Pope, Steven W. "Negotiating the 'Folk Highway' of the Nation: Sport, Public Culture, and American Identity, 1870–1940." *Journal of Social History*, 27(2)(1993):327–40.

Price, Marie and Courtney Whitworth. "Soccer and Latino Cultural Space: Metropolitan Washington Fútbol Leagues." In *Hispanic Spaces, Latino Places: Community and Cultural Diversity in Contemporary America*, ed. Daniel D. Arreola, pp. 167–86. Austin: University of Texas Press, 2004.

St. John, Warren. *Outcasts United: A Refugee Team, an American Town*. New York: Spiegel and Grau, 2009.

United States Census Bureau, 2000 Census. http://factfinder.census.gov (accessed 16 January 2015.

United States Census Bureau, 2010 Census. http://factfinder.census.gov (accessed 16 January 2015).

Weise, Julie. "Dispatches from the 'Viejo' New South: Historicizing Recent Latino Immigration." *Latino Studies*, 10(1–2)(2012):41–59.

Zentella, Ana Celia. *Growing Up Bilingual: Puerto Rican Children in New York*. New York, Blackwell, 1997.

_____. "'José, can you see?' Latin@ Responses To Racist Discourse." In *Bilingual Games: Some Literary Investigations*, ed. Doris Sommer, pp. 51–66. New York: Palgrave MacMillian, 2003.

Zolberg, Aristide R. *A Nation by Design: Immigration Policy in the Fashioning of America*. Cambridge, Mass.: Harvard University Press, 2006.

Beyond Apology and Assertion in *Beyond Bollywood*

Masum Momaya

What are the limitations and possibilities for museums charged with expressing national identity? Two Smithsonian exhibitions—*Beyond Bollywood: Indian Americans Shape the Nation* and *Many Voices, One Nation*—chronicle experiences of immigrants as explorations of American national identity. In doing so, they aim to broaden and nuance the public's understanding of "America" beyond the canon in museums of American history. But how, as curators, do we do this without falling prey to the same pressures advocacy groups face amid immigration debates, namely, to subtly apologize for the immigrants' presence, or to refute their condition as a "burden" and assert belonging?[1] At our disposal are the details of history, through which we show that not only have many immigrants shaped the United States, but they have literally and metaphorically taken beatings and are still doing so in the process. In the context of the national, public museum that is the Smithsonian Institution, is it possible to go beyond apology and assertion as we tell immigrant stories? In this essay, I consider the limitations of interpreting material culture in traditional ways and the possibilities for more nuanced narratives enabled by juxtaposing material culture with film and performance art.

From February 2014 through August 2015, the Smithsonian Asian Pacific American Center[2] showed *Beyond Bollywood: Indian Americans Shape the Nation* at the National Museum of Natural History (NMNH). The exhibition was featured in NMNH as part of the museum's ongoing commitment to cultural anthropology exhibitions, including those of communities residing within the United States. *Beyond Bollywood* was the Smithsonian's first broad look at the lives and experiences of Indian Americans and Indian immigrants over the span of more than 200 years. This included migrants from the South Asian subcontinent before 1947, the current nation of India post-independence in 1947, and the Indian diaspora countries globally.[3]

Drawing upon the experiences of generations of migrants, from farm workers and merchants in the nineteenth century and their descendants to the range of low- and high-skilled immigrants in the twenty-first century, *Beyond Bollywood* chronicled how Indian migrants have shaped America culturally through traditions of the arts, food, and faith, politically through participation in struggles for rights, and professionally through various occupations. This history was largely unknown to both Indian American and broader audiences alike. Many visitors—Indian American and otherwise—reported seeing themselves and their own immigrant family histories of building a life in a new homeland in the exhibition.[4] As I reminded visitors when I gave tours in the gallery, all Americans have histories of migration in our own families, whether recently or many generations ago.

Beyond Bollywood included more than 300 images, 36 works of art, and 24 historical artifacts. Amongst the artifacts were a turban of the late Balbir Singh Sodhi, a pamphlet—"What America Means to Me"—by former Congressman Dalip Singh Saund, and a doctor bag of Abraham Verghese, MD. The turban represented a moment of tragedy within ongoing violence toward Indian Americans, the pamphlet was a symbol of achievement for the community, and the doctor bag symbolized sacrifice, dedication, curiosity, and assimilation. Overall, these artifacts were three windows into the Indian American experience between the late 1950s and the early twenty-first century.

These artifacts were also part of a well-intentioned but perhaps overly cautious tradition at the Smithsonian and many other public institutions and cultural heritage organizations. We often represent the narratives of immigrants, people of color, women, lesbian, gay, bisexual, and transgender persons, people with disabilities, and the working class through the politically correct trajectory of struggle, assimilation, achievement, and contribution. In other words, interpretations of such objects often tell a story to the tune of "we came, we struggled, we worked hard, we made it, and not only are we not burdens but we give back, and now we are Americans." As curators, we are limited to a small number of words on any given object label, or text panel, and directed to write to a seventh-grade reading level. Moreover, when mounting a first-time exhibition of a community in such a public institution, we face pressures to start where the national conversation is, at least as a point of departure. Taken together, these factors make it difficult to have very nuanced conversations embedded in the materiality of the exhibition itself. It is possible, though, to enlist them as entry to more provocative conversations—beyond apology and assertion—by juxtaposing them with performance art, specifically theater, in the exhibition gallery. I will discuss this in more detail in the last section of this chapter, following an explanation of collecting and interpreting the artifacts themselves.

COLLECTING AND INTERPRETING ARTIFACTS

When research for *Beyond Bollywood* began in 2007, the Smithsonian's collection of 137 million objects did not have a single identifiable item of Indian American history. Thus began a seven-year journey to consult scholars, archives, community organizations, and individuals to find, borrow, and eventually accession objects from around the country, including the ones discussed in this chapter. Generally, the Indian American community was excited to work with the institution to have our histories represented, and also had strong opinions about *how* they should be represented. Some were concerned that the struggles of the community be placed front and center while others wanted an exhaustive rendering of the achievements. Thus, the community's sentiments mirrored the challenges we as curators face in conveying nuance while acknowledging that representation itself, especially for a community that has only had citizenship rights in the United States since 1946, cannot be taken for granted and is a significant step forward. Accessioning of artifacts mean that our history is held in the public trust and will be preserved and accessible to the public and researchers in perpetuity.

In addition to accessioning, the inclusion of these artifacts in *Beyond Bollywood* represented curatorial choice on how to render the experience of a specific yet non-monolithic immigrant community at this moment in U.S. history amid ongoing immigration debates. The setting of the Smithsonian—national, public museums in the nation's capital—also influenced curatorial choice. The national stage of the Smithsonian provides curators working on exhibitions such as *Beyond Bollywood* and *Many Voices, One Nation* with unique pressures and challenges to produce narratives beyond those politically benign ones of achievement, struggle, assimilation, and contribution. Ultimately, artifacts chosen for *Beyond Bollywood* set the stage for these narratives, but interpreting them still posed limitations to realizing these narratives fully.

Balbir Singh Sodhi (b. 1949) was the first person of South Asian origin killed in a hate crime after 11 September 2001 (Figure 1). Persons of Arab, Middle Eastern, and South Asian origin throughout the United States were targeted and

Figure 1.
Balbir Singh Sodhi, in Phoenix, Arizona, date unknown. Sodhi emigrated from Punjab, India, to the United States in 1989. He worked first as a taxi driver and then opened his own business, a gas station, in Arizona. Sodhi identified as a Sikh and wore a turban as part of his faith. National Museum of American History, Smithsonian Institution, gift of Rana Singh Sodhi.

Figure 2.
Balbir Singh Sodhi's turban. In the days following the 11 September 2001 terrorist attacks, hate crimes targeting Arab Americans, Muslim Americans, and South Asian Americans skyrocketed. Shot to death in front of his gas station in Mesa, Arizona, Sodhi was the first victim of post-9/11 hostility. National Museum of American History, Smithsonian Institution, gift of Rana Singh Sodhi.

attacked in hate crimes following 9/11.[5] Sodhi came to the United States from Punjab, India, in 1989. Initially residing in Los Angeles and San Francisco where he worked as a taxi driver, Sodhi eventually saved enough money to open up a gas station in Mesa, Arizona. On 15 September 2001, Frank Silva Roque, a local Boeing aircraft mechanic, shot Sodhi five times from a truck, killing him. The police arrested Roque the next day, and he was eventually sentenced to life in prison without parole. Sodhi's family donated his turban, along with other personal effects, to the National Museum of American History, and they have been accessioned into the national collection (Figure 2).

Dalip Singh Saund (b. 1899) was the first person of Asian and Indian origin and non-Abrahamic faith elected to the United States Congress (Figure 3). Also from Punjab, India, Saund migrated as a young man for graduate studies and later became a farmer. Following the passage of the Luce-Celler Act in 1946, Saund applied for naturalization and became an American citizen in 1949, the same year that Balbir Singh Sodhi was born. He served as Justice of the

Figure 3.
Portrait of Dalip Singh Saund by Jon R. Friedman, 2007. Saund was the first person of Asian and Indian origin elected to the United States Congress. Saund gained United States citizenship in 1949 and was elected to the House of Representatives in 1955. His portrait includes a range of icons at right, including the Statue of Liberty, Abraham Lincoln, and Mahatma Gandhi. Collection of the U.S. House of Representatives.

Peace in Westmoreland township, California, and in 1955 ran as a Democrat for an open House of Representatives seat against a well-known Republican aviator, Jacqueline Cochran. Cochran had wealth and long-standing Washington, D.C., connections. Still, Saund won the seat and was reelected twice. His family donated the "What America Means to Me" pamphlet, along with campaign bumper stickers and a book he had authored, to the National Museum of American History, and these artifacts have also been accessioned into the national collection (Figure 4).

Abraham Verghese (b. 1955) is a physician and author at Stanford Medical School and was part of a generation of Indian doctors that immigrated to the USA after the creation of Medicare and the passage of the Immigration and Nationality (Hart-Celler) Act in 1965 (Figure 5). Verghese received medical training in India and Ethiopia and completed his residency in Johnson City, Tennessee. It was common for foreign medical graduates to find residency placements in rural and urban poor communities. Verghese recounts,

> It was hard to get a job in a nice hospital unless you wanted to be a bathroom sweeper. Hospitals in poor and rural areas needed us foreign medical graduates. Compared to hospitals in India, I liked how organized everything was, especially all the charts and the nurses' notes. I had to ask someone how to tie my tie with a thinner knot so I could fit in. And the only way I could eat the bland hospital food was to put Tabasco sauce on everything.[6]

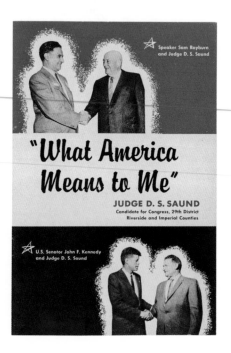

Figure 4.
"What America Means to Me," a campaign booklet of U.S. Representative Dalip Singh Saund, 1956. Saund was a public servant who carefully navigated difficult issues of race, nation, and identity throughout his long career. National Museum of American History, Smithsonian Institution, gift of the Saund Family.

Figure 5.
Physician and author Abraham Verghese, on 10 October 2009. Today, Dr. Verghese is a popular author as well as a practicing physician. Photo by Schleyer/ullstein bild via Getty Images. Used with permission.

Figure 6.
Doctor bag of Abraham Verghese, MD, 1980s. Dr. Verghese trained in India and Ethiopia before travelling to the United States for his residency appointment. He used this bag during his residency in Johnson City, Tennessee. National Museum of American History, Smithsonian Institution, gift of Abraham Verghese.

Verghese donated the doctor bag he used during residency to the Smithsonian Asian Pacific American Center, and it too is entering the national collection (Figure 6).

Saund's pamphlet represented the first in a string of high-profile achievements by Indian immigrants, earlier rendered as "underdogs" without privilege and resources. His story is one of contribution, too, as a public servant. In his era, few Indian immigrants were professionals. Verghese's doctor bag represented simultaneous experiences of isolation, trying to fit in, being embraced, and seeing fresh opportunities in a new homeland. Today, Verghese is one of a handful of physician-authors humanizing the medical profession by sharing its inner workings with broader audiences through popular writing. Sodhi's turban was a symbol of struggle and violence, rooted in ongoing discrimination, racism, and racially motivated hate crimes, including violence that persists today.

As curators, we create exhibits for the general public, sometimes up to 10 million visitors a year, and know that they walk in the door with a range of beliefs and assumptions. We assume that some may hold the same racist sentiments demonstrated by Roque and that others have experienced the deep pain of Sodhi and his family firsthand. Moreover, we also imagine that others—immigrants and people of color from many different backgrounds—are quite familiar with the range of emotions and experiences Verghese had in Johnson City, and that many take pride in seeing the achievements of their community—with Saund as an example. But, as much as these artifacts add dimension and meaning to the narratives, it was difficult to enlist them in pushing beyond apology and assertion, to have them symbolize more than achievement, struggle, assimilation, and contribution.

ARTIFACTS AS ENTRY, COUPLED WITH PERFORMANCE ART

In *Beyond Bollywood*, to move beyond apology and assertion, I deliberately juxtaposed objects with film, visual art, and performance art, including theater, to layer narratives of struggle, assimilation, achievement, and contribution with counter-narratives that further nuance immigrant experiences.

At first glance, Verghese's doctor bag seems like an affirmation of the model minority myth (i.e., "Indian Americans are smart, successful and rich"),[7] but Verghese's own biography, rendered through the object's extensive text label (quoted above), departs from that. And lest visitors viewed the object with assumptions about financial success and professional privilege unquestioned, diagonally opposite its case was a documentary film about discrimination faced by taxi drivers and photographic portraits of Indian American motel owners living and working in their motels.

Both Saund's pamphlet and Sodhi's turban were used as reference points in a play entitled *Living Beyond Bollywood*, created through a collaboration between me as curator and a local playwright and performed by a local theater company, the South Asian Performing Arts Network (SAPAN) Institute. The play was crafted to elaborate upon historical moments depicted through the gallery, drawing from both archival material and creative license in building out each of six vignettes. It was advertised in various local sources and performed multiple times per day on successive Saturdays over a three-month timespan, and over 1,100 people attended 24 performances. Some audiences deliberately "attended" the play while others who just happened to be there were "pulled in" to the performance as it moved around the gallery.

Some of the vignettes referenced the actual life of the object and others used the material culture as a starting point around which to build a scene. In one of the scenes, an actor portrayed Saund's campaign manager, teaching volunteers how to canvass and respond to frequently asked questions about the candidate, including those about his ethnic background and patriotism. The pamphlet was used as source material from which the dialogue was devised and was literally referenced in the scene. Similarly, the turban was referenced in two different scenes: one between mother and daughter discussing how dress can make one a target of racial profiling, the second in which the character of a Sikh young man tells his sister he has enlisted in the U.S. Army, referencing both patriotism and the current-day debate about whether Sikhs in the U.S. Army should be allowed to wear turbans (Figure 7).

Figure 7.
Actor Trisha Sanghvi of the SAPAN Institute performing in *Living Beyond Bollywood* at the National Museum of Natural History. Sanghvi portrayed a young woman whose brother had just enlisted in the U.S. Army. The play was performed in the *Beyond Bollywood* exhibition gallery as part of an integrated approach to engaging visitors in the museum. Photo by Shan Jalla.

The engagement of these objects with performance art—performed in situ in the gallery—helped provide nuance for the understanding of the artifacts themselves and broadened overarching narratives in the exhibition by presenting characters, based on historical figures, telling their stories with detail and emotion. Interestingly, if the theater was presented separately, it might be dismissed as partisan or visited more selectively. In *Beyond Bollywood,* combining film, visual art, and performance art with material culture allowed a single, powerful way of moving beyond apology and assertion in immigration narratives and presenting the community experiences as more nuanced than solely "struggling" or "achieving."

Through in-gallery theater, the complexity of the human and immigrant experience was highlighted with all its triumphs, travails, and tragedies in the present moment, with history literally as a backdrop—something difficult to achieve in textbooks, tweets, and the soundbytes of social media, not to mention the limited word counts of artifact labels in exhibition galleries. As our national identity as Americans—and our understanding of it—shifts, so too must our curatorial approaches, to encompass more creative, multidimensional engagement with material culture inside exhibition galleries.

NOTES

1. For more discussion of this, see Vijay Prashad, *The Karma of Brown Folk* (Minneapolis: University of Minnesota Press, 2001) and *Everybody Was Kung Fu Fighting: Afro-Asian Connections and the Myth of Cultural Purity* (Boston: Beacon Press, 2002).

2. For more about the Smithsonian Asian Pacific American Center, see http://www.smithsonianapa.org.

3. Countries that are part of the Indian diaspora include Australia, Belgium, Burma (Myanmar), Canada, Fiji, Guyana, Jamaica, Kenya, Malaysia, Qatar, Singapore, South Africa, Tanzania, Trinidad, Uganda, United Arab Emirates, and the United Kingdom.

4. "Visitor Experience Evaluation of *Beyond Bollywood: Indian Americans Shape the Nation,*" (Washington, D.C.: Smithsonian Institution Office of Policy and Analysis, 2014).

5. For more on this, see the "Post 9-11 Backlash" section of the website of South Asian Americans Leading Together, http://www.saalt.org/policy-change/post-9-11-backlash/.

6. Abraham Verghese, "The Cowpath to America," *The New Yorker,* 23 June 1997, 80.

7. For recent discussion of the model-minority myth, see Ellen D. Wu, *The Color of Success: Asian Americans and the Origins of the Model Minority* (Princeton: Princeton University Press, 2014).

Prashad, Vijay. *Everybody Was Kung Fu Fighting: Afro-Asian Connections and the Myth of Cultural Purity.* Boston: Beacon Press, 2002.

———. *The Karma of Brown Folk.* Minneapolis: University of Minnesota Press, 2001.

Smithsonian Asian Pacific American Center. http://www.smithsonianapa.org (accessed 4 November 2016).

Smithsonian Institution Office of Policy and Analysis. "Visitor Experience Evaluation of *Beyond Bollywood: Indian Americans Shape the Nation.*" https://www.si.edu/content/opanda/docs/Rpts2014/2014.12.BeyondBollywood.Final.pdf (accessed 4 November 2016).

South Asian Americans Leading Together. "Post 9-11 Backlash." http://www.saalt.org/policy-change/post-9-11-backlash/ (accessed 4 November 2016).

Verghese, Abraham. "The Cowpath to America." *The New Yorker*, 23 June 1997.

Wu, Ellen D. *The Color of Success: Asian Americans and the Origins of the Model Minority.* Princeton: Princeton University Press, 2014.

The Desert Colossus:
Fragments of Twenty-First-Century Undocumented Migration

Jason De León

Between 2000 and 2014, 12.2 million people were apprehended while trying to cross into the United States from Mexico without authorization.[1] During this period, 5.4 million border crossers were arrested in Arizona.

> *Fifteen-year-old José Tacuri looks up at an unbroken sky the color of the Pacific Ocean. He squints and wipes sweat from his furrowed brow. Jagged mountains like the serrated edges of enormous knives surround him. His knock-off Air Jordans and dark clothes are covered in a fine powder of red Sonoran Desert dust. Growing up in the cloud city of Cuenca, Ecuador, he and his cousins never imagined that there were places on earth that got this hot.[2]*

Much of the American public imagines the U.S.–Mexico border to be a well-defended line in the sand. They envision an impassable wall out of Emperor Hadrian's playbook that boldly divides two countries; crew-cut agents in starched green uniforms scan the horizon through high-powered binoculars in search of any movement. Some unsuspecting border crosser from a tiny village in Durango, Mexico, scales the wall only to trip a motion sensor buried in the dirt on the American side. Immediately a black Apache helicopter drops from the sky and blinds him with a search light. These exciting images, which make for great television, are largely the stuff of fiction.[3] Most of the 1,954 miles of U.S.–Mexico border are unguarded. This geopolitical boundary cuts through areas that are remote and desolate. It is a land where Border Patrol agents are often few and far between.

Although only 351 miles (18 percent) of the border has anything resembling a wall, man-made physical barriers (often referred to as "Pedestrian Fencing") are key components of enforcement architecture and security logic.[4] In the early 1990s, the federal government developed a policy called "Prevention Through Deterrence" whereby the U.S. Border Patrol began to heavily fortify urban zones.[5] This meant an increase in agents on the ground, more high-tech surveillance cameras, and a strengthening of the partitions dividing Mexico and the United States. The idea was that if it was too difficult to get over a fence in downtown El Paso, Texas, or San Ysidro, California, people would attempt to cross in more remote and less guarded areas. These are places where the harsh natural environment could act as a deterrent to movement and where migrants would be easier to catch. In these locales, border walls don't exist. Here the desert provides the federal government with a "tactical advantage." The fragment of fencing in the *Many Voices, One Nation* exhibit comes from the California border town of Calexico and was once used to separate this community from their Mexican neighbors in Mexicali. Prior to the introduction of reinforced steel walls in the late 1990s, which are significantly taller and more difficult to scale or breach, this simple chain-link fence was what you would have found in and around all official ports of entry for decades (Figure 1). What most people don't know is that this type of obstacle literally disappears as soon as you get to the edge of any American border town and make your way toward the surrounding unpopulated wilderness.

In places like southern Arizona, all that stands between undocumented migrants and the cities where they are seeking employment or looking to reconnect with family is the vast Sonoran Desert: hundreds of square miles of mountains, extreme temperatures, and more species of rattlesnakes than any other place on earth. Two decades of social science research has shown that "Prevention Through Deterrence" has failed to deter people from crossing, but has made the social process of clandestine migration more difficult and deadly[6] (Figure 2).

De León

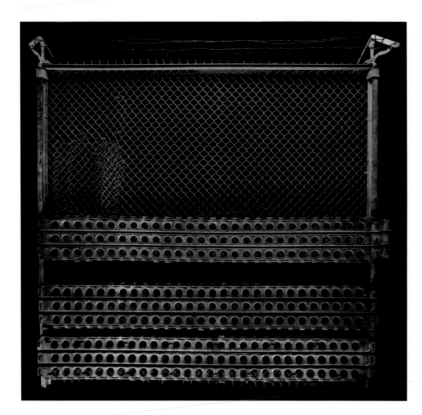

Figure 1.

Section of fence from the border between Calexico, California, and Mexicali, Mexico, mid-twentieth century. Standing approximately 11.5 feet high, this barrier has a mesh strip, called tarmac plates, along the bottom and barbed wire along the top. The tarmac plates were likely added after people cut through or dug under the fence. It was replaced with a more substantial metal barrier in 1997. National Museum of American History, Smithsonian Institution, gift of Armando J. Rascon.

The coyote [smuggler] in charge of José Tacuri's group leads them through a steep can-yon 10 miles east of the border town of Nogales. Here there is no wall separating Mexico from the United States, just a three-strand barbed-wire fence with an unlocked gate. The smuggler unties the wire that holds the gate closed and 25 migrants from Mexico, Central America, and Ecuador quickly pass through. Everyone is wearing dark clothes, carrying a backpack filled with food, first-aid supplies, and extra garments, and grip-ping a plastic bottle of water. These are the objects you need to survive the desert and avoid apprehension by the Border Patrol. Some have managed to bring a few meager personal possessions to remind them of home: a dog-eared bible, a love letter, a pair of their child's shoes. José is wearing a tiny wooden pendant around his neck that is in the shape of an owl. His girlfriend in Ecuador gave it to him for luck. It is June of 2013 and the morning temperature is slowly climbing toward the high 90s.

"Give me your tired, your poor, your huddled masses yearning to breathe free." Emma Lazarus's poem "The New Colossus" is one of the most iconic pieces of American writing ever produced and it is fundamentally and forever asso-ciated with U.S. immigration, Ellis Island, and the Statue of Liberty on whose pedestal it is engraved. While these words have long inspired the American ide-alism that we are a nation founded by a "melting pot" of immigrants who were welcomed with open arms, it fails to capture the cruel reality that the immigrant

Figure 2.

Sonoran Desert, Arizona, January 2014. The Sonoran Desert in southern Arizona is known for its harsh conditions including extreme temperatures, limited shade, and dangerous wildlife. Despite the hostile environment, many migrants undertake the treacherous journey across the southern border into the United States. Courtesy of Michael Wells.

experience has never been easy. Historians and those who were present at Ellis Island have noted that passing through that port of entry was often traumatic. Watchful health inspectors attempted to weed out the sick, deformed, and those likely to become "public charges." Immigrant bodies were subjected to a range of humiliating inspections for lice, trachoma, gonorrhea, or signs of lunacy, idiocy, or disability.[7] Some agents made extra cash by extorting bribes from those who would likely fail health checks.[8] The island was not the pristine beacon of hope that some have made it out to be. The grandfather of former governor of the state of Massachusetts and 1988 Democratic presidential nominee Michael Dukakis, who passed through Ellis Island in 1913, called it the "Palace of Tears, or sighs."[9]

Like the U.S.–Mexico border today, Ellis Island was a complicated space where politics, notions of race, and de facto and de jure discrimination shaped who could come through the "golden door." Writing about the health inspection that all immigrants were subject to, one physician commented on what he perceived to be the negative effects of an early-twentieth-century decrease in arrivals from western Europe and Scandinavia and an increase of "Jews, Slavs, the Balkan and Austrian races and those from the Mediterranean countries." He wrote:

As a class, they [non-Western Europeans] contribute little of lasting value but the work of their hands for which they are well paid…They do not amalgamate. They are here in no small degree for what they can get…Such is the type of newer immigration, and its changing and deteriorating character makes restriction justifiable and necessary. No one can stand at Ellis Island and see the physical and mental wrecks who are stopped there, or realize that if the bars were lowered ever so little the infirm and mentally unsound would come literally in hordes, without becoming a firm believer in restriction and admission of only the best…Restriction is vitally necessary if our truly American ideals and institutions are to persist, and if our inherited stock of good American manhood is not to be depreciated.[10]

Over time, the tense, humiliating, and often racist encounters between Ellis Island's gatekeepers and newly arrived immigrants have generally been sanitized or forgotten in the public's imagination.[11] In the twenty-first century, those who washed up on New York's shore 100 years ago are now described as noble and industrious immigrants wholly different from those who come across America's southern border today seeking a living wage and a better life.

In 2009, I started the Undocumented Migration Project (UMP), a long-term anthropological analysis of clandestine border crossings from Latin America to the United States.[12] Some of the goals of the UMP are to use archaeology to document and collect the items that people leave in the desert during the social process of migration, which is often characterized by extreme physical pain and trauma (e.g., dehydration, long distances walked over rugged terrain, sexual assault at the hands of bandits), and to draw historical linkages with other waves of immigration.[13]

In 2012, the UMP found this shirt depicting the Statue of Liberty (Figure 3). It was stuffed into a backpack that a migrant left behind in the Sonoran Desert 30 miles north of the border. It is a provocative object that materially represents a highly contentious and politicized social process while simultaneously referencing America's rich immigrant past. I am left asking two interrelated questions: What did the symbol on this shirt mean to the person who carried it through the desert? How much time will pass before the Latinos who arrive through America's desert Ellis Island become the noble and industrious immigrants who we then use to measure against newer (and less desirable) arrivals?

José Tacuri left Ecuador in April of 2013 to reunite with his parents in New York, both of whom had migrated five years before him. His mom and dad diligently sent money home every month to put food on the table and a roof over the heads of their five children. They migrated so that they could educate and provide for their kids, something that had become impossible for them to do in Ecuador where a living wage is hard to come by for most working-class people. José's parents couldn't bear to watch their children suffer in poverty.

Figure 3.
Front and back views of a shirt found in the Sonoran Desert in 2012, owner unknown. The Undocumented Migration Project documents and collects items left by migrants crossing the border. The Statue of Liberty design on this shirt is particularly poignant as a traditional beacon of liberty and freedom for immigrants. National Museum of American History, Smithsonian Institution, gift of the Undocumented Migration Project.

Figure 4.
Picture frame discovered in the Sonoran Desert in 2009, owner unknown. Uncovered by the Undocumented Migration Project, this frame was carried across miles of perilous desert terrain and never made it to its destination. National Museum of American History, Smithsonian Institution, gift of the Undocumented Migration Project.

The objects deposited by border crossers in the Arizona desert are the archaeological traces of a modern-day exodus. In the wake of the North American (1994) and Central American (2003) Free Trade agreements, along with a host of other economic, political, and environmental crises in Latin America, millions of people have left their homes in search of a better life for themselves and for their families. Some of the material traces of this migration, such as this empty picture frame, speak to both the high personal cost and the anonymity of this clandestine movement[14] (Figure 4). This frame also leaves many questions unresolved. Who is the "#1 Dad"? Is it the father who leaves his children behind

Figure 5.
José Tacuri, Cuenca, Ecuador, 2013. José Tacuri joined the many
migrants attempting to cross the border through the Arizona
Desert. The fifteen-year-old travelled from his home in Cuenca,
Ecuador, with the hopes of reuniting with his parents in New York
after a five-year separation. Tacuri has been missing since his
attempted crossing in 2013. Courtesy of Jason De León.

so that he can find work in a distant country? Does the "#1 Dad" wash dishes in the kitchen of your favorite downtown restaurant? Did the "#1 Dad" make it across the border or become one of the hundreds who die annually while trying to traverse the rugged Sonoran Desert? Whoever he is, how desperate must he have been to leave his own kids behind? What are the long-term emotional costs of this migration? We are only now beginning to understand the impact on families divided by transnational movement.[15]

Some of the artifacts that border crossers leave behind speak to these issues, but many stories remain untold or can never be excavated through archaeology alone. Perhaps all these objects can do is stand as physical reminders that millions of people have suffered in the Arizona desert so that they and their children can breathe free.

José Tacuri left Cuenca, Ecuador, in April of 2013. He entered the Sonoran Desert in June of that year. He was migrating to reunite with parents who had not hugged him in five years. He was migrating so that he could earn money to send home to support his girlfriend and his soon-to-be-born baby girl. José was left behind when he became sick and couldn't continue walking through the desert. He has not been heard from since. There is no physical trace of him, no artifact to put on display (Figure 5).

The bodies of over 3,000 border crossers have been recovered in southern Arizona since 2000.[16] It is unknown how many people have disappeared in the vast wilderness of the Sonoran Desert.

NOTES

1. Jason De León, *The Land of Open Graves: Living and Dying on the Sonoran Desert Migrant Trail* (Berkeley: University of California Press, 2015), table 1.

2. The italicized vignettes in this essay are constructed from interviews with members of José Tacuri's family, including his two cousins who were with him in the desert, and six years of participant observation in the Arizona desert and the northern border town of Nogales, Mexico. Humphreys and Watson call this type of account *semifictionalized ethnography,* or a "restructuring of events occurring within one or more ethnographic investigations into a single narrative." See Michael Humphreys and Tony Watson, "Ethnographic Practices: From 'Writing Up Ethnographic Research' to 'Writing Ethnography,'" in *Organizational Ethnography: Studying the Complexity of Everyday Life,* eds. Sierk Ybema, Dvora Yanow, Harry Wels, and Frans H. Kamsteeg (Thousand Oaks, Cali.: SAGE, 2009), 40–55, table 2.1; see also discussion of ethnography and fiction in: James Clifford, "Introduction: Partial Truths," in *Writing Culture,* eds. J. Clifford and G. Marcus (Berkeley: University of California Press, 1986), 1–26; Kirin Narayan, "Ethnography and Fiction: Where is the Border?" *Anthropology and Humanism* 24(2)(1999):134–147; and Didier Fassin,

"Revisiting the Boundaries Between Ethnography and Fiction," *American Ethnologist* 41(1) (2014):40–55. For more on the life of José Tacuri see De León, *The Land of Open Graves*.

3. For example, see National Geographic Channel's show *Border Wars*.

4. Marc R. Rosenblum, *Border Security: Immigration Enforcement between Ports of Entry*, Congressional Research Service Report for Congress (6 January 2012):16, http://fpc.state.gov/documents/organization/180681.pdf.

5. Timothy J. Dunn, *Blockading the Border and Human Rights: The El Paso Operation That Remade Immigration Enforcement* (Austin: University of Texas Press, 2009).

6. See discussion in De León, *The Land of Open Graves*.

7. Alan M. Kraut, "Silent Travelers: Germs, Genes, and American Efficiency, 1890–1924," *Social Science History* 12(4)(1988):377–94 and Daniel J. Wilson, "'No Defectives Need Apply': Disability and Immigration," *OAH Magazine of History* 23(3)(2009):35–40.

8. Kraut, "Silent Travelers," 379.

9. Kraut, "Silent Travelers," 382.

10. A. C. Reed, "Going through Ellis Island," *Popular Science Monthly* 82(1913):7–9.

11. For a discussion of American immigration and the dynamic nature of race, see Matthew F. Jacobson, *Special Sorrows: The Diasporic Imagination of Irish, Polish, and Jewish Immigrants in the United States* (Cambridge, Mass.: Harvard University Press, 1995) and *Roots Too: White Ethnic Revival in Post-Civil Rights America* (Cambridge, Mass.: Harvard University Press, 2005); Karen Brodkin, *How Jews Became White Folks and What That Says About Race in America* (New Brunswick: Rutgers University Press, 1998); Mae M. Ngai, *Impossible Subjects: Illegal Aliens and the Making of Modern America* (Princeton: Princeton University Press, 2004); Ira Katznelson, *When Affirmative Action was White: An Untold History of Racial Inequality in Twentieth-Century America* (New York: W. W. Norton, 2005); Robert L. Fleegler, *Ellis Island Nation: Immigration Policy and American Identity in the Twentieth Century* (Philadelphia: University of Pennsylvania Press, 2013); David R. Roediger, *Working Toward Whiteness: How America's Immigrants Became White, The Strange Journey From Ellis Island To The Suburbs* (New York: Basic Books, 2005).

12. For information on the Undocumented Migration Project, see http://www.undocumentedmigrationproject.com.

13. Audrey Singer and Douglas S. Massey, "The Social Process of Undocumented Border Crossing among Mexican Migrants," *International Migration Review* 32(3)(1998):561–92.

14. Ann E. Kingsolver, *NAFTA Stories: Fears and Hopes in Mexico and the United States* (Boulder, Colo.: Lynne Rienner Publishers, 2001); John R. MacArthur, *The Selling of "Free Trade": NAFTA, Washington, and the Subversion of American Democracy* (New York: Hill and Wang, 2000); David Bacon, *The Children of NAFTA: Labor Wars on the U.S./Mexico Border* (Berkeley: University of California Press, 2004); Jennifer L. Burrell and Ellen Moody, eds., *Central America in the New Millennium: Living Transition and Reimagining Democracy* (New York: Cedla Latin America Studies, Berghahn Books, 2012).

15. Kristin Elizabeth Yarris, "'Quiero Ir y No Quiero Ir' (I Want to Go and I Don't Want to Go): Nicaraguan Children's Ambivalent Experiences of Transnational Family Life," *Journal of Latin American and Caribbean Anthropology* 19(2) (2014):284–389.

16. See Jess Beck, Ian Ostericher, Greg Sollish, and Jason De León, "Scavenging Behavior in the Sonora Desert and Implications for Documenting Border Crosser Fatalities," *Journal of Forensic Sciences* 60, Issue Supplement 1 (2015): S11-20; see http://www.derechoshumanosaz.net/remembering-the-dead/ for count to date of migrant fatalities in Arizona.

Bacon, David. *The Children of NAFTA: Labor Wars on the U.S./Mexico Border.* Berkeley: University of California Press, 2004.

Beck, Jess, Ian Ostericher, Greg Sollish, and Jason De León. "Scavenging Behavior in the Sonora Desert and Implications for Documenting Border Crosser Fatalities." *Journal of Forensic Sciences* 60, Issue Supplement 1 (2015): S11–20.

Brodkin, Karen. *How Jews Became White Folks and What That Says About Race in America.* New Brunswick: Rutgers University Press, 1998.

Burrell, Jennifer L. and Ellen Moody, eds. *Central America in the New Millennium: Living Transition and Reimagining Democracy.* New York: Cedla Latin America Studies, Berghahn Books, 2012.

Clifford, James. "Introduction: Partial Truths." In *Writing Culture,* eds. J. Clifford and G. Marcus, pp. 1–26. Berkeley: University of California Press, 1986.

De León, Jason. *The Land of Open Graves: Living and Dying on the Sonoran Desert Migrant Trail.* Berkeley: University of California Press, 2015.

Dunn, Timothy J. *Blockading the Border and Human Rights: The El Paso Operation That Remade Immigration Enforcement.* Austin: University of Texas Press, 2009.

Fassin, Didier. "Revisiting the Boundaries Between Ethnography and Fiction." *American Ethnologist,* 41(1)(2014):40–55.

Fleegler, Robert L. *Ellis Island Nation: Immigration Policy and American Identity in the Twentieth Century.* Philadelphia: University of Pennsylvania Press, 2013.

Humphreys, Michael and Tony Watson. "Ethnographic Practices: From 'Writing Up Ethnographic Research' to 'Writing Ethnography.'" In *Organizational Ethnography: Studying the Complexity of Everyday Life,* eds. Sierk Ybema, Dvora Yanow, Harry Wels, and Frans H. Kamsteeg, pp. 40–55. Thousand Oaks, Cali.: SAGE, 2009..

Jacobson, Matthew F. *Roots Too: White Ethnic Revival in Post-Civil Rights America.* Cambridge, Mass.: Harvard University Press, 2005.

_____. *Special Sorrows: The Diasporic Imagination of Irish, Polish, and Jewish Immigrants in the United States.* Cambridge, Mass.: Harvard University Press, 1995.

Katznelson, Ira. *When Affirmative Action was White: An Untold History of Racial Inequality in Twentieth-Century America.* New York: W. W. Norton, 2005.

Kingsolver, Ann E. *NAFTA Stories: Fears and Hopes in Mexico and the United States.* Boulder, Colo.: Lynne Rienner Publishers, 2001.

Kraut, Alan M. "Silent Travelers: Germs, Genes, and American Efficiency, 1890–1924." *Social Science History,* 12(4)(1988):377–94.

MacArthur, John R. *The Selling of "Free Trade": NAFTA, Washington, and the Subversion of American Democracy.* New York: Hill and Wang, 2000.

Narayan, Kirin. "Ethnography and Fiction: Where is the Border?" *Anthropology and Humanism* 24(2)(1999):134–47.

Border Wars. Television Series. National Geographic Channel, 2010–present. http://channel.nationalgeographic.com/border-wars/ (accessed 14 November 2016).

Ngai, Mae M. *Impossible Subjects: Illegal Aliens and the Making of Modern America.* Princeton: Princeton University Press, 2004.

Reed, A. C. "Going through Ellis Island." *Popular Science Monthly,* 82 (1913):7–9.

Roediger, David R. *Working toward Whiteness: How America's Immigrants Became White, The Strange Journey from Ellis Island to the Suburbs.* New York: Basic Books, 2005.

Rosenblum, Marc R. *Border Security: Immigration Enforcement between Ports of Entry.* Congressional Research Service Report for Congress. 6 January 2012. http://fpc.state.gov/documents/organization/180681.pdf (accessed 14 November 2016).

Singer, Audrey and Douglas S. Massey. "The Social Process of Undocumented Border Crossing among Mexican Migrants." *International Migration Review* 32(3)(1998):561–92.

Undocumented Migration Project. http://www/undocumentedmigrationproject.com (accessed 14 November 2016).

Wilson, Daniel J. "'No Defectives Need Apply': Disability and Immigration." *OAH Magazine of History*, 23(3) (2009):35–40.

Yarris, Kristin Elizabeth. "'Quiero Ir y No Quiero Ir' (I Want to Go and I Don't Want to Go): Nicaraguan Children's Ambivalent Experiences of Transnational Family Life." *Journal of Latin American and Caribbean Anthropology*, 19(2) (2014):284–389.

Epilogue:
Our Polycultural Past and Future Century

Scott Kurashige

Each November, there arrives a momentous anniversary of the landmark moment when travelers from across the Atlantic first established relations with the indigenous inhabitants of what would become the United States. For decade upon decade and all across the nation, young and old alike have celebrated Thanksgiving in America to mark the first harvest of the Plymouth colony in 1621 and extol the values of harmony and goodwill that sustained our ancestors through trying times.

The historical event I seek to recover, however, occurred in an entirely different time and place. It predates the first Thanksgiving by nearly a century, although it is generally not the subject of commemoration or, for that matter, remembrance. With its quincentenary soon approaching, now is the perfect time to consider this alternative account of a first contact.

In 1526, 500 people sought to establish a colony on land that would possibly sit today within South Carolina. They were, to be certain, a group we would characterize in retrospect as diverse, but they became so under ignoble circumstances. Sailing out of the Caribbean from Hispaniola, the Spanish majority was headed by a wealthy aging patriarch named Lucas Vásquez de Ayllón and christened the settlement San Miguel de Gualdape. Roughly one-fourth to one-third of the group, however, consisted of enslaved peoples—some Africans and others Native Americans captured in a previous expedition to the region.[1]

San Miguel de Gualdape has been consigned to the dustbin of history, not even recounted like Roanoke as a first failed attempt at European colonization. The Spanish settlers grew cold, ill, and unable to provide for themselves. When their leader died, they fought viciously among themselves to assume power, further depleting whatever energy and resources they retained as winter approached. There are no reports leading us to believe that Native Americans could or would help save the colony. Some of the enslaved Native Americans escaped, including one the Spanish had named Francisco de Chicora and educated in Europe to serve as a translator. Other indigenous peoples from established communities in surrounding areas briefly harbored colonists who came to commandeer food, then killed them when they tired of their antics.[2]

Finally, the colonists relented. Only 150 survivors set sail for return. Eight more people froze to death on the journey home, and Ayllón's body was cast overboard. This was in no small measure a human horror story. Nevertheless, the events of 1526 proved pivotal for what they established. During the turmoil, a group of enslaved Africans rose up and burned down the home of one of the Spanish leaders. Peter Wood has characterized this event as "an act of slave arson which would mark the beginning of a lengthy tradition." Herbert Aptheker went one step further: in his paradigm-shifting book documenting the revolt of enslaved blacks, Aptheker argued that these "rebel Negroes" represent "the first permanent inhabitants, other than the Indians, in what was to be the United States."[3]

In a popular history book written for young readers, William Loren Katz projected that these black Maroons joined with Native Americans to form a new community—one whose duration is unknown but whose legacy is everlasting. "In distant South Carolina forests, two and a half centuries before the Declaration of Independence," he wrote, "two dark peoples first lit the fires of freedom and exalted its principles." They were, in other words, the originators of the struggle to build a free society made up of people of different hues and from different continents during the post-1492 era of conquest, slavery, and genocide and on land that would become the United States. "As such," Katz concluded, "they qualify as our earliest inheritance."[4]

What would it mean for those of us living in the twenty-first century to recognize Africans and Native Americans revolting against slavery and conquest as "our earliest inheritance"? With the nation in the midst of a great period of demographic transformation, cultural change, and political contestation, this is an exciting and eventful time to study, discuss, and debate our historical origins and antecedents. "The past is never dead," wrote the oft-cited William Faulkner. "It isn't even past." We are shackled by the burdens of history. Yet, we can also reawaken buried or neglected dreams and hopes when we reexamine and reimagine the past—just as every generation before us has done.

Our ideas about national heritage are anything but fixed or permanent. "The true history of Thanksgiving reveals embarrassing facts," writes James Loewen. Native Americans held harvest celebrations for centuries before the arrival of the Pilgrims. In fact, our modern holiday dates only to 1863, and "the Pilgrims had nothing to do with it until the 1890s."[5] What we assume to be foundation turns out to be scaffolding.

This volume and the exhibit that it accompanies speak directly to this watershed moment in history, when uncertainty reigns and change is guaranteed but our future course will be determined by choices and actions we partake of through our own free will. By shining the light on a multiplicity of experiences and foregrounding diverse perspectives, *Many Voices, One Nation* will help to redress the "diversity deficit" within our national institutions—the underrepresentation of diverse groups within those physical sites and textual representations that convey our national heritage. A consultant to the National Park Service reported that "of over 77,000 properties listed in the National Register as of April 20, 2004, only about 1,300 are explicitly associated with African-American heritage, 90 with Hispanic, and 67 with Asian."[6] This volume recognizes the heterogeneous and intersectional qualities that characterize diversity, race and ethnicity within historical events and discourse.

Through its potential reach to millions of onsite visitors and online viewers, *Many Voices, One Nation* promises to enrich our national dialogue and open our minds to connections and possibilities we may not have previously detected. For some readers and viewers, it may speak to stifled impulses they have previously felt—those times when they were learning about history and something seemed missing, distorted, or not quite right but they could not find the sources to reinforce their sentiment or were not in a position to challenge a voice of authority.

Taken together, this book and exhibition provide a vital response to those who assert that rising diversity threatens to tear holes in the nation's social fabric or has already done so. Harvard scholar Robert Putnam sparked a national conversation spreading from schoolrooms to the White House with his "Bowling Alone" publications lamenting the decline of civic engagement in the United States. Based on follow-up research, he named diversity as a prime culprit. "Diversity seems to trigger... anomie or social isolation," Putnam stated. "In colloquial language, people living in ethnically diverse settings appear to 'hunker down' – that is, to pull in like a turtle."[7]

Beyond mild-mannered social scientists lay firebrand critics of diversity. But regardless of temperament, those who set off alarm bells often harken back to a supposed golden age of social harmony that can never be found when one actually examines the historical record. Building relationships and finding common bonds—be it at the local, state, or national level—has always involved negotiation and struggle. In recent years, the issue of diversity in the K–12 curriculum has become the source of political debate that has sometimes reached a fever pitch. In 2010, Arizona passed legislation to curtail ethnic studies programs that politicians believed were or could be designed to "promote the overthrow of the United States Government," "promote resentment toward a race or class of people," serve "pupils of a particular ethnic group," or "advocate ethnic solidarity instead of the treatment of pupils as individuals."[8]

Ironically for many proponents of ethnic studies, the last three factors characterized the ethnocentric curriculum that they assert was once standard throughout all levels of education, prompting calls for ethnic studies from the 1960s onward. The past five decades have also given rise to multitudinous studies of difference, inequity, and exclusion based on gender, sexuality, class, ability, and religion. Transcending seeing diversity as a problem, these new fields of study have sharpened our sense of how and why, out of their interactions with people from diverse backgrounds, Americans have begun to produce new ideas of collectivity and new modes of civic engagement. Instead of seeing minoritized subjects as "objects" of diversity and add-ons to a preexisting narrative, they have acted to pose the epistemological questions that arise when we center the margins.

Scholars of diversity have challenged the preeminence of the traditional archive, dataset, and canon. They have sought to enhance our base of knowledge by helping to build community-based archives, launch oral history projects, recover overlooked authors and texts, deploy new ethnographic methods, and shine a light on social movements to uncover new forms of communicative action and new models of citizenship. Notably, as this volume more than amply demonstrates, curators have collected, presented, and interpreted objects that help us trace diverse histories reflected in material culture.

In this way, *Many Voices, One Nation* serves as a model of how such research fosters new forms of engagement with the public. Moreover, it seeks to connect with the increasingly diverse audience that comprises the twenty-first-century public. The exhibit is certain to educate visitors from around the world, but its planned long-term installation will also coincide with shifts in American self-conception. Over the past century, as essays in this volume detail, we have witnessed new waves of immigration and internal migration prompt new paradigms of social identity from the melting pot to integration and multiculturalism.

We are now deep in the midst of a paradigm shift from multiculturalism to what forward-thinking commentators have termed polyculturalism. Responding to being repeatedly asked, "So, what are you?" African American historian Robin D. G. Kelley responds as follows: "Although folk had trouble naming us, we were never blanks or aliens in a 'black world.' We were and are 'polycultural,' and I'm talking about all peoples in the Western world." Rather than seeing ourselves as members of mutually exclusive groups emanating from distinct cultures, Kelley asserts, "All of us are inheritors of European, African, Native American, and Asian pasts, even if we can't exactly trace our bloodlines to these continents."[9]

The concept of polyculturalism provides an alternative to the "postracial" conundrum. As election of the nation's first black president created unprecedented forms of both unity and division, it has become readily apparent that we need a new language to reflect changing realities. To see ourselves as immersed within a polycultural paradigm is to recognize the imperative to go beyond defining people and communities based on rigid categories, binary oppositions, and biological determinisms that are anachronistic now but have never captured the complex nature of our existence. Polycultural analyses, however, resist the urge to erase traces of difference, diversity, and oppression that has come to characterize hasty and ill-formed interpretations of the "postracial."

A polycultural discourse emphasizes our interconnectedness. At its best, it pushes us to appreciate social change and achieve social justice by highlighting the potential for breakthroughs. When we challenge ourselves to think and act through the tensions and contradictions that arise from diverse actors, it becomes more feasible and urgent to envision the affinities and solidarities that arise from many voices drawn together by the nation.

We begin to see immigrant contributions to American culture not as singular or assimilable but multiple and transformative, as in the case of Korean barbecue tacos sparking the food truck revolution. Furthermore, we know that U.S. citizens like Josephine Baker and James Baldwin traveled abroad to seek spaces of exile, while others facing expulsion or persecution, such as James Connolly, Ricardo Flores Magón, Vang Pao, and Edward Said, migrated to the United States as transnational subjects representing diasporic communities. And there are those in the islands of the Caribbean and Pacific—some granted U.S. citizenship and some perpetually denied—who were incorporated into the American cultural and political sphere through U.S. expansionism and still relate to the nation principally as colonial subjects whose status is the product of past wars and ongoing military interests.

We also recognize that our national heritage has been shaped by those whose struggle for liberation and self-determination led them to transgress the boundaries of the nation-state. As Sylviane A. Diouf's research demonstrates, the history of *marronage* foregrounds "people who defied slave society, enforced their own definition of freedom, and dared invent their specific alternative to what the country had delineated as being blacks' proper place."[10] The Seminole freedmen went a qualitative step beyond the typical Maroon colony to create an independent model of existence tied to an American Indian nation.

These are just some of the diverse strands that come into focus when we begin to listen to many voices. To presume there is only one voice would necessitate elevating one above the rest or drowning out those that do not fit prescribed expectations. It is rather the polyvocality that enriches our understanding of history and our untapped potential. Through reimagining the past, it becomes possible to see different trajectories toward a better and more just future.

NOTES

1. Woodbury Lowery, *The Spanish Settlements Within the Present Limits of the United States, 1513–1561* (New York: G. P. Putnam's Sons, 1901), 160–68; Gonzalo Fernández de Oviedo y Valdés, *Historia general y natural de las Indias* vol. 3 (Madrid: Impr. de la Real academia de la historia, 1851): 626–33. Special thanks to José Fusté for helping me to interpret sections from this text.

2. Douglas T. Peck, "Lucas Vásquez de Ayllón's Doomed Colony of San Miguel de Gualdape," *Georgia Historical Quarterly* 85(2) (Summer 2001):183–98.

3. Peter H. Wood, *Black Majority: Negroes in Colonial South Carolina from 1670 to the Stono Rebellion* (New York: Alfred A Knopf, 1974), 4; Herbert Aptheker, *American Negro Slave Revolts* (New York: International Publishers, 1963), 163.

4. William Loren Katz, *Black Indians: A Hidden Heritage* (New York: Atheneum, 1986), 25.

5. James Loewen, *Lies My Teacher Told Me: Everything Your American History Textbook Got Wrong* (New York: Touchstone, 2007), 90.

6. Ned Kaufman, "Historic Places and the Diversity Deficit in Heritage Conservation," *CRM: The Journal of Heritage Stewardship* 1(2) (Summer 2004), 68–85. http://www.nps.gov/crmjournal/Summer2004/article3.html.

7. Robert D. Putnam, "*E Pluribus Unum*: Diversity and Community in the Twenty-first Century," *Scandinavian Political Studies* 30(2) (June 2007):137–74.

8. Arizona House of Representatives, HB 2281 (2010).

9. Robin D. G. Kelley, "The People in Me," *ColorLines*, Winter 1999, 5–7.

10. Sylviane A. Diouf, *Slavery's Exiles: The Story of the American Maroons* (New York: New York University Press, 2014), 305.

BIBLIOGRAPHY

Aptheker, Herbert. *American Negro Slave Revolts.* New York: International Publishers, 1963.

Arizona House of Representatives, HB 2281 (2010).

Diouf, Sylviane A. *Slavery's Exiles: The Story of the American Maroons.* New York: New York University Press, 2014.

Fernández de Oviedo y Valdés, Gonzalo. *Historia general y natural de las Indias* vol. 3. Madrid: Impr. de la Real academia de la historia, 1851.

Katz, William Loren. *Black Indians: A Hidden Heritage.* New York: Atheneum, 1986.

Kaufman, Ned. "Historic Places and the Diversity Deficit in Heritage Conservation." *CRM: The Journal of Heritage Stewardship*, 1(2) (Summer 2004), 68–85. http://www.nps.gov/crmjournal/Summer2004/article3.html (accessed 18 November 2016).

Kelley, Robin D. G. "The People in Me." *ColorLines*, Winter 1999, 5–7.

Loewen, James. *Lies My Teacher Told Me: Everything Your American History Textbook Got Wrong.* New York: Touchstone, 2007.

Lowery, Woodbury. *The Spanish Settlements Within the Present Limits of the United States, 1513–1561.* New York: G. P. Putnam's Sons, 1901.

Peck, Douglas T. "Lucas Vásquez de Ayllón's Doomed Colony of San Miguel de Gualdape." *Georgia Historical Quarterly*, 85(2) (Summer 2001):183–98.

Putnam, Robert D. "*E Pluribus Unum*: Diversity and Community in the Twenty-first Century." *Scandinavian Political Studies*, 30(2) (June 2007):137–74.

Wood, Peter H. *Black Majority: Negroes in Colonial South Carolina from 1670 to the Stono Rebellion.* New York: Alfred A. Knopf, 1974.

Acknowledgments

We are so pleased to acknowledge the many contributions of our Smithsonian colleagues and scholarly communities.

This book is the result of many years of thought by curators Fath Davis Ruffins and William H. Yeingst in the Division of Home and Community Life at the National Museum of American History. Ruffins's vision for a pan-institutional initiative on the history and culture of migration in American life sparked the *Many Voices, One Nation* exhibition and this accompanying publication.

We extend our appreciation to the entire *Many Voices, One Nation* exhibition team, especially project director Nancy Davis for her incredible leadership. Bonnie Campbell Lilienfeld has provided critical support for the team and this publication. Our anonymous peer reviewers from the Smithsonian Institution Scholarly Press offered thoughtful comments, as did our colleagues Magdalena Mieri and Harry Rubenstein. Many thanks to Ginger Strader and Deborah Stultz at the Smithsonian Institution Scholarly Press, for their assistance and patience in the creation of this collection.

Support from our museum and institution leadership has been invaluable. Director John Gray and Associate Director of Curatorial Affairs David Allison encouraged this collection of essays and the exhibition to bring important untold stories into a national narrative. For production support for this book and for the larger Smithsonian immigration and migration initiative, we thank the Smithsonian Consortium for Understanding the American Experience and especially Senior Program Officer for History and Culture, Michelle Anne Delaney, who has been a dedicated champion of our work for many years.

Thank you to our partners from the Smithsonian Asian Pacific American Center, the Smithsonian Center for Folklife and Cultural Heritage, and the National Museum of the American Indian for contributing thoughtful essays and amazing objects. Conversations with colleagues at the National Museum of Natural History, the Smithsonian Center for Learning and Digital Access, the National Museum of African American History and Culture, the Anacostia Community Museum, and the Smithsonian Latino Center have greatly informed our work.

Connections with museum and academic colleagues across the country have expanded our vision and expectations for this project. Thank you to the institutions and individuals who shared objects and images. Many of the authors in this book first became collaborators during years of research and outreach. We thank them for their outstanding contributions to this volume.

We are most thankful for our superb museum colleagues. Christine Klepper and Molly Horrocks are excellent caretakers of the nation's artifacts. We are also grateful for the careful work of NMAH Preservation Services, Laura McClure, Cassie Mancer, and Bennie Brunton. Leslie Poster's editing expertise and keen eye for language brought us to the finish line. Photographer Jaclyn Nash's artistry and meticulous perfectionism made our objects glow on the page. We especially express our gratitude to Wanda Hernández for her dedication to this project.

It has been our greatest pleasure working with you.

Margaret Salazar-Porzio
Joan Fragaszy Troyano
Lauren Safranek

Contributors

Margaret Salazar-Porzio is Curator of Latina/o History and Culture at the Smithsonian's National Museum of American History and a specialist in twentieth-century visual and material culture of the Western United States, Pacific Rim, and U.S.–Mexico borderlands. Formerly an Associate Research Scholar at the Center for Institutional and Social Change at Columbia University Law School, she has received numerous research fellowships and awards. Salazar-Porzio was also a primary education teacher in Los Angeles, California, where she received a local Teacher of the Year award (2004).

Joan Fragaszy Troyano is a Research Associate and former Mellon/American Council of Learned Societies Public Fellow at the Smithsonian Institution. A specialist in immigration history, visual culture, and public understandings of the past, she is a member of the *Many Voices, One Nation* curatorial team. She has developed exhibitions and education programs across the Smithsonian and digital projects with the Roy Rosenzweig Center for History and New Media at George Mason University.

Lauren Safranek is Curatorial Assistant at the Smithsonian's National Museum of American History for the *Many Voices, One Nation* exhibition. Her scholarly work focuses on material culture and storytelling around recent immigration to the United States, and her public history products include exhibition development and curation, educational materials, public outreach, and the award-winning citizenship education website *Preparing for the Oath*. In 2012 she was a Goldman Sachs Junior Fellow at the National Museum of American History.

Davarian L. Baldwin is Paul E. Raether Distinguished Professor of American Studies at Trinity College in Hartford, Connecticut. He is the author of *Chicago's New Negroes: Modernity, the Great Migration, and Black Urban Life* and coeditor (with Minkah Makalani) of the essay collection, *Escape from New York: The New Negro Renaissance beyond Harlem*. Baldwin is currently at work on two new books, *Land of Darkness: Chicago and the Making of Race in Modern America* (Oxford University Press) and *UniverCities: How Higher Education is Transforming Urban America*.

Nancy Davis is Curator of Costume at the Smithsonian's National Museum of American History, where she is a specialist in technologies in the home, Asian influence on American material culture, and consumption and market studies. Previously the deputy director and chief curator of the Maryland Historical Society, most recently she co-curated the business history exhibition *American Enterprise* (2015). She is the project director and a curator for the *Many Voices, One Nation* exhibition.

Jason De León is Assistant Professor of Anthropology at the University of Michigan. As director of the Undocumented Migration Project, he is conducting a long-term anthropological study of migration between Mexico and the United States that uses a combination of ethnographic, visual, archaeological, and forensic approaches to understand this clandestine social process. A 2013 National Geographic Society Emerging Explorer, De León also co-hosted the Discovery Channel show *American Treasure* in 2011.

Gary Gerstle is Paul Mellon Professor of American History at Sidney Sussex College, Cambridge University. The author and editor of many books on the history of American political thought, institutions, and conflicts, he also has written extensively about immigration, race, and nationality. Gerstle has been elected to the Society of American Historians and Royal Historical Society, and from 2011 to 2012 was Goldman Sachs Fellow at the National Museum of American History.

Ramón A. Gutiérrez is the Preston and Sterling Morton Distinguished Service Professor of History at the University of Chicago. He is a specialist in Mexican-American history, Indian-White relations in the Americas, social and economic history of the Southwest, colonial Latin America, and Mexican immigration. A MacArthur Foundation Fellow, he has written widely on the history of the Southwest and race and ethnicity in American life.

Sojin Kim is a Curator at the Smithsonian Center for Folklife and Cultural Heritage. She previously held curatorial positions at the Natural History Museum of Los Angeles County and the Japanese American National Museum.

Alan M. Kraut is University Professor of History at American University and a Nonresident Fellow of the Migration Policy Institute. He specializes in U.S. immigration and ethnic history, the history of American medicine and public health, and Civil War history. He is the prize-winning author or editor of nine books and many scholarly articles. A past president of the Organization of American Historians, he is currently the chair of the Statue of Liberty–Ellis Island History Advisory Committee and President of the National Coalition for History. He frequently serves as a consultant to the National Park Service and documentary filmmakers, and as an adviser to museums, including the National Museum of American History. He is a fellow of the Society of American Historians.

Scott Kurashige is Professor in the School of Interdisciplinary Arts and Sciences at University of Washington Bothell. He is the author of *The Shifting Grounds of Race: Black and Japanese Americans in the Making of Multiethnic Los Angeles* (Princeton University Press, 2008) and coauthor with Grace Lee Boggs of *The Next American Revolution: Sustainable Activism for the Twenty-First Century* (University of California Press, 2011). He was a Goldman Sachs Fellow at the National Museum of American History from 2013 to 2015.

Bonnie Campbell Lilienfeld is Assistant Director for Curatorial Affairs and Curator of the Ceramics & Glass Collection at the Smithsonian's National Museum of American History. In addition to serving as a co-curator of the *Many Voices, One Nation* exhibition, she has curated exhibitions on topics including philanthropy, the Bracero Program, transportation, and ceramics.

Masum Momaya is an Independent Scholar and Research Fellow at the Chicago Council on Global Affairs. She has curated exhibitions for the Smithsonian Asian Pacific American Center and the International Museum of Women and published widely on the topics of race and immigration, women's rights, economic justice, and social justice.

Kym Rice is Director of George Washington University's Museum Studies Program. Her award-winning exhibitions include *Before Freedom Came: African American Life in the Antebellum South*, which won the Gustavus Meyers Award for contributions in the study of human rights in 1992. She served as coeditor of the two-volume work *The World of a Slave: Encyclopedia of the Material Culture of Slavery* (2011).

Fath Davis Ruffins is Curator of African American History and Culture at the Smithsonian's National Museum of American History. She is a specialist in ethnic imagery in popular culture, history of advertising, history of African American preservation efforts, and the origins of ethnic museums on the National Mall. Ruffins has curated or consulted on numerous major exhibitions around the country including an inaugural exhibition for the National Underground Railroad Freedom Center (2004), and served as the founding director for the *Many Voices, One Nation* exhibition.

Debbie Schaefer-Jacobs is Curator of the Education Collections and the Harry T. Peters America on Stone Collection at the Smithsonian's National Museum of American History. Her expertise is in material and visual culture of the American classroom, childhood artifacts, and nineteenth-century American prints. In addition to being one of the curators for *Many Voices, One Nation,* she recently contributed to *Smithsonian's Civil War, Inside the National Collection.*

Barbara Clark Smith is Curator of Early American Society and Politics at the Smithsonian's National Museum of American History. She has served as a curator on major exhibitions ranging from *After the Revolution* (1985) to *Jamestown, Quebec, and Santa Fe: Three North American Beginnings* (2008) to *American Democracy: A Great Leap of Faith* (2017). Her publications include popular and scholarly works, most notably reinterpreting the American Revolution in *The Freedoms We Lost,* published by the New Press in 2011.

John Kuo Wei Tchen is a Historian, Curator, and Writer. He is the Founding Director of the Asian/Pacific/American Studies Program and Institute at New York University and Cofounder of the Museum of Chinese in America, where he continues to serve as senior historian. He is author of several award-winning books, and regularly collaborates with filmmakers and media producers, artists, and collectors. Tchen was awarded the Charles S. Frankel Prize (renamed the National Humanites Medal) from the National Endowment for the Humanities. His current work is on American eugenics and its ongoing impacts on the political culture of the nation.

Christopher Lindsay Turner is Cultural Research Specialist at the Smithsonian's National Museum of the American Indian. He has been a curator of exhibitions relating to Native American histories of federal treaty relationships, the history of mixed-heritage communities, and American Indian musicians of note. His own work concerns the cultural politics of land, history, and environmental issues in the Haudenosaunee communities of his home, upstate New York.

L. Stephen Velasquez is an Associate Curator in the Division of Home and Community Life at the National Museum of American History. His research and exhibition projects include the Bracero Program, Latino collections, and food history.

Index

Page numbers in *italics* indicate illustrations and captions.

Academie Saint Jean-Baptiste, Pawtucket, Rhode Island, *171,* 171–172, *172,* 173
Addams, Jane, 143, 156n15, 179, 186, *186*
adoptions. *see* Korean orphans, U.S. adoptions of
AFL-CIO poster, *213*
African Americans and African immigrants. *see also* free blacks; slaves and slavery
    Antebellum expression, 111–121
    Black History Month, 152–153, *153,* 159n46
    Black History Week, 159n46
    in census (1790), 82
    charity and community-driven schools, 174n5
    Chicago, 181, 182–184
    citizenship denied to, 82, 95n5
    cowrie shell necklace, *30*
    historically black universities, 159n46
    housing discrimination against, 151, 182–184, 187–189
    literacy, 118n16
    lynchings, 127, 142
    Maroon colonies, 274
    military service, 147, *147,* 157n26
    museum exhibits, 4
    National Register, associated properties, 271
    as percentage of population, 219
    rice fanner basket, 35, *35*
    role in peopling of North America, 29–31, 36
    Statue of Liberty, response to, 126–128
    Statue of Liberty as, 133n2
    violence against, 142, 159n48
    voting rights, 138
The Afro-American Tradition in the Decorative Arts (exhibition), 117n1
agricultural workers, *ii, 217,* 217–218, 224n31
air traffic controllers, 225n33
Alexander VI, Pope, 75
Algonquian cultures, 33, 72
Alien Naturalization Act (1790). *see* Naturalization Act (1790)
Allen, Theodore, 140
Allen, Woody, 4
almanacs, 119n18
"America, Liberty Restored" (teapot), 69, *70,* 76

"America—A nation of one people from many countries" (Bourne), *144*
American Committee at the National Academy of Design in New York, 129
American Committee for the Statue of Liberty, 126–127
American empire
    conquest, 3, 14, 16, 81, 95, 270–271
    expansion, 3, 72, 82, 84, 91, 94, 95, 199, 274
    imperialism, 95
    incorporation, 13–14, 18, 49, 60, 81, 84, 88, 91, 95, 96n14, 197
American G.I. Forum, 158n37
American Indians. *see* Native Americans
Americanization efforts, 165–177
    American Indian boarding school system, 167, 174n3
    emergence, 141
    English language lessons, 165
    Ford Motor Company, *141*
    nostalgia, *168*
    patriotism in immigrant communities, 175n6
    pledge, *169*
    in public schools, 165–168
    South (region), 174n5
    tenets, 169
American Legion, 141
American Museum of Immigration, 131
American Revolution, 84
Americans
    national identity, 84, 131
    use of term, 38–40, 84
Anglo-Protestant conformity, 141–142
Angola, slaves from, 114
Ann (slave), 113
Anthony of Padua, Saint, 46, *46,* 48–49, 53
anti-Catholic prejudice, 17, 93–94, 142
anti-immigrant sentiment. *see also* nativism
    Ellis Island, 260–261
    immigrant responses to, 216
    post-9/11 violence, 246, 248–249, 252
    prevalence, 93
    racial hierarchies, 140, 142
    Siler City, North Carolina, 237
    toward undocumented immigrants, 216

Apache, 46, 53
Aptheker, Herbert, 270
Arab Americans and Arab immigrants, 248–249
Arizona
    ethnic studies programs, 272
    Spanish colonization, 52
    undocumented migration, 257, 258, 264, 264n2
artifacts
    collecting and interpreting, 247–252
    colonial New Mexico, 45–55
    "dumb traces," 45
    as entry, coupled with performance art, 252–254
    as framework for expanding social imaginaries,
        219–220
    as histories yet to be recovered and retold, 77–78
    interpreting beyond apologizing and asserting, 245,
        247
    museum labels, 219, 247
    objects of memory and journey, 57–67
    from "slavery times," 111
    stories they tell, 232–233
    Undocumented Migration Project, 261, 262, 262, 264
Asian Americans and Asian immigrants
    asylum seekers, 152
    countries of origin, 208
    National Register, associated properties, 271
    number of immigrants, 208
    population increase, 219, 223nn20–21
    prejudices against, 152
    segregation in U.S. Armed Forces, 147
    transformation from inassimilable into model
        minorities, 199, 202n10
Asian and Pacific American History Month, 153
assimilation, 141, 167, 172–174. see also Americanization
asylum seekers, 152, 208
Atlanta, Georgia, 232
Atlantic, 30, 31, 96n6, 125, 209, 269
    Basin, 29
    coast, 27, 58, 60
    Seaboard, 5
Atlantic Creoles, 29
Aupaumut, Hendrick, 61–62
Axtell, James, 38
Ayllón, Lucas Vásquez de, 269–270
Aztec empire, conquest of, 46, 51, 75

baby boomers, 150–151
baby formula, 150
Baddler (potter), 118n9
Baker, Josephine, 274
Balch, George Thatcher, 169, 175n12
Baldwin, James, 274
Baltimore, Maryland, 176n22
banks, 168, 168–170, 169, 175n10
Bartholdi, Frédéric Auguste, 123, 125, 125–126, 133n2
baseball, color line, 225n35
baskets, 35, 35

Baxter, Annette, 107, 107–108
Baxter, Emile, 107–108
beads. see Glengarry cap; wampum
Bellamy, Francis, 174n4
Bennett Law (Wisconsin, 1888), 176n21
Berlin, Ira, 88
Bethune, Mary McLeod, 149
Beyond Bollywood (exhibition), 245–255
    artifacts as entry, coupled with performance art,
        252–254
    collecting and interpreting artifacts, 247–252
    performance art, 253
Bhabha, Homi, 224n28, 224n30
bilingualism
    in schools, 169, 171, 171–173, 174
    state legislation, 176n21
    St. Jean Baptiste Church, 176n24
Bilingual Law (Ohio, 1839), 176n21
Black History Month, 152–153, 153, 159n46
Black History Week, 159n46
Blue-Back Speller (Webster), 167
Bollywood. see Beyond Bollywood (exhibition)
Booth, Charles, 185
border fence, 257–258, 259, 260
Border Patrol. see under United States
Boston, Massachusetts, 167, 168, 168, 175n9
Boston Provident (bank), 175n10
Boston Tea Party (1773), 69
Bourne, Emma, 144
"Bowling Alone" (Putnam), 272
Brace, Charles Loring, 175n10
Bracero Program, 222n12
Bradford, William, descendants of, 28
Bragg, Laura, 117n1
British Americans and British immigrants
    in census (1790), 82
    as "natives," 155n9
    role in peopling of North America, 5–6, 27–28,
        33–34
    view of North America as wilderness, 27
    Virginia, 33–34, 41n13
British Columbia
    Eagle Clan, Tsimshian people, 29, 60
    slavery system, 31
British East India Company, 69
British Empire
    domestic dissenters, 76
    exploration in western North America, 52
    industrialization, 77
    Treaty of Paris, 84
Brokaw, Tom, 157n25
Brown, Dee, 4
Brownlee, Charlotte, 197, 198, 201
Brown v. Board of Education, 151
Buddhism, 216, 216
Bureau of Education, 167
Burgess, Ernest, 180, 180–181, 183, 183–184, 187

Burgundy (sailing ship), 97n25
Bury My Heart at Wounded Knee (Brown), 4

Cabet, Etienne, 106–108
Calexico, California, 258, *259*
California
    Chinese immigrants, 94, 97n29
    Del Valle family, *87,* 87–88
    gold rush, 94
    Proposition 187 (1994), 215–216
    segregation, 159n40
    Spanish colonization, 52
Californios, 87, 87–88, 157n23
Cambodia, immigrants from, 208
Campbell's Wampum Factory, Park Ridge, New Jersey,
    32
Capote, Texas, 90, *91*
Capra, Frank, 157n26
Caribbean, 74, 75, 95, 145, 208, 269, 274
Carson, Cary, 41n13
Carte Tres Curieuse, 33
Carthage, Illinois, 106
Catechism of Catholic Education, 172
Catholics and Catholicism
    Americanization movement, 166, 172–173
    anti-Catholic prejudice, 17, 93–94, 142
    Mexican-Americans, 88
    parochial schools, 165–166, 170–173, 176n22
    population, 170
    promotion of own heroes, 175n7
Celler, Emanuel, 152
census (1790), 82, *83,* 95n2
Centennial celebrations (1876), 167
Central America, immigrants from, 212
Central American Free Trade Agreement (2003), 262
ceramics. *see* pottery
Champlain, Samuel de, 32, 74
Chaney, Michael, 116–117
Charleston, South Carolina, 34, *34,* 90
Charleston Museum, 117n1
Cherokees, 86, 158n30
Chesapeake region, English settlement, 33–34
Chicago, Illinois
    "Concentric Zones" map, *180,* 180–185, *183,* 187
    housing segregation, 182–183
    Hull House, 179, *186*
    Hull House nationality map, 181, *184–185,* 185–187
    King's attempted march, 152
    Negro History Week, 152
    organized labor protests, 181
    population, 181
    race riot (1919), 156n13, 181
    Residential Security Map of Chicago, Northern
        Section, October 1939–April 1940, *188*
    Social Research Map of Chicago, *183*
    tenements, 182–183
    as urban landscape model, 181–182

Chicago Defender, 127
Chicago School
    academic prominence, 180, 184, 187
    Chicago tradition, 187–189
    "Concentric Zones" map, *180,* 180–185, *183,* 187
    reasons for, 181–182
Chicora, Francisco de, 270
children. *see also* education; Korean orphans, U.S.
        adoptions of; public schools
    Korean culture, 196
    rocking chair, 103, *103*
    soccer teams, 231–240
Children's Aide Society, New York, 175n10
China
    economic influence, 209
    trade with U.S., 74, 76
Chinatown, New York City, *213*
Chinese Americans and Chinese immigrants
    bans on, 17, 94, 155n7, 199
    California gold rush, 94, 97n29
    citizenship denied to, 82
    Cold War, 152
    as garment workers, 212, *213*
    ill-treatment of, *94*
    number of, 97n29, 208
    Statue of Liberty, symbolism for, 130–131
Chinese Exclusion Act (1882), *17,* 94
Chinese porcelain, 73–75, *74*
Choctaws, 158n30
Christianization
    as goal of Spanish conquest, 46, 48–49, 53
    Korea, 197–200, 201, 202n9
    of Native Americans, 46, 48–49, 53, 61
Christmas cards, *148*
churches, bilingual, 176n24
Church of Jesus Christ of Latter-day Saints. *see*
        Mormons
Cibola County, New Mexico, 36–37, *37*
Ciesla, Dudek, 158n33
Ciesla, Hanka, 158n33
ciqi (Chinese porcelain), 73–75, *74*
cities, concentric zones, *180,* 180–185, *183,* 187
citizenship
    African Americans, 95
    Fourteenth Amendment, 154n2
    Indian immigrants, 247, 249
    Mexican citizenship, 96n14
    Naturalization Act (1790), 82, 155n7
    race and, 17, 96n14
    territories, 154n6, 274
The City (Park, Burgess, McKenzie), 179, 180
Civil Rights Act (1964), 91, 151
civil rights movement
    "A Yankee Doodle Tan (The 'Double V' Song)," *148*
    cultural shifts enabling legislation, 138–139
    interracial coalitions, 158n38, 212, *213,* 214
    opposition to, 138

progressive legislation, 206
veterans in, 158n37
violence against participants in, 151–152
Civil War, aftermath, 90–91
CIW. *see* Coalition of Immokalee Workers
Clark, William, *85*
Clarkston, Georgia
foreign-born population, 232, 235
Fugees soccer team, 231, *233*, 233–236, *234*, *235*, 238–240
refugee resettlement, 234–235
tensions between refugees and established residents, 233–235, 236, 238, 240
Clarkston Community Center, Clarkston, Georgia, 234, 236
Cleveland, Grover, 126
Cleveland Board of Education, *166*
Cleveland Gazette, 127
Cleveland Museum of Art, 117n1
Clinchy, Everett R., 156n17
clothes hanger, *108*
clothing and identity, 196–197
Coalition of Immokalee Workers (CIW), 216–218, *217*, 224n31
Cochran, Jacqueline, 250
"Code Talkers," 149
Cold War
as causal element in civil rights, 138
immigration, 152
racial segregation, 147–153
transformation of Asians from inassimilable into model minorities, 199, 202n10
Coles, Edward, 104
colonial history
New Mexico, 45–55
Pilgrims, 27, 28, *28*, 269, 271
San Miguel de Gualdape, 269–270
settler colonialism, 36
color-line problem, 137, 153–154, 219, 225n35
colors, racial associations with, 18
Columbian exchange, 46, 50, 53–54
Columbian Exposition, 174n4
Columbus, Christopher, *39*, 45, 74, 129
Comanche, 46, 53
communism, 151, 152, 199, 202n7
concentric zones map, *180*, 180–185, *183*, 187
Congress, U.S. *see under* United States
Congress of Racial Equality (CORE), 158n38
Connolly, James, 274
Constitution, U.S., 126, 145, 154n2, 154n4
continentalism, 5–6
Coppola, Francis Ford, 4
corbel (ceiling bracket), 38, *38*
CORE (Congress of Racial Equality), 158n38
Coronado, Francisco Vásquez de, 48
Cortés, Hernán, 51, 75
cosmograms, 114, 118n13

cotton plantations, 113, 117n7
Council Against Intolerance in America, *144*
couriers du bois (French hunters and trappers), 33
cowries, 30, *30*, 74
creamware pitcher, 39, *39*
The Crisis (NAACP magazine), 156n16
Cronin, Mike, 238
Crosby, Alfred B., 46
Cuadros, Paul, 232, 236, 238, 240
Cuenca, Ecuador, immigrants from, 257, 260, 261, *263*, 264, 264n2
cultural gifts movement, 142, 144–145, 156n17
cultural pluralism
American self-identification, 131, 138
assimilation conflicts, 173–174
coining of term, 145
cultural gifts movement, 142, 144–145, 156n17
opposition to, 138
widespread acceptance of, 154
culture wars, 216
curator/curation, 70, 72, 219, 231, 232, 245, 247–248, 252, 254, 273
currency, *75*, 75–76

Darwin, Charles, *143*
Daughters of the American Revolution, 141, 167
"Dave Day," 119n22
Davies, Thomas, 118n14
Declaration of Independence, 17
Del Valle family, *87*, 87–88
demographic shift (1965–2014), 219–220
"Descriptive Map of London Poverty" (Booth), 185
Des Sauvages (Champlain), 74
Dewey, John, 144, 156n17
Diouf, Sylviane A., 274
diversity. *see also* cultural pluralism
as backbone of the nation, 12
in school curriculum, 272
as strength, 145, 272
Time magazine cover, 18, *18*
triggering social isolation, 272
U.S. Armed Forces, 149–150
Doak, William, 224n26
doctors, immigrants as, 250–252
doctor bag, 246, 251, *251*, 252
Dominic, Saint, 46
Dominican Republic, immigrants from, 208
Dorchester, Massachusetts, 168, 175n11
"Double V" campaign, 147
Douglass, Frederick, 118n16
Drake, Dave, 111–121
biography, 111–112
cosigned pieces, 118n9
earliest vessel attributed to, 118n12
exhibitions of his work, 117n1
family, 119n22
literacy, 114–115

loss of leg, 118n9
as master potter, 113
name, 115, 117n2, 119n17
poetry, *112*, 114, 115–116, *116*
pottery, 111–116, *112, 114, 116,* 117 118n13, 119n25
research on, 117n1
as slave, ownership history, 112, 113, 117n3
surviving works by, 113, 118n11, 119n26
as typesetter, 114–115
verse pots, 111, 115–117, *116*, 119n20
Drake, Harvey, 112
DuBois, Rachel Davis, 156n17
Du Bois, W. E. B.
    biography, 137
    on color-line problem, 137, 219
    as *The Crisis* founding editor, 156n16
    as NAACP founding member, 144, 156n16
    portrait of, *138*
    on Statue of Liberty, 128
Dukakis, Michael, 260
Duke, David, 237
"dumb traces," 45
du Simitière, Pierre Eugène, 21n3
Dutch Americans and Dutch immigrants, 95n2
Dutch Empire
    fur trade, 31
    purchase of Manhattan, 71–72
    role in peopling of North America, 31–32
Dutch West Indies Company, 31–32

Eagle Clan, Tsimshian people, 29, 60
eagles, *58, 59, 82*
Ecuador, immigrants from, 257, 260, 261, *263,* 264, 264n2
Edelman, Larry, 129
Edgefield, South Carolina
    cotton industry, 117n7
    "Dave Day," 119n22
    newspapers, 114–115
    pottery, marks on, 114, 118n13
    pottery factories, 112–113, 118n7, 118n14
    pottery types, 117n5
    stoneware storage jar, 111, *112, 114*
    transportation features, 119n23
Edgefield Hive (newspaper), 115
education. *see also* parochial schools; public schools
    Academie Saint Jean-Baptiste, Pawtucket, Rhode Island, *171,* 171–172, *172,* 173
    American Indian boarding school system, 167, 174n3
    Americanization and, 165–177, *166*
    diversity in curriculum, 272
    English-only schools, 175n13
    language of instruction, 169–170, 176n21
    "Little Red School House Savings Bank," *168,* 168–170, *169*
    pluralism–assimilation conflicts, 173–174

private schools, 165
report card, *171,* 171–172
segregation in schools, 146, 151, 159n40
teaching tolerance, 144, *144*
Edwards Law (Illinois, 1889), 176n21
Eisenhower, Dwight, 150
elk hide, painting on, 46, *46,* 53
elk hunting, 50–51
Ellis Island (immigration station), 8, 134n21, 260–261
Ellis Island National Immigration Museum, 131
El Paso, Texas, 52
El Salvador, immigrants from, 208
An Emblem of America (Fairburn), 39, *39*
Empress of China (ship), 76
England, American rebellion against, 69
English immigrants. *see* British Americans and British immigrants
English language
    Americanization efforts and, *141,* 165, *166*
    English-only movement, 170
    English-only schools, 172–173, 175n13, 176n21
E Pluribus Unum
    contemporary interpretations, 11–12, 16–17, 19
    on eagle, *82*
    early use, 12
    on Great Seal, 1, *13*
    original interpretation, 21n3
    translations of, 1, 16, 21n2, 22n9
    as U.S. motto, 82
ethnicity
    competing beliefs about, 139–146
    shaping national identity, 81–82
ethnic studies programs, 272
ethnography, semifictionalized, 264n2
eugenics, 142
European immigrants and descendants
    in census (1790), 82
    Glass, Peter, 91–94
    segregation in U.S. Armed Forces, 147
    travel to America, 97n25
    U.S. incentivization of, 92
European Union, motto, 16, 22n11
Evers, Medgar, 158n37
exiles, 152

Fairburn, John, 39, *39*
Fair Food Campaign, 224n31
farm workers, *ii, 217,* 217–218, 224n31
Faulkner, William, 271
Federal Housing Authority (FHA), 188–189
F. Heppenheimer's Sons, *143*
Fischbach, Rota, 129–130
Fitzpatrick, Peter, 69
flags, "Stars and Stripes" (1777), 168–169
Florida agricultural workers, 216–218, *217,* 224n31
Ford, Gerald R., 152
Ford, Henry, 141–142

Ford Motor Company, English and Americanization classes, *141*, 141–142
Fort Marion, Florida, *86*
Fort Myers, Florida, 217, *217*
Fourteenth Amendment, 145, 154n2
France
    Louisiana Purchase (1803), 84
    Statue of Liberty, gift to U.S., 123, 125
Franciscan Order
    founding, 48
    indigenous labor, 51
    martyrs, 48
    New Mexico missions, 37, *47*, 48–49, 50, 52–53
Francis of Assisi, Saint, 48
Franco-American Union, 125, 126
free blacks
    Capote, Texas, 90, *91*
    kidnapped by slave catchers, 104
    literacy, 118n16
    New Philadelphia, Illinois, 6, 102–104, *103*, 106, 108
freedom
    American identity and, 8, 131
    Statue of Liberty as symbol of, 125, 129, 131, *132*, 132–133
Free Frank. *see* McWorter, Free Frank
free whites, as definition of Americans, 84
French Americans and French immigrants, 95n2, 106–108
French Empire
    fur trade, 31, 32–33
    Louisiana outposts, 52
    role in peopling of North America, 5–6, 31, 32–33
French/English Bilingual Curriculum Act (Louisiana, 1847), 176n21
French-speaking Canadians, *171*, 171–173, *172*
Freyre, Gilberto, 223n15
Friedman, Jon R., 249
Fugees soccer team, Clarkston, Georgia, 231–236, 238–240
    jersey, 233, *233*, 234
    soccer cleats, *235*, 235–236
    team, *234*
fur trade, 31, 32–33
future, 269–275

Garcia, Hector P., 158n37
garment workers, 212
Georgia
    Fugees soccer team, Clarkston, *233*, 233–236, *234*, *235*, 238–240
    Gullah culture, 36
Gerber baby formula, *150*
German Americans and German immigrants
    anti-immigrant sentiment toward, 17, *17*
    Glass, Peter, 91–94, 97n25
    marquetry table, *93*
    number of, 92, 97n25

Statue of Liberty, thoughts concerning, 129–130
    Wisconsin communities, *93*
German language, 176n21
"German Triangle," 92
Glass, Peter, 91–94, *93*, 97n25
Glengarry cap, *63*, 63–64
globalism, 205, 220n1
globalization, 78, 205, 207
global trade, 74, 76–77
global trans-local, 76–78
The Godfather (Coppola), 4
gold, Spanish quest for, 46
gold rush, California, 94
Grand Army of the Republic, 141, 167
Grant, Madison, 142, 156n14
Grant, Ulysses S., 126
Great Depression, 224n26
Great & Noble Jar (Baldwin), 117n5
Great Seal, *13*
Great Society initiatives, 206–207, 221n5
Greek immigrants, 129
Guadalupe Hidalgo, Treaty of (1848), 86, 87
Guatemala, immigrants from, 208
guest worker programs, 222n12
Gullah culture, 36

Haley, Alex, 4
Hall, Stuart, 224n28
hanbok (traditional Korean dress), 194–195, *195*, 196, 200, 201
Handlin, Oscar, 145
Harper's Weekly, 17, *17*
Hart, Philip, 152
Hart-Celler Act. *see* Immigration and Nationality Act (1965)
hate crimes, 248–249
Haudenosaunee (Iroquois), 63, 64
Hawaii
    annexation by U.S., 95
    Korean laborers, 199
Hawikuh Pueblo, New Mexico, 36–37, *37*
Helzner, Morry, 130
Henry, Aaron, 158n37
High Museum of Art, 114
Hill, Richard W., Sr., 64
Hinduism, 216, *216*
Hindu Temple Society of North America, 209–211, *210*, *211*, 223n15
Hispanic Heritage Month, 153
Hispanicization efforts, 48, 49–50, 52
Hispanics. *see* Latinos
Hispanos, use of term, 157n23
historically black universities, 159n46
Holt, Bertha and Harry, *194*
    children, 193, 194, *194*, *195*, 201n1
    immigration laws, 193
    private adoption agency, 194, 199

Holt, Betty Rhee
adoption, 193
hanbok (traditional Korean dress), 193, 194–195, *195*, 196–197, 200
Holt, Nathan, 194
Home Owner's Loan Corporation (HOLC), *188*, 189
Homestead Act (1862), 92
horses
iron spur, 46, *47*, 49, 51, 53
Pueblo Revolt, 52
strategic importance, 46, 51, 53
housing discrimination, 151, 182–184, 187–189
Howe, Irving, 4
Hudson, Henry, 71
Hughes, Langston, 144, *144*, 217
Huguenots, 40n9
Hull House, Chicago, Illinois, 179, *186*
nationality map, 181, *184–185*, 185–187
Hull House Maps and Papers, 181, *184–185*, 185–187
human ecology, theory of, 182
human rights, interracial coalitions, 212, *213*, 214, 216–218, 224n31
Humphreys, Michael, 264n2
hunting, by Pueblo Indians, 50–51, 52
Huron Indians, 32
H. Wilson Pottery, 90, *91*
hybridity, 209, 216, 224n28, 224n30
cultural fusion, 222
cultural mixing, 6, 46, 219, 224n28
mestizaje, 220n1

Icarians, 106–108, *107, 108*
identity, national, 131, 140, 196–197, 273
identity, personal, 206, 273
ILGWU (International Ladies Garment Workers Union), 212, *213*, 223n17
Illinois. *see also* Chicago, Illinois
communities of refuge, 101–109
Edwards Law (1889), 176n21
Icarian community, Nauvoo, 106–108, *107*, 108, *108*
Mormon community, Nauvoo, 104–106, *105, 106*
New Philadelphia, 6, 102–104, *103*, 106, 108
Illinois Military Tract, 101–102, 104
immigrants. *see also* anti-immigrant sentiment; *specific immigrants and groups*
American patriotism of, 175n6
booklets for prospective immigrants, *92*
difficulties upon arrival, 260
forced (*see* slaves and slavery)
military service, 64, *148*, 149, *149*
museum exhibits, 131, 245, 246–247
number of (1880s–1920s), 129
number of (1970–2000), 208
post-1965, 205–229
regulation, 95n1
Statue of Liberty's meaning for, 8–9, 128–130

tensions with established residents, 237, 238, 240
United States, draw of, 91–92
violence against, 142, 246
immigrants, undocumented, 257–267
arrests of border crossers, 257
artifacts, 261, 262, *262*, 264
border fence, *259*
causes of, 208
Great Depression, 224n26
number apprehended, 257
number of, 208
number of border crossers' bodies recovered, 264
restricted access to services, 216
vignettes, 257, 260, 261, 264
Immigration Act (1924), 140–141
Immigration and Nationality Act (1965)
civil rights movement and, 206–207
family reunification preference, 201, 208, 221n8
highly skilled immigrants, 221n8
immigrant wave triggered by, 7, 232
India, immigrants from, 250
numerical limits, 208
purpose, 7
signing of, 131, *207*, 208
sponsors, 152
Immigration and Naturalization Service, raids by, 237
immigration studies, Eurocentric bias, 8
Immokalee Statue of Liberty (Rodriguez), *ii*, 9, *217*, 217–218, *218*
India, immigrants from. *see also Beyond Bollywood* (exhibition)
1970–2000, 208
achievement, 246, 249–252
assimilation, 246
citizenship rights, 247
discrimination against, 252
Hindu Temple of North America, 209–210
Saund, Dalip Singh, 246, *249*, 249–253, *250*
Sodhi, Balbir Singh, 246, *248*, 248–249, 252
violence against, 246, 248–249, 252
Indian diaspora, countries of, 254n3
"Indian Discovery of U.S. Calvary" (Koba), 86
Indian Removal Act (1830), 62, 84, 86
indigenous Americans, defined, 155n9
Indonesia, motto, 16, 22n11
inequality
as natural, 181, 182, 184
race, ethnicity, and class and, 206
as unjust, 181
"In God We Trust" (motto), 21n3
Inouye, Daniel K., 158n37
International Ladies Garment Workers Union (ILGWU), 212, *213*, 223n17
internment camps, *148*, 149
interracial collaboration, 225n35
"Iowa as it is in 1855" (booklet), *92*
Ireland, John, 173

Irish Americans and Irish immigrants
    anti-Catholic prejudice against, 17, 93–94
    anti-immigrant sentiment toward, *17*
    census (1790), 95n2
    meaning of "white" and, 140
    as "natives," 155n9
    number of, 93
    as president, 154
iron spur, 46, *47,* 49, *49,* 51, 53
Islam, 159n48, 216, *216*
Italian immigrants, 130, 140

Japan
    economic influence, 209
    Pearl Harbor attack, *147*
Japanese Americans and Japanese immigrants, *148,* 149,
    208
Los Jets soccer team, Siler City, North Carolina, *236,*
    236–240, *238, 239*
Jewish Americans and Jewish immigrants, 128–129, 140,
    149–150, 151
Jingdezhen, Jiangxi province, China, 73–75, *74*
Johnson, J. C., *148*
Johnson, Lyndon B., 131, 206–207, *207,* 208, 221n5
Johnson City, Tennessee, 250, *251,* 252
Jones, Mark, 118n9
Jordan Matthew High School, Siler City, North Carolina,
    232. *see also* Los Jets soccer team
Jos. D. Lowe Company, *168,* 168–170, *169,* 175n9
Joseph, Rebecca M., 133n2

Kallen, Horace, 145, 154, 156n17
Kang, Sura, *197,* 198
Kassab, Aelyas, 130
Katz, William Loren, 270
Kelley, Florence, 186
Kelley, Robin D. G., 273
Kempner, Aviva, 158nn32–33
Kempner, Chaim, *149,* 149–150, 158nn32–33
Kennedy, John F., 154, 206, 221n5
Kent State University, 159n46
Keystone Manufacturing Company, *139*
Kim, Claire Jean, 225n35
Kinebrew, Carolyn, 133n2
King, Martin Luther, Jr., 152
King James Bible, 167, 170
Kiowa ledger art, *86*
KKK (Ku Klux Klan), 142, *142,* 224n26, 237
Know Nothing political party, 94
Koba (Kiowa tribe member), *86*
Korea
    clothing, cultural aspects, 196–197, 201
    Protestant Christianity in, 197–200, 201, 202n9
Korean immigrants, 152, 196, 200, 201, 208
Korean orphans, U.S. adoptions of, 193–203
    arrival in U.S., 193–194, *194*
    clothing, significance of, 196–197

hanbok (traditional Korean dress), 194–195, *195,* 196
    mementos, 200–201
    number of, 201n1
    press coverage, 197
    role of Christian missionaries in, 199–200
    transracial aspects, 195, 196
    U.S. obligation for, 197
Koverman, Jill, 116
Ku Klux Klan (KKK), 142, *142,* 224n26, 237
Kunert, Marie, 130

labor movements
    Chicago protests, 181
    ILGWU, 212, *213,* 223n17
    interracial coalitions, 212, *213,* 214, 216–218
    poster, 212, *213,* 214
    postwar period, 218, 225n33
    union busting, 218, 225n33
    white supremacist violence against, 142
Laboulaye, Édouard-René Lefebvre de, 125–126, 133n2
LaFayette (schooner), *89*
Lambert, Charles, *105,* 105–106
land rights, 62, 69–70, 84, 87, 101
Landrum, Abner, 112, 114–115
Landrum, B.F., 119n25
Landrum, Franklin, 113
Landrum, John, 119n25
Landrum's Pottery, Edgefield, South Carolina, 112–113
language
    Americanization efforts and, *141,* 165–177, *166*
    bilingualism, 169, *171,* 171–173, 174, 175n24,
        176n21
    English-only movement, 170
    English-only schools, 172–173, 175n13, 175n21
    language of instruction in schools, 170–173, 176n21
Laos, immigrants from, 208
La Sentinelle (newspaper), 173
Latinos. *see also* Los Jets soccer team
    anti-immigrant sentiment against, 237
    National Register, associated properties, 271
    population increase, 208, 219, 223nn20–21
    segregation in U.S. Armed Forces, 147
    use of term, 157n23
Laughlin, Harry H., 142, 156n14
Lazarus, Emma, 8, 128–129, 260
ledger art, *86*
Le Havre, France, 92, 97n25
Lenape wampum belt, *70–71,* 71–73
Lewis, Meriwether, *85*
Lewis and Clark Expedition, *85*
liberty, love of
    as bond between Americans, 8
    racial slavery and, 31
    rebellion against England, 69
    teapot, 69, *70,* 76
"Liberty enlightening the world" (lithographic print),
    128

Liberty Island, New York City, New York, *207*
Life magazine, 197
limestone capital, *106*
Lincoln Memorial Reflecting Pool, *12*
Lionnet, Francoise, 224n28
literacy, 114, 118n16
"Little Red School House Savings Bank," *168*, 168–170, *169*
Living Beyond Bollywood (performance art), *253*
Locke, John, 69–70
Loewen, James, 271
Los Angeles, *87*, 225n35
Los Jets soccer team, Siler City, North Carolina, *236*, 236–240, *238, 239*
Louisiana, bilingualism, 176n21
Louisiana Purchase (1803), 84
Lowe, Josephine Dwyer, 175n9
Lowndes, Mrs. Charles, *34*
Luce, Henry R., 202n7
Luce-Celler Act (1946), 249
Lutguts'amti (Tsimshian chief), *58*, 59–60
lynchings, 127, 142

Magnuson Act (1943), 199
Magón, Ricardo Flores, 274
Mahicans, 60–62
MALDEF. *see* Mexican American Legal Defense and Educational Fund
Manhattan, Dutch purchase of, 71–72
Manifest Destiny, 84, 86
Many Voices, One Nation (exhibition)
    artifacts, 14–15, 38
    background, 12–19
    as continental in scope, 5–6
    continuity between past and present, 5, 7–9
    many voices, 5, 6–7
    organization, 14
    purpose, 5
maps
    "America—A nation of one people from many countries" (Bourne), *144*
    Chicago concentric zones, *180*, 180–185, *183*, 187
    Hull House Maps and Papers, 181, *184–185*, 185–187
    nationality map, Chicago, Illinois, *184–185*
    Residential Security Map of Chicago, Northern Section, October 1939–April 1940, *188*
    Social Research Map of Chicago, *183*
March for Dignity, Dialogue, and a Fair Wage (Florida, 2000), *217*
Mark (potter), 118n9
Maroon colonies, 274
marquetry table, *93*
Martin, David Stone, *147*
material culture. *see* artifacts
Mayall, David, 238
McGuffey Reader, 14n2, 167
McKenzie, Roderick, 180

McWorter, Free Frank, *102,* 102–104, *103,* 106, 108, 109n3
McWorter, Lucy, 103
McWorter, Solomon, *102,* 103, *103*
The Melting Pot (Zangwill), 141
"Melting Pot" graduation ceremony (Ford English School), *141,* 141–142
melting pot metaphor
    alternative metaphors, 154, 215
    concept of, 209
    hybridity as replacement for, 216, 224n28
    multiculturalism as replacement for, 209, 211–216
    polyculturalism as replacement for, 273–274
    rejection of, 4, 145
    as solace to native-born Americans, 209
    "unmeltable" populations, 146
memory, Native American objects as, 57–67
Mendez et al. v. Westminster School District of Orange County, 159n40
Mesa, Arizona, 249
Mexicali, Mexico, 258, *259*
Mexican American Legal Defense and Educational Fund (MALDEF), 212, *213,* 214
Mexican Americans and Mexican immigrants
    Del Valle family, *87,* 87–88
    family reunification preference, 208, 222n12
    guest worker programs, 222n12
    names for, 157n23
    segregation of, 147, 159n40
    transition from Mexican to, 88
    white supremacist violence against, 142
Mexicanos, use of term, 157n23
Mexico
    border with U.S., 86, 87, 155n7, *259*
    citizenship, 96n14
    reales (coins), *75,* 75–76
    Treaty of Guadalupe Hidalgo (1846), 86, 87
    U.S. war with, 86
Middle Eastern origin, people of, 248–249
migrations, international. *see* immigrants
migrations, Native American, 57–67
Miles, Lewis, 114, *114,* 115, 116, 119n26
Miles Pottery, Stoney Bluff, South Carolina, 119n26
Military Boundary Tract, Pike County, Illinois, 102
Miller, Doris "Dorie," 147, *147*
Miller, James, 115
Ming Dynasty, 73–75, *74*
Missouri, expulsion of Mormons from, 104
Moore, Amzie, 158n37
More, Thomas, 106
Mormons, 104–106, *105, 106,* 108
mortgage loans, 189. *see also* housing discrimination
Mufleh, Luma, 231, 233–234, *234,* 235, 240
multiculturalism, 209, 211–216, 273
museums
    artifact label restrictions, 219, 247
    challenges in interpreting material culture, 219, 245, 252

performance art, 247, 252–254
    as well-intentioned but overly cautious, 246–247
music, *148*
Muslims, violence against, 159n48

NAACP. *see* National Association for the Advancement
    of Colored People
NAFTA (North American Free Trade Agreement), 262
NAREB (National Association of Real Estate Boards),
    187–188
Nast, Thomas, cartoon by, 17, *17*
Natchez, Mississippi, *89*
National Association for the Advancement of Colored
    People (NAACP)
    The Crisis magazine, 156n16
    founding, *138,* 144, 156n16
    objectives, 212
    poster, 212, *213,* 214
    segregation, fight against, 151
    veterans as members of, 158n37
National Association of Real Estate Boards (NAREB),
    187–188
National Conference of Christians and Jews (NCCJ),
    145, 156n17
National Council of Negro Women (NCNW), 158n38
National Housing Act (1934), 188–189
national identity. *see* identity, national
Nationality and Immigration Act (1952), 95n5
National Mall, art installation, 11–12, *12*
National Museum of American History. *see also Many
    Voices, One Nation* (exhibition)
    Holt family artifacts, 194, *195*
    Korean adoption in U.S. project, 201n2
National Museum of History and Technology
    A Nation of Nations (exhibition), 5–6, 7, 13
National Museum of Natural History
    Beyond Bollywood (exhibition), 245–255
National Museum of the American Indian (NMAI)
    objects of memory and journey, 57–67
National Organization for Women (NOW) poster, 212,
    213, 214
National Papier Mache Works, Milwaukee, Wisconsin,
    85
National Park Service, 131, 271
National Portrait Gallery, 72
A Nation of Nations (exhibition), 5–6, 7, 13
Native American History Month, 153
Native Americans. *see also specific nations and peoples*
    boarding school system, 167, 174n3
    Christianization of, 46, 48–49, 53, 61
    "Code Talkers," 149, 158n30
    on creamware pitcher, 39, *39*
    domesticated animals, 50
    first use of term, 62
    fur trade, 32–33
    "Indian Removal," 62, 84, 86
    land rights, 58, 62, 69–70, 84, 101

museum exhibits, 4
native societies, pre-European contact, 28–29
    in Northeast, 28
    objects of memory, 57–67
    peace medals, *85*
    population decline, 29, 95n3
    Seminole freedmen, 274
    settlers, contact with, 27, 29, 32, 36
    settlers, displacement by, 84, 101
    as slaves, 270
    in Southeast, 28
    Thanksgiving, 271
    treaties with U.S., 84
    violence against, 142
"natives," Northern European immigrants as, 140, 155n9
nativism/nativist. *see also* anti-immigrant sentiment
    anti-Catholic prejudice, 17, 93–94, 142
    Chinese Exclusion Act (1882), 94
    creation of Catholic schools as response to, 176
    defined, 137
    ideas, 154
    immigrant responses to, 216
    movements, 176, 215
    racial, 216, 224n26
    twentieth century, 215–216, 224n26
Naturalization Act (1790), 17, 82, 84, 155n7
"natural law," 69
natural rights, land rights as, 69–70
Nauvoo, Illinois
    Icarian community, 106–108, *107, 108, 108*
    Mormon community, 104–106, *105, 106*
NCCJ (National Conference of Christians and Jews),
    145, 156n17
NCNW (National Council of Negro Women), 158n38
Negro History Week, 152, *153*
The Negro Soldier (documentary film), 157n26
New Amsterdam, 31–32. *see also* New York City
The New Colossus (Lazarus), 8, 128–129, 260
"The New Face of America" cover (*Time* magazine),
    214–215, *215,* 223nn20–21
New France, 32–33, *33,* 40n9
New Mexico. *see also* Pueblo Indians; Pueblo Revolt
    colonial history, through artifacts, 45–55
    Hawikuh Pueblo, 36–37, *37*
    horses, strategic importance of, 46
    Pecos Mission Church, 38, *38*
    reconquest by Spain, 52–53, 54
    Santo Domingo Mission Church, *46*
New Mexico Territory Act (1850), 176n21
New Netherland, 32
New Orleans, Louisiana, *89*
New Philadelphia, Illinois, 6, 102–104, *103,* 106, 108
New Stockbridge, New York, 61–62
New York City
    Americanization movement, 167, 169
    Chinese immigrants, *213*
    garment workers, 212

history, 31–32, 71–72
   public schools, 169, 175n10, 175n12
New York State Women's Suffrage Association, 127
The New York Times, 126
Ngai, Mae M., 208
Nihei, Ken, *148*
9/11, hostility following, 159n48, *248,* 248–249
Nitti, Helen, 130
Nixon, Richard, 132, 152
Nobel Peace Prize recipients, 156n15
Nogales, Mexico, 260, 264n2
North American Free Trade Agreement (NAFTA), 262
North Carolina
   immigrant population growth, 237
      Los Jets soccer team, Siler City, *236,* 236–240, *238,*
      239
northern colonies, as "societies with slaves," 31
Northwest Ordinance (1787), 84
Novak, Michael, 4
NOW (National Organization for Women) poster, 212,
   213, 214
"#1 Dad" picture frame, 262, *262,* 264
Nussbaum, Martha, 20

occupational choice, race-based, 183
O'Conner, Alice, 186
Ohio, bilingualism, 176n21
"Old stock" Americans, 140–141, 155n9
Omi, Michael, 22n15
Oñate, Don Juan de, 50
Oneidas, 61
"One Shoe" (youth soccer player), 235
Orlando, Florida, 217, *217*
orphans. *see* Korean orphans
Ortiz, Fernando, 223n15
Osage people, *85*
"Out of Many, One" (Rodríguez-Gerada), 11–12, *12*

Pacific, 86, 209, 274
   coast, 58
   islands, 95, 145
   route, 75
Pakistan, immigrants from, 208
Pao, Vang, 274
Paris, Treaty of (1783), 84
Park, Robert, 179–180, 182–183, 186, 187
Parker, Sarah, *34*
Parker, Walter C., 19
Parmentier, Lillian, *171,* 171–172, *172*
parochial schools
   Americanization efforts, 166, 173–174
   Baltimore, Maryland, 176n22
   bilingual, 171–172, 174
   Providence, Rhode Island, 171–173
   reasons for, 170–171
   retaining heritage traditions, 165–166
Pastor, Manuel, 225n35

PATCO (Professional Air Traffic Controllers
   Organization), 225n33
patriotism, in immigrant communities, 175n6
Pawtucket, Rhode Island, *171,* 171–172, *172,* 173
peace medals, 62, *85*
Pearl Harbor, Honolulu, Hawaii, *147*
Peck Education Act (Rhode Island, 1922), 172
Pecos Mission Church, New Mexico, 37, *38*
Penn, William, *70–71,* 71–73
performance art, 247, 252–254, *253*
Pew Research Hispanic Trends Project, 219
Philip II, King (Spain), 48
Philippines, immigrants from, 208
Phillips, Ruth B., 72
physicians, immigrants as, 250–252
   doctor bag, 246, 251, *251,* 252
picture frame (#1 Dad), 262, *262,* 264
pieces of eight. *see* reales (coins)
Pierce, Bob, 199
Pike County, Illinois, 102
Pilgrims, 27, 28, *28,* 269, 271
Pitcaithely, Dwight, 133n2
pitchers
   1790 census on, *83*
   creamware pitcher, 39, *39*
   porcelain pitcher, *94*
Pittsburgh Courier, 147
"Plain Language from Truthful James" (poem), *94*
Pledge of Allegiance, 167, 169, 174n4
Plessy v. Ferguson, 145
pluralism. *see* cultural pluralism
Plymouth colony, 269
Plymouth Rock, 28, *28*
Polish immigrants, 129, 140
Polk, James, 86
poll taxes, 138, 154n4
polyculturalism, 273–274
porcelain. *see* pottery
Port Simpson, British Columbia, Canada, *58, 59,* 59–60
postcolonial theory, 224n30
posters
   Americanization Committee, Cleveland Board of
      Education, *166*
   labor movement, 212, *213,* 214
   World War II, 147, *147*
"postracial" conundrum, 273
Potosi, Peru-Bolivia, 75–76
pottery
   ciqi (Chinese porcelain), 73–75, *74*
   creamware pitcher, 39, *39*
   Edgefield, South Carolina, 111–113, *112, 114, 116,*
      117n5, 118n7
   H. Wilson Pottery stoneware jar, *91*
   marks on, 114, 118n13
   porcelain pitcher, *94*
   porcelain stem bowl, 73–75, *74*
   slave labor, 90

South Carolina, 117n1
 stoneware, 90, *91,* 111, *112,* 113, *114, 116*
 Zuni salt cellar, 36–37, *37*
Pottle, James, 103
poverty, 186, 187
prejudice, 17, 131, 140, 143–144, 149, 151, 152, 154,
  159n48, 170
presidential peace medal, 62
private schools, 165
Professional Air Traffic Controllers Organization
  (PATCO), 225n33
Progressivist reformers, 142, 144
Proposition 187 (California, 1994), 215–216
Protestant Huguenots, 40n9
Protestant values, promotion of, 165, 167–168
Providence, Rhode Island, 171–173
public schools. *see also* education
 alternatives, 170
 Americanization movement, 141, 165, 166, 173–174,
   175n12
 banking, 175n10
 curricula, 166–167
 first, 168, 175n11
 health issues, 175n12
 number of, 165
 prejudices against immigrants, 170
 segregation, 151
 textbooks, 167
Pueblo Indians
 animism, 50–51, 53
 Christianization, 48–49, 53
 crafts, 48
 Hispanicization, 48, 49–50, 52–53
 horse culture, *47,* 54
 hunting, 50–51, 52
 identity, 36
 iron spur, 46, *47,* 49, 51, 53
 motifs, *37*
 Spanish conquest, 50, 52
 Spanish reconquest, 52–53, 54
Pueblo Revolt (1680), 36, *37,* 46, *47,* 48, 51–52, 54
Puerto Ricans, 146, 147, 154n6
Puerto Rico, annexation by U.S., 95
Putnam, Robert, 271–272

quahog clamshells, 32, *32*
Queen Charlotte Islands, British Columbia, Canada,
  57–60
Queens, New York, 209–210, *210*
Quinney, John Wannuaucon, *60,* 60–63, 66n8

race
 citizenship and, 17
 color associations, 18
 color-line problem, 137, 153–154, 219, 225n35
 competing beliefs about, 139–146
 geography and, 183

interracial alliances, 206, 212, *213,* 214, 220n1
 migration and, 16–19, 81–82
 nation and, 18–19, 205–206
 occupational choice and, 183
 shaping national identity, 81–82
 Time magazine covers, 18, *18,* 214–215, *215,*
   223nn20–21
 upward mobility and, 183
race riots, 156n13, 181
Racial Formation in the United States (Omi and Winant),
   22n15
racial hierarchy
 Chicago neighborhoods, 186–187
 counteracting, 142, 144–145
 early twentieth-century ideas, 139
 eugenics, 156n14
 land value, 187–189
 in laws and customs, 145–146
 maintenance of "national character" and, 140–142
 nativism's connection to, 216, 224n26
 theories of, *143*
 white supremacism, 137, 140–142, 144–146, 152,
   156n14, 237
racial inequality, as natural, *180*
racialization, defined, 22n15
racial profiling, 253
racism/racist, 90, 91, 108, 127, 130, 147, 151, 152, 214,
   216, 219, 224n27, 237, 252, 261
Rancho Camulos, California, 87–88
Randolph, A. Philip, 147
Razaf, Andy, *148*
RCNL (Regional Council of Negro Leadership), 158n37
Reagan, Ronald, 131, 134n32, 225n33
reales (coins), *75,* 75–76
real estate industry. *see* housing discrimination
redlining, *188*
Refugee Relief Act (1953), 193–194
Refugee Resettlement Act (1980), 240n6
refugees
 annual cap on, 240n6
 postwar exemptions for, 152
 resettlement locations, selection of, 235
 tensions with established residents, 233–236, 238,
   240
 Vietnam War, 208–209
 youth soccer, 231–240
Regional Council of Negro Leadership (RCNL), 158n37
religion and spirituality, 209–210. *see also specific*
   religions
report cards, *171,* 171–172
Residential Security Map of Chicago, Northern Section,
   October 1939–April 1940, *188*
Rhode Island, bilingual education, 171–173
rice plantations, 34, 35, *35*
The Rise of the Unmeltable Ethnics (Novak), 4
rocking chair, 103, *103*
Rodriguez, Kat, *ii,* 9, *217,* 217–218, *218*

Rodríguez-Gerada, Jorge, 11–12, *12*
Roediger, David, 140
Roman Catholicism. *see* Catholics and Catholicism
Romeo (potter), 118n14
Roosevelt, Theodore, 170
Roots (Haley), 4
Roque, Frank Silva, 249, 252
Rosenblatt, Brooke, 133n2
Ross, Betsey, 168–169
Roth, Philip, 4
rowels, *49*
Rucci, Angelo, 130
Ruffins, Fath Davis, 21n6
Russian immigrants, 128–129, 130, *149,* 149–150
Rypinski, Celia, 129

Said, Edward, 274
salt cellar, *37*
Sanghvi, Trisha, 253
San Miguel de Gualdape (settlement), 269–270
Santo Domingo Mission Church, New Mexico, 46, *46,* 53
SAPAN (South Asian Performing Arts Network)
     Institute, 252–253, *253*
Saund, Dalip Singh, 246, *249,* 249–253, *250*
savings banks. *see* banks
schoolhouse flag movement, 167, 174n4
schools. *see* education
Schuyler, Georgina, 129
SCLC (Southern Christian Leadership Conference), 151
Scottish Americans and Scottish immigrants, 95n2, 155n9
Scottish military regiments, 64
segregation
     Cold War, 147–153
     fight against, 151
     housing, 182–184, *188*
     laws and customs, 145–146
     laws prohibiting, 151
     as natural, 182–184, 187
     post–Civil War, 91
     public places, 146
     in schools, 146, 151, 159n40
     signs, *146*
     state laws, 145
     as states' rights, 152
     U.S. Armed Forces, 147
     World War II, 147–153, *148*
SEIU (Service Employees International Union) poster,
     212, *213,* 214
Selig, Diana, 144–145, 156n17
semifictionalized ethnography, 264n2
Seminole freedmen, 274
Senna, Danzy, 214–215, 223n21
La Sentinelle (newspaper), 173
September 11, 2001, hostility following, 159n48, *248,*
     248–249
Sermons for Feast Days (Saint Anthony of Padua), 48
Serrano, Orlando, 224n31

Service Employees International Union (SEIU) poster,
     212, *213,* 214
settlement houses, 142, 144
settler colonialism, 36
Shawano County, Wisconsin, 62
Sheboygan County, Wisconsin, 92
sheet music, *148*
Sikhs, 246, 248, *248,* 252, 253
Siler City, North Carolina
     foreign-born population, 232, 237
     Los Jets soccer team, 231–232, *236,* 236–240, *238,*
        239
     tensions between immigrants and established
        residents, 237, 240
silver mining, 75–76
silver peace medals, *85*
slaves and slavery
     abolition of, 126
     agricultural methods, *35*
     buying one's family out of, 102–103, 104
     citizenship denied to, 82
     cowrie shells as currency, 30, *30*
     diversity of slave experience, 88, 90, 96n19
     education of, 118n16
     as forced migration, 88–91
     hiring-out, 90
     horrors of, 88, 113
     identification tag, *90*
     internal slave trade, 88
     known by first name, 117n2
     legal importation, end of, 88, *89*
     literacy, 114, 118n16
     number imported, 88
     as pottery factory employees, 113, 118n13
     regional differences in impact of, 31
     revolts, 270
     rice plantations, 34
     role in peopling of North America, 27, 29–31
     San Miguel de Gualdape, 270
     self-identity through art, 111
     ship manifest, *89*
     slave catchers, 104
     Statue of Liberty's symbolism, 8, 9, 123, 125
     stoneware storage jar, 111, *112, 114*
     time awareness, 115
     transcontinental slave trade, 88
Smith, Joseph, 104–106
Smithson, James, 77
SNCC (Student Nonviolent Coordinating Committee),
     151
soccer
     Fugees soccer team, Clarkston, Georgia, *233,* 233–
        236, *234, 235,* 238–240
     Los Jets soccer team, Siler City, North Carolina, *236,*
        236–240, *238, 239*
     refugee and migrant children, 231–240
     total registration for youth soccer, 241n11

Social Research Map of Chicago, *183*
social work, 187
sociology
    academic *vs.* applied, 187
    Chicago School, 179–182
    emergence as discipline, 179
    as science of society, 181
Sodhi, Balbir Singh, 246, *248,* 248–249, 252
Sonoran Desert, Arizona, 9, 258, *260,* 262, *262,* 264
Sons of Liberty, 69, 70
Sons of the American Revolution, 141
Soraci, Tony, 133, 134n32
The Souls of Black Folk (Du Bois), 219
South (region), U.S.
    Bureau of Education, 174n5
    new migrations, 231–243
    segregation laws, 145
    slavery, 31, 88, 90
South Africa, motto, 16, 22n11
South American immigrants, as garment workers, 212
South Asian immigrants. *see* India, immigrants from
South Asian Performing Arts Network (SAPAN)
        Institute, 252–253, *253*
South Carolina
    European settlers, 34
    Gullah culture, 36
    rice fanner basket, *35*
    San Miguel de Gualdape (early settlement), 269–270
    slaves brought illegally to, 114
South Carolina Railroad, 119n23
South-Carolina Republican (Pottersville), 114–115
Southern Christian Leadership Conference (SCLC), 151
southern colonies, as "slave societies," 31
South Korea, immigrants from, 208. *see also* Korean
        immigrants; Korean orphans
Spako, Theodore, 129
Spanish, use of term, 157n23
Spanish Empire
    colonization of Texas and California, 52
    conquest of America, 45–46
    domesticated animals, 51
    goals in conquest of America, 46, 48, 49–50
    horse culture, *47,* 51, 53
    indigenous labor, 46, 48, 49–50, 51
    motto, 16
    Pueblo Revolt (1680), 36
    reconquest of New Mexico, 52–53, 54
    role in peopling of North America, 6, 31
    San Miguel de Gualdape (settlement), 269–270
Spanish language, 176n21, 176n24
Spanish missions, 37, *37,* 46, *47*
sports, 231, 238, 241n11. *see also* soccer
Springfield, Illinois, 156n13, 156n16
Springfield, Missouri, 127
spurs, 46, *47,* 49, 51, 53
Stamp Act, *70,* 76
Starr, Ellen Gates, *186*

statehood, path to, 84
Statue of Liberty
    as African American, 133n2
    African American response to, 126–128
    as American icon, 123–135
    American Museum of Immigration, 131
    celebrating end of slavery, 8, 9, 123, 125, 126
    Centennial Celebration, 134n32
    in Congressional portrait, *249*
    dedication ceremonies, 126, 131
    exhibitions of, 126
    as French gift to U.S., 8, 123, 125
    fund-raising for, 125, 126–127, 128–129
    idea for, 125, 133n2
    immigrant concepts concerning, 129–130
    Immigration and Nationality Act (1965), signing of,
        207, 208
    Immokalee Statue of Liberty (Rodriguez), *ii,* 9, *217,*
        217–218, *218*
    "Liberty enlightening the world" (lithographic print),
        128
    location, 126
    maquette (terra-cotta and tin model), 123, *124,* 125
    meaning of, 8, 124
    The New Colossus (Lazarus), 8, 260
    protests and occupations, 131–132
    renovation (1980s), 134n29
    size, 126
    suffragette's response to, 127
    symbolism, complexities of, 126, 134n29
    symbolism, freedom, 125, 129, 131, *132,* 132–133
    symbolism, immigrant experience, 8–9, 123, 125,
        128–130
    symbolism, national identity, 131
    symbolism, transnational, 130–131
    on undocumented immigrant's shirt, 9, 261, *262*
    Vietnam War protesters, *132*
    welcoming all newcomers, 139
Sterling, Illinois, *139*
St. Jean Baptiste Church, 176n24
St. Louis, Missouri, 156n13
stoneware pottery, 90, *91,* 111, *112,* 113, *114, 116*
St. Raphael Academy, Rhode Island, 173
Student Nonviolent Coordinating Committee (SNCC),
    151
sub-prime mortgages, 189
suburbs, 151
suffragettes, 127
sunstone, *106*
Supreme Court, 145, 151, 152
Sutter's Mill, California, 94
Swaney, Lee, 234
Swedish descent, people of, 95n2
Syrian immigrants, 130

Tacuri, José, 257, 260, 261, *263,* 264, 264n2
Taft-Hartley Act (1947), 225n33

Taiwanese immigrants, 152
Taylor, Alan, 29
teapot, 69, *70,* 76
Tejanos, use of term, 157n23
territories, U.S., 84, 154n6, 274
Tewa, 36
Texas, Spanish colonization, 52
textbooks, 167–168
Thanksgiving, 269, 271
theater, in museum exhibitions, 247, 252–254
Third Plenary Council of Baltimore (1884), 176n22
third space, defined, 241n24
Thirteenth Amendment, 126
Thomas Davies pottery, Edgefield, South Carolina, 118n14
Tiananmen Square protest (1989), 131
time awareness, 115, 119n23
Time magazine
    "America's Changing Colors" cover, 18, *18*
    "The New Face of America" cover, 214–215, *215,* 223nn20–21
tobacco, 34
"Together Against Discrimination" poster, *213*
Toledo, Luis Colón de, 76
tolerance, teaching of, 144, *144,* 145
Topaz Relocation Center, Utah, *148*
tourist market, Tuscaroran whimsies, *63,* 63–64, *65*
trade, international, 74, 76–77
trade cards, *139, 143*
Trail of Tears, 86
transatlantic slave trade. *see under* slaves and slavery
transculturalism, 223n15
transnationalism, 209–211
transportation, segregation in, *146*
Travelers Insurance Co., *128*
Treaty of Guadalupe Hidalgo (1848), 86, 87
Treaty of Paris (1783), 84
Tsimshian nation, 29, 57–60, *58, 59*
Tulsa, Oklahoma, 156n13
turbans, 246, *248,* 249, 252, 253
Tuscarora, *63,* 63–64, *65*
24th Amendment, 154n4

UMP (Undocumented Migration Project), 261, *262*
Uncle Sam, 84, *85,* 139, *139*
undocumented immigrants. *see* immigrants, undocumented
Undocumented Migration Project (UMP), 261, *262*
unions. *see* labor movements
United Daughters of the Confederacy, 174n5
United States
    as "a nation of nations," 138
    Armed Forces, 127, 147, *149,* 149–150, 157n26, 253
    border fence, 155n7, 257–258, *259,* 260
    boundaries, 86, 87, 96n6
    census (1790), 82, *83,* 95n2
    Congressional members, 158n37, *249,* 249–253, *250*

Constitution, 126, 145, 154n2, 154n4
currency, 75
Diplomatic Medal, *13*
formation of, *70,* 84
future demographic shifts, 219–220, 223n21
ideals, 8
"Indian Removal" policy, 62, 84, 86
motto, 21n3, 82
population growth (1970–2000), 208
Supreme Court, 145, 151, 152
territories, 95, 139, 154n6, 274
Treaty of Guadalupe Hidalgo, 86, 87
Treaty of Paris, 84
University of Chicago sociologists, 179–180, 182–183, 186, 187
The Uprooted (Handlin), 145
urban growth, concentric zones, *180,* 180–185, *183,* 187
Urban League, 158n38
Utopia (More), 106

Velasco, Don Luis, 46
Verghese, Abraham, 246, 250–252, *251*
Vietnam, immigrants from, 208
Vietnam Veterans Against the War, 131–132, *132*
Vietnam War, *132,* 152, 207, 208–209
Virginia, English settlement of, 33–34, 41n13
Virginia Company, 33–34
Vlach, John M., 117, 117n1
voting rights, 138, 154n4
Voting Rights Act (1965), 91, 151
The Voyage to Icaria (Cabet), 106

wampum
    commercial value, 60, 73
    inheritance, 66n8
    Lenape wampum belt, *70–71,* 71–73
    as messaging device, 61
    in negotiation and agreements, *60,* 61, 72–73, *73,* 74
    non-Native American production, *32*
    use by Dutch, 32, 60
War of 1812, 101
Washington, George, *39,* 168–169
Watson, Tony, 264n2
Weber, Max, 181
Welsh immigrants, 155n9
West, peopling of, 6, 84
West African cosmograms, 114, 118n13
West Virginia, U.S.S., *147*
"What America Means to Me" (campaign booklet), 246, 250, *250*
whiteness, use of term, 140, 145
whites, as percentage of population, 219
white supremacism
    Cold War, 152
    counteracting, 142, 144–145
    as crucial for national stability, 137
    eugenics, 156n14

in laws and customs, 145–146
　maintenance of "national character" and, 140–142
　Siler City, North Carolina, 237
Why We Fight (film series), 157n26
Wilson, Hiram, 88–91, *91*
Wilson, James, 90
Winant, Howard, 22n15
Wisconsin
　Bennett Law (1888), 176n21
　German communities, *93*
　Mormon-run sawmills, 105
women
　civic groups, 174n5
　discrimination against, 214
　Haudenosaunee, 64
　Icarians, 107, *108*
　ILGWU, 212, 223n17
　missionaries, 198
　multiracial, 214–215, *215*
　NOW, 212, *213*, 214
　reformers, 187
　savings banks, 175nn9–10
　suffrage, 127
　Tuscaroran, *65*
Wood, Peter, 270
Woodson, Carter G., 152, *153*
World of Our Fathers (Howe), 4

World Relief, 235
World War I, 158n30
World War II
　as causal element in civil rights, 138
　Christmas cards, *148*
　death camps, 158n33
　"Double V" campaign, 147
　as greatest generation, 157n25
　internment camps, *148*, 149
　military service of immigrants, *149*
　racial segregation, 147–153, *148*
　U.S. immigration policy and, 199

"A Yankee Doodle Tan (The 'Double V' Song)," *148*
Yeingst, William, 21n6
YMCA, 141, 234
Youn, Hui-Sung, 201
Youth's Companion magazine, 167, 174n4
youth soccer. *see* soccer
YWCA, 141

Zacatecas, Mexico, 75–76
Zangwill, Israel, 141
Zolberg, Aristide R., 95n1, 221n6
zones. *see* concentric zones map
Zuni, 36–37, *37*